B   Doyle, Clive,
Doyle   1941-

A journey to Waco.

$38.00

DATE			

PRAISE FOR *A JOURNEY TO WACO: AUTOBIOGRAPHY OF A BRANCH DAVIDIAN*

"The federal assault on the Branch Davidian community will forever remain an ignominious moment in American religious history. This book offers a personal account of Branch Davidian life and the tragic demise of the Branch Davidian community by one of its important surviving members. Clive Doyle's witness, as told to Catherine Wessinger and Matthew Wittmer, is a welcome and necessary corrective to official legitimations of those fateful events." —**David G. Bromley**, Virginia Commonwealth University

"As one of the few remaining survivors of the catastrophic federal siege of the Branch Davidian sect in 1993, Clive Doyle provides us with a humanizing and sometimes humorous biographical narrative, as well as a deeply compelling story of those who lived and died at Mt. Carmel. It provides a starkly different portrait of the Branch Davidians than the self-serving version offered up by government officials in the days and weeks after the worst federal law enforcement disaster in U.S. history." —**Stuart A. Wright**, Lamar University

"This is not an academic book, but it is a book that academics and anyone who has ever wondered how the terrible tragedy at Waco in 1993 could have come about should read. The book does not answer this question, but it does give a remarkably gripping account of how one of the 'survivors' came to join David Koresh's Branch Davidians, what his life was like, what Koresh taught, and how the siege and fire were experienced from inside the compound." —**Eileen Barker**, London School of Economics

"This autobiography offers an authentic and fresh look into the history and culture of one of the most important new religious movements in America of the late twentieth century. It also provides a compelling insider's account of the events that led to the demise of the group, which is very different than the official federal reports. Doyle's memories are more than worth reading. They are instructive and enlightening. I highly recommend this book." —**Yaakov Ariel**, University of North Carolina at Chapel Hill

"The Branch Davidians have been demonized in the popular mind as dangerous, or at least deluded, fanatics. Clive Doyle now shows us just how wrong that view is. Telling his story, he shows just how human and normal his fellow members were, and how they were victimized by overly zealous law-enforcement agents." —**Timothy Miller**, University of Kansas

A Journey to Waco

A Journey to Waco

Autobiography of a Branch Davidian

Clive Doyle with Catherine Wessinger
and Matthew D. Wittmer

ROWMAN & LITTLEFIELD PUBLISHERS, INC.
Lanham • Boulder • New York • Toronto • Plymouth, UK

Published by Rowman & Littlefield Publishers, Inc.
A wholly owned subsidiary of The Rowman & Littlefield Publishing Group, Inc.
4501 Forbes Boulevard, Suite 200, Lanham, Maryland 20706
www.rowman.com

10 Thornbury Road, Plymouth PL6 7PP, United Kingdom

British Library Cataloguing in Publication Information Available

Library of Congress Cataloging-in-Publication Data

Doyle, Clive, 1941-
  A journey to Waco : autobiography of a Branch Davidian / Clive Doyle with Catherine Wessinger and Matthew D. Wittmer.
    p. cm.
  ISBN 978-1-4422-0885-8 (cloth : alk. paper)—ISBN 978-1-4422-0887-2 (electronic)
  1. Doyle, Clive, 1941- 2. Branch Davidians--Biography. 3. Waco Branch Davidian Disaster, Tex., 1993. I. Wessinger, Catherine, 1952- II. Wittmer, Matthew D., 1971- III. Title.
  BP605.B72D69 2012
  299'.93—dc23
  [B]
                                                        2012014525

♾™ The paper used in this publication meets the minimum requirements of American National Standard for Information Sciences—Permanence of Paper for Printed Library Materials, ANSI/NISO Z39.48-1992.

Printed in the United States of America

Dedicated to
Shari Doyle, my youngest daughter, forever eighteen.
To my mother, Edna Doyle, who passed away at eighty-five.
To Bonnie Haldeman, my dearest friend.
And to my oldest daughter, Karen Graham, the only one still living of my
immediate family at the time of this book being published.

Excerpt from "A Soliloquy for Shari"

She's one amongst so many names,
Her life cut short amidst the flames,
No helping hand.
That she is dead and she is gone,
It's hard for me to carry on,
Or understand.

Shari. How I miss her so,
It's impossible to let her know,
It's just too late.
I wish it did not have to be,
If only she were here to see,
But that is fate.

O God, there's nothing I can do,
But hope, and pray, and wait on you,
And wonder when
The resurrection will take place,
And I'll see her happy smiling face
Once more again.

Dad (9/15/93)

Contents

Acknowledgments   xi

A Short Introduction to the Branch Davidians and
Clive Doyle—Catherine Wessinger   1

1   Telling My Story and the Story of the Branch Davidians   9

2   From Australia to Texas—Meeting the Branch Davidians   11

3   Living with the Branch Davidians   39

4   Branch Davidian Theology   75

5   The Mount Carmel Conflict: The ATF Raid, the Fifty-One-Day
Siege, and the FBI Assault   99

6   Jail, Two Trials, and Changes at Mount Carmel   163

7   Survivors of the Siege—Where We Are Today   181

Appendix   Reconstructing Mount Carmel Center: Proportion
and Memory—Matthew D. Wittmer   189

Notes   199

Works Cited   243

Index   249

About the Authors   265

Acknowledgments

Catherine Wessinger thanks her parents, Bryson and Ellen Lowman, for a financial gift that supported her 2004–2005 sabbatical, during which she conducted most of the interviews with Clive Doyle on which this autobiography is based. Those funds also paid for the transcription of thirty-one audiotapes of interviews with Clive—two recorded in 2003, twenty-five recorded in 2004, and four recorded in 2006. She thanks her mother for a financial gift that supported her 2011–2012 sabbatical, during which this autobiography was edited and produced. She is grateful for her parents' support in so many ways.

Loyola University New Orleans provided a research grant in 2004 that paid for part of Catherine Wessinger's expenses incurred in traveling to Waco. She thanks Dr. Jo Ann Cruz, dean of the College of Humanities and Natural Sciences, for release from teaching one course in spring 2011, which enabled the editing work on this autobiography to begin.

Matthew D. Wittmer served as the primary information technology expert in our work with Clive Doyle. Completion of this book was facilitated by Matthew's getting Clive set up with a laptop computer. Matthew also assisted by doing most of the work inputting Clive's corrections into the transcripts. Knowing that she is collaborating with a librarian, Catherine has appreciated Matthew's constant reminder to think of the archives.

We thank Ron Goins for serving as Clive's technical assistant in Waco, and also for serving as occasional photographer.

Catherine thanks her son, Clinton Wessinger, for digitizing the audiotapes of the interviews with Clive Doyle as well as selected audiotapes of negotiations and surveillance audio recorded in 1993 by the FBI, and audiotapes of Bible studies given by David Koresh, Lois Roden, and Steve Schneider.

Catherine thanks Richard and Julieta Ruppert, friends who offered hospitality in Houston on her drives between New Orleans and Waco. She is grateful to Richard Ruppert for his advice about the legal issues involved in the disputed ownership of the Mount Carmel Center property.

Numerous people transcribed the audiotapes of the interviews with Clive Doyle. Catherine thanks the following people for their hard and careful transcription work: Clinton Wessinger, Scotland Green, Dena Schwartz, Sarah Vandergriff, Andrew Polaniecki, Erin Proven, Deborah Halter, and especially Alanda Wraye, who transcribed twenty of the thirty-one tapes.

The thirty-one transcripts included much more material than could be included in this volume. The corrected transcripts will be placed in the Texas Collection at Baylor University.

Catherine thanks Lee Hancock, reporter with the *Dallas Morning News*, for donating her collection of primary documents to the Loyola University New Orleans archive in 2004, where they were stored for six years, giving Catherine the opportunity to go through them. In 2010 the Lee Hancock Collection was moved to the Southwestern Writers Collection, Texas State University, San Marcos. This collection contains important documents and memos internal to the Federal Bureau of Investigation, the Bureau of Alcohol, Tobacco, and Firearms, and other federal agencies, as well as Texas Rangers reports, relating to the Branch Davidian case. Joel W. Minor has done a fine job of advertising the presence of the Lee Hancock Collection at Texas State University, San Marcos. The valuable finding aid available on the Internet was compiled by Margaret DeBrecht. The Dick Reavis Papers are also located in the Southwestern Writers archive.

Catherine and Matthew thank Ellen Kuniyuki Brown, former director of the Texas Collection, Baylor University, for facilitating research and duplication of audiotapes, videotapes, photos, and documents in several Branch Davidian–related collections of materials. Staff at the Texas Collection have provided nothing short of excellent research accommodations to access the materials in their Branch Davidian archive. Texas Collection staff deserve a commendation because courteous assistance to any records pertaining to traumatic events ensures that the public can discover the complexities and humanity often overlooked in events that have received sensational media attention. The Mark Swett Collection is an important and accessible source of audiotapes of the negotiations with the Branch Davidians in 1993 as well as surveillance audiotapes recorded by the FBI. The proceedings of the 1994 criminal trial are also in the Texas Collection, which hopefully one day will receive in-depth study by a researcher.

Matthew and Catherine are grateful to Ken Fawcett for providing us with digitized audio files of the more than twenty-four hours of the 911 call made by Wayne Martin to the McLennan County Sheriff's Department on February 28, 1993, and also for digitized video Ken Fawcett captured from live satellite feeds from February 28 through April 19, 1993. These materials have been placed in the Texas Collection, Baylor University. We thank Ken Fawcett for permitting us to make photocopies of documents in his possession and for sharing the extensive video footage of the property he recorded during and after the siege in 1993.

We thank Eugene V. Gallagher for his helpful comments on historical material contained in the endnotes in chapter 4 on Branch Davidian theology and Stuart A. Wright for checking the material in the notes for chapters 5 and 6 on the events in 1993, the two trials, and the Danforth Report.

Matthew Wittmer thanks Catherine Wessinger for her ongoing support of his work on researching and documenting Branch Davidian history. He also thanks Cathy for extending to him the opportunity to be a co-editor of this book, for supporting the idea to create line diagrams to enhance Clive's narrative, and for referring in this book to Matthew's webpage created to record the history of the Mount Carmel property.

Matthew thanks Ellen Mahoney, Rourk Reagan, Jeffrey Allen Price, and Jason Kafil for their assistance with, and recommendation to use, Adobe Illustrator to create the line diagrams in this book.

Matthew thanks Clive Doyle for over a decade's worth of conversations about his recollections and experiences in the Mount Carmel Center buildings—conversations that began in 2000 when Clive started exhibiting Matthew's wooden memorial model of the building in the property's Visitor's Center that Clive created and maintained between 1998 and 2006.

We are both grateful to relatives of deceased Branch Davidians who have given us permission to publish photographs of their loved ones in Clive Doyle's autobiography. These are Sandy Connizzo, whose son, Michael Schroeder, was killed by ATF agents on February 28, 1993, as he attempted to return to his family and friends at Mount Carmel Center; Ofelia Santoyo, who lost her daughter, Juliette Santoyo, and five grandchildren, Audrey Martinez, Abigail Martinez, Joseph Martinez, Isaiah Barrios, and Crystal Barrios, in the fire; Angelica Sonobe Cregge and Crystal Sonobe Cregge, whose parents, Scott and Floracita Sonobe, died in the fire; and of course, Clive Doyle, who provided photos of his family and friends, many of whom died in 1993, and some of whom are survivors like himself. As told in Clive's account here, his youngest daughter, Shari, died in the fire.

We thank Stuart A. Wright for permission to use the photograph taken of Livingstone Fagan in London in 2008.

We wish we could have included more photographs of the members of the Branch Davidian community in this book, so we call the reader's attention to the photographs of David Koresh, his wives, and their children in *Memories of the Branch Davidians: The Autobiography of David Koresh's Mother,* by Bonnie Haldeman, and the photographs of Wayne and Sheila Martin and their children and a collage of Branch Davidian children in *When They Were Mine: Memoirs of a Branch Davidian Wife and Mother*, by Sheila Martin. We thank our spouses, Ken Richards and Holly Jerger, for serving as sounding boards as we have puzzled over the complexities of the Branch Davidian case and for their love and support through the years as we have interfaced with the people and historical traces of the Branch Davidian community and the events that occurred in 1993.

Catherine and Matthew are grateful for the privilege of getting to know Branch Davidian survivors, especially Bonnie Haldeman, Catherine Matteson, Sheila Martin, and Clive Doyle, whom we have come to know the best. We have been living and dying with the Branch Davidians as we have become engrossed in their stories, grieved the loss of loved ones who died in 1993, grieved those who passed subsequently, and grown older together. We thank Clive for the privilege of working with him to bring his story to publication.

Catherine Wessinger   Matthew D. Wittmer
New Orleans   Los Angeles

A Short Introduction to the Branch Davidians and Clive Doyle

Catherine Wessinger

On Sunday, February 28, 1993, a little-known Christian community living on property named Mount Carmel Center located within the rural outskirts of Waco, Texas, suddenly became famous when its members got into a shoot-out with Bureau of Alcohol, Tobacco, and Firearms agents. The seventy-six ATF agents were attempting to carry out a "dynamic entry" into the community's residential building to deliver an arrest warrant for the community's leader, David Koresh, and execute a warrant to search the building, which housed approximately 130 people of all ages, from babies to the elderly. Not all members of the community were present at the building on February 28. The members were Americans, Canadians, Australians, British, and one Israeli. The community was a racially and culturally diverse group. Many of the members had Seventh-day Adventist backgrounds. The allegation in the affidavit written to obtain the warrants was that community members were converting semiautomatic weapons to automatic weapons without paying the tax to obtain the permit to do so legally. Four ATF agents and five of the community's members died as a result of the shoot-out, twenty ATF agents were wounded, some severely, and four Branch Davidians were wounded, including David Koresh, who initially believed that he was dying. Later that day, a sixth community member, a young father anxious about his wife and children, was shot and killed by ATF agents as he attempted to return to Mount Carmel on foot.

The shoot-out immediately became a controversial incident that gained international attention. Press coverage instantly attributed a sense of notoriety to the community based on federal agents' allegations and the presumed guilt of community members in relation to the deaths of the ATF agents. Virtually no attention was initially focused on the nature of the raid

1

carried out by the ATF agents. Before the community's telephone lines to the outside world were cut off by FBI agents who arrived to conduct what would become a fifty-one-day siege, David Koresh and the members alleged that the ATF agents shot first and that bullet holes in the metal front door, the outer walls of the building, and the ceiling in the central tower would prove that the ATF agents had done most of the shooting and that ATF agents had fired down at the residence from National Guard helicopters. They pointed out that no effort was made to knock on the door and serve the warrants peacefully. In fact, prior to the raid, when David Koresh had learned through his gun dealer that ATF agents were interested in his weapons purchases, he had invited ATF agents to come to the residence openly and inspect his weapons. David Koresh could have been arrested on one of the many occasions when ATF undercover agents came to Mount Carmel to interact with him or when he left the property, which he did regularly. During the siege, after all telephone lines were cut off with only a line remaining for communications with FBI negotiators, the members consistently made these allegations to the negotiators and to two attorneys, who were permitted to enter the building and examine the number and nature of the bullet holes.

News reporters who rushed to determine the identity of this religious group found a receiver's deed on file indicating that the property had been purchased in 1973 by the trustees of the General Association of Branch Davidian Seventh-day Adventists, so the news reports began calling the Mount Carmel community the Branch Davidians. The Branch Davidians, founded by Ben Roden, had been living on the property since 1965, but the 1973 receiver's deed had formalized the transfer of the property from the previous owner, the General Association of the Davidian Seventh-day Adventists, to the Branch Davidians. Ben Roden (1902–1978) was the founding Branch Davidian prophet, and his wife, Lois Roden (1905–1986), succeeded him as prophet. Lois Roden was succeeded by a young man, Vernon Howell (1959–1993), who arrived at Mount Carmel in 1981 when he was twenty-two years old. By 1984 Vernon Howell was regarded as the next Branch Davidian prophet and, even more, as the end-time Christ. In 1990 he changed his name legally to David Koresh.

Because federal agents had been killed on February 28, 1993, FBI agents took charge of the case. FBI negotiators spoke by telephone with David Koresh, Steve Schneider, Koresh's primary spokesperson, and virtually all the Branch Davidians, including the children. Between February 28 and March 23, twenty-one children and fourteen adults came out of the building as a result of negotiations. March 5 was the last day that a child came out. Audiotapes of the negotiations indicate that agents were happy whenever children were sent out. On the other hand, whenever adults came out, the FBI tactical team punished the remaining Branch Davidians by cutting off the building's electricity and blasting high-decibel and irritating sounds at the building, where infants, children, women, and men remained. Bright spotlights were shown at the residence through the nights to prevent the use of a flashlight to signal SOS messages. The building was surrounded by tanks, concertina wire, and snipers. The tanks made threatening maneuvers around the building, occasionally ramming it, crushed and removed vehicles parked around the building, and ran over the grave of the Branch Davidian who had been killed on top of the water tower during the ATF raid. FBI agents made obscene gestures at the Branch Davidians looking out the windows. Toward the end of the siege, whenever a Branch Davidian would walk out of the building, whether to get a breath of fresh air or to pick up supplies being delivered by one of the tanks, agents would throw dangerous percussion grenades ("flash-bang" grenades) to drive him back into the building.

Despite the psychological warfare tactics being applied against them, David Koresh and Steve Schneider told the negotiators that the Branch Davidians would come out and be taken into custody after Passover. The eight-day Jewish holiday concluded on April 13. On April 14 David Koresh sent out a letter stating that after he wrote his short interpretation of the Seven Seals in the New Testament book of Revelation, they would all come out. On April 16 he reported that he had completed writing his interpretation of the First Seal. Despite this breakthrough in negotiations, Attorney General Janet Reno was told that the negotiations were stalled, so she approved a plan for the FBI to use the tanks to gas the residence slowly over two days. However, the plan approved by Reno included a provision stating that if the Branch Davidians fired at the tanks inserting CS gas, the FBI commanders present at Mount Carmel could accelerate the gassing. Once the assault began, the commanders on the ground had complete decision-making power.

CS gas is a virulent form of tear gas that burns the skin and respiratory passages and can cause suffocation through excessive production of mucus in the lungs. Its instructions state that it should be used outdoors, not indoors in enclosed spaces. The United States has agreed in an international treaty not to use CS gas in warfare.

The gassing began on the morning of April 19 at 6:00 a.m. Almost immediately an FBI sniper-observer reported seeing gunfire directed toward tanks, which were driving into the building, so the FBI commanders ordered the acceleration of the CS insertion. The chemical powder that turns into CS gas was delivered through sprayers attached to the booms of the tanks. "Ferret rounds," small rocket-shaped canisters that spray gas, were also shot into the building. The tanks demolished the building by driving through it in multiple areas. The mothers and small children took refuge in what was considered the safest part of the building, a concrete vault located at the base of the central tower. The door to the vault had been removed in

1992 when a walk-in refrigerator had been placed inside the vault, which was next to the kitchen. At 11:31 a.m. a tank drove through the front of the building to where the open entrance of the vault was located and gassed that area until 11:55 a.m. The tanks continued driving through the building and breaking it up until the first fire was seen at 12:07 p.m. in the front window of the room on the second floor of the building's southwest corner. A few minutes later the entire building was engulfed in flames.

Only nine people, including Clive Doyle, escaped the fire. Fifty-three adults and twenty-three children ages fifteen and younger, including two babies born during the assault, died in the fire. Taken together, the deaths of eighty-two Branch Davidians and four ATF agents mark the Mount Carmel conflict as having the largest loss of life in a law enforcement action on American soil.

Afterward, the government was very concerned with avoiding liability and the appearance of federal agents attacking American citizens and visiting foreign nationals, so officials put all the blame on David Koresh and the Branch Davidians. This was reinforced through the judge's manipulation of the jury's verdicts in a criminal trial in 1994. The jury found all eleven Branch Davidian defendants, including Clive Doyle, innocent of conspiracy to murder federal agents. Clive Doyle and two other men were found innocent of all charges. The jury found seven defendants guilty of other charges. At the sentencing, the judge declared that the jury had intended to find five of the defendants guilty of conspiracy to murder federal agents, applied that verdict, and gave the men extremely lengthy sentences—forty years—which were later reduced to fifteen years after appeals to the Supreme Court.

During the trial, government prosecutors alleged that the Branch Davidians had illegally converted automatic weapons—the reason for the ATF raid—but this was never proved because the weapons put on display in the courtroom were covered in plastic wrap. The prosecutors would not let the defense team's gun experts examine the weapons unwrapped.

In 1995 congressional hearings on the case were highly politicized. ATF agents, FBI agents, and Attorney General Janet Reno sought to minimize government responsibility for the deaths. Branch Davidians sought to testify to what they had experienced. Democratic senators and representatives sought to protect the administration of President Bill Clinton (Democrat) by demonizing David Koresh.

Branch Davidian survivors and relatives of those who died brought a wrongful death civil lawsuit against the government that went to trial in 2000. In the run-up to the civil trial, a story published in the *Dallas Morning News* revealed that contrary to congressional testimony that FBI agents did not use pyrotechnic devices (utilizing a spark and therefore capable of igniting a fire) on April 19 to deliver CS gas, in fact two pyrotechnic devices had been fired at a tunnel early in the morning. This prompted Attorney

General Janet Reno to appoint former senator John C. Danforth (Republican) as special counsel to investigate whether there was criminal wrongdoing on the part of federal law enforcement agents in the actions against the Branch Davidians. The Danforth investigation occurred at about the same time as the civil trial. Both the civil trial and the Danforth Report published in 2000 exonerated federal agents from any responsibility for the deaths of the Branch Davidians.

Throughout all of these events, the Branch Davidians in general have not had the opportunity to tell their side of the story on their terms. The demonization of David Koresh and the dehumanization of the Branch Davidians in the media, based on characterizations made by ATF and FBI agents during the siege and after, and reinforced by the media application of the pejorative stereotype associated with the term "cult," have made a lasting impression on the general public. When I first got to know survivors living in and near Waco in 2004, they were keenly aware that when they gave interviews to reporters there was a good chance that the story would depict them as "cultists."

I recently told an educated person old enough to remember the conflict in 1993 that I research the case. She replied, "It is too bad that people get involved in cults." This kind of response, although a compassionate one, is a major reason Clive Doyle's autobiography needs publication. Colleagues in the field of new religions studies and I have argued that "cult" is a pejorative term that dehumanizes believers and demonizes leaders by imposing a stereotype that prevents open-minded investigation into what a group believes and practices. After the events at the Branch Davidians' Mount Carmel Center in 1993, new religions studies scholars have argued that the "cult" stereotype shaped the perceptions of ATF agents as they formulated and carried out the paramilitary raid on February 28. FBI agents who took control of Mount Carmel Center conducted the fifty-one-day siege, subjected the Branch Davidians to psychological warfare tactics, and carried out the tank and CS gas assault on April 19, utilized press briefings to reinforce the public perception that the Branch Davidians were a "cult." The Branch Davidians' side of the story was not presented in the news media in 1993 and for a time afterward. Clive Doyle's narrative, told in this volume from the perspective of one who lived through the events in 1993, survived the fire, and navigated the aftermath, provides a compelling alternative to the one-sided narrative promoted by the government.

April 19, 2013, will mark the twentieth anniversary of the fire, and with the passage of time the public's memory of the violence at Mount Carmel is fading. By the time this autobiography is published I will be teaching students who were born after 1993. It is important that American citizens, as well as citizens of other countries, not forget what happened to the Branch Davidians so that they will be vigilant in demanding that their law enforcement agents refrain from using excessive force against citizens. It is important that law enforcement agents learn the lessons of the Mount Carmel conflict so that they do not contribute to similar incidents in the future.

David Thibodeau, who with Clive Doyle survived the fire, published his autobiography, *A Place Called Waco: A Survivor's Story*, in 1999. In 2001 I met David Thibodeau and the other survivors—Clive Doyle, Edna Doyle, Sheila Martin, Kimberly Martin, Catherine Matteson, Bonnie Haldeman, Ofelia Santoyo, and Concepción Acuña—in Waco. During my sabbatical in 2004–2005 I had the privilege of interviewing Clive, with whom I recorded thirty-one audiotapes, and Sheila, Bonnie, and Catherine, with whom I recorded four audiotapes each. The corrected transcripts of Catherine Matteson's interviews have been placed in the Texas Collection archive at Baylor University. I edited the transcripts of the interviews with Bonnie Haldeman to produce *Memories of the Branch Davidians: The Autobiography of David Koresh's Mother* (2007). Bonnie was a strong and caring woman. She was murdered by her mentally ill sister on January 23, 2009, as Bonnie was attempting to take her sister to the doctor. A copy of Bonnie's book was placed in her hands before her coffin was closed. Sheila Martin's transcripts were edited to produce *When They Were Mine: Memoirs of a Branch Davidian Wife and Mother* (2009). Sheila's grief for the deaths of her husband Wayne and her four oldest children in the fire, and for the death of her fifth child, Jamie, in 1998, is tempered by her gratitude for God's gifts and what she learned from David Koresh, and her devotion to her surviving children, Daniel and Kimberly, who are now young adults.

It has taken another sabbatical for me to work with Matthew Wittmer on Clive Doyle's corrected transcripts to produce this autobiography. The thirty-one transcripts contain more information than could be included in this book. The corrected transcripts and a finding aid will be placed in the Texas Collection, Baylor University.

Clive Doyle was baptized in the Seventh-day Adventist Church in Australia when he was ten years old. Clive and his mother, Edna Doyle, became Davidians in 1956, when he was fifteen. As Davidian Seventh-day Adventists they accepted the teachings of Victor Houteff, who had passed away in 1955. They read themselves into becoming Branch Davidians under Ben Roden in 1964, when Clive was twenty-three. Clive and three other young Australian Branch Davidians were called to Mount Carmel Center in 1966, when he was twenty-five. While living at Mount Carmel with Ben Roden as prophet, Clive married, had two daughters—Karen and Shari—divorced, and gained custody of the girls. His mother, Edna, came to Texas to help him raise the girls. Clive was living and working at Mount Carmel when Ben Roden died and his wife, Lois Roden, became the next prophet. When Vernon Howell, later named David Koresh, came to Mount Carmel in 1981, Clive and Edna were among the Branch Davidians who gradually shifted their allegiance from Lois Roden to him. There were conflicts with the Rodens' son George, and they left Mount Carmel for a time. Clive was among the Branch Davidians who traveled, worked, and proselytized in California, Australia, and Hawaii. He was with the Branch Davidians when they returned to Mount Carmel and was periodically at Mount Carmel as they built the large building that figured prominently in the events of 1993. He was present for the ATF raid, the siege, and the tank and CS gas assault on April 19. He was among nine Branch Davidians who survived the fire, but his eighteen-year-old daughter, Shari, perished. He was a defendant in the criminal trial, was acquitted of all charges, returned to Waco, and lived at Mount Carmel from 1999 to 2006.

Clive's life story constitutes an autobiographical history of the Davidians and the Branch Davidians. Clive tells an intelligent, informed, and engaging account of his experiences. We have included material in endnotes to provide additional information, often from original documents provided by Clive and other sources. Matthew Wittmer's essay on "Reconstructing Mount Carmel Center" in the appendix provides maps and floor plans of the building that address and amend discrepancies in previously published diagrams. Clive's recollections inform various details in the ground level layout and second floor diagram of the building. This is Clive Doyle's autobiography in his own words.

1

Telling My Story and the Story of the Branch Davidians

Everyone has a story. The knowledge in everyone's experience, I don't care who they are—high or low, educated or uneducated, rich or poor—is interesting to someone. Many people have lots of information, whether it's how to fix things, household hints, or family trees. Everyone has information they've learned or that is part of their makeup from a lifetime of living. It's a shame that a lot of it is lost when someone dies. Certainly over the period of my life I've learned a lot of things, and I've experienced a lot of things that I hate to think are all down the drain when I pass on. That's one reason for recording my story.

In the particular case of the Branch Davidians, there are few people who really understand our religious point of view: what our desires are, what our learning was all about, what our goals and hopes are based on. There are also very few survivors, and they are dying fairly rapidly. We've lost a couple every year at least.[1] There are so few of us left that it would be good for posterity to record our history, our experiences, why we believe the way we do, what it is based on, and what David Koresh was trying to teach.[2]

There are so many stories out there about who we are and what happened in 1993, from the government on down to the guy on the street with an opinion based on what he heard. Those stories are very distorted. Some people may have no opinion at all because they don't know anything. For those who are interested, I think the story from our perspective needs to be recorded and laid out as close to factual and accurate as possible.

Every Branch Davidian is going to tell his or her story differently, and everyone is going to explain their beliefs on different levels. That was something that concerned David Koresh. He started out with a group of people studying, studying, studying, and learning, learning, learning—but he was frustrated because some of us were still so ignorant on certain issues. I find that when you study under a church or a particular program for years, you end up getting into the "parrot mode," where you give the answers that are expected and not too much thought goes into them. You say what you think will please your questioner. David squelched that a lot of times. In fact, Ben Roden, the founder of the Branch Davidians,[3] would squelch that. He quizzed us: When you get to Israel, how are you going to deal with this situation?[4] How are you going to answer this question? We would repeat back to him some of the stories he had told us about his personal experiences in Israel, and he said: That isn't going to do any good. They've already heard my answer. They've already got a comeback for that. You don't want to be a parrot.[5]

During my life I've run into that word, "parrot." Judges, government officials, and people like that to whom I have had to give answers don't want pat answers. I remember going down to San Antonio many years ago for hearings about my becoming an American citizen. One of the questions was about my view on military service. I answered: I gave you our official church booklet on it, that is my position. The man said: I don't want to know what your church promotes. I want to know what you espouse. I had to speak for myself. It's so easy to fall into the parrot mode of repeating back the pat answers. A lot of times they're very hollow. They're maybe even insincere, because you haven't put any effort into them—you're just repeating things you have heard or read.

Many people judge us by what they hear from the media or from people who are against certain things. If you want to learn what a Republican is all about and what he believes, you don't necessarily go to a Democrat to find out, because you're going to get a slanted view; they're going to bring up the negatives or the failures.

We were taught that if someone comes with a message based on the Bible, instead of trying to fight it, instead of trying to put it down or trying to prove it wrong, we should study the Bible to perceive whether the message is true, whether it has any merit: Study to see if it's so.

A certain stigma is attached to small groups. There are certain prejudices. I hope that the Branch Davidian survivors or anyone else who writes something on us will provide people with another side than the one they've been presented by the media, the government, or whatever official version they have received, even the one from their own pulpits.

If people read this account, they will at least gain a different perspective on who David Koresh was, where he was coming from, who we were, and why we believe the way we do. Most people think "cult" about us and think we are people who were brainwashed and deceived. They think our church members don't know what they're doing or where they're going. Hopefully, my story can open their eyes. I'm not saying that readers have to accept what we believe, but at least they will come to an understanding of the way we perceive things.

2

From Australia to Texas—Meeting the Branch Davidians

EARLY LIFE IN AUSTRALIA

Early Years in Grandparents' Home

I'm a war baby. I was born February 24, 1941, at what they called the Women's Hospital in Melbourne, Australia. In those days a woman didn't go home twenty-four hours after having a baby. The mothers usually stayed in the hospital longer. Then they were sent to a recovery facility where they could stay another week or so. Of course, this is all hearsay, from what my mother told me after the fact.

After I was born my mother brought me back to her family home. My father had left her prior to my birth. Both my uncles were in the army during World War II, so they weren't home. My grandmother and grandfather, my mother, and I lived in the family home in a suburb of Melbourne called Kensington.

My mother worked in a garment factory for twenty-odd years to support us. While she was at work my grandmother took care of me. I don't remember my grandmother because she died by the time I was eighteen months old, maybe even before that. I only vaguely remember my grandfather.

We lived on a corner. In one direction it was all residential, but across the road from our front door it was all factories. They were obnoxious factories that made soap and candles, and there were factories that tanned hides, so the area had lots of odors.

The kids at least had the advantage of having a brick wall to hit a tennis ball against. I never played real tennis in my life, but we used to bounce the ball off the factory walls and play out in the street.

We got along with our neighbors. On Friday nights or Saturday nights the whole neighborhood would gather in someone's house to sing and play music. Someone would have a piano, or maybe a violin or an accordion. Our whole neighborhood was pretty social in those ways. You don't see much of that these days.

I spent several years in what they call a crèche. It's a French word for a day-care center. After my grandmother died there was no one to take care of me, so my mother put me in one of those. I don't remember a whole lot about it except they had little canvas cots with fold-out legs that we were supposed to sleep on in the afternoon.

At about the age of five I went to the local state school. I had to walk maybe a couple of miles. All the neighborhood kids went there, so quite a number of us went together. We had to walk past lots of factories and over a bridge that spanned a canal to get there.

I was a very timid child. I was shy and introverted, easily influenced I guess, because I remember sneaking with kids who would get me to go with them to smoke cigarettes. I was probably six or seven. We'd sneak off behind the school or behind a shed in the schoolyard and smoke a cigarette. I never developed a smoking habit from that. We'd just do it to try it out.

. I remember that a tannery caught fire across the road from the school. They brought us all out to watch it burn in case the fire jumped the road and caught the school on fire. We were all lined up along the fence watching. It was probably my first major fire.

At home it was very, very dark. The house had black wallpaper with little bitty flowers, but it was predominantly black. We had electricity, but for whatever reason we took a candle in a little candleholder if we went out of the kitchen to go up the hall to the bedrooms.

My mother's maiden name was Serjeant, which was the French spelling as opposed to the English, even though a lot of our people came from England. My mother's name was Edna Margaret and she had two brothers, Harold and William. William's name was shortened to Bill. My grandfather's name was Phillip John Serjeant. My grandmother's maiden name was Margaret Bruce Patterson Spice.

My grandfather remarried some lady whose name I don't know, but I recall people calling her a land shark. She had married several men in her life and had somehow finagled all of them into signing everything they owned over to her.

I was maybe six years old when I came out of school one night and my mother was there waiting for me. She had my little metal pedal car with her. Normally she wasn't off from work when I got out of school, but she was there at the school gate waiting for me, and we went home together. I pedaled and she walked. When we got to a certain street, she said: We're not going that way, we're turning here. I said: That's not the way home. She said: We're not going home.

I found out as I grew up that this step-grandmother had us evicted. The police came round and told my mother that she had to get out. My older uncle, back from World War II, was evicted also. The other uncle had married, so he was living elsewhere.

My mother said: We're turning up here. We're going somewhere else tonight—which was strange to a little kid.

Childhood

We went up a long road, and we ended up in the park. I can't remember the name of the park, but it was the park that had the Melbourne Zoo in it. During the war the army had put up a number of barracks in the park. After the military had finished using them, each one was divided into three living spaces with plywood walls.

We were the middle tenants in one of them. There was a little potbellied stove in the middle of the floor where we did all of our cooking. To do laundry you went up to the laundry building, which had troughs and boilers for boiling clothes. I don't recall how we got on for bathing, but I think we mostly took little baths in tubs on the floor.

That first night when I pedaled to the new place, my uncle was already there. I walked in and there were mattresses on the floor. I just sat down. I was tired after all that pedaling. I don't even recall eating or staying up. I just crashed on the mattress and went to sleep.

We stayed there about eight months. We never went to the zoo the whole time we lived next door to it.

At some point my mother arranged to rent a house from the housing commission, which had cheap houses for poor families. Today in the United States they'd probably call it a project. Most of the houses—single-family dwellings and duplexes—were in a new subdivided area out on the edge of the city.

So we moved into a house that had cheap rent in a suburb called Essendon. Essendon was where the Melbourne airport was at that time. Our house was the last on the street, and from there on were grassy fields. All the streets that were parallel ended at these fields. So for a little kid there were lots of places to play. We were on a hill, and at the bottom of the hill was the Maribyrnong River. It was kind of a muddy thing, but it was a river.

There were caves, where sand had been mined, on the edge of the river a mile or so from the house. Kids would play in the caves, even though they were off-limits because some kids had been hurt in them. It was a pretty good life for a while as far as having places to play and things to do.

Our greatest entertainment at the time was the movies. When I was out of school during the summer, Mother would take me to the city on her way to work. She would give me the equivalent of a quarter, which was enough for the whole day. I'd go to the movies starting at 8:00 or 9:00 in the morning and she'd pick me up after 4:30 at night. I could see three or four shows in that time. I was a little kid in the big city all by myself.

Mother worked in a garment factory that made women's wear such as corsets and swimsuits. She packed them in boxes to send to stores or overseas.

Occasionally Mother took me to work. I had inherited from her the love of reading. She loved to read, I loved to read. I was shy and introverted. The bench or table where she worked had a shelf about six or eight inches off the floor where all the empty boxes were put. I would take a book and burrow in among the empty boxes and sit in there and read all day. It used to frustrate the people she worked with: Oh, that poor kid, making him sit in there. She would say: He's not being punished—he likes it. He just gets in there and goes into another world.

After we moved to Essendon I kept going to the same state school up until the fourth grade. I had to walk down to the bottom of the hill to catch a bus, which took me to the railway station, where I caught a train to the Kensington station, from which I walked to school. After I turned ten I changed to another school on the other side of Melbourne. So I had to take the train into the city. I then changed to another train that took me out the other side of town. From there I still had to walk a couple of miles to get to the school.

The area we lived in was predominantly Catholic, and the Catholics hated the Protestants, and probably vice versa. But the Protestants were in the minority, so we were always the ones getting beaten up and worked over. At the top end of our street, where we lived, there were maybe four or five Protestant families. Catholics dominated the rest of the street. Just to go to the bus stop you had to run the gauntlet. I've been shot at, had rocks thrown at me, been pulled off my bicycle, and beaten up. I've even been banged over the head with a brick. That all happened to me over a period of time.

A Baptist church rented some rooms in the local school closest to where we lived and used them for a Sunday school. They went around the neighborhood canvassing as to which parents would send their kids.

My mother let me go to some of those Baptist Sunday school classes. My mother said we were Presbyterians, but we never went to a Presbyterian church as far as I know. She sent me off to Sunday school to get me out of her hair while she did the laundry.

Mother told the story that I came home one day and asked her to shake my hand. She humored me. When she shook my hand, I said: "You've shaken hands with a servant of the Lord." I'd given my heart to Jesus that day. That kind of impressed her, but she didn't start going to church. I joke about it now, saying, "When I was nine, I gave my heart to Jesus. He's been trying to hold me to it ever since," you know, keeping me reminded of my commitment.

The family next door called themselves "brethren." They had a lot of Adventists in their extended family, but they were very anti-Adventist themselves. They had four daughters. The two oldest girls came over to our place one night and said that about half a mile away on a vacant lot: They're putting a tent up. I asked: Oh, what is it? I thought maybe it was the circus. They said: There are going to be some meetings down there and we'd like to go, but Mom and Dad won't let us unless an adult goes with us, and they won't go. They were trying to cadge my mother into accompanying them, so Mother agreed.

FINDING THE SEVENTH-DAY ADVENTISTS

It turned out to be a Seventh-day Adventist evangelistic meeting. We sat right in the front row. After that first night the girls' parents wouldn't let them go back, but my mother and I went every night. We thought it was great.

Seventh-day Adventists put on these kinds of meetings. They have a good speaker present prophecy based on the scriptures. We had never heard anything like it in our lives, so it was very impressive. Sometimes they showed slides. These types of meetings might have a choir, although they didn't have a choir at that first one we attended. You know, it's entertainment. This was way before television, so it was something going on in town to do. We were fascinated by it. Within several months we decided to be baptized and join the Seventh-day Adventist Church.

It was 1951, and I was ten years old. I was the second-youngest person in Australia, up to that time, to be baptized into the Seventh-day Adventist Church. People quizzed my mother: He's kind of young. Do you think he knows what he's doing? She answered: I think he knows what he's doing.

We were pretty happy as Adventists. We were not disgruntled members. We were not the kind of people who would miss a meeting, sneak out early, or any of that. We went to Adventist camp meetings, and if the meeting was going to be, say, ten days long, we would get there early. When the meeting was over we would stay an extra week to help them fold up the tents and that kind of thing. Mother was in the choir and held office in our church. So we were not into being disgruntled or looking around for something else. We weren't even interested particularly in more light.[1]

One of the things that made an impression on us when we first became Adventists was that Seventh-day Adventists were pretty much focused on 1964 as the year when the Lord would come. It wasn't official; it was just kind of a feeling that went through the ranks. I don't think the Church ever made it an official statement, but the grassroots feeling was that Christ should return by that time, based on statements that had been made in

scripture that the gospel was to be preached to all the world in this generation and then the end would come. They tabulated that a generation was
120 years, "as in the days of Noah." So 120 years from 1844 (the beginning
of the church) would bring you to 1964.

There were green banners hanging in the front of the churches with the
Seventh-day Adventist aim, mottoes, and different things printed on them.
One of them was the statement about spreading the gospel to all the world
in this generation. In other words, they were making an effort to evangelize
the whole world by the time this generation was over in 1964, which they
perceived as being at the end of the 120 years. Not too long after 1964 those
banners got removed.

ADVENTIST SCHOOL

A woman Bible worker would come around to see us in between meetings
with the minister whom we first heard preaching. She came to our house
and would have Bible studies or go through a lesson with us. She kept urg-
ing my mother that I ought to be going to a Seventh-day Adventist school
instead of a state school. My mother said to her: State school is free. Church
schools are expensive. I can't afford it. The woman kept pushing, and finally
she said: If you'll send him to the Adventist school, I'll pay part of his tu-
ition. So my mother finally gave in.

I went to a Seventh-day Adventist school, which turned out to be on the
very opposite side of Melbourne. I did that for six years.

I was not a good student in school. I was good as far as behavior, on most
occasions anyway, but I was not necessarily an A student. I had to work
for anything I got, and I did not get straight A's at any time that I recall. I
might've hit an A once in a while. But I loved school. In ten years, I think I
missed half of one day for being sick.

I missed half a day one time for being late. I had walked to the bus stop,
caught the bus to the station to catch the train into the city. My connect-
ing train never came. We asked around: What's going on? There had been
a wreck or something way out on the line. Three or four of us decided to
walk to school from the city. We didn't know the way, so we followed the
railroad tracks. We picked up rocks and threw them at puddles and goofed
around a little bit. We got out to school about twelve or one o'clock in the
afternoon, and we got hauled down to the principal's office because they
figured we had been playing hooky. We were all set for a whipping, because
in those days you got a whipping if you did anything. We told them our
story, and of course they didn't believe us. But they decided to ring the railway company, which confirmed that there had been no trains coming out
that way all morning. Then they held us up to the other kids as examples
for how much we wanted to go to school.

In the Adventist school, the students wore uniforms. High school begins in seventh grade in Australia. They don't have what you call middle schools in the United States. In Australia, back then, when you went from the sixth grade to the seventh grade you were entering high school. It's a major culture shock. In seventh grade we went from geography and history and health and those kinds of things that little kids learn, to social studies, algebra, Latin, trigonometry, logarithms, and metalwork or shop.

The uniform for the Adventist school was expensive, so I found myself going to school with a knitted sweater that Mother had made rather than a store-bought one. I wore short pants until I was about fourteen. Everyone else got into long pants at ten or twelve. I was two or three years behind everybody.

I was never in the "in" crowd in school. I'd go to school and all the kids would have marbles, and I wouldn't have any. By the time I got it in my head, "Hey, marbles are the big thing this week," I'd show up, say, Thursday or Friday with marbles, and everybody had switched to tennis balls or some other knickknack. I was always behind on that kind of stuff.

I got picked on. You would think that since it was an Adventist school, everyone believed the same and we would all get along, but that wasn't the case. There were cliques. There were rich kids, ministers' sons, doctors' sons, and so on. I got beaten up nearly every day. Most of the time I'd try to run away. If I stood up to them, they made fun of me until I cried.

If I got out of school late, they would be waiting for me. If I got out early, they would run to catch up with me walking to the station. It didn't matter which direction I went in, they would somehow manage to waylay me and give me a hard time. I had every reason to hate school, but I didn't. I didn't like getting beaten up or teased, but I didn't hate school.

One time I was out on the playground at lunchtime. Our school didn't have swings, it had trapezes. A trapeze was a big A-frame with a swing made out of bars. I was out in the playground eating my lunch, and there was this one group of kids—ministers' sons, rich kids—that used to pick on me all the time. This one kid came up and started needling and teasing me, and I said: Why don't you leave me alone? He mimicked me, so I ran off. I ran over to the trapeze and shimmied up the bar. I got up there and stood on the crosspiece. He came climbing up the bar after me, and when he got level, for once in my life I let fly and punched him in the nose. He bled like a stuck pig, and slid all the way down to the ground. I thought: They're going to kill me tonight. He's going to tell all his friends and I'll be lucky to make it to the station.

I never had another ounce of problem out of any of them. It was kind of weird. I was expecting revenge and I never had any more trouble. They were in higher grades than I was, and eventually they left the school and weren't there anymore.

At the end of eighth or ninth grade, at age fourteen, most kids were expected to leave school, unless you were going to be a professional. If you weren't going to go to a university to become a lawyer or a doctor or something like that, you were expected to drop out. Then you would go get a job in some trade, some factory that made something, and if you signed up as an apprentice they would send you to a technical college one day a week. So you did slave labor for about five years until you got your trade papers or license.

All my friends left at the end of the ninth grade. I stayed and did one more year, and I would have gone on to finish high school because I wanted to be a doctor. That was my dream. But I chose to drop out of school after Mother and I were excommunicated from the church for studying the tracts put out by the Davidians.

HEARING THE DAVIDIAN MESSAGE

At the end of my tenth-grade year in Adventist school, Mother and I became acquainted with a man who was giving out Davidian literature. As a result, we were among thirteen people who were—in a single night—kicked out of our Seventh-day Adventist church. Most of them were the officers of the church, and the reasoning behind being disfellowshipped was that we were studying *The Shepherd's Rod* tracts by Victor Houteff.[2]

Seventh-day Adventists didn't like Davidians and called them "Shepherd's Rods" because of the book that Victor Houteff published named *The Shepherd's Rod*, volumes 1 and 2. Davidians got called a lot of things, including "Hotrods" and "Twigs" or "Sticks." But "Shepherd's Rods" and "Hotrods" were probably the worst, and the most common, names we used to hear.

In Australia summer vacation is in December, January, and February. In the summer of 1956 in December, which was at the end of my tenth-grade year in high school, I went to an Adventist youth convention in Nunawading, a sort of mecca for Seventh-day Adventists. People from all over the South Pacific turned up, and there were thousands of young people there. During a break in the meetings several of us were going off the property to go swimming in a quarry. In the course of crossing the front road, we looked down toward the front gate of the campground, and there was this huge crowd of people—hundreds of people—gathered around a white car. The white car had a sign on the top of it held up with guy wires. We couldn't see what was on the sign. We didn't know anything about it; we hadn't heard any rumors going around that something was going on at the front gate. We were oblivious until we saw this crowd. For some reason I made the remark: Oh, they are probably some offshoot[3] or cult. I don't know why I said that because I didn't know too many cults in those days.

So we went off to go swimming. We came back, finished out the camp meeting, and came home. There was very little buzz that I can recall about this car that attracted so much attention down at the gate.

Mother and I attended a little Seventh-day Adventist church in a neighborhood called Moonee Ponds. It had very few people who came to church regularly—maybe forty or fifty on a good day—which was about half the members on the church rolls. When it came to the prayer meeting on Wednesday nights, attendance was worse—it was down to about eight.

We went to the prayer meeting one Wednesday night and were kind of milling around outside waiting to go in and get started, and this white Jaguar pulled up. The signs painted in red on the doors and trunk were permanent. Most of them were one-liners like "666 is not the Pope." The sign mounted on the top of the car read "Hear ye the Rod." I don't know whether it had "and who hath appointed it" or just "Hear ye the Rod." This was taken from Micah 6:9. The idea was to catch your attention by these short statements on the car.

We went: Uh-oh, what is this guy doing at our church? How does he even know our church exists? We were just a little dinky church, not a big or popular one. We went into the meeting.

It turned out there were two or three people there who hardly ever came to prayer meeting. They had come out of guilt, because some other church member was putting on a big party at their house. These people were invited to the party and they were going, but they felt guilty going to a party when there was a prayer meeting at church they weren't attending. I don't know why they didn't feel guilty any other time, but they showed up that night out of guilt, reasoning: We'll go to prayer meeting and then we'll go to the party.

So the prayer meeting proceeded. The couple with the white Jaguar, the man with his wife, sat in the back. They didn't say a word, and no one introduced them. When the prayer meeting was over, the elder of the church let the people going to the party get away, and then he said: I want you all to come to my place. I invited this couple to come here to let them speak, but in view of the fact that we had some other people here who would have tattled on us, I'm inviting you all to my house if you want to listen. Of course those people probably tattled on us anyway, because they probably recognized this couple and their car. We all went back to the elder's house. The man with the white Jaguar spoke for what seemed liked several hours, into the early hours of the morning.

His name was Daniel Smith. I don't remember his wife's name. He was a big Scotsman with all of his fingers and part of his thumb on one hand missing. He was kind of a gruff person. He could be friendly, but he came across pretty stern at times. He spoke, and we were pretty impressed with what he presented, so he was invited to come back and give us some more studies.

When we became Adventists the minister who had baptized us into the church was Frank Braden. He was a nice man, his wife was nice, and as Adventists we got along great with him. So out of respect and out of curiosity we contacted Frank Braden about the Davidian teachings. Because we trusted him, we wanted Frank Braden to present a rebuttal to what was being presented by Daniel Smith. I don't know if Mother contacted him directly or if the other people listening to Daniel Smith did. They asked Frank Braden: Would you be willing to come by the house? We want you to hear something.

Frank Braden came to a meeting at the elder's house, and then Daniel Smith showed up. Before Daniel Smith could even start speaking, Frank Braden said: There is something you ought to know about this man. . . . We stopped him and said: We don't want to know about this man. We want you to listen to him and then give us your opinion of whether it's right, wrong, or what you think of it. Frank Braden was indignant. He didn't even want to be in the same room with Daniel Smith. Frank Braden didn't come across very well and fell in our estimation as to his qualities as a minister and as a student of the Bible.

Once Frank Braden left the house the cat was out of the bag, and it got around pretty quickly. Here was this group of people from our little wooden church listening to Daniel Smith about the teachings of an offshoot founded by Victor Houteff in America called the Davidians. Most of the people who were listening to Daniel Smith were officers in the Moonee Ponds church: head elder, youth leaders, Dorcas leader. The Dorcas women are the do-good women in the church who collect clothes and food. The Dorcas Society is named after Dorcas in the book of Acts.[4] My mother was librarian. Most of them held offices and were the backbone of this little church. So this was a big thing.

We received notice that there was going to be a church meeting and we all had to be there. The hint was that they were going to disfellowship us. They were scared to death we would vote ourselves to stay. They figured that we had enough votes to vote ourselves to stay in. So they dragged everybody they could to this meeting, including people who had not been to church in years. We agreed among ourselves ahead of time: We are not going to fight this. If this is what they want to do, let them do it.

There was one man who tried to speak in our defense. He was a member of the Seventh-day Adventist Church but not a member of our congregation, so they wouldn't let him speak. There were a couple of others who supported us. It turned out that they were so offended by how it was handled that they left that church or just gave up belonging to the Seventh-day Adventist Church altogether.

One of the questions brought up at that meeting was: Why are we being disfellowshipped? They said that one of the reasons was that we were no longer supporting the church with our tithes and offerings. We replied that 40 percent of Adventists don't pay tithes. They answered: Right, but the difference is that they never have, but you have and you stopped. They had to make an example of us. So our listening to Daniel Smith split the Moonee Ponds church down the center, and the church voted us out.

There were thirteen of us ousted from our little church. It actually included more people, including children who were not baptized and some others. I had been baptized at ten so I was one of the thirteen. I've seen this happen to individuals over the years since, but the only other time I saw a group being disfellowshipped was in Hawaii, where the church ousted all of the people who joined David Koresh.

FIRST JOB IN AUSTRALIA

It was summer vacation. I was in a state of flux. I wondered: Now what do I do? I'm kicked out of the church. If I go back to the Adventist school I'm going to be the brunt of all kinds of persecution. I was almost sixteen and I wasn't sure what I would do.

My uncle came and said: What are you planning on doing? I answered: I don't know. It's kind of up in the air now. He said: I can get you a job where I work. So he took me to a cabinet shop. Both of my uncles worked there, making television cabinets. Television had just come in and the cabinets were made of wood. The shop also made cocktail cabinets and different kinds of entertainment centers, but mostly television cabinets. I went there and was offered a job as an apprentice.

The owner of the shop explained to me: We only have one apprentice every five years. We don't have any other kids working here, and the boy that was here has just finished the course, so he's going on full pay. I was hired, and I had to sign an apprenticeship contract.

I think I got paid about eight dollars a week, but they sent me to Melbourne Technical School one day a week to learn cabinetmaking. Half the day was math, and half the day was model making. I didn't do very well in model making.

The students who attended the technical college full-time were antagonistic toward the kids who came in one day a week for technical subjects. The classrooms were used for other subjects, so whatever you were working on would be stolen, smashed up, or thrown in the trash, so you would have to start over from scratch when you came back the next week. I kept getting further and further behind on some of the projects, so my boss picked on me.

I was a gopher at the shop. They were not helping me too much to learn the cabinetmaking trade. It was assembly-line work. I got to work with some things, but mostly I swept the floor, cleaned up after the tea or coffee break, ran errands, and on Fridays I went to buy lottery tickets for all of them. It got so bad that I really dreaded going to work.

SPREADING THE DAVIDIAN WORD IN TASMANIA

In 1958 I had been an apprentice for eighteen months. This was the year Australian Davidians figured things were going to happen in relation to the forty-two-months prophecy put out by Florence Houteff.[5] Daniel Smith was basing the prediction about 1958 on the date of Victor Houteff's death on February 5, 1955.

My mother asked: How can God judge Seventh-day Adventists for not heeding the Davidian message when most of them haven't heard of it or they haven't had a chance to read it? I decided to quit my job. Mother and I were going to go to the island of Tasmania, which no one had touched as far as the Davidian message was concerned.

I had a hard time quitting my job though. My boss made all kinds of threats: You'll never work again. We'll blackball you. You'll never work in this business again—which I never did, at least in Australia. But Mother and I felt that going to Tasmania was important. Time was running out. If God was going to judge not the world, but the Adventist Church, then it just wasn't fair to let the Adventists in Tasmania get killed or go to hell without at least a chance of learning the Davidian message.

To get to Tasmania we took an overnight boat. The Melbourne harbor is a bay enclosed with two narrow necks of land called the Heads that come pretty close together. Inside the bay the water is fairly calm, but outside it is rough.

We had gotten a cheap cabin. The propeller shaft for the boat went right through our cabin. You could hear the propellers and the engines all night long. It was enough to drive you nuts. Plus we were underwater. When we looked out the porthole, it was just water. We couldn't see sky or anything.

People told us: The best way to get through the trip is to go to bed early and be sound asleep when you go through the riptide, then you won't notice it. Well, that didn't work. Mother and I took turns going down the hall to the bathroom to throw up.

We eventually arrived at the island of Tasmania. The island of Tasmania is shaped roughly like a heart, and we landed in the middle of the north coast.

My mother had borrowed the biggest suitcase she could find. We had packed it full of books because we thought: They're going to want to know what we believe, so we'll give Bible studies, and we'll use all of Ellen White's writings,[6] and we'll use Davidian writings, and we'll use the Bible to prove our points. I was just a teenager lugging this huge suitcase all over the island. It weighed a ton.

We were there for a month and went to every Adventist church that we could find and handed out literature. A lot of the Adventists in Tasmania wouldn't talk to us. We did get invited into some homes. While we got to talk to some people, we never gave a Bible study the whole time we were there. People would visit with us and be polite. They maybe felt sorry for us, but they would not actually get down to the nitty-gritty: Let's open the Bible up and look at what we are here for.

A funny episode was when my mother and I went to Launceston, the second-largest town in Tasmania. When we got there we made inquiries: Where is the Adventist church? We learned it was out of town. We went to the bus company and we were told: Oh yeah, we go past there. So we went out there on a Sabbath morning. It was way out in the sticks, but it was not bush. It was just fields going for miles.

The bus driver pulled up on the side of the road—it was not a regular bus stop at all. He said: This is it. We stood up. There was nothing to be seen. I asked: Are you sure this is the right place? He said: Oh yeah. You see that over there on the horizon? That's the place. We looked and looked, and there was not a soul to be seen. He swore up and down that was the place where we had to go.

So we got off the bus. We trudged through the fields carrying all this literature to hand out, because we didn't know how big the church was. As we got closer we could see it was a school. There were no cars, no evidence of anybody being there. The bus was going way out of town and probably wouldn't come back until that night. We were going to be stuck out there all day for nothing.

As we got close, we saw a car pull into the driveway. We followed the car around the driveway, and we found all kinds of cars in the back. We knocked on the door. We didn't just walk in because we weren't sure what was going on. We knocked. Lo and behold . . . guess who opened the door—the kid I had punched in the nose back in school! His father was an elder of the church.

We walked in and every seat was filled. They just had folding chairs because it was a rented room in a school. They didn't offer us seats. We had to go find some chairs and drag them in there and sit down. They were really cool, austere, toward us.

After that we journeyed by train down to Hobart, which is Tasmania's capital. We got there at maybe one or two o'clock in the morning. We went

to the Salvation Army, hotels, place after place, just trying to get a room. There was no room anywhere, no room in the inn. So Mother and I got on a bench in the park.

The only policeman I saw the whole time we were in Tasmania was this huge guy—he must have been about six and a half feet tall—who came out to the park and said: What are you doing? This is illegal. You can't sleep on a park bench. We explained that we had been everywhere and couldn't get in, but we were willing to stay on the bench. We said: This doesn't bother us. We are used to doing this. We will survive. Don't worry about it. He said: It's my job to worry about it because you are breaking the law. I'll get you a place.

He took me to the YMCA. They gave him the same story: We're full. No rooms. He said: I know for a fact that not every bed in this place is taken. You may not have a separate room, but I want you to make room for this young man. So they made me go into a room that had two beds but only one person in it. I got in there with a young guy. I didn't get much sleep because he was excited that he had company. We stayed up most of the night and talked. Just to make conversation I asked: What do you do for entertainment or fun in this town? This was the capital city of the state of Tasmania. He said: Well, we ride bicycles. Even though I was, you might say, a strict Davidian who was not too much into the world[7] anymore—we had already withdrawn from movie going and dancing and that kind of stuff—I was tickled that here was a guy whose biggest thrill was riding a bicycle.

The policeman took my mother back to the Salvation Army. They let her in, but they let her know she was not welcome. They charged her full price for the room, and then she didn't get breakfast in the morning. She had to be out within a few hours because she arrived way after midnight and you had to be out by six or seven in the morning.

We decided we would go up and do the north coast on the west side of the island. We had gone to the major towns in the east and down through the middle. There was a string of little towns along the coast on the north shore.

We went to the railway station in Hobart and asked for two tickets. They sold us two tickets all the way to the very northwestern corner of the island. We got on the train, which went all the way up the center of the island and hit the coast. Then we were told: Everybody off. This is the end of the line. We asked: What do you mean this is the end of the line? We booked a ticket all the way to Stanley. He said: This train doesn't go to Stanley. We haven't had a passenger train go to Stanley in fifteen years. We said: They sold us tickets to go to Stanley. We argued back and forth and finally we were told: If you wait around we have a freight train that goes out there. So we rode in the caboose, or the guard's van, as they call it in Australia, with the guard.

He had a little potbellied stove, a pail, and maybe a stool, and that was it. In Stanley, we visited as many Adventists as we could find. We figured we had covered the island as best we could and it was time to go home. Mother said: We're not going to fall for that train trick again. I'll call the bus station and we'll get bus tickets. Sure enough, they were willing to sell us two tickets to Devonport, in the middle of the north coast where the boat went back to Melbourne. We were told that we had to be out on such-and-such a corner at, like, seven in the morning, where we would be picked up.

So we got up. It was almost dawn. We were standing out there waiting for the bus to come, and a station wagon pulled up. The man asked: You waiting for a ride? I answered: We have bus tickets. We're okay, you can go ahead. We thought he was offering us a ride. He said: I am the bus. So we got in. He stopped all along the way, picking people up going to work. It was like carpooling except that the station wagon was already full and our extra two seats technically weren't available. People were sitting on each other's knees.

We went back to the mainland, back to Melbourne, and within a short time after that the 1958 deadline passed. That was our figuring as to when Florence's forty-two months would come to an end. Nothing happened, so that was somewhat disappointing.[8]

MOVIES, THE BAKERY, THEATRE, AND LEAVING THE DAVIDIAN MESSAGE

I was about eighteen at the time of the 1958 disappointment. My best friend Ian left the Davidian group and went out to do his own thing shortly after that. I had a crush or off-and-on relationship with his younger sister Lesley. She left after him because, I guess, he influenced her.

I rationalized it in my mind that I was being a hypocrite by going to meetings when I had so many questions bothering me. Why go through the pretense of being faithful if you are not really 100 percent a believer?

One of the things that influenced me the most was Cecile B. DeMille's movie *The Ten Commandments*. Several of us—contrary to Adventist and Davidian standards against going to movies—went and saw *The Ten Commandments*. We liked it so much we went back and saw it a second time a week later. I had been raised on movies when I was a little kid before becoming an Adventist. I had pretty much gone without movies from, say, age ten for about seven or eight years while I was an Adventist and a Davidian. I guess going to that movie, even though it was supposedly a religious movie, was kind of like starting smoking again after you have given it up. I began to question why I was going to the Davidian meetings when I was not as much into it because of the 1958 disappointment. So I took Lesley to see a Walt Disney animal movie. I justified it since it wasn't an acted movie, it was a nature film. It was called *Perri*, and it was about a little squirrel.

When I quit going to Davidian meetings I tried telling myself: I am not really giving up everything. I still believe in the Sabbath. I still believe in not doing this and doing that, living a good life. I had certain beliefs I was not going to give up, I thought. But, of course, you get out there and get caught up in what everyone else is doing, and you end up doing a lot of things you did not plan on doing when you first thought you would experiment out in the world.

I remember going to see a Tarzan movie after that. I justified that to myself: There are animals in a Tarzan movie, so that is not too bad. They have got a couple of people in it, but it is basically elephants, chimpanzees, and crocodiles. Before I knew it I was going to all kinds of movies. I quit going to the Davidian Bible studies on Saturdays.

When I came back from Tasmania I was out of work for about a month. I finally found a job at a bakery. I worked there for about two and a half years, and it was during that time that I quit going to church and the Davidian meetings.

I worked all hours at the bakery; every day was different. Most mornings I started around 4:30 a.m. Mondays were earlier. We would do a double shift on Friday, so that started the night before.

I was rushing to work one morning on my bicycle and unbeknownst to me they had been digging and doing some roadwork the next street over, and the trucks that had been hauling the rocks away had been dribbling them along the road. My bike hit one of those rocks—it stopped and I kept going—and I came up with a broken arm. So I had to be off at the bakery for three to four weeks. A young boy by the name of John Wheatley was hired to take my place.

After my arm healed I got my job back. They laid John off, but they kind of kept him on a string: Don't go get another job. You can replace anybody who is sick, or you can fill different positions when people take a day off. He didn't live far from the bakery, so I got to know him. He was kind of a persecuted, lonely kid. I have had a tendency all my life to favor the underdog. If someone is a little strange or maybe retarded or has a physical problem, I tend to side with or defend them because I have been picked on all my life and beaten up. I tend to champion or play a friendly or protective role toward others. So we got to be friends. He had a great love for movies, too, so we started going to movies a lot more.

My two uncles had quit working at the cabinet shop. They ended up working backstage in live theatre. The theatre they worked for was called the Tivoli. It was a circuit. There was a Tivoli in every capital city in Australia. Occasionally the Tivoli had a musical, but mostly it was like vaude-ville—different acts, singers, dancing. My uncle either got me a free ticket or he got me a backstage pass.

The first time I went to the Tivoli and saw the show, I just fell in love with theatre. My uncle let me know there was a position I could get. For a while I worked at both the theatre and the bakery, which after six months was killing me. The theatre did eight shows a week. We would get off at about 11:00 or 11:30 at night, and sometimes I would go straight to the bakery and work a shift. Most people at the bakery would work all night and sleep all day, but I didn't. I would go to town, shop, run around with friends, so it was getting to me.

I finally gave up the bakery and went into the theatre, I won't say full-time, because I got what work I could. It was very minimum pay. I did it because I liked it, not because it was a well-paying job. I supplemented by working for other theatres, filling in for other people, or when they were building a show I worked during the daytime constructing and painting.

Edward Everett Horton was an older American actor, and the word going around was that the next show was going to be a one-man show centered on him. They let us know that everyone, except the heads of the depart-ments, would be laid off because we would not be needed.

By that time my uncle was living in Sydney, which is about 600 to 650 miles from Melbourne. I thought: I'll go visit my uncle until the Horton show is over, and then I'll go get my job back. When I drove to Sydney I didn't know where my uncle lived. I didn't have an address, and I didn't know what his circumstances were. All I knew was that he worked for the Tivoli in Sydney. I headed for the theatre figuring I would find him there.

My uncle was surprised when I kind of just showed up. He asked: Where are you staying? I answered: I'm not staying anywhere, I just got here. I fig-ured I would stay with you. He said: I've got a hotel room and it's not big enough for two. If you like, I can talk to the proprietress. I'm sure she has other rooms. I said: I don't have a lot of money. Is there any possibility of getting work so I can afford to pay for a hotel room every night? He said: You are out of luck. They hired on for a new show just the day before you got here, and they've got everybody they need.

He took me back to the hotel room, and I think I might have slept in his room on the floor that first night. Then we went and talked to the woman who ran the place, and she said there were other rooms and I could have one for so much a week. I said: I might stay one week, but that is about as much as I can afford.

My uncle went off to work the night after I got there. He came back and asked: Do you still want a job? He said that one of the guys they just hired broke his arm or his leg. He said: You can have his job, but it's not in the department you are used to working in. It was in what they call mechanist, which was hanging scenery that they pull down on ropes. Prior to that I worked in props—the property department. The theatre's backstage crew had an electrical department, a mechanist department, and props.

I went to work there, and shortly after that I got a message from my boss at the Tivoli in Melbourne: Come back, we need you. Edward Everett Horton only lasted a couple of weeks. We need you back here. I said: I just committed to a show in Sydney. As soon as it is over I'll be back.

I think the show in Sydney lasted three months. When I got back I supplemented my income by working for other theatres and filling in for people who took days off. I worked three months on *The Sound of Music* doing electrical at another theatre because they had their mid-week matinee on a different day than the Tivoli.

While I was in Sydney my uncle was involved with a girl who was part of the show. I ended up falling in love with her, too. It made him mad. There was nothing happening between us in Sydney, but he got mad to the point that he dumped her. He was mad at me in a protective way because he said: She has got a bad reputation. You don't need to get involved with her. I told him: Hey, nothing is happening. We are just friends.

When the show transferred from Sydney to Melbourne, he and I drove back to Melbourne to work at the Tivoli there.

GIRLFRIEND

On opening night this girl, who was part of the show and had traveled to Melbourne, came to me and asked: Can you do me a favor? I replied: What is it? I had not seen her since there was this big blowout about my uncle and her and me. She said: I have all this luggage that I got from the railway station. I rented an apartment at the beach and I need someone to take it down there in a car. I said: Sure, I can help. Once I took her down there we ended up going together for a whole year practically. I moved in with her eventually.

Of course, my mother was a little distraught that I had left the Davidians, was working in the theatre, and was involved in this situation. None of that pleased my mother at all. She prayed continually that I would come back, kind of like the prodigal son.[9]

My girlfriend's jealousy and hounding got me to quit the theatre. I got back on at the bakery and worked there for another year. During that time I was having problems with this girl because of her jealousy. She was very violent. She was suicide prone and was always trying to kill herself. There were all kinds of stressful situations.

My mother had been saying: I wish you would start going to church again, I wish you would read the Bible, I wish you this, that, and the other thing. An Adventist evangelist was going to hold some meetings in the city. Mother was going, and she wanted me to commit to go and listen to him.

In the meantime the show ended that my girlfriend had come from Sydney to be in. She was not needed in any of the next shows, so she was out of a job for a while. So she went into dancing at clubs and private parties and what have you. She would make more money in four or five minutes than I could make in two weeks.

Mother had been pressuring me. She wanted me to hear this Adventist evangelist. I kept putting it off and putting it off. One night I took my girlfriend to a club where she danced. She wouldn't let me go into the club. She didn't want me there watching her. So most of the time I sat out in the car and waited.

On the last night of this evangelistic series, Mother had begged: Come. This is the last meeting. This is the last chance. Will you come? Will you come? Will you come? I wouldn't give her a definite yes or no.

I guess it played on my mind. I was sitting out in front of the club and thought: I'll drive over to where this meeting is being held. I don't plan on going in. I'll just show up and make my mother feel happy. As I was driving toward this place I was thinking: Nah, I don't really want to go. But I found myself still heading in the right direction. As I was heading down the street that the building was on, I was thinking: Nah, I'm not going in, I'll just drive past. Well, as I drove past, Mother was standing right on the curb looking at all the cars to see if I was coming. Of course she spotted the car and spotted me. I was seen. Now I had to commit. So I went in there. I was in a beard, long hair, leather jacket—the whole deal. My mother was ecstatic; her prayers had been answered.

RETURN TO THE CHURCH

It was a huge hall, longer than it was wide. The place was packed. I said: Let's sit in the back. Mother said: No, no, no, let's get near the front so we can hear. We found two seats maybe two-thirds of the way down. I was livid with myself for letting Mother pressure me into coming and feeling guilty that my girlfriend was back there at the club thinking I was sitting outside waiting for her when I had actually gone off to this. So there was a turmoil in my mind.

I don't remember what the preacher said, except that at some point I just started crying. The reason I was crying was because it hit me: You have already made the first step back to God. I felt like I was making a fool out of myself, so I jumped up and ran out. Of course, Mother chased me out of the building in the middle of the meeting. Everybody could see. I said: I shouldn't have come. I shouldn't have come. I've got to go back and pick up my girlfriend. So I left. Mother was ecstatic because she also knew that I had broken the ice.

I got back and told my girlfriend where I had been. I said: I think I'm going back to church. She thought that was neat: Oh, we haven't gone to church together, let's do it! So we went off to a Seventh-day Adventist church, because Davidians at that time and even up to the present day continue to attend Adventist church service on Saturday mornings. They have their meetings in the afternoons. That is the kind of a thing they have kept up for seventy years or more.[10] Anyway, we went to church.

Shortly thereafter I said to my girlfriend: I wasn't thinking of going to church just as a tryout, as a new experience we could share. I'm thinking of going to church regularly. She agreed. I think we went the next week, and after the church service we went to the Davidian meeting as well. The Davidian meeting was a little more intimate, with people sitting around in a circle studying the Bible.

After that she began to balk: You are just tied to your mother's apron strings. Do you love me or do you love her more? I said: You have to make a decision. We either go together or I go without you.

The following week she got all ready to go. We headed off and she threw a fit in the car. She said: Stop the car. She used to pull that kind of stunt on other occasions over other situations. I would stop the car, she would get out and maybe run into a park or begin walking. I would beg her to get back in the car: Don't be stupid. Sometimes I would drive around the block. By the time I came back around, she woke up to the fact that she was stranded somewhere, so she would get back in the car and off we would go and things would work out.

That was what I did that day. I said: We are going to be late if you don't get back in the car. We can talk about this later. Get in the car. No, she was not getting in the car. So I drove down the road and around the block. By the time I got back she had disappeared. I went to the meeting and, of course, I was sitting there the whole time wondering what had happened to her, where she was, and whether she was okay. It turned out that she had hitchhiked and jumped in the first car that came by after I left, and she ended up back home.

My mother and the Davidians were all saying: You can't serve God and live in this situation. You are not married to her, so you should not be living together.

I went to the apartment one night when she wasn't there. I wrote her a note saying something to the effect: I can't continue living with you. I still love you, but I can't go on this way and serve God as well. I got my things and left. I felt so bad that I used to go back and see her. It took a while to bring about a complete break, but that was the beginning of the way back.

There are things that happen in your life that seem bad or that most people would frown on or judge negatively, but if you go back and look at it in a positive light, it was the means of getting me to rethink where I was headed and what I was doing. Everything was going wrong financially, and my relationship with this girl wasn't that good. She was cheating, being argumentative and suicidal, so I said: This is not working. So I came back to the church about 1963–1964.

DISCOVERING BEN RODEN AND
THE BRANCH DAVIDIANS IN TEXAS

About 1964 there was a meeting in California trying to get the Davidians reorganized.[11] A couple came and talked to us about going and representing all of the Davidians in Australia at that meeting. So Fred Steed and his wife went to California. He made a phone call back to Australia and said: God has a man here.

When Fred Steed came back he brought a bag full of literature that Ben Roden, founder of the General Association of Branch Davidian Seventh-day Adventists,[12] had handed out at the meetings in California. He shared them with us, and we got all excited. We were impressed that, hey, this man's got a message from God, as opposed to all the other ones who were writing and trying to get a following.

Fred Steed and his wife thought they were prophets, the two witnesses in the book of Revelation.[13] He tried to play down the impression he'd given us on the phone, because once we got the literature we figured he was talking about Benjamin Roden. He brought the literature back to Australia, so we thought he was impressed with Brother Roden.[14] Fred Steed tried to downplay that later because he never accepted Ben Roden. He said: When I said, God has a man here, I was talking about myself.

We found out that the Branches, similar to the Davidians, directed most of their efforts of evangelism and teaching at Seventh-day Adventists and Davidians. We basically read ourselves into Branch Davidian beliefs.

We began writing to Ben Roden in the United States, and we learned that he was taking people to Israel. After Victor Houteff died in 1955, Ben Roden started teaching and preparing people to go to Israel. He had taken a group over in 1958, and he approached the Israeli government with the concept that God's kingdom would be in the Middle East. To the Davidians, Ben's taking people to Israel by plane or boat was blasphemy. They believed they were going to go to the kingdom miraculously. God's kingdom would be full blown, and they would just be stepping into paradise.

What Ben envisioned was small groups going to Israel like pioneers, so when he was there in 1958 he negotiated with the government. He impressed them that there were Christians in the United States who were interested in the welfare of Israel and the setting up of God's kingdom according to the Bible's prophecies. Israeli officials asked Ben how many anticipated bringing over. Ben was thinking of the 144,000 in Revelation,[15] but he rounded it off and said: Oh, about 150,000.

He said that the Israelis jumped on the idea and told him to bring the people. Ben said the government's position was that as fast as you bring them we'll provide housing; we'll subsidize them for the first couple of years until they can get on their feet and make a living, open up settlements where they can produce their own food or make a living in some form. So Ben went over to Israel from around the fall of 1958 until he came back for the spring sessions that the Davidians were having in Waco, Texas, in 1959 leading up to Florence Houteff's prophecy about April 22. That's when the Davidians were expecting the fulfillment of Ezekiel 9. They were expecting the chastisement of the Adventists and they were expecting to go to Israel in "God's chariot," some heavenly vehicle that would take them over to where God's kingdom would be all set up.

When Ben Roden arrived at Mount Carmel Center east of Waco, the Davidians were in the middle of all this 1959 expectation. He said they were praying day by day for a sign that things were going to happen, and he went to them and said: I'm your sign. He used scriptures like Ezekiel, in which Ezekiel is told to do certain things and he would be a sign to Israel, and they were to do what he did or take note of what he did.

By that time most of the Davidians in Australia had dropped away. Probably in all of Australia there were only about one hundred Davidians in the late 1950s during Florence Houteff's tenure. There were probably about thirty or forty in our group. Especially after the 1958 disappointment in Australia, some of the young people and some of the older people quit coming to the meetings. So the Davidian group that I returned to around 1964 was pretty small, maybe two or three families.

Initially Ben Roden wasn't well received by the Davidians in Texas. They thought that actually traveling to Israel was blasphemy. They pretty much kicked him off the Mount Carmel property, so I guess he went back to Odessa, Texas. In the meantime his wife, Lois Roden, had gone over to Israel. She was over there for about four years holding that Davidian group together.

After 1959 the Davidians in Texas grew discouraged. They had the 1959 disappointment when nothing happened like they expected. Between 1959 and 1962 they pretty well all gave up, sold most of the Mount Carmel property, took the assets, and split them up among the approximately seventy people still there at the property, and took off.

They left seventy-seven acres of the Mount Carmel property. For some reason it did not get sold at that time. They left it in the hands of a lawyer in Waco by the name of Tom Street Jr. to dispose of.[16] In 1964, about two years after they had abandoned the place, a man from Colorado by the name of Atwood made a bid to buy the property. He put up about twenty-five thousand dollars. Then he contacted the scattered Davidians, trying to get them to back him financially and help him to buy the property. He couldn't raise the money needed, and he ended up losing his deposit.

Ben Roden then put up twenty-five thousand dollars. He came down from Odessa, paid the money, and went out to Mount Carmel. He went to the caretaker, who was a former Davidian, and asked for the keys, but the man wouldn't give Ben the keys. That's how Ben got into litigation, trying to get his money back, or trying to prove that the property was his, or trying to expose the fact that all of this liquidation was illegal.

In the meantime, we were in Australia reading the literature that Ben had given out at the meeting in California in 1964, which talked about groups he was taking to Israel and encouraged us to get ready to go there. Several of us began studying Hebrew with a Jewish family to prepare to go should we be called upon.

WAITING TO GO TO ISRAEL: RESERVE BANK OF AUSTRALIA, NATUROPATHIC STUDIES, PLANT NURSERY

I left the bakery in 1963 and went to work for the federal government of Australia with the Reserve Bank, printing money, stamps, and treasury bonds. One day I told the foreman or somebody higher up: I can't guarantee how long I'll be here because I plan on going to Israel. The next thing I knew, men in suits came down from the main office upstairs to talk to me. They said, in effect: You've got potential and you can go a long way in this business. You can work your way up. I thought to myself: There are about twenty or so older guys working just on this floor who have been here forty years and they are only one step higher up the ladder than I am. I thought: These are vague, vain promises just to keep me around because I'm a good worker. I was told: We will give you a raise if you stay. I said: I would love the raise and I will promise to stay until I leave. They accepted it and gave me the raise.

After this meeting with the big bosses, several people came to me and said: In the forty years we have been here we have never seen the top brass come down and beg someone to work here. The big brass were almost bending over backward to keep me, so that made an impression on everyone, but I was embarrassed. There was a continual ad in the newspaper for jobs with the Reserve Bank, and the turnover was about 90 percent a year. Very few people lasted more than a year.

While I was working at the Reserve Bank, an Adventist family from Austria moved into a house around the corner from where I lived. I got to be friends with them. The mother was really big into herbs and natural healing, and she was pushing her teenage boy to attend classes at a naturopathic college in Melbourne. He wasn't all that interested, but she was pressuring him, so he said: I will go and enroll only if you can talk Clive into going. I was a little older than him. She begged me to go with him. So I went with him to apply.

They were glad to get him because he had graduated from high school. He said: I'm only enrolling on condition you take this guy, too. They asked me questions and said: You don't qualify. You haven't graduated from high school. My friend said: If you don't take him I'm not enrolling. So they let me in. He dropped out after about two weeks, but I stayed. The college was located across the road from the Reserve Bank where I worked.

I think about forty people were in the class the first year. These were night classes. I worked at the bank during the day, and then I would go across the road. They had a clinic on the first floor and the classrooms were upstairs. People would come in and lecture on different subjects: chiropractic, iridology, herbology, and chemistry. Some of them taught at the university.

I noticed that out of the forty students in that year's class, there were two Adventists, two former Adventists who were members of another Adventist faction, and myself who had been connected to the Seventh-day Adventist Church. I thought: The whole Adventist Church is supposed to be interested in health,[17] but they don't have a program like this. Out of the thirty-five people who were not related to Seventh-day Adventism, a lot were what today would be called New Age—teacup readers, palm readers, etc. I found that many of them were interested in nature worship and health. I used to say to one of the Adventists: This is weird. God says His people are to be the head and not the tail.[18] Here we are with all this knowledge that we have had for years about health and diet and not smoking, and we are going to the world to get an education in something we should already know all about. But I stayed in the classes.

In 1965 Ben Roden contacted our group and requested that the four young people go to Israel. Lesley Shaw, my former girlfriend and the sister of my best friend, had come back to what were now Branch Davidian meetings. Her brother Ian, my best friend, never came back. She had an older brother, Edward Shaw, who stayed in the group the whole time I was gone. The four young people contacted by Ben Roden were Lesley, Edward, myself, and a teenager named Rod Somerton. We were about the only young ones left among the Davidians and later the Branch Davidians in Australia.

We quit our jobs and prepared to go to Israel. We were told we would go to Israel and stay with a family of Branch Davidians until we joined a *moshav*. A kibbutz is a communal village where everything is shared. A *moshav* is where people have their own house, a little bit of property to themselves, but also work communally on a major agriculture- or business-type project.

At the end of the letter from Ben Roden it said something like: But do not leave until further instructions arrive. We waited, and we waited, and we waited, and nothing came. So we ended up having to get jobs again, and we worked for about another year in Australia.

Jean Smith, a woman who was in the Branch Davidian group, lived out in the country. She told Lesley and me that she could get us jobs at a plant nursery near where she lived. She talked to the nursery owner and told him about the fact that we kept the feasts[19] mentioned in the Bible and we would need certain days off. Then she took us there for an interview. The owner asked me: What do you know about growing plants? I answered: Nothing much. I have had a vegetable garden once or twice. He said: Good. That is the way I like my workers. I get people coming in here who have had training or worked in other nurseries, and they have their own ideas about how to do things; I want my workers to do it my way. So he hired me.

He and his wife were Christian Scientists. He let me know early on: Mrs. Smith told me all about what you believe. I have my religion. I don't want to talk about your religion. You do the work you are asked to do, and everything will be fine. I said okay.

Within a couple of months I knew the Latin names of all the plants and could identify them. Most of the plants we were growing were native trees and shrubs. They were not just flowers. I pretty much ran the place because he would go off for five days a week selling. He would load up all the best plants in the morning and go out and sell them.

His wife was sickly, and she stayed in the house a lot. He had some women working, doing the potting, so I was basically the only guy he had working there for quite a while. I did the watering, selecting, labeling, and setting out new areas for plants. Both of them fell in love with Lesley and myself.

At the end of the growing season he laid the women off, but he kept me on. He said: I am so overwhelmed with work, going out and selling all the time. I have got to get seed planted and I haven't taught you how to do it. I would do it myself, but I can only do it at night, and I'm so tired I am not going to get much planted. I said: I will help you. He said: I appreciate that, but I can't afford to pay. We are barely making ends meet. You have to realize that in seasonal work there is nothing much coming in during the winter. That is why I laid the women off and I will get them back in spring. I am barely making enough to pay you from week to week, so I can't afford to pay you any overtime to be here at night as well. I answered: I didn't ask you to pay me. I am willing to work for nothing just to help you out. Otherwise, come spring, there won't be anything for us to do because there won't be any young plants coming up. That set him back; he had never heard that before, I guess. We agreed that on two nights a week I would help him for free. We went out to the potting shed and planted seeds in the seed trays, and we wound up talking religion all night long.

He brought it up and as we stood side by side at the tables, religion was about all we talked about. He would tell anecdotes and funny stories. At the end of the first week in which I worked the two extra nights, he came up and gave me my money. It was more than normal, so I said: I think you made a mistake. He said: Oh no, that is for the two nights you worked. I replied: I agreed to work for nothing. He said: I know you did and I appreciate it, but I feel I need to pay you anyway. So I got extra pay out of that.

FLYING TO TEXAS

After about a year at the nursery—by that time Lesley and some other women had come back to work during the spring and summer of 1966—we received another communication from Ben Roden that we were to make plans to come to Mount Carmel Center, outside Waco, Texas, as preparation to going to Israel. So I told the nursery boss: We have been waiting for this, so I am giving you notice. Well, he cried and his wife cried. They gave me a camera for the trip. I don't know what they gave Lesley. They were really sad to see us quit.

The four of us young people rushed around to get our plane tickets. We went to the airport to purchase tickets to the United States. We didn't know where Waco was—we knew it was in Texas, but that was all. We were told: Planes fly into Dallas. We said okay, and they booked us to fly to Dallas. While we were talking about booking into Dallas, we were told: You can't just fly one way into the United States. You have to have a return ticket. We said: We don't think we will be coming back to Australia. We are going over there to get information and then we will be going to Israel. So we ended up buying tickets to fly all the way to Israel. That way we would have an exit ticket to please the American government. Then we were told: We can't sell you the tickets until you have a visa from the American embassy.

We rushed down to the American embassy, which was five or six miles out of town. There was a very officious woman working the counter that day. She said: I need to see your plane tickets. I answered: We don't have the tickets because the airline said we can't get the tickets until you give us the visas. We showed her our money: Look, we have the money. She replied: No, you must have the tickets.

We went back and forth all day between the airline office and the embassy, two or three times. Every time we went back to the embassy she was there. I said: They won't give us the tickets. We went back to the airline and explained what you said, and no one will give us the tickets. She said: I won't give you the visa. The second-to-last time we went to the airline, we said: This woman is not budging. This is a stalemate. You won't sell us tickets without the visa, and she won't give us a visa without the tickets. So they wrote a letter on airline stationery. It said we had paid for the tickets, but the airline was not giving them to us until they saw the visas.

We went rushing back to the embassy, and the woman was not there. The new woman was as sweet and cooperative as could be. In no time flat we had the visas and off we went back to the airline: We got 'em! We got 'em!

We were told: There is one last thing. Have you had your shots? We said: No. The ticket agent said: We are not supposed to give tickets to you unless you have had shots. I have always been leery of inoculations and I would rather not have them. I had to sign a form saying that in the event that I got smallpox or whatever in my travels, I would not sue the airline. We all signed that form.

We finally got the plane tickets and we were off—Edward Shaw, Lesley Shaw, Rod Somerton, and myself. Rod was about sixteen, I think. He had to get a letter from his mother saying that he could leave the country in our company, he was not running away from home, and we were not abducting him. We got all that taken care of.

A big crowd of people came to the airport to see us off. The Jewish lady we had been studying Hebrew with in Melbourne, all the people who knew us, all came to wish us well on our journey. And off we flew into the wild blue yonder toward Sydney.

It was getting dark by the time we arrived in Sydney. We changed planes and then we flew on to Suva, Fiji. I think we got there around twelve or one o'clock in the morning. We were thinking: Oh, this is exotic! We had never been out of Australia. In fact, I had never been on an airplane before. This was all new, exciting. We were thinking: We will be able to see the island of Fiji. Even though it is night we are going to look around. As we were landing, the youngest boy, Rod, developed a nosebleed. We spent the whole hour or so of the layover in the bathroom trying to get his nose to stop bleeding.

Then we flew to Hawaii. We were telling each other: We didn't see anything in Sydney, we didn't get to see anything in Fiji, they are telling us there is a two-hour layover in Hawaii and we are getting there in the daylight. We are going to be the first ones off this plane, we are going to run over to get our bags, we're going to go through customs, open the bags, show them everything, and we will have all the rest of the time to look around. Even if it is only in the airport, we will get to see a bit of Hawaii.

We did get out of the plane quickly. We breezed through customs. We thought: Good, we have more than an hour to get out and look around. We had to go through a turnstile after customs. A man in a uniform stopped us: Will you follow me please? He took us into a little room where we were quizzed about the fact that we had not had our shots. We showed them the forms we had signed. We pleaded: We had plans so, please, can we hurry this up? They went through all the different diseases they were on the look-out for and made us sign some more papers saying that if we felt sick after we got to where we were going, we would report it.

We had already heard the last call for the plane when they finally let us out. We asked: Where is the gate for boarding our plane? They told us that it was at the far end of the airport. So we went lugging our suitcases and running the full length of the airport.

When we got to the outside of the terminal, there was no sign of the plane, there was no sign of anything. We asked someone and we were told that an airport bus would be along shortly to pick us up. We waited, and waited, and waited. Finally, a little golf cart pulling a trailer with seats pulled up. We jumped on but . . . we were the only four there. We said: Quick, we have got to get to flight so-and-so. He said: Don't worry. He just sat there. And he sat and he sat. We asked: What's the holdup? He answered: There are two other people. They're running late, also. They will be here any minute. We asked: Are we going to miss our flight? We were getting panicky. He said: Don't worry.

Eventually two people showed up. They jumped on and the whole six of us took off. We rode all the way back to the other end of the airport, practically to where we had been when we got off the other flight. The plane was already getting ready to line up to take off. He drove us way out to the plane. We got on the plane, flew into San Francisco, switched planes, and flew to Dallas.

When we left Australia, one of the men in the Branch Davidian group said: I will call Mount Carmel and let them know you are on your way and when you will arrive. However, he forgot to call. We arrived in Dallas at the old Love Field airport at one or two o'clock in the morning. There was no one there but skycaps, and they were all black people. We were thinking: Texas is pretty laid back, countrified, we ought to be able to understand them, we've watched cowboy movies. The skycaps sounded like they were talking ninety miles an hour. We could not understand a word they said. We found out later that they were talking slowly compared to people up north, for instance, New York City. To us it was a foreign language.

3

Living with the Branch Davidians

ARRIVING AT MOUNT CARMEL

We made a phone call to Mount Carmel, and they didn't know we were coming, let alone that we had arrived. They were all in bed. We were told: Sit tight.

We sat and we sat. Eventually George Roden, son of Ben and Lois Roden, his wife, Carmen, and a guy from California, Ernest Farrell, came in a station wagon and picked us up. We then found out that Waco was one hundred miles away. We didn't know that when we booked our flights. We thought that Dallas was the main stop close to everything. The people at the airline didn't tell us, and they should have.

It was daylight when we got to Waco. George didn't want to take us out to Mount Carmel because they had no place for us to stay, so they put us in a motel downtown. Later on in the day Lois Roden told us they had been surprised that we came so fast because they had been begging other people to come to Mount Carmel and they never showed up. We were there within a few days. But the other surprise was that they thought we were all boys. They had been corresponding with us and they thought Lesley was a boy.

So now they had another problem. First Ben and Lois put us into one house[1] and then they thought that didn't look good, so they took Lesley out and had her live in their house with them. They felt responsible for bringing in young people, but we weren't little kids. The only one who was a kid was Rod. I was twenty-six. Lesley was about twenty-four, and Edward was the oldest one at almost twenty-eight.

The Rodens tried to mother us. They let us know shortly after we got there that they were doing it not only out of concern for us and regard for our parents back in Australia, but also because they had lost their middle children. The only two of their children who were with them at Mount Carmel were George, who was married and had his own family and house at Mount Carmel, and Rebecca, who was eleven. Ben and Lois Roden had lost three boys and their oldest daughter, who had left the church and were either in jobs or in school. They had never been to Mount Carmel Center. I think they lived in Odessa, Texas. And here we were, three boys and a girl. So the Rodens kind of took us under their wing in a replacement kind of sense.

By the time we got to Mount Carmel in November 1966, the Rodens had already been through some litigation about the property. Quite a number of people, mostly from California, who had accepted Ben Roden as a messenger had moved to Mount Carmel, and now the four of us from Australia had joined the community.

Ben Roden didn't have the same kind of organization that Victor Houteff had at the Old Mount Carmel in the city of Waco. There were about seventy people living and working at Old Mount Carmel full-time in its heyday, and it was almost like Victor Houteff created work for people.[2] He had what they called the Davidic Levitical Institute to train young ministers. He also had all kinds of secretaries working in the office. They had secretaries who answered letters and secretaries who dealt with the finances. They had people whose only job was to keep track of the weather and people to keep track of visitors. They had someone who critiqued every sermon given by the ministers and wrote up reports on them. Victor Houteff had publishing and mailing. He had what they called mercantile, their own store. They even printed money and used cardboard coins. If people had to go to town and buy things, of course, they exchanged it, but those who worked there were paid in the Mount Carmel currency, which they could use in the store there on the property. When Ben Roden set up his Branch Davidians at New Mount Carmel, he didn't have as many people and he didn't have the kind of system that Victor Houteff built up.

When I came to New Mount Carmel, which was purchased by Florence Houteff after she sold the Old Mount Carmel property, I found some of the records from Old Mount Carmel in the Administration Building. They had a book that recorded all the Davidian funerals. Victor Houteff was very methodical; everything was tabulated.

When I arrived at Mount Carmel under Ben Roden, I lived and worked full-time on the property. There were quite a number of people who went into the city of Waco and worked. The number of people at the new Mount Carmel property fluctuated a good bit. There were quite a lot of people at Mount Carmel when we arrived, but shortly after that some of them left. And some who had been at Mount Carmel and gone away came back. It kept fluctuating. I'd say there were maybe forty people at Mount Carmel Center on average in any given year.

Ben Roden had cows for milking, and he had horses. He eventually got goats, so we had quite a dairy going. We didn't raise cattle for meat because we were vegetarian. When we got to the point where we were producing more milk than we could use, we found that we couldn't sell it because it wasn't pasteurized. So we donated a lot of milk to the Methodist Boys Ranch, which is just down the road from Mount Carmel. They accepted it gladly. They said the health department would not allow the boys to drink it, so they used it in cooking. That way it got heated.

The four of us who came from Australia and quite a number of single individuals who lived and worked at Mount Carmel on a full-time basis ate at the Rodens' house. Lois Roden, Carmen Roden, and some of the other women cooked for all of the workers who were full-time. The families in which the husband or the wife worked downtown ate in their own homes. It was only the full-time workers at Mount Carmel who ate communally. There were times later on, a couple of years later, when we all ate communally. That was an experiment for a while, but it didn't last long. It tended to peter out, kind of like the school. If we had people who could teach in the school, we had our own school. If teachers left and there was no one to take their place, then we sent the children to public school in Axtell, a little town nearby.

PRINTING AT MOUNT CARMEL

Two or three families from California had just left before we arrived, and one had been involved with printing Sabbath school lessons with a mimeograph machine. Someone informed Ben Roden that I had done printing for the Australian government, so I was asked to pick up the slack. The presses I worked with in Australia used big engraved intaglio plates. At Mount Carmel they did not even have offset printing at that time. We typed on a stencil that I then put on the mimeograph machine in order to print.

Ben Roden told a story that when he first started writing, he wrote a letter to Florence Houteff and the Davidian Council, which he believed God dictated to him. He sent this letter to people around the country who were interested in his message. Some of the people in Miami told Ben: Instead of sending boxes of copies of the letter to us, why don't we just reprint it down here? When they read Ben's letter, they thought there were some typos in it, so they corrected them. One was the phrase, "I AM hath sent me unto you." They figured that was bad English, so they corrected it in the copies of the letter they put out. When Ben found out about it he was upset. He said: They have totally missed the point of what is being said. They think that I, Ben Roden, said this, but I took this as dictation from God. I AM is the one who is saying it.[3] So Ben Roden for many years did not want other people printing his material.

After I came we did all the printing at Mount Carmel. Ben Roden didn't want anyone else doing the printing for the Branch group. It all had to be done where he could supervise it for quality control, you might say.

We used the mimeograph for probably a couple of years, and then we upgraded to offset presses. Once we got into offset printing, the format of Ben's tracts and literature improved. We went to color. We went to booklet form instead of the big, long legal-size papers that were just stapled in the corner. We had folded books and folded literature. By the time printing at Mount Carmel was at its zenith, we had four presses. We had our own darkroom and camera and plate-making system. We did our own binding and addressing.

I ran the printing and mailing departments. For the first couple of years I worked in the dairy as well, milking the cows in the morning, which later on branched out to milking cows and goats. If there wasn't enough help around, I fed the horses. But most of that work was done early in the morning and late at night, so in between was mostly the printing work.

Seventh-day Adventists hold camp meetings in the summer during school vacation. Leading up to every summer we printed thousands of pieces of literature and mailed them in the winter and early spring. Then, during the summer, groups of people would hit the roads and go to camp meetings, especially on weekends, and hand out literature. They either put the literature on the cars or handed them personally to people. If a meeting was held at an Adventist college, we might go into the dorms and stick them under all the doors.

I tended to dread the beginning of the summer because I had gone all winter without any public contact as far as witnessing. I pretty much stayed in the print room. So I had to get back into coming face to face with people in the public, which at some places was kind of like meeting the enemy, because some of them would get in your face and want to beat on you. Especially up in Arkansas there was one camp meeting, which was held at a Seventh-day Adventist college, where they'd throw our people off a bridge into the creek. It got pretty nasty, but not all of them were that way. Probably the hardest ones for me were when a couple of white people would be sent to a black camp meeting. There was no way to blend in; they knew who you were right off the bat. You stuck out. But once I got into the swing of it and broke the ice, it got to be something that I looked forward to.

INITIAL PROBLEMS WITH GEORGE RODEN

Years after we arrived at Mount Carmel, George Roden told me he was responsible for the four of us from Australia coming there. He had told his father, Ben: There is so much work here, I can't handle it all on my own.

I need help. George's idea of getting help was to ask us to come. George regretted that because he was very, very jealous of our replacing his brothers and sisters. I can understand his jealousy a little bit. The Rodens tended to play the mother/father figure, especially to us.

George resented us right off the bat, plus he resented the fact that we worked. Anything we could do to help we pitched in, and that showed him up because George was lazy. He did some work, but only if it suited him. He was erratic and overbearing even back then. It got worse over the years. We did not learn for a long time that George had Tourette's syndrome.

George's younger brother Benny told me that when George was in school he picked fights and got beaten up. Then Benny would have to rescue George to get him out of trouble. So George had been a thorn in the family's side for a long time. He was very arrogant.

I think they let him get away with a lot of things because he was sick, so he grew up to be a bully. If you complained about something George said or did, you would be told: You have to understand that George is sick. I know a lot of sick people, but they are still responsible for some of the things they do. George was not crazy[4]; he was not retarded. Letting him get away with things didn't help his situation at all.

So George was very resentful of us. Very few people at Mount Carmel would stand up to him. He was so big and such a bully that most people cowered in his presence. If they didn't, he would beat them into cowardice. I have seen him beat up a few people.

George would confront me. I had been shy and introverted for so many years, so one thing about going out into the world and getting involved in theatre was that I started to come out of my shell. All through my life I have sided with the underdog. So if I saw George do something, or if he was getting onto someone smaller or sicklier than himself, I would get into it with him—not because they were right and he was wrong, but because he did not need to be a bully. I sided with the other person most of the time, and that got me into conflict with George, which was mostly verbal. George resented me because he did not like my standing up to him.

It turned out that we never did get asked to go to Israel. We kept staying at Mount Carmel. George hated Edward, he hated Rod, and he hated me. He did not seem to mind Lesley too much. He hated her taking the place of his sister and living in his parents' house, but he tolerated Lesley a little better. George gave Edward a hard time and eventually manipulated Ben into deciding to send Edward back to Australia. Edward was gone in almost a year.

Then George beat up Rod. Rod and I were working in the dairy milking the cows, and George came up looking for Rod. Rod was not milking at the time. He was sitting on the fence. George went out there, and they got into it. I don't know what Rod said to him, but the next thing George was beating him up. He hauled Rod off the fence, threw him to the ground, kicked him in the head, and a few things like that. Of course, after that Rod wanted to leave, so within a week he left and went to Canada.

So that left two out of the original four of us from Australia.

MARRIAGE AND CHILDREN

Just before coming to Mount Carmel I had started going out with Lesley again. We had an off-and-on relationship for years, but when we were out in the world we did not have any relationship because she found herself another guy and they were going to get married, which never ended up occurring. Just before coming to the United States we made a pact that we would put plans for marriage on hold until we saw how things worked out going to America and Israel.

But when we got to Texas, the Rodens were looking for a way to get their family back. They wanted Lesley to win their son John back; at least, they were suggesting that maybe Lesley could marry John. Edward could marry their daughter, Jane. Their kids were not interested in this, and Jane and John married other people. So that didn't work out, but Ben and Lois were pushing it. Of course, I resented that because they knew I had my sights on Lesley.

About 1969 to 1970 I had been sending literature all over the world to address lists, especially Davidian address lists, that we had found in the Administration Building. Davidians were big on getting names and addresses of Adventists, especially the ministers. Over the years I've run into ministers who have told me: I've got stacks of your literature this high. I didn't read them, but I've got them. So I sent some literature to a man by the name of David Joyce in Australia. It piqued his interest, and he wrote and asked if there were any Branches in Australia. He was told there were some in Melbourne. So he came down to Melbourne from the next state, New South Wales, and got together with the group that included Lesley's mother. He told them that he had a dream that he was going to meet a girl, and that she was the reason he had come to the Branch Davidians. Lesley's mother interpreted: The girl in your dream must be my daughter. I guess somewhere in the back of their minds, Lesley's parents never forgave me for living with my girlfriend from the theatre; I was not good enough for Lesley, I guess. So they put it in his mind that there is a girl from Australia in America, and she is the one in your dream. It was arranged with the Rodens that he would come over and study. So this David Joyce showed up at Mount Carmel. I don't know whether Lesley's mother had written to her, or whether he told her what he believed God had showed him, but he convinced Lesley that they ought to be together.

In the meantime, I had been teaching school at Mount Carmel as well as doing a lot of other things. A family from Arizona had moved onto the property. They had brought a trailer and were living in it. They had three children, two boys and a girl. The two youngest ones began going to school at Mount Carmel.

I can't remember now whether it was the girl, Debbie Slawson, who asked me, or her mother: Debbie is having problems with math. Can you come and help her after school? I thought about it. The mother said: Come over. I'll cook you a meal. So I went over there and they cooked me a meal and I helped Debbie with her homework.

Over the period of a year I kind of got smitten with Debbie. She was quite a bit younger than me, by about thirteen years. But her mother and stepfather kept pushing the issue that we were an item. She was a teenager, maybe sixteen or so by then.[5] Even though I liked her, I took the attitude: I am going to wait. I am not in a hurry.

Debbie's stepfather's family in Idaho was going to have a family reunion, so there was talk that they were going to attend. They were getting their plans ready and unbeknownst to me her mother had gone to Lois Roden. I don't know how she put it, maybe, "Debbie and Clive like each other," or "Clive hasn't had a vacation in four or five years. It might be nice if he could come with us," or something like that. No one told me anything to start with.

Debbie came to see me in the print room and said: We are leaving in a couple of hours. We said our goodbyes. I gave her a kiss on the cheek, or maybe on the lips, and said: Have a good trip. See you when you get back. And she left.

Shortly thereafter, Lois Roden came and asked: How would you like to go with the Slawsons to the family reunion? I had not given it any thought. She said: If you would like to go, you'd better go pack a bag.

So I went and told the Slawsons: Lois Roden just suggested that I tag along. Is that okay with you? They said: Oh, yeah. So I packed a bag. We got in the car—the mother, Debbie, and I. The older brother had already left Mount Carmel and run off. The younger brother had gone to visit friends in Colorado, and the plan was that we would pick him up along the way. Lois told me: I would give you some spending money for the trip, but I don't have any money right now. Barbara Slawson, Debbie's mother, said we would go downtown first to pick up her husband, who was working for an air-conditioning company in Waco. Lois said: Since you are going in that direction, I'm going to go to the bank and get some money for Clive. Can we meet somewhere?

We met Lois in the Kmart parking lot, and she gave me some money. Then she started giving me a little speech about marriage. I asked: What are you bringing this up for? She said: I understand that you and Debbie like each other. I said: Yes. Lois asked: What are your plans? I said: I'm in no hurry. She said: Oh, okay. Have a good trip.

We got in the car, picked up Debbie's stepfather, Athan Slawson, and off we went. All of a sudden, Debbie's mother said: I talked with Lois Roden about you and Debbie. I said: Yeah, apparently you did. She brought it up back there at the store. She said: If you are planning on getting married this is the time to do it. I thought: Really, what did Ben Roden have to say? The mother implied that Lois Roden had condoned it, that if we were going to get married, do it while we were on this trip. That was kind of sudden, but Debbie and I were by then thinking about it.

We got to Idaho, and Debbie's mother rushed us over to get the blood test done and to put in for the marriage license. They ordered a cake, and we headed to the reunion. I forget which day of the week we got there, a Thursday or a Friday. On Saturday we went to church. There were no big plans actually spelled out, but we could see that things were moving in a certain direction.

We were in a Seventh-day Adventist church, and all of a sudden Athan Slawson went walking up the aisle toward the preacher in the pulpit. I guess the preacher was doing the preliminaries before he actually started preaching, or maybe it was at the end of the sermon. Athan walked up to the preacher, and I thought to myself: What on earth is he doing? He said to the preacher out loud so that everybody could hear: I've got a favor to ask. The preacher was looking at us because some of them knew we were Branch Davidians, so they wanted to know: Is this guy wanting to speak about his theology? Is he going to start handing out literature? I don't know what was going through their minds, but I could see everybody with a "What is going on?" expression on their faces. Athan pointed to us: You see this young couple back here? They want to get married. I'm asking you, will you do it? We just about crawled under our seats from embarrassment.

We had to wait until Monday to get the license, so we agreed to do it on that day. The die was cast: we had the preacher, we had all the blood tests done, and we were just waiting for the license. On Monday some of the church people came, and we had the ceremony out in the garden. We got married on August 17, 1970.[6]

When we left Idaho we went to Athan Slawson's brother's place in Oregon. We went through the redwoods and stopped in California at Tillie and Raymond Friesen's place in Dinuba.[7] While we were there I called Mount Carmel. It turned out that the Rodens were on a trip, so Lesley answered the phone. I told Lesley I just got married, and it took her by surprise.

Sometime between my calling and our return to Mount Carmel, Lesley contacted the Rodens to tell them. I don't know exactly what was said, but the story got turned around to where Debbie and I had eloped. That did not sit well with me. If the Rodens were not happy with it, or if they had not said anything, I might have balked about the marriage and said: I will wait until I can check this out.

We came back through Phoenix. The Slawsons were from Arizona, so they knew a couple of families in Phoenix who were interested in the Davidian message. I don't know whether they already had Branch Davidian studies by that time or not, but we stopped there on our honeymoon on the way back to Texas. That was where I first met Catherine Matteson.[8]

We came back to Mount Carmel and set up in a house as a married couple. All kinds of stories were going around. Debbie and I had eloped. We got married just so I could stay in the country. In fact, one woman in west Texas was putting it out that we had to get married because Debbie was pregnant. This woman said: They had that girl, Karen, real quick. Karen was born about eleven months after we got married! The woman just brushed off the facts and said: That's close enough.

We thought Karen was going to be born on the Fourth of July. We had gone to Lake Waco with the Slawsons to watch the fireworks. While we were watching the fireworks, Debbie's stepfather and her younger brother thought it would be funny to add a few fireworks of their own, so they began throwing firecrackers in Debbie's direction. Debbie was upset: Don't do that! Here she was, pregnant, the baby was going to be born any minute. I got mad and yelled at them, and they thought it was hilarious and they just did it more. I ended up picking up a chair and throwing it at them, and the next thing, Debbie's water broke. Everybody sobered up. We jumped in the car and rushed back to Mount Carmel.

We had arranged for a midwife. There was a black lady down in the Bellmead area in Waco [see figure 1 in appendix] who was going to come and take care of Debbie. We got back to Mount Carmel, and I went rushing down to Bellmead to get the midwife.[9] She was in bed, and it took forever to get her up. All the doors and windows were open, I guess because it was summer, but they had about four or five radios going full blast in the middle of the night. Everybody was in bed, sleeping through the noise. I was knocking on the door, and they couldn't hear a thing. I banged forever before someone finally came. I said to the midwife: Quick, quick, my wife's water has broken. She's going to have the baby any minute. After I brought her out to Mount Carmel and the old lady looked at Debbie, she got mad at me: She's not ready for this baby. She's not dilated enough. But she stayed because I had brought her out there. She sat there until five o'clock in the morning, when Karen came. Karen was five or six hours too late to be born on July the Fourth. She came along on July 5, 1971. Debbie's mother helped the midwife, and I helped assist.

I picked the name Karen from Leon Uris's book *Exodus*. I had read it sometime before that and liked it. I had an affinity with the girl's plight in the story, so I thought that was a neat name. That is where Karen got her name. Shari was born three years later on August 1, 1974.

David Joyce and Lesley got married. They went back to Australia, and they changed their last name to Ben David. He was David Ben David, and she changed her name to Abigail Ben David.[10] They were in Australia for a while, and then they moved to Israel. So Lesley finally got to Israel. Edward got to Israel. I still haven't gotten there, even though we had tickets way back in 1966.

BEN RODEN'S BRANCH DAVIDIANS AND THE MOUNT CARMEL PROPERTY

Between 1966 and 1973 Ben Roden and the General Association of Branch Davidian Seventh-day Adventists were in and out of court trying to get clear ownership of the New Mount Carmel property because we were, you might say, Davidians.[11] We were claiming that the property ought to be ours since we were church members.[12] Ultimately in 1973 we had to rebuy the property, or at least buy out the Davidians who were asking for repayment of a percentage of their "second tithes" that had gone into the property.

The court determined that since there were too many individuals who didn't agree with those of us—the Branch Davidians—who were on the property, Ben Roden should buy out the interest of the Davidians who had left. So a waiver form and a claim form were sent in 1973 to the former Davidians.

The claim form stated that the court had ruled that the property should be sold and that the people contesting the sale of the property to Ben Roden and the General Association of Branch Davidian Seventh-day Adventists should be paid a percentage of what they had paid in second tithes over the years. A lot of the Davidians took that route. A lot, probably hundreds of former Davidians, signed the waiver form, which said they didn't want their money back and they were willing for it to go toward the purchase price of the property. You might say that those waiver forms were the initial payment on the property. Ben Roden had to pay forty thousand dollars or so to the ones who wanted some of their second tithes back. From then on, the General Association of Branch Davidian Seventh-day Adventists owned the property,[13] and the Davidians had no further legal interest in it.

DIVORCE AND GAINING CUSTODY OF THE GIRLS

My marriage to Debbie did not go well. Debbie's great-grandmother—the grandmother of her stepfather—came to Mount Carmel and stayed about six months. Then the grandmother wanted to go visit her granddaughter out in California. So the Slawsons ended up driving her out there and staying. Athan had some health problems and they stayed in California so that he could get some treatments. Eventually he started working out there, and they never came back to Mount Carmel, although they continued to be Branches.

After they left Mount Carmel, Debbie would say: I need to go visit Mom and Dad in California and take the girls to see their grandparents. She started wanting to go visit them more and more. She would get out there and not come back. I would have to go get her. That went on for a while.[14]

On one occasion Debbie left Mount Carmel in January 1976. Months later she was still gone. Her stepfather called me and said: If you want to save your marriage, you'd better get out here right now. When I asked why I was told: Debbie is looking around at other men. If you want to save this marriage you'd better get out here. I talked to Brother Roden and told him the situation. He said: Go ahead and go. It was June when I went out to California.

It turned out that Debbie was living at her parents' former apartment in Glendale. They had given up the apartment to let her live there, and they had moved to a new one up the road in Burbank. I knocked on the door, and my little daughter Karen opened the door and looked out. I heard Debbie ask: Who is it? Karen said: It's just Daddy. Debbie came to the door and said: You can't come in. You can't stay here. You need to go to my parents' place and stay with them. So I went and stayed with my in-laws. I would go over to Debbie's apartment and visit the kids. I talked to Debbie about the situation, and it was pretty obvious she was not interested in coming back to Mount Carmel.

It seemed like the marriage was over, so I said: There is no point in my hanging around. I didn't come out here to visit your parents, I came to visit you. I came to see what the situation was and what we could do about it. I am going back to Mount Carmel. I will probably leave in two or three days.

A little later Debbie asked: When are you planning on leaving? I said: Maybe at the end of the week. Debbie said: I've been thinking. Would you like to take the children back to Texas with you? I said: Of course I would. She said: I told them it is just for a visit. You've got to promise me that you will have them back here in the fall, because I have registered Karen to start school. I said okay. I wondered: What brought that on? All of a sudden she was anxious for me to take the kids.

Debbie thought about it some more and said: You are a workaholic. You will not be able to take care of them on your own, because you will always be at work. How are you going to take care of them? I said: I will find a way, I will work it out. So she went back and forth on it all day: Okay, you can take them—no, you can't. It won't be good for them. Finally she said: If you have somebody to take care of them, I'll let them go.

I called Ben Roden and said: Debbie doesn't want to come back, but she is going to let me take the kids on condition that I find someone to help me take care of them while I'm at work. He said: Call your mother in Australia and see if she can come over. I did, and Mother was there in a couple of days.

So off we went to Texas. The kids had been gone six months. Shari had not yet turned two and she didn't recognize me when I first went out to California. Karen was getting up toward five years old.

I called Debbie several times a week and let her talk to the kids. I was talking to her one day and she said something about: I've got to go, I've got to fix Jim lunch. She said that Jim was a guy who lived somewhere with his mother and that he was visiting with friends in the apartment across the hall. The next time we talked on the phone, I heard this Jim mentioned again. I asked her if Jim was living with her, and she said yes. I told Ben Roden about it. I said: I promised Debbie I would bring the kids back before school started, but this is not the same situation that existed when I picked them up and brought them here. He said: Don't take them back. You need to get custody.

I was talking to Debbie over the next month or two, and it came out that she was pregnant by this other man. I got a lawyer and filed for custody of Karen and Shari. He filed the papers, and within a day or so he received papers from the lawyer Debbie had hired seeking a divorce. If her papers had been filed first, Debbie, being the mother, would probably have gotten custody automatically, but we had filed first. Debbie's parents were still sympathetic to me, so they wrote an affidavit saying that they felt the children would be better off with me.

We never went to court over it. For a while Debbie kept saying: If I was to come back, would you have me back? Talking out of my emotions, I said: Of course I would. She said: I might come back, but this is not your baby. Would you accept this baby? I said: I will love it and raise it just as I do the two we had together. It is not the baby's fault that it is on the way.

As the time of birth got closer, Debbie finally said: I decided to give the baby Jim's name, so I need this divorce in a hurry. There is no time to fight it out in court. We will exchange signatures. I will give you the children if you give me the divorce without a fight. That is what we ended up doing, and I got custody of Karen and Shari.

GETTING KAREN AND SHARI BACK THE FIRST TIME

Debbie and I talked on the phone even after the divorce went through. I would call her up and let the kids talk to her. Apparently it didn't work out with Jim, and they split up.

The kids were supposed to visit their mother twice a year. She could come to Waco once a year, and we had to take them to California once a year. We were to stay at the grandparents' place while the girls visited with their mother. She could take them out during the day, but she had to bring them back to me at night.

When we went out to California for a visit, Debbie was with a new guy. Things seemed fairly okay. Debbie asked if she could keep the kids over-night. I said: Okay, bring them back tomorrow. I think she did the first time. Several days later she asked if the kids could stay overnight again. I let them, and she didn't bring them back.

Debbie's mother went to where they were living and came back and told me that she had bad news—they were not there. My mother and I went over, and the place was abandoned—no furniture, no car, back door wide open, nothing was there.

First we went to the Glendale police. We were told we were in the wrong jurisdiction: I had to go to the area from where the kids were taken. We did that, and they said the procedure was to go back to Waco and report it to the sheriff's department, who would notify the attorney general in Austin, Texas, and the attorney general in Austin would notify the attorney general in Sacramento, California, the attorney general in Sacramento would notify the police, and the police would notify us. The kids weren't even considered missing persons until after forty-eight hours.

We started to leave, and a detective walked up and said he was sorry the rules were such that they couldn't help us much, but off the record, if we ever saw the kids in a shopping mall or on the street and had a chance to take them, we should grab them and head back to Texas right away. We went back to the grandparents and told them we had to go back to Texas and we would be leaving in a couple of days.

The day before we were to leave, I said to my mother: I want to go back to that apartment where they were staying. We parked out on the road and walked up the driveway. The apartment was in the back of a complex. As we walked up the driveway we passed the garage, and I saw through the win-dow that their car was in there. I went to the door and found it was locked. I listened for voices in the apartment. I went back to my mother and said: I can hear voices. Let's go back to the car.

I drove to the corner of the block and kind of hid around the corner and watched the front of the apartment. I didn't know how long we were going to have to wait, but we were praying about it. I think it was a Friday because I was saying to Mother that the Sabbath was coming. In the back of my mind I was wondering if I could get the girls out of their beds at night. I had all kinds of scenarios going around in my mind.

All of a sudden out came my ex-wife, this guy, and the three girls. They had them all by the hand. They were going for a walk, which was the answer to our prayers, because we probably couldn't have gotten ahold of them otherwise. They turned in our direction. I let them get about halfway toward us. Then I turned the motor on and came flying around the corner. I aimed the car at them—not to hit them—I figured they'd panic and let their hands go and run in different directions and we would get the girls and take off.

They didn't let go. They hung onto the girls, turned around, and started running back to the apartment like crazy. I followed them up the driveway, jumped out of the car, and chased them. They got to the door and couldn't get it open. They had locked themselves out. I tackled him and Mother went for the girls. I think she got Shari in the car and was trying to get Karen. Debbie was pulling Karen in one direction and my mother was pulling in the other direction. I was fighting him. I was holding my own even though he was a lot younger than I was, but he started swinging me into the apartment wall, which was made of stucco. Every time I whacked up against the wall, great clumps of skin were coming off. I was bleeding all over the place. We ended up down on the ground.

Once Mother got the kids in the car, Debbie came back and started pulling on me and screaming to the neighbors to call the police. Someone yelled out: They're on their way! So I quit fighting and laid there until the police came. They told me to get up and they quizzed me about the whole thing. They said I should be ashamed for scaring the kids. The girls were in the car, crying after seeing me get beaten up and their mother flailing around. I said: Yeah, it's not good, but I did what I thought I had to do. They said: You are the guardian. We are going to let you take the kids. They said: Get in the car and we will make sure they don't follow you. We did not go back to the grandparents' place. We left for Texas right then.

LOIS RODEN, VERNON HOWELL, AND GEORGE RODEN

Ben Roden died on October 22, 1978. Before he died, he started to listen to his wife, Lois, give Bible studies. In 1977 she had a vision that showed that the Holy Spirit is feminine, so this became an important part of her message, which we accepted. Even before Ben died we regarded Lois as a prophet.

Vernon Howell came to Mount Carmel in 1981 when he was twenty-two years old. Lois took him to Israel in 1983. That year he began to give Bible studies and he gained a hearing from those of us at Mount Carmel. Lois began to indicate that Vernon, who changed his name to David Koresh in 1990, would be the next prophet.[15]

George Roden had been out of the church and away from Mount Carmel since 1979. Lois took George to court in 1979 and got a court order that he could not be on the property and that he could not hold himself out as president of the General Association of the Branch Davidian Seventh-day Adventists.[16] She did that because George was beating on her, stealing things and selling them, smashing up the Administration Building, wearing guns and threatening people, and manhandling different people and hurting them. It got so bad that Lois finally got the court order. About 99 percent of the Branches sided with her.

George became very, very jealous in 1983 when he heard that David had come to Mount Carmel and that Lois was favoring him as the next prophet. George at that time was out in California with his sister, Jane. Lois got a phone call saying that her daughter was dying. Lois said: I'm going out to California because my daughter is in bad shape. David said: The Lord showed me that this is a ruse; this is not something you should do. Lois ignored David and went anyway. She got out there and sure enough, it was a means of getting her out there.

After Lois returned, David said: Everyone here at Mount Carmel has been listening to what God is saying at this time for the last five to six months. David said that Branches from all around the United States, and maybe even the ones overseas, should be invited to come to Mount Carmel to hear what he had been teaching. So Lois and David put out a joint letter inviting everyone to come to Mount Carmel for Passover in the spring of 1984 to hear David.[17]

In the meantime, George decided he would come to Mount Carmel to give this Vernon guy a hard time. George didn't like the idea that David might be the heir apparent. George brought his guns when he came back to Mount Carmel, and he parked a trailer to live in about two-thirds up the main driveway, out in the field. His mother, Lois, didn't file a complaint with the sheriff's department. She let George back on the property.

When George was getting after David, George's brother Benny asked me: How are you getting along with George these days? It was seventeen years after I had arrived at Mount Carmel in 1966. I said: It's probably calm right now because he has some other dog to kick. In other words, George had somebody else to go after. George was still after me, just not to the same degree. I was not in the front of the battle.

In 1983 David told Lois to quit publishing *SHEkinah*,[18] but she went ahead and published a final copy,[19] which I, as the printer, already had in the works. She put a picture of herself in it, and when it was printed it looked like she had two black eyes.[20] David made the remark to Lois: You are supposed to be the eyes of the church, you are the seer, you are the prophet, and this picture signifies symbolically that you are blind. You have got these glasses that reflected the light wrong.[21] David said that Lois had lost her wisdom, or that she had lost her eyesight. She had lost Inspiration.[22] As a result of disobedience to God, Lois had caused all this trouble.

She had allowed George back onto the property. She hadn't shown a firm stand or set an example for the members who were undecided and unaware of David's message.

In the months leading up to Passover in 1984 George put out all kinds of terrible stories. Some of them were pretty sick. One of the first things he said was that David had raped his mother.[23] He put out stories that David's father-in-law, Perry Jones,[24] and I were doing homosexual acts with David, which wasn't true. He accused David of putting drugs into the Emblems—the grape juice and cracker[25]—which wasn't true. The stories scared many people.

Later I talked with some Branches in California who sided with George without even coming to hear David. I asked why they sided with George, whom they had hated for years. It turns out he had embarrassed them by accusing them of all kinds of things. George was pretty brutal. They said: He was the best of a bad lot. I replied to them: If you think David is the devil, and you *know* George is the devil, why take a side at all? They would have been better off to stay neutral. That particular group never accepted David. They didn't stay with George long either. George ran everyone off.

So the word was going out to the field that all these horror stories that George was telling had merit: Beware, don't go to Mount Carmel, or if you do go, be aware of what you are going to run into.

Passover 1984 came along, and quite a number of people came. An awful lot of them stayed away. I asked them years later why they didn't come, and they told me they were scared. But a lot came, and most of the ones who came ended up hanging around with George at the front of the property.

At the beginning of Passover[26] David began holding his meetings. George wouldn't let us use the chapel. George took over his mother's house and wouldn't let us even go down there most of the time to visit. The Administration Building had burned down in 1983. So David held his meetings at the back of the property at Perry Jones's house. David even rented places away from Mount Carmel to hold his meetings. A very few came to hear David, and they had a real prejudicial chip on their shoulders. Most of them were not going to listen to David without being upset. By the end of the week the sides had pretty well jelled. There were those who were for David, and there were those who turned against him. Lois Roden came to David's meetings. Sheila Martin came to the meetings with her little son Jamie, and she ended up accepting David's message.[27]

DAVID HELPS GET KAREN AND
SHARI BACK THE SECOND TIME

I think it was in 1984 that Debbie came to Waco and asked if we could meet them at the park. I said: I've got some business to take care of in town, but I'll try to meet you at 4:30. When we got through with what we had to do, Mother said: Don't go to the park. The kids said: We don't want to go, Daddy. I said: I gave my word. Let me drive by and see if she gave up, because we are running behind.

I kind of circled the park. I came down one street, went all the way around, and then saw Debbie, her boyfriend, and her youngest daughter sitting on some park benches close to the road. We got out and sat down and were talking for a while.

All of a sudden, from behind, out rushed Debbie's brother straight past me. He grabbed Karen and took off running down into the park. Mother immediately grabbed Shari and started for the car. In the meantime, the boyfriend started pummeling me. I was holding my own, blocking his punches, and working my way back, trying to help Mother. Halfway down the park, the brother looked back and called: Come on!

They were not following him, so he put Karen down. He rushed back and started hitting me from the rear in the kidneys. I went down from the pummeling from the two of them. I fell kind of on the brother's leg, so he went down, too, punching me in the kidneys. The boyfriend threw Mother onto the ground, and they ran off with Shari.

All kinds of people were around as witnesses. When they were gone, we had to walk about a block. No one would let us use a phone. We finally got a phone in a restaurant and called the cops. They took about forty minutes to get there even though they were only half a mile or so away. They finally got there, and by that time all the people who said they would be witnesses were tired of waiting and left. The people working concession stands decided they didn't know anything or see anything. I think one said: I saw something. I thought it was just a family fight. It *was* a family fight! The kids were being stolen and people were being hurt. That was the final episode of the girls being taken. It was seven weeks before we managed to get them back.

David came to my mother one day and said that God had told him that if he and I would go out the next weekend that God would go with us. He said that was all the message was. David said: God hasn't indicated that we'll find them. David said to my mother: Do you have any extra money? I don't want to use a vehicle they are familiar with.

We bought a little station wagon for about three or four hundred dollars. We set off and ended up going to East Texas. We had no addresses, but in my mind I knew that my ex-wife's brother was living in the vicinity of Canton. We arrived in Canton and went to the sheriff's department first. They had no report from Waco and were not concerned much to help us. We went to the post office and it was closed. We could hear people working in the back, so I banged and banged on the door. They yelled at us: We're closed! They eventually came and opened the door, and we told them we needed an address for the man who was my ex-wife's brother. They said: We don't deliver mail to him. We don't have him listed. I said: I'm sure you do. They said: Well, we don't deliver to his address. He gets his mail care of someone else.

They were very reluctant to give us any information at all, but eventually they gave us an address on a rural route where his wife's mother lived. We asked: Can you tell us how this route runs? They gave us the most vague directions ever—go to this big tree and turn right and there's a white house. We tried to follow the directions for about four hours and asked people in their front yards for directions.

Eventually, we were going up a road that was narrow and overgrown. As the road curved to the left I saw a big sign: Eggs for Sale. It rang a bell in my mind, because my ex-wife's brother and his wife had come to Mount Carmel and asked if we were interested in buying eggs. Her mother raised chickens. I thought: Wow, this might be it!

As the road curved around it took you from the side of the house around to the front, but you couldn't see anything because of all the bushes until you got right in front of the house. When we did, there were small children playing out on the front lawn. I saw my youngest daughter, Shari, sitting on the front steps with her head in her hands. She wasn't playing with the other kids; she was just sitting there.

David was driving and we decided to go past and come back. We did, and I said: Let me jump out and go grab Shari. He said: No, let's go back to town and get the police to do it legally now that we know she's there. Being the father and I hadn't seen them in almost two months, I wanted to take this opportunity, but he prevailed.

We went to the police station in town this time, because the sheriff's deputies had not been interested. As the police listened to the story of where we had found my daughter, they said this was not a police matter because it was out of their jurisdiction. It was a county matter and we needed to go to the sheriff's department. We said: We already went there. They didn't seem like they wanted to help. The police officer said: Don't worry, I'll get them over here. He called, and two deputies came over. We had to tell the whole story again, and I was chafing at the bit because time was passing. As we were describing the area where we saw Shari, one of the deputies said he knew where it was. He lived out there, and that address was his neighbor's house.

We got in the squad car. The deputies knew where they were going. They pulled into a driveway that led up to the side of the house, and we couldn't see the door or the front yard from the car. They told us to stay in the car and they would go talk to them. One of them came back to the car after a while and said there were no children in there and no sign of any children, and the woman was pretending she didn't know anything about what we were saying. I said: We saw them just an hour or so ago. He said: She's pretending she doesn't know anything. Let me make one more try. He went back around to the front, and then he brought out an older gentleman. The old man was kind of scared. He was real nervous and said he did not want to be involved. He had only just married this woman and the kids were her relatives.

It turned out that when we had seen the children playing in the yard, they had only come outside for a minute or two, because they were making so much noise that the old man had kicked them outdoors. Right away his wife jumped on him to get them back in the house. In the meantime, while we had gone to town to get the police, the mothers—my ex-wife and her sister-in-law—had come back from shopping and had picked them up and returned to Debbie's brother's house. The old man finally told us where the brother lived. We headed out there, and the deputies called for backup. I think we had four squad cars.

We went out to the boonies somewhere, and the house was set way back off the road. It had a long driveway. All the squad cars pulled in. They stopped well back from the front door. The deputy said: You stay in the car. I saw them knock on the door and the door open, but then the deputies were blocking my view. I learned later that my oldest daughter, Karen, had opened the door. She would have been about twelve or thirteen. Shari was eight or nine.

The next thing we saw was the sheriff's deputies step into the house. They asked for my ex-wife. No one answered. The cousins were all in the room, so the deputies didn't know which kids were which. They repeated the question, and one of the little boys, a little bitty kid, said: That's her, standing right there!

The next thing we knew the sheriff's deputy came out with the two women in handcuffs and the two girls. They asked David to get into a different squad car. They put the girls in the back seat with me. I asked: What is going to happen to the women? The deputy said that they were under arrest and they were going to take them down and lock them up. The women weren't looking too happy.

We went back to town. We signed some papers, and we got to take the kids back to Waco. We had tried to work through the system in Waco and we had to go find them ourselves, but we got to bring them back. It was a real miracle in a sense. We had nothing to work with when we left Mount Carmel to look for them. It wasn't like David had a vision that said, go here, this is where they are. All David said was: God said if you go this weekend I'll go with you. So we had my daughters back.

LIVING IN WACO

Once I had my daughters back I decided I was not taking them to Mount Carmel because of the situation with George; I figured that word of our coming back to Mount Carmel would get to my ex-wife's people.

We got a motel room downtown one night, and then we made other living arrangements. That's how we found the place on Herring Avenue in Waco. A lady let us live on a vacant lot she had with a little cabana-type trailer on it. Mother and the girls slept in the trailer, and I slept out on the grass. Eventually the lady let us rent a big two-story house a few doors up the street. It was being broken into and furniture was being stolen, so she let us live there.

I made several trips to Mount Carmel by myself, and each time I got a few things. I was gradually moving out. One day George blocked me from coming onto the property and said: You don't live here anymore. You've chosen to leave. They had dumped all the things left in our house outside the fence in a ditch. It wasn't a lot. That's how we ended up moving from Mount Carmel in June or July 1984.

Shortly after David's series of meetings in the spring, and because George was toting guns and carrying on the way he was, David and Rachel, his wife,[28] chose to leave Mount Carmel. Others left Mount Carmel as well. George was getting rough. George pushed Catherine Matteson off a porch. He got physical and made threats. Perry and Mary Belle Jones left. I had left with my daughters and my mother. I think the last ones to move were the Kendricks. Over a period of time, most of the residents of Mount Carmel moved off the property. Most of them settled in the Herring Avenue area.

My mother and I and the girls had moved into the house on Herring Avenue, and David pulled a school bus that he had bought into our backyard, where he lived with Rachel, who was pregnant with their first child, Cyrus.[29]

David did a bit of traveling during this time. He went to Israel for the second time in January 1985 and took Rachel with him.[30]

The message that David had received was getting out. New people were joining, and our numbers were growing. As more and more people came, they tended to move into the house with us. Eventually the lady who owned the house became concerned about wear and tear on the property. So we needed to find another place to live.

MORE HARASSMENT BY GEORGE RODEN

Lois Roden used to come over to the Herring Avenue house for Bible studies. One Friday she called and said: Why don't you all come out to Mount

Carmel? You have cramped quarters and limited bathrooms. You can have showers out here and fellowship. So we took her up on that invitation.

By that time the Houtmans[31] had moved out from Massachusetts in a school bus. David had me drive the school bus with women and children and only a couple of other men out to Mount Carmel. I drove through the front gate. As I drove past George's trailer, he suddenly ran out with two other men, and they all had guns. I couldn't hear what they were saying. I just kept going. He shot out all the tires of the bus on that side, so I drove around the curve in the driveway on the flat tires and pulled up at the Kendricks' house.

Since we were stranded, we ended up staying overnight. Most of us slept on the bus. A few went into the houses. The next day we called a tire company in town to send someone to fix the flat tires. The guy came out and said: Wow, all of them on one side. That's unusual. He was getting ready to fix the tires, and in the course of my explaining why they were all flat on one side, he said: I've got to make a phone call. He disappeared and didn't come back. We called the tire company again and said we thought he was too scared to be out there, so they sent someone else. I think it cost about $800 to get those tires either replaced or repaired.

Lois Roden was very apologetic to us, and she was a little bit scared. She asked us not to file charges against George. When we left we went back to where David was downtown.

Life in Waco was a little hairy because sometimes George would follow us. One time when David asked me to take Rachel somewhere, George was in town, recognized the vehicle, and decided to follow me. I couldn't shake him so I finally parked near the door of the police station. George walked right in hollering. I explained to the police that he was a nuisance. They held him while I left and drove home. We did not let George learn where we were living.

LOIS RODEN'S CHOICE

Even though she kept contact with us up until she took sick, Lois made a choice. She saw her whole congregation[32] worldwide being torn apart. She considered Vernon as having one part of that congregation, and she saw George tearing away as many as he could from her part of the congregation and pushing them in another direction altogether. There were a few undecided people in between, who were probably thinking: We know all about George and we don't want to go with him; and we don't know Vernon—who is he and where did he come from?

So Lois decided that she would make up a third party that would be the center of all this polarization. She thought maybe she would be the means whereby she could win them all back. She picked up all the ones who were undecided. You might say she got the third vote. She figured she would be a refuge for them.

Lois continued to come to David's meetings. Also, David traveled to visit her at different locations. One time we heard she was in Odessa, Texas, and several of us went out there with David and they studied the Bible together.

People at Mount Carmel who knew that Lois Roden was sick and then died on November 10, 1986, kept it from us. She just sort of dropped out of the picture. After we learned of her death, quite a number of the Branches who had sided with her and did not want to have anything to do with George came over to David. Some were from Canada. There was a man from Florida and several others.

SOJOURN IN MEXIA, TEXAS

David got us all to move to Mexia, a little town about thirty miles or so from Waco on Hwy 84, which is the road that goes up to Palestine, Texas. It is on the north side of Waco, where highways 84 and 31 run together. When they divide, 84 goes to the right to Mexia, and Highway 31 goes left to Corsicana and Tyler.

We moved to an abandoned campground at Mexia that had some buildings on it. David had met somebody who said we could stay there. It was a bad place. There were big holes in the walls and the roofs leaked. During that time David was looking for property we could acquire.

David and Rachel and their new son, Cyrus, were at Mexia. I had my mother, Karen, and Shari. I think Catherine Matteson was there with Perry Jones and Mary Belle Jones and their youngest daughter, Michele Jones. I'm not sure whether the Kendricks went to Mexia or not. I think Raymond and Tillie Friesen were there. The Houtmans and Sylvias from New Bedford, Massachusetts, came to Mexia. Jimmy Riddle was there also.

Sheila and Wayne Martin came to stay with us in Mexia during the 1985 Passover.[33] Then they left to return to North Carolina and prepare to move their family to Texas. By the time they came back in early May, we were at our camp in Palestine.

We stayed at the campground in Mexia for several weeks. We didn't consider our stay in Mexia as anything permanent.

LIVING AT THE CAMP AT PALESTINE, TEXAS, 1985–1988

David had a motorcycle and was going out looking for property. One day I was on the back of Floyd Houtman's motorcycle and Jimmy Riddle was on the back of David's, and we looked at quite a number of locations thinking we would buy something. Floyd couldn't change gears very well. Every time he changed gears we banged heads. We went all over the place. David would say: What do you think of this?. But we didn't make a decision that day.

Later David and I went to Athens, Texas, and saw a real estate agent. It seemed that David had already seen the place at Palestine because he was just signing papers.

Then we went out to this piece of property. It was twenty acres that was longer than it was wide.

It had a very intricate way to get into it. You'd never know it was there because it was overgrown with pine trees and underbrush. Before going out there, we stopped at a hardware store and bought an ax, a hatchet, and a couple of other tools. When we got there, David said: I want you to cut a trail wide enough for a vehicle, but I don't want it straight in. Wind it around a bit so you can't see all the way through from the front. I'll be back. And he left me there.

I started cutting trees down and making the trail, which he had already marked. I cut a trail maybe a hundred yards, and then it was dark and he had not come back. I sat down with my back against a tree, and the next thing I knew worms were coming down out of the tree. They were on my head and going down the back of my neck. I put the motorcycle helmet on and zipped up all my clothes. I couldn't see a thing and there was nothing much to hear except animal and night noises.

It was probably 3:00 or 4:00 in the morning when I saw headlights. David was back with one of Stan Sylvia's removal vans. Stan was in the flea market business, and he sold furniture and antiques. I guess David got Stan to empty the van out and they loaded it with lumber. We had the van unloaded by the time it started to turn dawn. David set the guys he brought with him to work constructing a building and took me back to Mexia to sleep.

It turned out that we built a long cabin-type of building. We framed it with two-by-fours and two-by-sixes, and we covered it with scraps of logs from a closed-down mill that was near the entrance of the trail going into the property. We were told that we could have as many scraps as we wanted. They were half-round boards, so the building looked kind of like a log cabin. The building was fairly long with a kitchen at one end, and the rest of it was a meeting hall. We slept in there until the buses were brought and cabins built to live in. It became our main meeting hall when we had meetings indoors.

Moving to Palestine was an experience. My mother had bought a white school bus that was packed to the gills with all the furniture and things we had brought from Mount Carmel. Raymond Friesen had bought a tractor.

Apparently it had gotten a flat tire and they had removed the big wheel off the back on one side and had it fixed. The tire was not balanced, and the tractor rode along like it had an egg for one of the wheels. Raymond drove that tractor the whole way to Palestine, and we followed him in the bus so that no one would run into him. We were crawling along at five or ten miles per hour. It was a two-hour car trip that took us most of the day. We were driving along with blinking lights and our heavy load on the bus. Everyone else passed us and went ahead to the camp.

I got a job working in Waco where I was in charge of a roofing crew. Several of the guys worked for me and we stayed in Waco all week and went back to Palestine on the weekends. We returned one time and they had moved the camp. Everything had been dismantled and moved. On the left-hand side of the property was a big wide easement with high-tension electricity pylons running along it, so they had set up a new camp way down, almost to the very back of the property. They had the buses in rows and they had a tent set up. I think they moved the building, too, because there was nothing left at the old location when we got there.

No one cooked on their own in the camp because it was a fire hazard. Actually it was kind of a miracle that there were no fires. Whether you were living in a bus, or a tent, or a cabin, there was no electricity. We went through that whole Palestine experience without ever making an open fire to cook or to stay warm. One time David took me with him to buy potbellied stoves for warmth. We got leftover wood from the mill, which got us through a couple of winters.

Sheila and Wayne Martin and their family came to Palestine.[34] People came from Australia and stayed, although not permanently. There were a couple of families from South Carolina.[35] There was a guy who came a couple times from Canada. When there was a feast day, people came from other states. The camp probably had eight or ten buses and a dozen or so cabins, as well as a tent. By the time we moved back to Mount Carmel in 1988, there were many people doubled up in the buses. On feast days we had Bible studies.

I remember David had a big baptism. Most of us had been baptized before and we thought one baptism was all you needed. Victor Houteff taught you shouldn't need to be baptized again just because you have accepted more light or new information. Davidians don't get into a lot of baptizing of people from the Adventist church because they've already been baptized. That being said, I remember one time Ben Roden had a big baptism at Cameron Park in Waco. It was mostly for young people who had never been baptized. I chose to be rebaptized at that time. Lois Roden at one point decided everyone needed to be baptized again, because many people had been backsliders. She pretty much baptized everybody. I think George was there and he refused.

At Palestine David had a big corrugated metal tank that we filled with water from a neighbor. We used that water for bathing unless we went to a motel or truck stop and took showers. For the baptism, they filled the tank with water from the creek, and it was red from the mud. David baptized all the people who were there. David's wife, Rachel, was in California. David said Rachel was going to be upset that she missed it, and he was going to take a bottle of the red, muddy water to California for her. I don't know if he did that. I don't recall that he ever baptized anyone after that. I don't really understand the significance of why he never did it again for the new ones, but he let us know that this baptism was a very special experience for us and it had a lot of significance.

We stayed on that property in Palestine from about 1985 to 1988. The Palestine property was still in our possession right up to 1993,[36] but almost everyone moved back to Mount Carmel early in 1988. The property at Palestine was rugged, but it was beautiful. Everybody loved it despite its being crude.

You might say that David established a base at the camp at Palestine. Some of the men, women, and children would stay there all year long. A lot of the men, and some of the women, would go out to California and get jobs. Some of us went to California with David to work. That's where we ran into Marc Breault, and he introduced David to people in Hawaii.

While we were in Palestine David made a trip to Hawaii, and some of the people from Hawaii moved to the camp. We made contact with other groups, and other Branch Davidians started to come to Palestine. We also made contact with Australian Branch Davidians, and some of them came to Palestine and stayed for a while. David also made a trip to northern California to a German Reform Seventh-day Adventist camp meeting. As a result, several women joined our group: Jean Borst, Trudy Meyer, and Ofelia Santoyo. Jean brought her son Brad, who was with us until he was about eighteen. When Ofelia came she brought her mother, Concepción Acuña.

David was traveling back and forth to California. During 1986, when David and some others were traveling around, I spent most of the year working in Waco running a roofing crew. We worked roofing in Waco for about a year, and then we made our way out to California.

IN CALIFORNIA WITH DAVID

As more people came to live at the Palestine camp our expenses grew. We needed money for building, to feed people, and so on. David said to those who had accepted his message when he first started: You pretty much understand what this is all about. You don't have to be at all the meetings. You can go out and get jobs and send money back to provide for your families, or to provide for these new ones so they can stay and hear. So those who could get jobs started out working in Waco or Palestine. Eventually, we found that California was an easier place to get jobs. It paid more than Texas, so a lot of us went there.[37]

When I first went to California we lived at Don and Jeannine Bunds's house north of Los Angeles near Pasadena. Don had a job and Jeannine worked as a nurse. David, Rachel, and Cyrus were there.

One time when David and I were headed back to Texas, the truck broke down in Loma Linda. David was very mechanical. He could fix vehicles, he was a carpenter and a musician. Just about anything he set his hand to do, he could do pretty well. It took him about a week to fix that truck. When he finally did, he decided it would not just be the two of us going, he would take Jimmy Riddle and Perry Jones, too.

We got a little farther than Loma Linda when we decided to stop and visit Rosie, an older lady who was someone Perry had met. When we pulled into her property we saw that she had a camper that fit on the back of a truck. In the course of visiting Rosie, David said something like: That camper sure would be handy. Is there some kind of a deal we can make, or can we borrow it? She let him borrow it. When we were ready to head out, David turned to Jimmy Riddle and said: Jimmy, I want you to stay and help this lady. She has been so generous and has given us the loan of this camper. I'm sure there are some things you can do to help her out. Jimmy's face kind of fell, because his mother was back in Texas. He was looking forward to going back just like the rest of us. David said: You're not too happy with being left here all by yourself. David then said: Would you feel better if Clive stayed with you? So both of us were dropped off in Mentone, near Redlands. We lived at Rosie's place and worked for her doing repairs and garden work. She had a big property with an orchard. She was a very nice lady.

By the time David came back from Texas and brought the camper back, we had learned that Rosie had lots of rental properties: houses, trailers, apartments. She took Jimmy and me down the road one day and pointed out house after house that she owned. She wasn't sure if she still owned some of them or not. She had places all over Mentone and Redlands.

David asked if she had any rental places available because we were living with the Bundses in Los Angeles and we wanted our own place. She said she had a place in San Bernardino. It was occupied, but the tenants were going to be moving out.

We went to look at it. A woman was living there with a Filipino husband. It wasn't a great house. The dog had torn a hole in the carpet, things like that. David said to Rosie: You already have people in that house. She said: Oh, but they are going to be moving. She basically gave them their walking papers, because she was unhappy with them. We found out later that this woman had been born there. The house used to belong to her father and he had sold it to Rosie. Rosie moved them out and moved us in.

While we stayed in the rented house in San Bernardino, the ones with jobs supported the rest of us. Those of us who did not have jobs witnessed to the homeless. We went down to San Diego and handed out literature. Jimmy Riddle and I were still doing work for Rosie, which went toward our rent. We were always in the mode of showing our gratitude to Rosie by doing work for her. We did that for many months.

Bonnie Haldeman, David's mother, came out and stayed at Rosie's house because she needed someone to housesit. During that time Bonnie worked in a nursing home run by two women, and she also cleaned houses.[38]

San Bernardino is on the other side of the freeway from Loma Linda. Loma Linda is a big Adventist area. It was during those days that we went to surrounding Adventist churches to give Bible studies and talk to people. That's where David met Marc Breault. As a result of meeting Marc, connections were made with people in Hawaii.

ATTRACTING PEOPLE FROM HAWAII AND AUSTRALIA

The first people who came over from Hawaii stayed at the San Bernardino house first, and then when we went back to Texas they went with us, a few at a time. As more families came to the Palestine camp, David started building.

I think that the first cabin was built in California and was then trucked to Palestine, but from then on the cabins were constructed in Palestine. People were told that if they wanted to live there they had to build their own houses and we would show them how from the model of the one already made. They were quick and nothing fancy—they were relatively small—they had a bunk-type loft for sleeping.

David and I made a trip from California to Australia in 1986. I spent two months in Australia and returned after Passover. David only stayed, I think, two weeks on that first trip. As a result of that trip quite a number of the Branch Davidians from Australia eventually came to Palestine. When David went back to Australia two more times he attracted quite a number of young people, some of whom came to the United States to join us.

SHOOT-OUT WITH GEORGE RODEN
AT MOUNT CARMEL IN 1987

In 1987 George Roden dug up the coffin of Anna Hughes, who had been buried in the cemetery located on the Mount Carmel property. George issued a challenge to David: If you can raise her from the dead, I'll acknowledge you as the prophet and leader. But if I can do it, you should acknowledge me as supreme leader. David said he wasn't into that.

David contacted the McLennan County Sheriff's Department. David asked: Isn't it a crime to dig up bodies in the cemetery? They indicated that they didn't want to go out there and check on his story. They told David that they needed proof for what he was alleging. So David got somebody to go to Mount Carmel to photograph her coffin, which was in the church. It had an Israeli flag draped on it and was sitting on a couple of sawhorses.

David went back to the Sheriff's Department with the pictures. They said: How do we know anything is in the coffin? We need more proof. As David was leaving he was told: George Roden is crazy and anyone going out to Mount Carmel should be armed. We knew George was armed. That was pretty obvious.

David got some weapons and he and some of the guys went to Mount Carmel looking for the coffin. He found it had been moved from the church and was hidden in a shed.

I was in Hawaii at the time. Several of us had gone over to Hawaii in the latter half of 1987 to run a bakery. David was always looking for opportunities where we could be employed.[39] So I heard about what happened at Mount Carmel later.

To shorten the story a bit, George started shooting at some of the guys who went with David, and in order to rescue them David retaliated by shooting in George's direction. As a result, eight of our guys, including David, went to jail.[40]

While they were waiting for the case to come to trial, George got himself arrested for writing letters to the judge, the sheriff's department, and lawyers telling them they were going to die of AIDS as God's punishment. The judge locked George up for contempt of court for about eight months. David took legal steps to find George in violation of Lois Roden's restraining order to prevent George from holding himself out as the president of the General Association of the Branch Davidian Seventh-day Adventists and from taking possession of Mount Carmel and related property, so the court gave George ninety more days in jail.[41]

While George was in jail, David contacted those of us who were in Palestine, and we moved back to Mount Carmel in the early part of 1988.[42] After that they had the trial for the shoot-out, which resulted in all of our guys except David being found not guilty. In David's case there was a hung jury. So they all ended up being released.

RESHAPING MOUNT CARMEL

When we moved back to Mount Carmel in 1988 I think there were thirteen little houses with some barracks behind them.[43] The barracks were used for storage in the Rodens' day. Over the years one had been made into a house, and several had burned.

When we returned we found chemicals and paraphernalia that were used to make methamphetamine in one of the houses.[44] Some of the houses were in such bad shape we couldn't use them.[45] We cleaned the houses up, tried to salvage some with roofing repairs and paint jobs, and we rehung doors or put new doors on to make the houses habitable. David took photos of the whole property showing the way we found it when we came back. He made a booklet of the beat-up condition with a few words under each picture. David titled the booklet "Let George Do It."

A few houses were occupied by people who were not willing to pay rent to David. David told them: You are welcome to stay, but you will not be paying rent to George. One by one they chose to leave. Amo Roden was the first to leave.[46]

We were threatened by a number of different people. Some of these were ex-convicts, I guess George's friends, who had vested interests at Mount Carmel— a drug lab, pornography, whatever was going on. So for a time we locked the gate at night. A couple of our guys would stay up by the gate in a guard shack [see figure 2 in appendix] keeping an eye out. A shotgun was kept in the shack in case it was needed. At certain times our people stayed down near the dairy in the back of the property [see figure 2 in appendix] and watched so someone did not sneak onto the property and do some damage.

Even under Ben Roden there had been a lot of vandalism. We stood guard then, too. We did not have guns at that time, but people were coming onto the property at night, smashing the doors in on the storage buildings and doing things like that. It got to where we were walking the property at night until the sun came up. Mount Carmel has had a lot of threatening situations through its history. When I first came to Mount Carmel people used to drive down Double EE Ranch Road [see figure 2 in appendix] and shoot into the buildings.

David made one last trip to Israel. That was when Pablo Cohen joined. People were still joining from California. With David traveling farther and farther, to England and to Australia again, we had quite an influx of people coming to celebrate Passover during these years. Probably around 1991 David started saying that we didn't want to get too many more people and that we needed to consolidate before we started bringing in any more.

That was about the time that David decided we needed to build a large building to handle our needs.[47] When we started working on the building we gradually demolished the buildings that were already at Mount Carmel[48] and used some of those materials along with new lumber to construct the new building. The foundation of the church near the front gate was partially sinking, so the church was the first structure that we demolished. David used the wood from it to start work on a communal eating hall. As we added to the building, David began to demolish the worst of the little private homes.

After the cafeteria was built, David added the chapel. Then a gymnasium with a basketball court was built. When more people came from England and California we didn't know where we were going to put them, so the gymnasium was divided into two floors for residential rooms, and this became the front portion of the building on the north end [see figure 3 in appendix].

The building evolved and kept being added to. Towers were built. We built a swimming pool out back. The last thing was the storm shelter in a huge pit being dug north of the building. [See figure 3 in appendix.] It was not finished by the time of the ATF raid on February 28, 1993.

I wasn't involved in burying the school bus to make a tunnel from the north end of the first-floor rooms to the storm shelter [see figure 3 in appendix]. That was done while I was in California. They buried the bus so we could go down through a trapdoor at the end of the hallway [#8 in figure 3] and walk through the bus to the shelter. The seats of the bus were taken out. It was just a tunnel. There were no escape tunnels, unlike the many stories that have been told.

LIFE AT MOUNT CARMEL

We believed that our property, Mount Carmel, was a place that God provided in the wilderness outside of the Holy Land. The wilderness is anything outside of the Holy Land or what is likened as God's vineyard. We thought of Mount Carmel as a training ground and haven.

There were people who came to the Rodens. There were people who came to David. We learned pretty quickly that some people have bad habits—they smoke marijuana or do drugs or have a drinking habit. Sometimes people we invited to come had these problems and we tried to help them understand that they could not bring that sort of stuff with them. In order to help them overcome those problems, we realized we couldn't have them living in the city of Waco or wherever they had come from, because of the influence peer pressure had on their addictions. Everybody living at Mount Carmel was focused on encouraging people with addictions to kick the habit, go cold turkey or whatever. Mount Carmel specifically was a place that prepared people to be able to go to Israel.

There have always been mixed nationalities in the Branch and under Lois.[49] David stressed that nationalistic issues, pride in one's country as opposed to somebody else's country, issues over color, are not pleasing to God.

David told a story of when he went to England to speak. A lot of the British who eventually came to Mount Carmel were black. David told us that the meeting was in someone's house somewhere near the Adventist college just north of London.[50] The first thing David said was: God hates black people. He said you could see everyone bristle. People didn't know him, they didn't know whether to jump up or walk out in protest. He said: I paused just long enough for that to sink in. Then I said, God hates yellow people. And God hates red people. And God hates white people. Of course, they were starting to think, well it's not so bad, He hates them all. This didn't fit their image of God; God is love. David recalled: So I paused. Then I said, What God wants is children of light. God is spirit, God is light, and God is love. He's not hung up in color and you don't need to be either.

When people from abroad came to Texas, David said: You don't need to be flaunting your patriotism for whatever country you are from. You don't need to be flaunting your education, or the color of your skin, or the fact that you were a businessman and somebody else was just a peon. God's not into that and we won't tolerate it here. We are all children of light. We are all children of God and we are all equal. Except for the fact that David had Inspiration, we were all one body. He stressed that on numerous occasions.

People who came or were invited to come made that effort, but a lot of them came with their heads in the clouds or with cameras, thinking they were tourists if it was their first time. David straightened everybody out pretty quick. He said: What did you come for? Did you come here because this is a golden opportunity to see America? Well, you came for the wrong reason. If you came here thinking that you'll listen to a couple of studies and then go down and see the Alamo and then go out to Disneyland, you came for the wrong reason.

He got that across with several different illustrations. He would say: The Spirit is the only thing that you should be here for. You should be here to learn, that's why you came. If you want to do all these other things, you might as well leave now and go have your fun. Take your pictures and go back to where you came from, and you'll be able to show everybody your wonderful trip. But if you are here to study, you need to get your priorities straight.

So people came, and some of them came back more than once. Over a period of time we saw and we believed that it was the Spirit of God that controlled all this. There were very few issues that arose where there was friction amongst people. By the time David built the big building and divided it into small rooms, you would have four guys living in a room with bunk beds. I was in a room with Paul Fatta's son Kalani and two black guys from England—Phillip Henry and Dabo, or Abedowalo Davies. Dabo was Nigerian. Phillip Henry was from the big Henry family that was at Mount Carmel. There were two brothers and three daughters and the mother. All of them came over from England.

A couple of the British who came over were white. Most of the black English people came originally from Jamaica, and some were from Nigeria and Guyana. Our idea was that everyone was coming to Mount Carmel for a reason and we needed to see the importance of that reason. That is what was stressed as important in David's meetings.

Some people could swing the pendulum to the other side to where they wanted Bible studies all the time. David would say: We are all going to go out and work together. Or, we are not going to work today, we are going to swim in the swimming pool. People might come down to the chapel expecting a Bible study, and David would say: We are going to show a movie. Some would walk out and go back to their rooms.

Once David sent for one of the people who left like that. The guy came back, and David asked: What's the deal? He said: I came for a Bible study and you are going to show a movie, or you are going to play music, so I figured I would go back to my room and wait until time for the Bible study. David said: No, we are all one body. This movie, or playing this instrument, that is the Bible study for tonight. It's to see whether you would separate yourself from the body because you are not interested or you've heard it before or you might have seen the movie. You are withdrawing from the body and that is not what we are trying to learn here.

Sometimes people messed up. One guy got into the kitchen late at night and helped himself to a bunch of cookies. David called us all together and said: If we are a body it doesn't matter whether the hand takes the cookie—the eye is involved, the mouth is involved if he eats it, the stomach gets involved because it goes down there, it ends up in the bowels, and everything else is involved, the legs are involved because they took you to the kitchen. If you can picture yourselves as all parts of this one body, it's no good that the stomach is saying, "I didn't eat the thing. It just landed on me after a while." The eyes can't say, "I didn't take it, I didn't reach out and take it, I saw what he had done." You can't separate things. Let's say if somebody does a sin. Then we all end up paying for it if we are one body.

Of course, everybody wondered: What's going to happen here? This guy has done what he wasn't supposed to do. Nobody was supposed to go help themselves to the kitchen in between meals. Everybody was sitting there thinking: Where is David going with this? Our brother has gone down and stolen, he has helped himself, he's broken the house rules. David asked: Do you all think he needs punishment? Everybody was thinking: I don't know if he deserves punishment or not. David said: He deserves punishment, he has broken the rules. There should be some kind of way of dealing with it. While he deserves punishment, he's also a part of this group, so then the whole group is going to be punished. If we are all going to be punished, but most of us didn't do it, it doesn't seem fair, does it? So David sent someone down to the kitchen saying: Get a bunch of cookies. We will all eat cookies.

That kind of lesson sticks with you more than a sermon, scripture this and scripture that. Many of David's lessons were taught by illustration and little enacted play-type things or situations that were brought out in that kind of mode. Nobody remembers Christ's sermons. They remember his stories called parables. They listened to them and went home. The disciples were thinking: Interesting, cute, but what about these stories? They asked Christ: Why do you always talk that way? Why do you always speak to them in parables? He said: So they won't understand.[51]

The parables are for understanding, but Christ said so they won't understand, and they were not interested enough to find out. They all went home after it was over. That's all they got. What Christ said was kept from them. It was sealed. Even to the disciples who asked—Will you explain it to us? What does this mean?—Christ answered with parables: Well the sower is this, and the seed is this, and the soil represents this.[52] He'd give an additional explanation or lesson, but he did not tell them what it was all about because they could not comprehend it. What he was talking about—the final harvest, the gathering in of all these people—might not even apply for two thousand years. They only learned as much as they could deal with and what perhaps pertained to the job they were sent to do at that time.

It's kind of like information is given on "a need-to-know basis,"[53] like you hear on TV. The only part we are going to tell you right now—this was two thousand years ago—is what you need to know to do your job and that's it: He's leaving; you are leaving; the Romans are still here; the Kingdom is not yet set up.

MOUNT CARMEL IN 1992

The last full year at Mount Carmel was 1992. The ATF raid took place on February 28, 1993. A lot of us were out in California at the beginning of 1992. David made a call for as many as possible to come to Mount Carmel for the Passover of 1992. So we went a little early. I think maybe we left about late February, maybe early March. By we, I mean most of the ones in California: Jeff Little, Don Bunds, Floyd Houtman, Jimmy Riddle, Cliff Sellors, and myself.

Most of us had jobs in California. I was working with a multitape dubbing company called AME, which stood for Andrew McIntyre Enterprises. I was in charge of client inventory, which meant I had to receive all of the supplies, for instance, sleeves for tapes, labels, and boxes. I logged the supplies into the computer and stored them in a retrievable warehouse setup. Orders would be issued for what they needed in packaging each day. I kept track of it all and pretty much ran the whole thing by myself.

I quit that job when we came back for the Passover season of 1992. Most of us traveled together in a convoy of several cars. My eldest daughter, Karen, didn't come. She and a couple of other people stayed out in California to watch over the two houses that we had out there.

Not too long after we got to Mount Carmel a lot of people came in from England and other places. Just about most of David's followers came for the Passover in 1992. By the time everybody got there and we had the meeting, there were probably about 150 people.

Marc Breault, who had left Mount Carmel and moved to Australia, had been putting the word out that we were all getting together that Passover to commit suicide. After the meetings for Passover week were over, David rang the sheriff's department and said: We're still here. I don't know what you've been told, but we are still here.

After that Passover, Don Bunds and a young guy from California and maybe one or two others were sent out to California to get a truckload of things; it might have been equipment for the machine shop. While they were out there, unbeknownst to us, the young man was persuaded to see Rick Ross.[54] When they returned to Mount Carmel the young man stayed for a short time and then went back to California. A lot of the information that came out in the criminal trial in 1994 could only have come from somebody who had been at Mount Carmel in 1992, about eight months prior to the ATF raid on February 28, 1993. That was probably why ATF agents thought David's bedroom and the guns were in the two rooms over the chapel [#21a and #21b in figure 4 in appendix], but several months before the raid David had moved the guns, and he had also moved to a different bedroom.

After that Passover season in 1992, probably about twenty people returned to wherever they came from. I think a couple of families went back to England. We ended up with about 130 people who stayed on throughout the year.

Sometime in 1992 I was sent to Florida with an older gentleman, Bill Worrow. This old guy had been with David for a while; he was an old-time Davidian and Branch Davidian who was among the ones who joined David after Lois Roden died. He told David he was going back to Miami to sell his house and then come back. They sent me with him to do repairs on his house. I was working on his house and I got the feeling he had some issues with David. He didn't like it that David had introduced him to eating meat again, because he'd been a vegetarian most of his life. There were probably a couple of other things that he was having difficulty with. When it came time that I felt we were finished with the repairs, I ended up coming back on my own.

When I returned they had built the swimming pool at Mount Carmel. We used the swimming pool throughout the summer of 1992. Then we built the gymnasium at the back side of the building behind the chapel. [See figure 3 in appendix.]

David had guys, especially Paul Fatta, going to gun shows and selling guns, MREs—which are Meals Ready to Eat—and military supplies like boots and uniforms. They were going to gun shows probably every week-end. A room in the large building was made into a sewing room [#18 in figure 3 in appendix] where the women sewed ammunition vests, which were sold at the gun shows. The label on the vests had the name Mag Bag. Any mail and deliveries coming to the Mag Bag business were directed to a building we rented off of Farm Road 2491 by the Loop,[55] where we did auto repair [see figure 1 in appendix]. Bob Kendrick and Mike Schroeder were the two main ones who worked down there quite a bit. Sometimes they slept there overnight to keep an eye on the place. That building is still out there. It's blue now.

DAVID'S BIBLE STUDIES

There were times when David told people: Don't take notes. He would say: Listen, because while you're writing you're missing the next sentence. There were times when people would ask him: Can you slow down? You're going too fast. David answered: I'm telling it to you as I'm watching it. It was like he was watching a movie. He said: If I slow it down then the events in this scene, this vision, will get ahead of me. You're just gonna have to keep up. If you pay attention, if you listen, it will come to you when you need it. You will end up getting it.

A lot of times my mother would be asked to take care of the children or do some job during a Bible study. She'd tell David: I don't want to miss something. He told her: You will get it. Don't worry about missing a meeting, or missing several meetings. You will get it. We'd been taught for years that the Spirit can bring to your mind all the things you have heard, if you need them, in due course. It doesn't mean you've got a good memory and it doesn't mean that you can recall just when you want to, but the Spirit will bring it out.

Sometimes when David finished giving a study, he would say to people: You, you, you, and you come on upstairs and we'll have a little extra. For a long time I held back from asking to sit in on these sessions. I thought they were just for the women, because that's who he seemed to pick at first. But I noticed that as time went on he was inviting more and more people and some of them were actually asking: Can I go?

One night he was getting ready to head upstairs [to room #21a in figure 4 in appendix] and people who had been going regularly were headed up there. I asked him: Is this kind of restricted, or would it be okay if I come up? He said: Sure. So I wound up attending the last session, because he never had any after that, none that I know of. That had to be before the latter part of 1992, because David moved out of those rooms over the chapel [#21a and #21b in figure 4] in October or maybe November.

4

Branch Davidian Theology

DAVID KORESH'S APPROACH TO SCRIPTURE

David started presenting his first series of meetings, titled "The Serpent's Root," on September 8, 1983. They were recorded on seven audiotapes.[1] That was his first speaking to us from the pulpit in the church at Mount Carmel. Unlike my having to wrestle with Lois Roden's message about the Holy Spirit being feminine—which took a month or more—I heard him speak two or three times and I was convinced that this was of God.[2] Other people maybe took a little longer. Within a fairly short time, everybody had joined. He gave five of the studies in "The Serpent's Root" series, and then he and Lois went to Israel. When he came back, he gave the last two studies on October 10 and 15.

David made scripture come alive. He showed that all of the prophets in the Bible were writing more for our day than for their own time. Even though some of what they wrote pertained to their time, the prophecies projected into what they called the Last Days or the Day of the Lord.[3]

The more David studied with us, the more we began to see that the Bible is not a bunch of different subjects and chapters. He taught that there were no chapters and verses in the ancient manuscripts. The translators were the ones who added the chapter divisions and numbered the verses.

David pointed out with the book of Isaiah that it was written under the reign of four kings of Judah (Isaiah 1:1). The first five chapters were written under the reign of Uzziah, king of Judah. Chapter 6 was written under Jotham. Chapter 7 to 14:27 was written under the reign of King Ahaz. From then on, the rest of Isaiah's book is written under King Hezekiah. So most of the book of Isaiah is written toward the end of his ministry as a prophet under the fourth king of Judah, Hezekiah, the son of Ahaz. David said that chapter 40 to the end of Isaiah in chapter 66 is all one vision. It's not divided up into little subjects. Most of it describes prophesied consecutive events.

It is the same with the book of Revelation in the New Testament. David taught that Revelation is being shown to John in a vision in which he sees a book sealed with Seven Seals in the right hand of the One on the throne (Rev. 4:1); he sees the Seven Seals being opened, and everything you see from that point on is pretty consecutive as far as the order in which it will be fulfilled. It says that the things that John sees are a revelation of Christ. It is information about what Christ—this Messiah figure, whether it's Jesus Christ or somebody else called Christ—is going to do in the Last Days. David made a big point that he saw himself as the Lamb opening the book to us. He did not open it to everyone else. He opened it to us. I believe it was opened to him and he passed it on to us.

BOOK OF REVELATION

David taught that all the books of the Bible meet and end in The Revelation of Jesus Christ to John, the last book in the Christian Bible.[4] The book of Revelation is like the summary, the wrap-up of all the Bible's prophecies. John is given a revelation by God, not by Jesus Christ, but *of* Jesus Christ. In other words, the Father gave it to the Son, who through his angels gave it to John. John wrote it out and sent it to the churches.

In Revelation 4:1 John is told: *Come up hither, and I will shew thee things which must be hereafter.*[5] He sees *a strong angel* (Rev. 5:2), asking, *Who is worthy to open the book, and to loose the seals thereof?* John is ultimately told that only the Lamb can open this book. When the seals are broken, you see all these pictures one after the other. Scholars have tended to interpret these pictures as catastrophic events, either in the past or perhaps yet to happen in the future. But David stressed the point that John tells us this is a revelation of Christ, not of world events per se.

CHRISTOLOGY AND THEOLOGY

David taught that the name of Christ of two thousand years ago was not Jesus, but Yahshua. We don't call him Jesus, although if I'm reading the King James Version of the Bible I will read "Jesus." We see him as God. David explained that when Christ said, *I and my Father are one* (John 10:30), he meant they are one. God is a dual nature, male and female. The female is what we call the Holy Spirit, the Holy Ghost, or the Shekinah.[6]

In the Old Testament the focus is on the Father figure. In the New Testament it has been on the Son figure, with a little mention of the Spirit. People haven't gotten the Spirit straight in their minds; they don't know whether to call it a he or an it, because the Greek word used in the New Testament, *pneuma* (breath, spirit), is neuter. They don't know whether it's real or an influence, or whether it's just a power or a person. She has a major role to play in the final events. At the time She is made manifest, then the focus will be more on Her than on Him.

The Rodens taught a Trinity concept. It wasn't until Lois brought out the feminine that we called it the Family, in the sense of the Trinity being Father, Mother, and Son. David began teaching differently from the Trinity or Holy Family taught by the Rodens. He said that God is One made up of two halves: the Father figure and the Mother figure, who are one in purpose and in unity. He said that when Jesus Christ was here two thousand years ago as the Son, Christ was the Father who had taken on flesh. Christ was an extension of Himself, and when his work here as a human was over, he went back to heaven and returned to the light of the godhead.

Shekinah or Wisdom[7] is Christ's Mother. Christ in the flesh on earth is projected from both the Father and the Mother. Down here he is an embodiment of both Their natures. He is born a man, but he has both the Mother and Father, the fullness of the godhead, within Him bodily. We believe that the human part of Him as flesh is limited; it can't be everywhere at once and doesn't know everything.

When the Spirit comes down at the time of Judgment it will be manifested who She is, and what role She will play in the judgments of God. In Isaiah 42:14 God says, *[N]ow I will cry like a travailing woman; I will destroy and devour all at once.* In other words, you'd better watch out, you don't want to get Mama mad. We believe that the Spirit will take on flesh to contend with that other woman, Babylon the Great (Rev. 17–18).

The *woman clothed with the sun, and the moon under her feet, and upon her head a crown of twelve stars* in Revelation 12:1 is the Holy Spirit. We recognize the Spirit that spoke from the mercy seat on the Ark of the Covenant between two golden cherubim (Exodus 25:16–22) as Shekinah, also known as El Shaddai, "the great-breasted one."[8] Moses was told by God on the mountain to build a sanctuary after the pattern he showed him in the vision.[9] The concept of who is sitting in the sanctuary is feminine. Later on, the apocryphal title was Shekinah. Before that it was Wisdom (*hokhmah*), and Spirit and wind (*ruah*). All those words are feminine in Hebrew.

In Revelation, John sees that woman in heaven initially. At some point She comes down to earth, where the dragon tries to attack Her and destroy Her Son (Rev. 12:1–6). Adventists interpret that woman to be the New Testament Church. They say the son described in this passage as being born is Jesus, and He is caught up to Heaven after they crucify Him. David said that is not a correct interpretation. The event in Rev. 12:1–6 is still in the future. You can see a similarity to Yahshua's life, but Mary didn't come from heaven. David taught that the Spirit is the real Mother of the man-child, but that role, as John was told, was to be in the hereafter. Christ was already dead and gone back to heaven before the time of John the Revelator, who was writing about 90 A.D. He was told that what he was seeing is in the future. We believe that the feminine part of God will also manifest in the flesh and play a visible role in the final end.

Prior to the Last Days, when God chooses to visit earth in the form of flesh, which he did two thousand years ago, that extension of Himself is likened to a Son, or what we call Christ.[10] David said that when Christ went back to heaven, he ascended back into the Father, so it is actually Christ who is sitting on the throne in Revelation. The man who was here two thousand years ago doesn't exist as a separate entity in Heaven.

David's concept is that the Son figure is only when God extends himself to earth, which we believe He did more than once. David taught that when Christ came two thousand years ago it was not his first appearance. People used to ask David about the second coming of Christ and he'd say: I don't count the comings in the same way you count them. The coming you're looking for is not the second coming. It could be the third or the fourth or the fifth.

When Sodom and the cities of the plain were overrun by the four kings (Gen. 14), Abraham's nephew, Lot, and his family were taken captive. Abraham put together 318 of his trained servants as an army and rescued them. Abraham divvied up the loot among those who helped him, but he didn't take any for himself. An individual called Melchizedek, king of Salem, brought bread and wine like a sacrament and blessed Abraham. David said Abraham is called the friend of God because he talked face to face with God when He came and visited from time to time in one form or another. But David said that when Abraham met Melchizedek he paid homage to him. He acknowledged that this man was higher than him and paid him tithes (Gen. 14:18–20). David said that was not some blink on, I'm here/blink off, I'm gone, visit by God or an angel. This man actually lived in that town and Abraham looked to him as more than just a human. David said Melchizedek was God taking on flesh in the days of Abraham.

David opened up the book of Job and said that when God allowed the devil to bring afflictions and catastrophes on Job, and his three friends were commiserating and advising him, their approach was to say you must have done some terrible thing for God to do this to you. A young man named Elihu spoke to them and said (paraphrasing): I don't have the years that you older ones have, but I beg you to listen to what I have to say. I've been respectful, I've listened to you, but now you listen to me. You're all wrong. He even reprimanded Job (Job 32:2–38:24). David said that was God speaking with authority.

Whether Christ has been on Earth in other earlier times in other places, I don't know.

Then of course, Yahshua, the baby who was born to Mary, was God come in the flesh two thousand years ago. David taught that when Christ went back to heaven he went into the Light or into God and became one again. Christ said, *he that hath seen me hath seen the Father* (John 14:9). Then David said: Nobody has seen God, but if you have seen me, then you have seen the Father.

It's hard to get your head around understanding the meaning of that, but that is how David presented it. He didn't really preach a Trinity, but he did acknowledge that when there is an extension of God in the flesh, that Son, Christ, continues to pray as if there is a Father in heaven. Things like *Father forgive them; for they know not what they do* (Luke 23:34) are communications back and forth.

David used to pray a lot, especially when he was feeling down, or if he was feeling like things were not working out. His prayers would be along the line of, "Father, get up off the throne and come down. We need you to fulfill your Word." It's not like he did away with God. He still looked to God as Father. David was always still looking to God for intervention or guidance.

Many of the apostles in their writings say that when Christ ascended up on high, he sat on the right hand of the Father (Acts 2:33; Hebrews 1:3; Romans 8:34). When you get to the book of Revelation and you have the entity that most people think is the Father sitting on the throne, of course, it doesn't show a human figure. It is kind of a symbolic description, with flames up and flames down from the loins and rainbows and all kinds of symbolic terminology, but there is no Son figure in there. There are not even two thrones for Mother and Father. There is one throne in the Judgment scene. What you see in the right hand of the "Father" is a book (Rev. 4:2–6; 5:1).

The way I try to explain it to people is that John, the youngest of the apostles, had a deeper or more spiritual insight into who Christ was than Matthew, Mark, and Luke. These three presented a storybook Jesus born in a manger, doing miracles, teaching, dying on the cross, being resurrected, returning to heaven—not that it is wrong.

But John presented Christ in this way by saying, *In the beginning was the Word, and the Word was with God, and the Word was God.* [. . .] *All things were made by him: and without him was not any thing made that was made* (John 1:1, 3). *And the Word was made flesh, and dwelt among us . . .* (John 1:14). This is the personage that most Christians call Jesus Christ. I don't know how to explain it, because Christ on the cross actually prayed to God, his Mother and Father, as a separate entity outside of Himself. On the other hand, we are told that He was the fullness of the godhead bodily within Himself. But

He addressed God as an outside entity or Father figure. It's a little hard to explain and perhaps for people to comprehend.

David said that when God wants to experience what we as humans are going through, He projects Himself into flesh, whether it's two thousand years ago or some other time in history. For whatever time He lives here in the flesh, God gets personally involved. At those times He takes on flesh as a human being, but when He goes back to heaven, He goes back to being God, because He is not bound to that flesh. This manifestation of God is different from prophets who are human beings who are inspired by the Spirit or a channel for the Spirit to speak through.

I believe David was a manifestation of God. When David first started to teach, we looked on him as a prophet. But the more we studied and the deeper we got into the prophecies, we believed that he was the manifestation of God or the Messiah figure predicted for the Last Days. The more we studied and the more we saw this Messiah figure for the Last Days and began to talk about the Seals in the book of Revelation being opened, and the only one who could open them was the Lamb, we began to see David as fulfilling that role. By the time of the ATF raid on February 28, 1993, we looked at David as being in a category higher than a prophet.

I believe that everything about David was foreordained, or at least known by God in advance. He was permitted to go through certain experiences and situations in his life,[11] but I don't think he was just a wicked sinner who was all of a sudden called out of the blue, as many prophets seem to be. It could have been from birth, it could have been from a very early age, but I think his role was somewhat foreordained right from the beginning.

Most people phrase the question as: Do you believe David is Jesus? Technically, no. Early on in his ministry he'd say: You need to keep your eyes focused on the rock, that figure on the throne in Revelation 4 and 5. He'd say: Keep your mind in heavenly places. You will not see or understand my message down here in the flesh, which is almost impossible to understand. You've got to look at what God's saying from God's point of view, through God's eyes. He said that when a study is being given, or when you are just going about your work during the day, keep your mind on the One on the throne with the book in His hand. For years, Adventists and other Christians figured that is the Father sitting on the throne. We believe that, too. But David said: That is Christ, from two thousand years ago, sitting on the throne. He is the Father.

David began to see himself as this latter-day Messiah, or the Lamb who takes the book out of the hand of the One on the throne and begins to open it (Rev. 6). David took on the role of a son to the Son, in a sense.

People ask, "Did David teach he was Jesus?" No. "Did he think he was God?" God, in the sense of God coming down in human form, he probably did. It's kind of hard to get the distinction across to somebody who never heard him speak, but like I said, he always prayed to somebody else; he always prayed to the Father.

David taught that God is singular in the sense that He's one, but He's a unified one of two parts, male and female. When God who is Spirit, who we say lives in heaven, chooses to come down to earth in a visible form, where He can relate to us and we can relate to Him, He takes on flesh. That is as an extension of Himself. In that case, that projection is called the Son of God.

David said that God the Father and God the Son are one and the same. They are just two different manifestations or two different aspects. To say there is only one Christ is in a sense true. I don't like to say that Jesus or Christ is reincarnated from generation to generation, or at different times in history. It's not like a human coming back periodically. It is a totally different personage that God takes on, like putting on a different suit.

David taught that when we get to heaven, Christ will take us into His closet and show us all the different garments He has worn, and show us that He has been here on earth on more than one occasion under different names. David said, When I come back I will not look like I do now, but you will recognize me.

God is Spirit, but God takes on flesh at times, and he is still God when he is in the flesh. David taught that God chooses to experience his creation personally at different times, as opposed to learning vicariously through watching or from filling a person with the Spirit and then conveying a message to them. God actually takes on flesh from time to time, so that God knows by experience what it is like to be in this body, or this carcass.

David did not see the Lamb in Revelation as being Jesus Christ. Jesus Christ is the Father on the throne.

The Lamb is going to be married (Rev. 19:7–9). Ultimately in the Kingdom, we'll have the Mother and the Father concept, and the Son and His Wife concept. There will be four.

Some people believe that fourth one is already around. I don't buy that. I don't know when She is going to show up or even where She comes from, whether She comes out of His side, from within Himself somehow. That's how I lean right now, that his bride will be of Himself, just as Eve came from Adam (Gen. 2:21–24). I don't think at this point that She exists as a separate entity any more than the Son exists as a separate entity in the flesh at this time.

God allows time to go on, and God allows some terrible things to take place—little children dying, famines, and genocide, and all of those kind of things that are going on in our world, more and more as each generation comes along. So David prayed at times for God to come down. We believe that God will come down personally, but you'll also have this latter-day Messiah figure, this human being through whom God works. They work together from the point where the 144,000 stand with the Lamb on Mount Zion (Rev. 14:1). It's the same Lamb who in Revelation 5 opens the book. The scene has transferred from Him being up there in heaven opening the book to where He's down here on earth and people are going to Mount Zion where He stands. The rider on the white horse is the Lamb,[12] and so is the rider on the red horse, and the one on the pale horse, and the one on the black horse (Rev. 6:2–8).

The Lamb is also the Seventh Angel in Revelation 10:1–3, 5–7:

> *And I saw another mighty angel come down from heaven, clothed with a cloud: and a rainbow was upon his head, and his face was as it were the sun, and his feet as pillars of fire:*
> *And he had in his hand a little book open: and he set his right foot upon the seas, and his left foot on the earth,*
> *And cried with a loud voice, as when a lion roareth: and when he had cried, seven thunders uttered their voices.*
> [. . .]
> *And the angel which I saw stand upon the sea and upon the earth lifted up his hand to heaven,*
> *And sware by him that liveth for ever and ever, who created heaven, and the things that therein are, and the earth, and the things that therein are, and the sea, and the things which are therein, that there should be time no longer:*
> *But in the days of the voice of the seventh angel, when he shall begin to sound, the mystery of God should be finished, as he hath declared to his servants the prophets.*

You have in Revelation this individual, the Lamb, who is called into being. John is told, no one who has lived, nobody in heaven, nobody on earth, and nobody under the earth is worthy to open that book in the hand of the One on the throne (Rev. 5:3). John is looking at a vision off in the future, but he is looking at it like a preview. He is not saying he sees Jesus standing off to the right or in front of the throne. He is not even saying Jesus is the book. You kind of gather that when John is told that no one can open the book, he is upset. He has been brought to heaven to be shown things and now they are locked up. He is told, *Weep not: behold, the Lion of the tribe of Judah, the Root of David, hath prevailed to open the book, and to loose the seven seals thereof* (Rev. 5:5), but you don't see a lion, symbolic or otherwise, in the picture.

In the next scene you see a Lamb *as it had been slain* (Rev. 5:6) in the midst of the throne or standing before the throne. The Lamb had to come from within this flame, this God concept, this Father or judge figure. It is another projected image. God has the ability to transport or transpose Himself into a figure that is actually real, that you can touch and talk to. The Lamb is real. The Lamb is not in the scene to begin with. The Lamb appears out of nowhere, you might say. God projects Himself into being that Lamb. All of a sudden this is the one who can open the book. Everyone in the scene—the four beasts and the twenty-four elders (Rev. 5:8–14)—is happy He is able to open the book, because He is the reason for their being in heaven. The Lamb goes up and takes the book from the hand of the One on the throne (Rev. 5:7).

Right now, I'm of a mind to believe that when Christ went back, he went back into being the Father, or part of the Father as a male and female God-being. I don't say that at his death David walked back into God and became God. As far as I know he is buried and waiting for resurrection.

When he is resurrected he will judge the world. He will judge countries at large based on what they profess. This is what David said. The things David was teaching, the things he was told to do by God, were all for Judgment. David said: The very things that they will accuse me of are the things they themselves are doing. They'll kill me or they will try to kill me for this, but they themselves are going to be asked by God, "You killed this man because he had more than one wife. You killed this man because he had a lot of kids, or you killed this man because he had guns, or you killed him because he drank a beer, or he didn't look like a prophet, so he must be a liar." David said: Fine, and where were you at? What has your religion done for you?

RESURRECTION AND THE WAVE SHEAF

David used to say about his dying and being resurrected and coming back that he would not look like he did then. It's kind of a weird concept, but we don't know what he will look like. David told us: When I come back, you who know me now will know me then and will recognize me.

I believe that in the resurrection the bodies are not just awakened. They have to be re-created. You wouldn't want people who are rotted or the people charred in the fire at Mount Carmel to come back as they are. I believe that at death the life force goes back to God and the DNA is in his computer to make the identical model.

Everything was enacted in the days of Christ as far as fulfilling the harvest times and the harvest symbols. That's what Christ's parables are about, farmers going out to sow seed, some of them falling on stony ground, and all these stories you hear (Luke 8:4–15; Matt. 13:3–23; Mark 4:2–20; also Matt. 13:24–30, 36–43 for the parable of the wheat and the tares).

The wave sheaf was a sampling of the first ripe grain in the spring that God asked to be brought up to the sanctuary at Passover time, where it was waved by a priest before the Lord (Lev. 23:10–14). They were to go out into the barley field and handpick one here and one there, finding the ripest, the tallest, and the fullest heads. They were told not to put the sickle to the grain until they gave to God what was His. He claimed the first of the first fruits.

I believe that the wave sheaf has been that group in every generation who were first to acknowledge God's instructions and obey God, sometimes at the cost of their lives. At the least, they sacrificed themselves by being so dedicated that their whole lives revolved around God's service, as opposed to those represented by the rest of the grain in the field who will be saved, although they are not quite as developed, not quite as devoted. The people who stepped out in faith ahead of everybody else are distinct.

So all of the wave sheaf is an offering that's made, whereby having been presented to God the go-ahead is given to harvest all the rest who are going to be saved, represented by the remaining crops that are going to be brought in. That's what the salvation of souls is all about. You have to present to God the most faithful, those who have given their lives for their faith. Whatever religion it was, whatever timeframe they lived in, they're given as a promise for all those they represent in their generation. The wave sheaf is the first of the first fruits.

Revelation talks about the first resurrection (Rev. 20:4–6) and the second resurrection (Rev. 20:12–13), but there are many resurrections in the Bible. A lot of them precede the first resurrection described in Revelation, so technically it's not the first. Other resurrections in the Bible are in Daniel 12:2 and Ezekiel 37:1–14, valley of dry bones. You've also got the resurrection of Christ and the wave sheaf on the Sunday morning after the crucifixion.

David showed that when Christ was resurrected two thousand years ago, other people were resurrected with him. The gospel of Matthew says that when Christ died on the cross there was an earthquake. Graves were opened, but nobody came out until the Sunday when he came forth from the grave, and then a multitude of people came forth with him. Those resurrected with Christ were the martyrs all the way back to Abel up to John the Baptist. They were resurrected to acknowledge Christ. They went to Jerusalem and said, he is risen and we are risen with him. According to Matthew 27:52–53, *the graves were opened; and many bodies of the saints which slept arose, and came out of the graves after his resurrection, and went into the holy city, and appeared unto many.* Christ and those resurrected with him are wave sheaf.

We believe that Christ took them to heaven on Sunday and offered them before the Father as trophies of His victory over death and the grave. Not everybody who lived in the Old Testament time was in that group. Only those who were martyrs and some of the prophets were taken by Christ to heaven at that time.

Paul said, *For as in Adam all die, even so in Christ shall all be made alive. But every man in his own order: Christ the firstfruits; afterward they are Christ's at his coming* (1 Cor. 15:22–23). Paul wrote, *And if Christ be not raised, your faith is vain; ye are yet in your sins. Then they also which are fallen asleep in Christ are perished* (1 Cor. 15:17–18). Paul is saying that Christians have faith in Christ's resurrection, which offers life beyond the grave, a chance to be resurrected just like Christ was.

The twelve apostles followed Christ. As his students they were with him 99 percent of the time. But at the time of Christ's resurrection they were not wave sheaf because they were not ripe. They weren't even converted until after his resurrection. Even though they followed him for three and a half years, they did not have a clue by the time he was dead, because they were still asking: I wonder if he was the real one? Maybe we picked the wrong guy to follow. Christ had to come back from the grave and teach them for forty days (Acts 1:3–9) to get them ready to receive the Spirit, or be cooked symbolically into loaves of bread on the day of Pentecost (Acts 2:1–6). From then on they went out and converted Jews. After the stoning of Stephen (Acts 7:58–60), they went to peoples they called the gentiles— Romans, Greeks, and others.

Even though the apostles weren't worthy to be taken to heaven with Christ when he left, because they hadn't gone through their baptism of fire or violent deaths—they hadn't become martyrs—they ultimately would, and being the first martyrs of the Christian era, they're in line for the next resurrection of wave sheaf that will be taken up.

I believe that no one has gone to heaven since the translation of Christ. People from every generation, going all the way back to Abel, went to heaven with Christ when he went up. They were martyrs, a special class of saved people. They are not all who will be saved. Just like the wave sheaf is the ripest, they are handpicked from the field. The rest of the barley in the field is still good, but this is a special group.

There will be an earthquake in the beginning of the opening of the Sixth Seal (Rev. 6:12). That is the time of the resurrection of the remaining wave sheaf, those who died since the resurrection of Christ. The Judgment starts with the resurrection of the Lamb and the wave sheaf. This first resurrection in Revelation is not everybody who has died who is going to be saved. Other righteous people will be resurrected later.

When David comes back and the resurrection of the wave sheaf takes place, I believe it includes all those who were martyred after Christ's resurrection. A living wave sheaf will be added to all the dead who will be resurrected as the final wave sheaf. The living wave sheaf consists of the ones who are still alive who qualify as wave sheaf. Millions of other people will be resurrected later, but this first group needs to be brought up so that in the Judgment you have somebody from every generation in order that people will be judged by their peers. I can't judge somebody who lived in the 1100s. I don't know what was in people's hearts and the circumstances they lived under in the days of the Crusades, or in the days right after Christ ascended, or even while he was alive. We believe there are 200 million people (Rev. 9:16) in the wave sheaf, including those who died under David, who were martyred because they followed the most present truth.

Now that doesn't wipe out everybody else—there will still be a harvest. The wave sheaf is just a little handful out of a whole field. And the wave sheaf is only one grain out of multiple grains in different fields. When the wave sheaf is presented to God, you don't burn the rest of the field and say, "We've got all we need, and God's happy with it." No, the rest is gathered into the barn, which is the Kingdom here on earth that everyone is going to be gathered into.

I used to tell my mother and Catherine Matteson: Don't be judging anyone, thinking I'm going to be in this group and everyone else is going to be lost. Scripture teaches that the harvest is the ingathering of souls. God is interested in saving His creation. Joel 2:32 says, *And it shall come to pass, that whosoever shall call on the name of the Lord shall be delivered: for in mount Zion and in Jerusalem shall be deliverance, as the Lord hath said, and in the remnant whom the Lord shall call.* All who will take hold of that offer to be saved will make it. But they are at different levels of understanding; you might say they are harvests from different fields. Christ told His disciples: *And other sheep I have, which are not of this fold: them also I must bring, and they shall hear my voice; and there shall be one fold, and one shepherd* (John 10:16).

That's a relatively new concept for us in the Adventist, Davidian, and Branch Davidian traditions. David opened the door to a much more loving God, even though there is still Judgment. Compared to the Davidians, David taught that God is love. Sometimes you have to go full circle and go through all the other aspects of God's nature to get back to what He really is, love. He wants to save, and that's what He is going to do. He is going to beat the devil, and show the forces of evil up for what they really are and that He is not an arbitrary dictator forcing everybody to kowtow to His will. When it is all over, people will ultimately acknowledge that the way He played it was fair, and that what He was presenting or wanting us to do was for our own good.

In Revelation 5, the scene in which the Lamb appears to open the seals, there are four beasts and twenty-four elders. The four beasts are described in Revelation 4:7, *And the first beast was like a lion, and the second beast like a calf, and the third beast had a face as a man, and the fourth beast was like a flying eagle.* These first four beasts in Revelation represent four categories of people from this Earth, maybe from four different timeframes, who have been redeemed. We were taught that the lion represents those from creation up to the time of Moses and the Exodus. The calf represents those who lived under the sacrificial system. The man symbolizes those who were saved during the Christian era, and the eagle represents those yet to be gathered while still living who will be translated without seeing death. These make up the wave sheaf, the martyrs from all the ages. They have to be in heaven when the seals are opened as part of the Judgment. Somebody from every generation has to be able to judge that God dealt with that generation fairly, that He gave everybody a good chance, or He has a good reason for saving them or not saving them.

DAVID KORESH'S CHILDREN AS THE TWENTY-FOUR ELDERS

The twenty-four elders introduced in Revelation 4:4 are part of the wave sheaf: *And round about the throne were four and twenty seats: and upon the seats I saw four and twenty elders sitting, clothed in white raiment; and they had on their heads crowns of gold.* David taught that the children he had by his wife and other women were special children. He said they were born for Judgment. He compared them to the twenty-four elders in Revelation 4:4, 10–11; 5:8; and 14. David didn't have twenty-four children as far as I know. Just how that will be taken care of in the Last Days, whether it includes miscarriages, I don't know.[13] I don't believe they will be the only ones represented by the twenty-four elders and the four beasts, but they will be part of that group. The fact that the wave sheaf, as I mentioned before, amounts to 200 million individuals, you will have more than just the children that David produced, unless you consider that all those saved are God's children.

David believed those babies were special and that they would be part of the Judgment. He also taught something that I don't even know how to relate to, to be honest. He said they had been here before, and chose to come back to play a role for Judgment's sake.

After those children were killed in 1993, before some of them knew right from wrong, I asked how could they judge the world? An eighteen-month-old or an aborted fetus does not have wisdom to judge. If they have been here before, maybe they know how to judge the world because they have lived a life of some kind.

It may be that the world has judged itself by what was done to the children. The killing of the children is the judgment. People made choices for which God is going to call them to account. If federal agents were so concerned for the children, then why did they cut off the electricity, bombard them with noise, and gas the place? Everything done to the adults affected the children as well.

When it is said that the children are for Judgment, it depends on how you think it through. Maybe they will take on adult forms at the time of Judgment. I don't know how it is going to work. The twenty-four elders are not, in some ways, shown as the judge in the scene in Revelation, they are the jury. The jury does judge. I think the judgment they could pass on the world is from the point of view, "What did you do to us?"

MARRIAGE OF THE LAMB

John records at the beginning of Revelation that he was told, *Write the things which thou hast seen, and the things which are, and the things which shall be hereafter* (Rev. 1:19). John is writing this at the end of the first century. The marriage of the Lamb prophesied in Revelation will be in the future when the Lord sets up His Kingdom. Revelation 19:7 says, *Let us be glad and rejoice and give honour to him: for the marriage of the Lamb has come, and his wife hath made herself ready.*

The marriage of the Lamb is the wedding of the Son figure and his perfect mate. I believe that His perfect mate comes from within Himself; God takes on flesh in order to live with us, and therefore the Spirit takes on flesh, too, as His complement. The Lamb is a figurative expression for the extension of God in the flesh, and the bride is the extension of the Spirit. The female part takes on a visible body to finish the work of the salvation of mankind at the final ingathering.

There were women in the past and currently who think they have a shot at being the bride. I think even some of the women who married David thought they had a shot at it. On numerous occasions he pretty much let the wives, or the women who were aiming to be wives, know that they were not Christ's or the Lamb's perfect mate. Just because they committed 100 percent here on earth doesn't mean they will have the job down the road.

Initially the wedding is between the Lamb and his bride; but the concept of His marrying the Church—the wave sheaf—is also implied in Revelation. The wave sheaf, those who gave their all, even their lives, to God, are the only ones who go to the wedding in heaven.

The wave sheaf go to heaven at Passover time and are accepted of God, and then the harvest or the Judgment begins from that point on. Once they are accepted, then people can begin to be gathered. All those who are saved, or gathered in, after the acceptance of the wave sheaf are not at the wedding, but they are invited to the reception, the marriage supper of the Lamb.

After the wedding between the Lamb and his bride takes place in heaven, in the Judgment scene it says the four beasts and the twenty-four elders are given harps to *sing a new song* (Rev. 5:8–9, 14:2–3). The 144,000 who stand on Mount Zion with the Lamb hear voices from heaven teaching them a new song (Rev. 14:1–3). Revelation 15:2–4 says that the ones who have the harps are the people who have overcome the beast (the two-horned beast) that preceded them in chapter 13.[14]

THE HARVESTS

People have been likened to grass or grains all through the scriptures. In the harvest you couldn't go out and reap your crops until after the Passover time in the spring. At Passover, the feast of unleavened bread, a wave sheaf of barley, the first grain to ripen, was presented to the priest to wave before the Lord's presence in the sanctuary. The wave sheaf was the most advanced of the barley, handpicked one here and one there. It would be presented to the priest as a thank offering to God of what they were about to receive in the harvest. Once that was done they went out and gathered all of the grains that had grown through the winter and had ripened by the springtime— barley, millet, wheat, oats. They were all first fruits because they were the first harvest. Later on in the spring the farmers planted vegetables and fruits. They were the second fruits, or the summer fruits, and they were harvested through the summer and the fall.

Fifty days after the wave sheaf was offered at Passover was Shavu'ot, the Festival of Weeks, or Pentecost (Lev. 23:15–21), which is in the early summer, somewhere in the vicinity of June. From the wheat harvest, a symbolic amount was taken out and made into two loaves of bread that were offered to the Lord as the culmination of the first fruit harvest. Leviticus 23:20 says, *And the priest shall wave them with the bread of the first-fruits for a wave offering before the Lord.* The wave loaves represented the harvest already gathered.

The two wave loaves represent the 120 disciples in the days of Christ. They also represent the 144,000 in the Last Days. In the United States we elect so many senators and so many representatives from each state to go to Congress to be our spokespersons, supposedly taking care of our business. The 144,000 are the selected representatives from the twelve tribes, from the first fruits. They are likened to the flour that's made out of wheat into two loaves of bread. They represent all of the first fruits. *These were redeemed from among men, being the first-fruits unto God and to the Lamb* (Rev. 14:4).

The concept is that after the marriage of the Lamb in heaven in the presence of the wave sheaf, there is a transfer from heaven to earth, and technically heaven is where God is. God is down here on earth for the Judgment. Everybody on earth beyond the wave sheaf is called to come learn about God.

The earth is the Kingdom. It is the dominion under the sun—that's what Daniel 7:27 says, *under the whole heaven.* It is the territory that the worldly beasts or nations have ruled over. It's taken away from them and given to the saints, so their home, Eden restored, is here on earth.

Victor Houteff made a statement in the beginning of his *Leviticus of the Davidian Seventh-day Adventists*, "With the emergence of this vanguard and its army, the first fruits from which are elected the 12,000 out of each of the twelve tribes of Jacob, 'the 144,000' (Rev. 14:1; 7:2–8) who stand on Mount Zion with the Lamb (Rev. 14:1; 7:2–8), the reign of the antitypical David begins."[15] In other words, after the wave sheaf is waved and after the first fruits are gathered and made into wave loaves, the reign of antitypical David, or the latter-day King David, begins. With the resurrection of the wave sheaf and the gathering of God's people, culminating in 144,000 standing on Mount Zion, the Kingdom is pretty well set up. It's got a lot of people in it.

In Matthew 24 Jesus said to the disciples admiring the temple (paraphrasing): This is all temporary. It is going to be gone. That's when the disciples asked: When shall these things be? What will be the signs of thy coming and the end of the world? Jesus spoke about famines, pestilence, and false prophets, but be not deceived; don't worry about wars and rumors of wars, they are not the signs. Famine, drought, disasters go on all the time; they are not the signs of my coming. He said, *Now learn a parable of the fig tree; When his branch is yet tender, and putteth forth leaves, ye know that summer is nigh* (Matt. 24:32; Mark 13:28–29). The summer Christ was referring to is the ingathering of the summer fruits.

Once Pentecost is over, marked by the gathering of the 144,000 in Revelation, we believe that all these other people—the summer fruits—will also be gathered. We see the harvest of the summer fruits as the time that the *great multitude* in Revelation 7:9–17, and which Isaiah and other prophets talk about, is brought in from all nations to come before the Lamb and God on the throne.

As a result of going to where the Lamb stands on Mount Zion (Rev. 14:1), the 144,000 receive the outpouring of the Spirit, and then they go out and bring in all their brethren, the summer fruits. People from all cultures and all countries are invited to come into the Kingdom, and that's the way Zechariah 14 ends up. The Lord's people are told to come up to the Feast of Tabernacles, Sukkot, in the fall.

Passover in the spring is for the resurrected and the living wave sheaf. Pentecost in the early summer is for the government of God to be reinstituted, which is the 144,000. The Feast of Tabernacles in the fall is for the summer fruits. The 144,000 and the summer fruits—the great multitude—are harvested from those who are living. The resurrection of the blessed, the dead who are saved, will be added to that number later, before the millennium.

The same story is presented in Zechariah 14, where the Lord is seen coming down and driving out the armies that are devastating Jerusalem. There is an earthquake that splits the Mount of Olives and creates a great valley (Zech. 14:4). It says that then people should *flee to the valley of the mountains* (Zech. 14:5) where the Lord's feet stand. After that the land under Jerusalem *will be lifted up* (Zech. 14:10), so in Revelation 14:1 you have a group of people called the 144,000 standing with the Lamb on Mount Zion. They are represented by the wave loaves. They are there on the day of Pentecost. Why are they on Mount Zion? Not because it's a good place to vacation, not because it's the greatest place in the world necessarily, but because He's there. They follow Him there.

What happened two thousand years ago was that Christ gathered the 120 disciples, got them ready to receive the Spirit, and then said if you wait in Jerusalem the Spirit will be poured upon you, which it was at Pentecost. They then had the power and ability to go out and bring in three thousand in one day, and five thousand on another day, and finally they went to the gentiles and so on with a great influx of people into the Church.

We believe that will be repeated on a larger scale in the Last Days. The 144,000 will stand on Mount Zion at Pentecost, where the Spirit will be called down upon them, and they will then go out and gather the summer fruits, just like it talks about in Joel 2:28–29: *And it shall come to pass afterward that I will pour out my spirit upon all flesh; and your sons and your daughters shall prophesy, your old men shall dream dreams, your young men shall see visions; And also upon the servants and upon the handmaids in those days will I pour out my spirit.*

So the bulk of the harvesting, the gathering in of souls in the Last Days, will be under the work of the Spirit, which is brought to view symbolically by the angel at the altar in Revelation 8:3–5. In spite of the King James Bible referring to that angel as "he," we believe this angel represents the Spirit. We believe that She is in control, or at least they are working together; the Husband and the Wife come down so they are visible.

David stressed over and over that you don't want to be trying to put God in a box or limit his performance. If you say God will save only Branch Davidians, or God will save only Seventh-day Adventists, or God will save only Baptists, or God will save only Christians—which most Christians think—David said: You're limiting God, you're putting God in the losing position. Let's say, according to the mindset of most Christians, God gets every one of the Christians and the devil gets all the rest, that means the devil has the majority. David asked: You mean the devil wins? He gets all of the millions upon millions of other people, and only Christians are saved? He said: God's got a few tricks up his sleeve. God's in the saving business, He wants to save all who will be saved. He has been nurturing these people in other countries. We believe God raised up what we call teachers of righteousness in other countries. We believe God raised up Muhammad, he raised up Buddha, he raised up major teachers of thought. We believe God inspired them to speak out on various issues, or various philosophies, in order to bring the people up out of the low state they're in to a higher state. God wants to save everybody.

TWO BEASTS, THE ASSYRIAN, AND BABYLON

In Revelation 13, initially there are two beasts. The first one, shown in Revelation 13:1–8, has seven heads and ten horns and comes out of the sea. It has crowns on the horns, and one of the heads is wounded to death by a blow that should have killed the beast. It says the whole world wonders at its survival. The wound heals, and people worship this beast. We call this beast the leopard-like beast. It's a composite beast, made up of the descendants of the four beasts in Daniel 7:3–8: the lion with eagle's wings, the bear, the leopard, and the one with iron teeth and ten horns. The beasts in Daniel represent the ancient empires—Babylonians, Persians, Greeks, and Romans. The leopard-like beast has the body of a leopard, the mouth of a lion, the feet of a bear, and it has seven heads and ten horns, and upon the horns are ten crowns (Rev. 13:1–2). It's a descendant of the ancient empires that had ruled over God's people in the Old Testament and up into the New Testament. It makes up what we might call "the world," specifically the Western world—Europe and the Middle East—primarily the world that revolved around where God's people were, whether they were Israelites or Christians. Of course, there are Christians now all over the world and there are Jews all over, so it gets more encompassing, but the descendants of those original empires are primarily in what we call the Old World, and also the New World because they migrated. It's the English-speaking or the Christian nations primarily.

So in Revelation 13 the world that came into being when the ancient Roman Empire broke up into the nations of Europe and their empires is depicted as the first beast that John sees. Revelation 13:2 says about the leopard-like beast: *And the dragon gave him his power, and his seat, and great authority.* The devil is symbolized in Revelation 12:3, 9 as a red dragon with seven heads and ten horns and seven crowns on the heads.

Revelation 13:11 talks about a second beast with *two horns like a lamb, and he spake like a dragon,* which comes up out of the earth. We call this the two-horned beast or the lamblike beast. The two-horned beast patterns his power and authority (Rev. 13:12) on the beast that preceded him, since his people are primarily from those old European nations. The two-horned beast tries to present itself as Christian, emulating the Lamb, but it speaks as a dragon, which is the devil. The United States plays the role of the two-horned beast, two horns referring to the two dominant political parties. The two-horned beast thinks to persecute God's people.

The Assyrian is described in the Old Testament as plundering the Holy Land, but to be punished by the Lord (Isaiah 10:5–6; 7:17–25; 8:1–10; 10:5–34; 14:24–28; 30:27–33; 31:3–9; 37:21–36; Nahum 1:1–15; 2:1–13; 3:1–19; Zephaniah 2:13–15; Zechariah 10:10–11). I think the Assyrian is primarily the United Nations, but the United States leads the United

Nations as its larger participant and financial supporter. God will judge Americans for all the opportunities and benefits and blessings they have had. They will have to answer for what they have done with their blessings in the Judgment. The Assyrian is going to be judged by God.

It's the Assyrian, or all nations (because of the coalition of nations that he puts together) that go into Jerusalem in Zechariah 14. If you read all of the scriptures about the Assyrians coming into the land, or what the king of the north is going to do in the Last Days, you see him going into the Holy Land, and he comes against Jerusalem. It says he comes in with good intentions. They think they're coming in to preserve peace. They are trying to stop a threat they feel from other nations surrounding Jerusalem, so the United States and its allies go in, like the United States has done in Iraq, Afghanistan, and other places. *Howbeit he meaneth not so, neither doth his [the Assyrian's] heart think so; but it is in his heart to destroy and cut off nations not a few* (Isaiah 10:7). The next thing you know, things get out of hand. They're ransacking the buildings, they're dividing the city into two halves, they're raping the women (Zech. 14:1-2).

God says that Jerusalem is the apple of his eye (Zech. 2:8). It's the city of David for one thing, and David was called the beloved.[16] God has plans for Jerusalem, and these people, the Assyrian, are interfering. It says the Lord is finally going to get up and come down from heaven, and His feet are going to stand on the Mount of Olives (Zech. 14:3-4).

In Zechariah 14 it tells you that after all of this invasion, which causes a lot of terrible things to happen in Jerusalem, *Then shall the Lord go forth, and fight against those nations as when he fought in the day of battle. And his feet shall stand in that day upon the mount of Olives, which is before Jerusalem on the east, and the mount of Olives shall cleave in the midst thereof toward the east and toward the west, and there shall be a very great valley; and half of the mountain shall remove toward the north, and half of it toward the south* (Zech. 14:3-4).

We see in the Bible that this earthquake is literal, it creates literal situations such as the valley and an outlet for the Dead Sea, and we believe it also involves resurrection. We also see in the Sixth Seal in Revelation 6:12 that there's an earthquake.

The wave sheaf consists of the 200 million martyrs since the beginning of this earth's history (Rev. 9:16), who are part of the army of the Lamb sent to kill a third part of mankind in judgment (Rev. 9:14-21). The wave sheaf are the horses in Revelation 9:17-19; the riders are angels. The Judgment on the Day of the Lord is described in Joel 2: *They shall run to and fro in the city; they shall run upon the wall, they shall climb up upon the houses; they shall enter in at the windows like a thief. The earth shall quake before them; the heavens shall tremble; the sun and the moon shall be dark, and the stars shall withdraw their shining* (Joel 2:9-10).

Not only does the Assyrian flee out, but the inhabitants of the land flee out—Jews, Arabs, Catholics, Copts, anyone who is not willing to acknowledge God and welcome God's intervention.

In the book of Isaiah the order of the events is given: God deals with the Assyrian, sets up the Kingdom, and then Babylon appears. In Isaiah 10 it talks about the Assyrian and God's judgment on the Assyrian; God likens the Assyrian to a tree, and He's going to cut down that tree (Isaiah 10:15). The Lord is going to *lop the bough* of Assyria *with terror, and the high ones of stature shall be hewn down* (Isaiah 10:33). Isaiah 11 describes the Kingdom, where the *wolf also shall dwell with the lamb, and the leopard shall lie down with the kid; and the calf and the young lion and the fatling together; and a little child shall lead them* (Isaiah 11:6). Isaiah 13 talks about the *burden of Babylon* (13:1), God's judgment on Babylon. Many, many years ago, Victor Houteff said that in between the fall of Assyria and setting up of Babylon the Great, God sets up his Kingdom. It's laid out there in Isaiah in order.

Revelation shows the same thing. Revelation 13 describes a period of time where God deals with Assyria. Before you get to Revelation 17 and 18, where Babylon is shown in its power, you have the 144,000 taken to Mount Zion by the Lamb, and then God's Spirit is poured on them and they go out to gather in other people (Rev. 14:1–6). The Kingdom is started. It may not be worldwide yet, because the territory hasn't been taken away from all nations, but the Kingdom has begun.

When God chases the Assyrian out of the land, there will still be a United States, the country is still operating. The prophecy about what is ultimately going to happen with Assyria in the Last Days is that *there shall be an highway for the remnant of his people, which shall be left, from Assyria* (Isaiah 11:16) to Jerusalem so they can learn God's ways.

A highway can take heavy traffic and suggests that millions of people will be saved from America and other countries. That makes God more a God of love than a lot of people want to give Him credit for. Even though there is judgment and sternness, God says: If you love me you will keep my commandments, you will want to please God. He says: You will do it not because I'm ordering you to do it. It is for your own good. If you keep my commandments, you will have health and lots of babies, no birth defects, plenty of animals, you will have all aspects of well-being in the Kingdom.

I think God is preparing people because the only way we are going to have peace, or the Kingdom, is for us to get along. It will entail war to some degree, although there is one prophecy that talks about when the nations are judged they *shall beat their swords into plowshares* (Isaiah 2:4); their interest moves to making food rather than making war. On the other hand, there are prophecies that indicate that wars will be fought, at least initially.

THE KINGDOM

The people who attend the marriage of the Lamb in heaven, the wave sheaf, are the ones who have been learning about it maybe for years, over the work of several prophets, leading up to it actually happening. The other people who are called to the Kingdom may not even know there is going to be a Kingdom. Some may have misconceptions. Most of the people in the Kingdom live here on earth. The wave sheaf go with Christ to heaven. All the others who are gathered into the Kingdom do not go to heaven at all.

Zechariah 14:4–10 says that the Mount of Olives, where the Lord stands, will split north and south to create a valley. Then it says the whole area becomes a plain that is lifted up. That is where the Kingdom will be located. The 144,000 will *follow the Lamb whithersoever He goeth* (Rev. 14:4) and stand with him on Mount Zion (Rev. 14:1).

The 144,000 are going to the marriage supper—the reception—which will be on earth, as described in the parable of the ten virgins in Matthew 25:1–13. The 144,000 are represented by the five virgins who are ready with oil for their lamps. The other five virgins, who are not prepared with oil for their lamps, are shut out of the marriage feast (Matt. 25:10).

Zechariah 14 says that after the Lord runs off the Assyrian, the message is going to go forth to *every nation, and kindred, and tongue, and people* (Rev. 14:6), who are the summer fruits, to come up to Jerusalem to keep the Feast of Tabernacles. If they don't go, for instance, if the family of Egypt doesn't go, or if other people don't respond to that invitation, it says they will receive the plagues and the rain will be cut off (Zech. 14:17–19).

The marriage feast is the Kingdom with everybody being invited. The first group that comes does not fill it, and the 144,000 go into the streets and lanes and invite others who come and do not fill it, so they go out to *highways and hedges* (Luke 14:23, in the parable in 14:16–24), and eventually God has saved as many as He can. *Blessed are they which are called unto the marriage supper of the Lamb* (Rev. 19:9).

Because God's people are scattered in every country, and there are good people trying to follow the truth and love God scattered in every religion and every country and every nationality, God has been blessing those countries with rain, etc., but once the Kingdom is set up and the invitation goes out for the people to come to it, then those who refuse or delay making the move will find the blessings cut off. This is done in order to give them the incentive to make the right decision.

We believe that when the Kingdom is set up, heaven will descend to earth, and Christ or God will actually live here. The earth will become the center of the universe. Heaven will be on earth, and He will dwell among us.

We believe that this earth will become the center of the universe, because They, the Husband and the Wife, are going to live here. That doesn't mean that They are confined here. The wave sheaf, we believe, gets to visit all over the universe. They go wherever Christ goes, but earth will be the headquarters.

So the whole concept of science, that everything revolves around something, is going to be changed to where it all revolves around this planet, or at least this solar system. According to Revelation, everything gets thrown out of whack, and there will be no sun and no moon. They will not be needed, *for the glory of God did lighten it, and the Lamb is the light thereof* (Rev. 21:23).

As David taught it, in the Kingdom, especially for those who go to heaven, one's true partner will be of oneself. That perfect mate, identically matched, has to be developed in this lifetime. Your whole life is geared to becoming more like God, more in His image, your mind aiming to be like God. By the time you get your reward, you will receive a perfect match from within. God will not have to find someone who suits you.

BABYLON THE GREAT

When the Lord comes down on the Mount of Olives and drives the Assyrian out, the Assyrian does not realize he is fighting God. The two-horned beast, the head of the coalition we call the Assyrian, wants to make an image or a copy of the first beast, the leopard-like beast, before the wound (Rev. 13:14–15), whatever the wound is. This means that the Assyrian puts together a larger coalition of nations, which ultimately becomes Babylon the Great. The governments of the world, in the name of peace, try to put together a new world order,[17] a one-world government, where everybody comes together. This is Babylon the Great in Revelation 17 and 18. Babylon is confusion.[18]

The copy of the beast is going to be the new world order: nations getting together to persecute God's people. This is what the devil does. He can't attack God. God is too big, too powerful, for him. He goes after God's children.

Babylon the Great is put together by the two-horned beast, and everyone is told they have to worship this image on pain of death. If you don't worship, and if you don't get his mark and his number, you will not be able to buy and sell (Rev. 13:15–18). It all has to do with economics and the merchants selling their wares in the name of religion.

If you read in Revelation 17 about the beast that the woman, Babylon the Great, rides, it looks like the leopard-like beast in chapter 13 that precedes the two-horned beast. It is *scarlet coloured* and has seven heads and ten horns (Rev. 17:4, 7–12, 16).

God said that Babylon is *the hold of every foul spirit, and a cage of every unclean and hateful bird* (Rev. 18:2)—every dirty bird, as we used to say. Babylon is full of dirty birds. David said that we're all dirty birds because we are part of the system that exists. Even though God brands them as unclean and hateful birds or spirits, He still says: *Come out of her, my people* (Rev. 18:4). They are invited to come out of Babylon and join God, and many people do.

God's people are called to come out of Babylon *that ye receive not of her plagues* (Rev. 18:4). In other words, God has a place of refuge, a place where they will be protected while God destroys Babylon the Great. Many of the prophecies liken it to the Exodus when the Israelites came out of Egypt. In Egypt their coming out was preceded by plagues on the Egyptians. The plagues did not fall on Israel, because Goshen was protected land (Exodus 9:26).

In our day, you have God's people scattered all over the world in different religions. It is not a case of getting one's head straight and rethinking one's doctrines and not being a part of the world by living in a commune and not shopping at Walmart. Adventists think they will give up dancing, drinking, and smoking, and therefore no longer be part of Babylon. The real coming out of Babylon all through history has been a physical move. When King Cyrus of the Persian Empire gave the decree for the Jews to go home after the Babylonian exile, some left and some didn't.

Revelation 18:11–19 says that when Babylon falls, merchants weep and wail because nobody buys their merchandise anymore. It sounds complicated, but once you catch the picture in your mind, I think you can see how it has played out over the years. And of course, the major fulfillment of it is still in the future.

Later, in Revelation 19:20, the two-horned beast and the false prophet are put in the lake of fire. God's going to do it! Much later on, after the millennium, the devil is cast in the lake of fire where the beast and false prophet are (Rev. 20:10).

ARMAGEDDON, THE MILLENNIUM, GOD'S KINGDOM

At the very end there is a war. The powers, Gog and Magog (Ezekiel 38–39; Rev. 20:8), which come against the Kingdom, are not going to win that one either. Once God gets on a winning streak, He is going to play it out to the end.

The battle in Zechariah 14 and Joel 2 is not the battle of Armageddon (Rev. 16:16). We really don't get into discussing the battle of Armageddon all that much, because it's way down at the end of the Judgment, at the end of the harvest period of time. The battle of Armageddon takes place during the sixth plague. The seventh plague starts out with an announcement, *It is done* (Rev. 16:17). It is followed by the final destruction of Babylon, an enormous amount of violence in nature, mountains and islands moving as a result of a major earthquake, and an outpouring of hail (Rev. 16:18–21). Those who did not accept the invitation to come out of Babylon into God's Kingdom are killed.

Revelation 20:6 refers to the resurrection of the blessed, those who were dead but are brought to life to be included in God's Kingdom: *Blessed and holy is he that hath part in the first resurrection: on such the second death hath no power, but they shall be priests of God and of Christ, and shall reign with him a thousand years.*

The millennium in Revelation 20:1–6, during which the devil is bound in a bottomless pit for one thousand years, comes after the plagues and the last battle, whether you think it's a millennium of peace or a millennium of desolation. I prefer to believe it is a Kingdom where God's people own the world. That battle is the last gasp of those who want to resist God's plan and God's way of salvation.

The final resurrection, at the end of the millennium mentioned in Revelation chapter 20, is the raising of all those who are lost to hear their judgment and to partake of the second death. Verse 6 seems to imply that the wicked are included in the first resurrection, but the phrase in verse 5, *This is the first resurrection,* refers to the previous statement in verse 5, *the rest of the dead lived not again until the thousand years were finished.* After all those wicked who refused to submit to God's mercy are destroyed, the Kingdom will have fulfilled Daniel's prophecy: *And in the days of these kings shall the God of heaven set up a kingdom, which shall never be destroyed: and the kingdom shall not be left to other people, but it shall break in pieces and consume all these kingdoms, and it shall stand for ever* (Dan. 2:44).

Clive Doyle, Karen Doyle, and Shari Doyle. Photo courtesy of Clive Doyle.

Shari Doyle and Karen Doyle at Mount Carmel. Photo courtesy of Clive Doyle.

Edna Doyle with her granddaughters, Karen Doyle and Shari Doyle. Photo courtesy of Clive Doyle.

Shari Doyle at the camp at Palestine, Texas. Photo courtesy of Clive Doyle

David Koresh and Clive Doyle in Melbourne, Australia, January 1, 1986. Photo courtesy of Elizabeth Baranyai/Sygma/Corbis.

Judy and Steve Schneider in Hawaii in 1987. Photo courtesy of Clive Doyle.

Scott and Floracita Sonobe with baby Angelica at the camp at Palestine. Photo courtesy of Angelica Sonobe Cregge and Crystal Sonobe Cregge.

Scott Sonobe, Greg Summers (wearing lei), Peter Hipsman (looking over the shoulder of Jimmy Riddle), Jimmy Riddle, and Neil Vaega with Joann Vaega in Hawaii in 1987. Photo courtesy of Clive Doyle.

Livingstone Fagan in London in 2008. Photo courtesy of Stuart A. Wright.

David Jones with his parents, Perry Jones and Mary Belle Jones, at Mount Carmel Center. Photo courtesy of Clive Doyle.

Michael Schroeder with his stepchildren, Christyn Mabb, Scott Mabb, and Jacob Mabb, and holding his infant son, Bryan Schroeder, at Mount Carmel Center. Photo courtesy of Sandy Connizzo.

Joseph Martinez, Isaiah Barrios, and Crystal Barrios, the three youngest children of Juliette Santoyo and grandchildren of Ofelia Santoyo. Photo courtesy of Ofelia Santoyo.

Fiery flying serpent on the David Koresh T-shirt, drawn by Cliff Sellors. The fiery flying serpent, a seraph mentioned in Isaiah 14:29, was on the back of the black T-shirt, and a stylized silhouette in white of David Koresh playing the guitar with the caption "David Koresh—God Rocks" was on the front. Photo courtesy of Clive Doyle.

Aerial photo depicting the building at Mount Carmel Center before the ATF raid on February 28, 1993. The shot is taken from the chapel side of the building. The swimming pool has been constructed, but it does not contain water. The storm shelter is under construction. The fuel tanks near the southwest corner of the building are visible. The front fence where the dogs were kept can be seen. This photo depicting the residence surrounded by Branch Davidians' vehicles and projects reveals their busy community life. Photo courtesy of Clive Doyle.

This is a composite photo of the front of the building taken by federal agents late in the siege. It can be determined that the photos were taken during the siege because a sheet with Bible passages written on it is hanging from a central tower window. The Branch Davidians' flag is flying from the flagpole, with its depiction of the fiery flying serpent in blue and white and the seven seals in red. Perspective is flattened in this composite photo. The telephone pole in front of Clive Doyle's window (third from the left) appears to be closer to the building than it actually was. The parked vehicles also appear to be closer to the building than they were. A tank has already knocked down the tree that was in front of Clive's window and has removed some of the vehicles. On the right of the photo, the side of the gymnasium, located behind the chapel, has been folded out to make it visible. On the left side of the photo, the dairy barn, located far behind the residence, appears to be immediately adjacent. The satellite dish, mounted on the roof over David's rooms on the second floor behind the chapel, is visible. The water tower can be seen behind the building on the north end. Government exhibit in 2000 civil trial.

Aerial photo taken on April 19, 1993, showing a tank demolishing the front door and foyer of the building. This would have been the tank that was driving through the foyer and entering the chapel to release CS gas. Destruction to other areas of the front of the building can be seen. The tank has already driven through front bedrooms to spray CS toward the vault at the base of the central tower. Part of the roof of the gymnasium, located behind the chapel, has collapsed as a result of tank penetration and demolition. Government exhibit in 2000 civil trial.

Aerial photo taken on April 19, 1993, showing the damage done to the gymnasium by a tank. Government exhibit in 2000 civil trial.

According to heat-sensitive FLIR footage taken over the building on April 19, 1993, the first fire started at 12:07 p.m. in the second-floor bedroom on the southwest front corner of the building. By 12:11 p.m. there were significant fires in the gymnasium behind the chapel and the cafeteria area behind the central tower, and the fire on the southwest corner had spread. These three burning areas can be seen in this aerial photo. Government exhibit in 2000 civil trial.

Aerial photo taken on April 19, 1993, from the chapel side of the building showing the spread of the fire. The opening toward the back end of the chapel, with rubble on a concrete slab, is where four men would escape the fire, with Clive Doyle being the last one. Government exhibit in 2000 civil trial.

When Ruth Riddle jumped from the second floor of the front of the building, she broke her ankle. Government photos verify her account told to Clive Doyle that she fell down when she tried to walk. Contrary to FBI statements to the media, the photos do not show Ruth attempting to run back into the building. The government photos show that two FBI agents ran to pull her away from the burning building. Here Ruth is shown lying in the open back of a tank, being attended by an agent, while the flames consume the building. Government exhibit in 2000 civil trial.

Clive Doyle, wearing the McLennan County prison jumpsuit, being led to a court appearance. The burns on his hands are visible. Photo courtesy of Clive Doyle.

Clive Doyle with his daughter Karen shortly after his release from jail. Photo courtesy of Clive Doyle.

Clive Doyle and Edna Doyle at the April 19, 1995 memorial service at Mount Carmel Center. Photo courtesy of the Joe Roberts
Collection, Texas Collection, Baylor University.

Sheila Martin, Clive Doyle, and Bonnie Haldeman in the yard of her home near Chandler, Texas, in August 2008 with Clive and Bonnie's dogs. Photo by Matthew D. Wittmer.

Sheila Martin and Clive Doyle visit the Mount Carmel property on April 18, 2010. The chapel, which was built in 2000 by volunteers for the use of the Branch Davidian survivors, is seen in the background. After Clive moved off the property in March 2006, the property and the new chapel have been under the control of Charles Pace, who leads a Branch Davidian group that rejects David Koresh. In 2009 Pace moved the memorial crape myrtle trees planted by Clive Doyle and others to new locations along the driveway. He also moved the memorial stones that had been placed under each tree to an arrangement by the front gate. Earlier, in March or April 2006, Pace destroyed the tree and memorial stone for David Koresh. Photo by Matthew D. Wittmer.

Paul Fatta, Kathy Jones, Clive Doyle, Sheila Martin, Ofelia Santoyo, and Mary Jones at the April 19, 2010, memorial in Waco. The framed photograph on the left end of the table depicts Catherine Matteson, who passed away in 2009. Sheila Martin's book, published in 2009, is placed in the center of the table. A framed drawing by Matthew D. Wittmer of the Branch Davidians' flag, which was consumed in the fire, is on the right end of the table. Photo by Matthew D. Wittmer.

5

The Mount Carmel Conflict

The ATF Raid, the Fifty-One-Day Siege, and the FBI Assault

THE BRANCH DAVIDIAN COMMUNITY IN 1992–1993

The fact that so many people of different backgrounds lived crowded into the small area at Mount Carmel—sometimes three and four to a room—and got along so well demonstrates to me that the Spirit was in control and able to bridge differences of race, understanding, and financial background. Our community included people from all over the world. About 130 were at Mount Carmel in 1993, but others were in California, out at the camp at Palestine, in a trailer a couple of miles from Mount Carmel [see figure 1 in appendix], and other places.

Australians

The Gents belonged to a Branch Davidian group in Australia. George Roden protested when David came on the scene at Mount Carmel in 1981, and he put out horror stories about David.[1] The Branch Davidians in Australia balked at these stories, and none of them came to Mount Carmel for Passover in 1984 to hear David teach.

Elizabeth Baranyai was a member of the Australian group. She mentioned in a letter to me that she had asked in a Branch meeting: Why are all of you condemning Vernon Howell when you have never listened to him? I shared this with David, and he suggested that we call one of the leaders of the group to see if he could come to Australia to speak to them. We called Jean Smith, and she said: If you come we'll give you a place to stay and we'll listen. David and I went to Australia in February of 1986.

On our first Sabbath in Australia we met at the home of Jean Smith's son, Guy. It was located outside Melbourne, a little bit in the country. Many people came that day. We met the Gents and several other families. David played his guitar and sang. David's music didn't go over with the Branches because they were very conservative, but they listened, and then David started to talk. No more than an hour into it people began to fidget and walk in and out. David continued. Finally someone interrupted and said: We don't go more than an hour. David continued, and that offended a lot of them. David didn't hit it off with Guy Smith either, and we were staying in his house.

The Gents invited David to come to their house while I remained at the Smith home. David stayed about two weeks in Australia and then returned to the States. I stayed two months. When David left his room at the Gents' house, he said I should move in there. Lisa and Bruce Gent had two children each by former marriages. Lisa had Michelle and Ian, Bruce had twins, Nicole and Peter. Lisa took me over to meet Peter, who was living at another address. When David visited Australia again, Nicole was away at college.

As a result of David's first visit to Australia, Jean Smith, Lisa and Bruce Gent, a lady named Myrtle Alloway, Elizabeth Baranyai, and a few others decided to come to the United States to listen to David, and ultimately they joined us there.

David visited Australia twice after that, and the young people began to listen to him. Peter Gent and Nicole Gent came to live at Mount Carmel. By 1993 Lisa and Bruce Gent had already moved back to Australia. In 1993 Peter and Nicole were twenty-four years old. During the ATF assault on February 28, Peter was the one on top of the water tower who was shot and killed. Nicole had two children with David. In 1993 Dayland, a boy, was three years old, and Paiges, a girl, was one. Nicole was pregnant with a third child, whom we count among the children who died in the fire because she was close to term. Nicole and all her children died in the fire on April 19, 1993.

Aisha Gyarfas, age seventeen in 1993, was the daughter of Elizabeth and Oliver Gyarfas. Australia is full of immigrants. This family was from Hungary. On one of David's trips to Australia, Elizabeth and Oliver said Aisha wanted to join. She had a little girl with David, Startle Summers,[2] who was one year old at the time of the fire. Aisha was pregnant and aborted a baby during the fire. Her pregnancy was about a month behind that of Nicole Gent.

At the time of the ATF raid, Aisha's brother, Oliver (nineteen), was at Mount Carmel. He was one of the three men who went outside the front of the building and across the driveway during the siege and buried Peter Gent's body. Shortly after that, Oliver, along with Kevin Whitecliff and

Brad Branch (Americans, thirty-one and thirty-five), were negotiated to go out. Ultimately Oliver was not charged; he was released and went back to Australia.

They were the main ones from Australia in 1993. Most of the others who had come from Australia had already left Mount Carmel for one reason or another. Marc Breault (American) had married Elizabeth Baranyai. When he moved to Australia to be with her, he made an effort to undo David's work from there.[3] Most of the Australian adults and even the young people who had accepted David's teaching were swayed by Marc Breault. Nicole Gent, Peter Gent, Aisha Gyarfas, and Oliver Gyarfas all stayed, much to the chagrin of their parents, and much to the suffering of these two families after the fire, losing three of their children and five grandchildren.

Graeme Craddock (thirty-five) was an electrical engineer and physics high school teacher in Australia. He moved to Mount Carmel in 1992. He survived the fire by taking shelter in a cinderblock utility building next to the water tower. In 1994 he was convicted in the criminal trial. When he was released from prison in 2006 he was deported to Australia.[4]

British

Most of the people from England were people whose families originated in Jamaica. Alrick George Bennett (thirty-five), whom we called Rick, was very tall. He had some building skills, so he and Neil Vaega (thirty-eight, Samoan American) were involved in heading up building projects. David had ultimate control of the projects because they were David's vision, but these two supervised what was to be done. I don't know much about Susan Benta (thirty-one). I think she was also Jamaican. They died in the fire on April 19.

I believe that Beverly Elliott (thirty) was a cousin of Livingstone Fagan (thirty-four). She was engaged to Winston Blake (twenty-eight), a fairly heavyset young man. He was killed in the ATF raid on February 28. Four bodies of our people who died on February 28 stayed inside for several days before I buried them.[5] Several days after the raid, Beverly came downstairs and I could tell she was still distraught. She said: Please take me to Winston. I want to see his body. I said: No, you don't. It is better to remember him the way he was, and anyway he has already been buried. She thought he was still lying in his room. We talked and then she went back upstairs. I don't know whether I consoled her or not. She died in the fire.

Yvette Fagan (thirty-two) was Livingstone's wife. Doris Fagan (age fifty-one) was his mother. They were from Jamaica. Livingstone had a master's degree in theology from Newbold College, which is a Seventh-day Adventist college north of London, and he had been a Seventh-day Adventist minister.[6] They had two children, Renae (six) and Nehara (four), who were sent out on the evening of February 28.[7] David sent Livingstone out on March 23 with a message for the FBI agents. Yvette and Doris died in the fire. Livingstone was sent to prison and served fifteen years.[8]

The Henry family also had a Jamaican background. Zilla (fifty-five) was the mother, and there were five children: Diana (twenty-eight), Paulina (twenty-four), Phillip (twenty-two), Stephen (twenty-six), and Vanessa (nineteen). The father never joined David, and I think he made efforts to get them back. I have seen him in documentaries made in England. He is very distraught because he lost his whole family.

Livingston Malcolm (twenty-six) was a Jamaican from England and a cousin of Bob Marley. Diane Martin (forty-one) was not related to Wayne and Sheila Martin (Americans). John-Mark McBean (twenty-seven) was a ministerial student from Newbold College.[9] Bernadette Monbelly (thirty-one) also had a Jamaican background. Sandra Hardial (twenty-seven), I believe, was a policewoman back in England. Most of these people were formerly Seventh-day Adventists. They died in the fire. John-Mark McBean's sister, Janet McBean (twenty-five) survived because she was in California with a few other Branch Davidians.

Bernadette Monbelly, Marjorie Thomas (thirty), and two or three others had some training as nurses. I was asked to go upstairs to the women's section one day because Bernadette needed a back adjustment. All these women were standing there watching me do it, and they were cringing at the sound of joints cracking. I asked: What kind of nurses are you? Marjorie Thomas escaped the fire on April 19, but she was severely burned. She eventually went back to England.

Rosemary Morrison (twenty-nine) had a daughter, Melissa (six). There were negotiations to send Melissa out, but she didn't want to leave her mother. Both of them died in the fire. They, too, were Jamaican.

Sonia Murray (twenty-nine) was Jamaican, but I don't know much about her. Abedolwalo Davies (thirty) was from Nigeria. We called him Dabo. They both died in the fire.

Victorine Hollingsworth (fifty-nine) was a British citizen, originally from Guyana. She had been a Branch Davidian before David's time. She came out during the siege on March 21 and has since died.

Derek Lovelock (thirty-seven) was a British citizen. He was one of the nine survivors of the fire. He was burned on his arm and spent about six months in jail. He was released after the death of his father and returned to England, where he still lives today.

Clifford Sellors (thirty-three) was white. His father was in the military, and I think he was born in Hong Kong or some place where his father was stationed. Cliff was an artist. He drew fantasy-type art. He liked to draw evolutionary concepts—not that he believed in evolution. He drew political cartoons. Cliff was with us in California for a while, where he took a course in airbrushing. From then on he painted gas tanks on motorcycles, helmets, and guitars. He painted David's guitars. He also did sign work for businesses. He painted the Ranch Apocalypse sign for Mount Carmel. During the siege, David asked him to rework all of Victor Houteff's charts that were used for Bible studies. Cliff died in the fire. I doubt whether any of his work is left, unless there's a motorcycle somewhere with his airbrush work on it. [See fiery flying serpent in photospread.] Everything that was inside the building at the time of the fire is gone.

Theresa Nobrega (forty-eight) died in the fire. Theresa's daughter, Natalie (eleven), was negotiated out during the siege, and she went to live with her father in England.

Renos Avraam (thirty-two) was a British citizen of Greek-Cypriot extraction. He was one of the nine survivors of the fire and spent about twelve or thirteen years in prison. Upon his release he returned to England.[10]

Norman Allison (twenty-eight) was a young guy who came to Mount Carmel in 1992. Most of us knew him by the nickname Bro. I don't know what brought him—whether it was curiosity, or whether he was invited by someone. He was a new guy we had never heard of prior to the 1992 Passover. He came over with people from England. His love was rap music, and he wanted to get ahead in the music world. He stayed probably most of 1992 and then went out to California. He was gone for a while, and early in 1993 he decided to come back to Mount Carmel. He arrived downtown and made a phone call to David and asked if he could come back. Instead of saying yes, David said: Why don't you go stay at the building we have rented for the car repair business?[11] So he went over there.

That is how Bro ended up at the shop with Mike Schroeder and Woodrow ("Bob") Kendrick on February 28 when the ATF raid happened. They tried to walk back to Mount Carmel later that day, and Mike Schroeder was shot and killed. Norman Allison was captured by ATF agents, and Bob Kendrick turned himself in. Norman Allison, Bob Kendrick, and I were the three defendants in the criminal trial who were acquitted of all charges.

Canadians

Novellette Sinclair (thirty-six) was a black woman from Canada. I first met her in Toronto. She was bilingual, and I think she worked as a translator in schools or government offices. She was good friends with Bonnie Haldeman, David's mother. They did cleaning work together, and they shared living space in a school bus at the Palestine camp.[12] Novellette died in the fire.

Gladys Ottman (sixty-seven) and Ruth Ottman Riddle (thirty-two) were Branches under Lois Roden. They lived in Canada and ended up joining

David after Lois Roden died. Gladys exited Mount Carmel during the siege. Ruth stayed till the end and was one of the nine who survived the fire. In escaping the building, she jumped from a second floor window and broke her ankle. She was part of the criminal trial and was sentenced to five years in federal prison. Upon her release she was deported back to Canada. She has since remarried and has a small child.

Israeli

Pablo Cohen (twenty-eight) was Jewish and came to Mount Carmel from Israel, but he was born in Argentina. Pablo met and studied with David on David's last trip to Israel. Pablo loved music. When David left Israel he loaned Pablo an electric bass guitar, saying that Pablo could bring it back to him. So Pablo showed up at Mount Carmel one day with the guitar and began playing in David's band. He died in the fire.

Americans

James Lawter (seventy), who had been a Davidian in the days of Victor Houteff, had actually gone to Israel under Ben Roden and also went to Israel under David. His hometown was Asheville, North Carolina. He came out during the siege and has since died.

Raymond Friesen (seventy-six) was Canadian-born, but he was an American citizen. He lived in California most of the time I knew him. He was an old Branch Davidian from way back, and before that he and his wife, Tillie Friesen, had belonged to what is known in the church family as Reformed Seventh-day Adventists. This group in Germany broke away from the Seventh-day Adventist Church in the days of World War I over the issue of serving in the military for the kaiser. Raymond died in the fire.

Tillie was not staying at Mount Carmel in 1993. Three older ladies, Tillie Friesen, Trudy Meyers, and Concepción Acuña, had been sent by David to live in David Jones's trailer in a trailer park at Beaver Lake [see figure 1 in appendix], a couple of miles from Mount Carmel. The building at Mount Carmel didn't have hot and cold running water, indoor showers, indoor toilets, or air conditioning and heat, so David sent them to the trailer so they could be comfortable. Mary Belle Jones, Perry Jones's wife, was staying there to look after them, but she said she needed help, so my mother, Edna Doyle, went to stay there also. Of these women, only Mary Belle is alive today. Tillie Friesen, Trudy Meyers, and Edna Doyle are buried in the Mount Carmel cemetery. Concepción Acuña is buried at the pauper's cemetery, the McLennan County Restland Cemetery in Waco, where her granddaughter and five great grandchildren, who died in the fire, are buried.[13]

Catherine Matteson (seventy-seven) became a Branch Davidian when she heard Ben Roden teach in Phoenix, Arizona. When Lois Roden was the prophet, Catherine was her assistant. When David began to teach, Catherine was among our group who believed that the Spirit of Prophecy had moved from Lois to David. After the ATF raid on February 28, 1993, David sent her out on March 2 at 8:10 a.m. She came out with Margaret Lawson (seventy-five) and Daniel Martin (six) and Kimberly Martin (four). Catherine wanted to stay, but David sent her out to deliver an audiotape of his explanation of the Seven Seals of the book of Revelation to FBI agents. David had agreed that we would come out after this audiotaped Bible study had been played on radio in prime time, but then God told David to wait. Catherine and Margaret were charged with using weapons, including automatic weapons, to murder and attempt to murder federal agents, but the charges were dropped the next day.[14] Catherine passed away in Waco in 2009 at age ninety-three, and she is buried in the McLennan County Restland Cemetery in Waco.

Janet and Bob Kendrick (sixty-two) were Branch Davidians from California who lived at Mount Carmel under Ben Roden by the time I arrived. Janet was at our Palestine property at the time of the ATF raid. Bob was at the repair shop and along with Norman Allison and Mike Schroeder tried to get into Mount Carmel later on the afternoon of the raid.

Bonnie Haldeman (forty-nine) was David's mother. She joined us in 1985 when we were living at the Palestine camp. She traveled to California to live there in one of our houses and work. She and Jimmy Riddle traveled to Hawaii three months before I went over to operate a bakery that had been donated. After we left Palestine to return to Mount Carmel in 1988, Bonnie lived there in one of the little houses. Later, her husband, Roy Haldeman, and David's brother, Roger Haldeman, moved to Mount Carmel. Bonnie and Roy left Mount Carmel in 1991 and lived in Waco while she attended nursing school. They were living in their home in Chandler, Texas, when everything happened in 1993. Roger was not at Mount Carmel in 1993; he had left a month or so earlier.[15] Bonnie took care of a lot of people, and one of these was her mentally ill sister, who stabbed her to death on January 23, 2009, when Bonnie stopped by to take her to see the doctor.

Quite a number of the young guys who joined—Jaime Castillo (twenty-four), David Thibodeau (twenty-four), Mike Schroeder (twenty-nine)—were all drummers. David tried to get them to expand their skills to other instruments. Most of them became quite versatile. Jaime Castillo and David Thibodeau escaped the building at the time of the fire. Jaime Castillo was arrested, convicted in the criminal trial, and released from prison in 2006. He died in 2008 from complications caused by hepatitis C. David Thibodeau was not charged and now lives in Maine.

On February 28, the day of the ATF raid, Mike Schroeder was at our car repair business down the road from Mount Carmel, which the reporters subsequently called the Mag Bag. He was shot and killed later in the day in the creek bed on the property behind Mount Carmel as he attempted to walk back to Mount Carmel to join his wife, Kathy Schroeder (thirty-four), and children. Mike and Kathy were from Florida. Kathy had three children from a previous marriage, Scott Mabb (eleven), Jacob Mabb (nine), and Christyn Mabb (seven). Mike was the father of Bryan (three). The children were sent out during the siege on March 1, and Kathy came out on March 12. Kathy served three years in prison. Mike's death was not investigated properly, and no charges were brought against the ATF agents who shot him.

The Andrade sisters, Katherine (twenty-four) and Jennifer (nineteen), were Argentinian, but they came from California. I think Kathy went with David, along with Steve Schneider, the last time he went to Israel. Kathy had a daughter with David, Chanel Andrade (one). They all died in the fire.

One of the Americans who came from Hawaii was a man named Neil Vaega (thirty-eight). He was born in the United States, but his parents were Samoans from New Zealand. Neil's wife, Margarida Vaega (forty-seven), was Chinese. They both died in the fire. They sent out their daughter, Joann (seven), on March 2.

Mary Jean Borst (forty-nine) had been with the Seventh-day Adventist Reform Movement before coming to join David's group. We called her Jean. She brought her son, Brad, with her. He was just a kid at the time. He left Mount Carmel before 1993. Jean Borst died in the fire.

Trudy Meyers had been at Mount Carmel many years before David arrived and then returned to Mount Carmel when Mary Jean Borst and Ofelia Santoyo came. In 1993 Trudy was elderly and living in David Jones's mobile home with Ofelia's mother, Concepción Acuña, Edna Doyle, and Mary Belle Jones. Ofelia Santoyo (sixty-two) was living at Mount Carmel and came out during the siege on March 21. She now lives at Mount Carmel with the Branch Davidian group led by Charles Pace.

My daughter Shari Doyle (eighteen) was at Mount Carmel in 1993. She died in the fire. Her older sister, Karen, was in California along with Janet McBean (twenty-five) and Stan Sylvia, looking after a house in Pomona.

Jeannine Bunds and the Bundses' daughter, Robyn Bunds, left Mount Carmel in 1990. Robyn had a son, Wisdom (now called Shaun), with David. Robyn's brother, David Bunds, and his wife, Debbie, had already left. The only one remaining at Mount Carmel was the father, Don Bunds (fifty-five), and he went out early on the morning of February 28, so he was not present for the ATF raid. He was arrested off the property. He has since died in California.

David met Lisa Marie Farris (twenty-four) at a music store in California. She died in the fire. When David went to music stores he would get into conversations with the salespeople. To protect their jobs he would buy quite a lot of merchandise while he told them about scripture. David did that in restaurants, too. If a manager or waitress showed an interest, David would take thirty or forty people there. If at some point they backed off, we would not go there anymore. Everything David did was for the purpose of sharing what he believed God was giving him. Whenever there was a good prospect of a potential member, he gave that person his attention. If they didn't want it, he stopped; he did not make a nuisance of himself. Just about anyone in Waco who knew David will say that he talked Bible to them.

David met Brad Branch (thirty-four) in a bar. Brad had a Pentecostal background. Brad started talking about the Bible and was surprised that David listened. Brad said that after about an hour he finally took a breath, David said a few things, and he discovered that David knew the Bible. Brad then came out to Mount Carmel for Bible studies. He said that he learned more from David than he had all the years he spent in his church.

Peter Hipsman (twenty-eight) and Greg Summers (twenty-eight) were roommates in Hawaii. They were both originally from New York. Greg did office work where Judy Schneider worked. I don't know what Peter did. Greg and Peter developed a comedy routine and would do their bits for us during our entertainment evenings. David encouraged everyone to participate. He said that shyness was basically pride—you wanted to be perfect and you did not want to embarrass yourself. Peter Hipsman was killed in the ATF raid. Greg Summers died in the fire.

Lorraine Sylvia (forty) was born in England, but she was an American citizen and wife of Stan Sylvia (fifty). We called her "Larry." They came from New Bedford, Massachusetts. Their daughter was Rachel (twelve), and their son was Joshua (seven). Larry had a daughter with David named Hollywood (one). I remember that Larry got up and sang one night and she sounded like Judy Collins. Others performed rap. Even in the music at Mount Carmel there was a broad spectrum among us. Stan was not at Mount Carmel in 1993 because he was in California. Joshua was sent out during the siege. Larry, Rachel, and Hollywood died in the fire.

Floyd Houtman (sixty-one) was from New Bedford, Massachusetts. He had been a Branch Davidian for many years going back to Ben Roden. There were Branch Davidians with Ben and Lois Roden in the Boston area, New Hampshire, and New York.

Floyd was not a highly educated man. He was a very humble factory-worker type of guy. I first met Floyd in 1979. Floyd and Stan Sylvia were buddies from way back. They had initially refused to come down in 1984 to listen to David because of the stories they were hearing from George Roden.

David made a trip up there, taking Novellette Sinclair with him. Once they heard him, Floyd and Stan joined, and they brought their families. They came down around the time that we moved away from Mount Carmel to Waco because of George Roden. They moved with us from downtown Waco to Mexia, then to Palestine, Texas. There were times Floyd and Stan were in California.

Floyd and his wife had three children. At the Palestine camp the two boys and the girl set up a pulpit, and the older boy played David. I remember the second boy getting upset because he wanted to be David, too. His wife later took the children and left. Floyd was at Mount Carmel in 1993 and died in the fire.

Sherri Jewell (forty-three) had lived in Hawaii and had been connected romantically with Paul Fatta (thirty-seven). I don't think they were going together when we met them. The first time I met her was in California. She was a schoolteacher. Sherri was a beautiful woman who was part Japanese. Her daughter Kiri Jewell lived with her at Mount Carmel for a while, but the girl's father gained custody in 1992.[16] Sherri died in the fire.

Paul Fatta (thirty-five) had been a very successful businessman in Hawaii. He was not an expert on guns, but he handled much of the business at gun shows, which helped provide income for our community. The guys who went to the gun shows in Texas sold guns, ammunition, Meals Ready to Eat (MREs), ammunition vests sewn by the women, and other paraphernalia. Paul and his son Kalani (fourteen) left Mount Carmel about two or three hours before the ATF on February 28 to take merchandise to a gun show in Austin.[17] At the 1994 criminal trial, Paul was convicted of charges relating to the guns and sentenced to fifteen years in prison. He was released from prison in 2006.

Perry Dale Jones (sixty-four) was from California. He had been a Davidian way back in the days of Victor Houteff because his father had been a Davidian. Helen Rogers, the mother of his wife, Mary Belle Jones, was also a longtime Davidian, since the 1930s in the Los Angeles area. Helen Rogers had accepted David when he first started teaching but died shortly thereafter. Perry and Mary Belle were in Ben Roden's Branch Davidian group from its inception. I knew Perry for almost thirty years. Mary Belle was living in the trailer owned by their son, David Jones (thirty-eight) [see figure 1 in appendix], looking after some older Branch Davidian women, so she was not at Mount Carmel during the events in 1993. Perry and Mary Belle Jones were David Koresh's in-laws because he was married to their daughter, Rachel (twenty-four). On February 28 Perry was standing behind David when he went to the door to meet the ATF agents as they rushed up. He was shot and died later that day. Mary Belle Jones continues to live in Waco.

David Michael Jones was the oldest son of Perry and Mary Belle. He was the mailman that you hear about in the accounts of what happened on February 28. He was shot on February 28, but he didn't tell us. It wasn't until well into the siege that one of the nurses was talking to some of us, and she said she had just finished an operation to take a bullet out of David Jones's backside. He was too embarrassed to tell people that he had been hit. David Jones was a very quiet, introverted person. You had to try hard to get him to carry on a conversation. His children, Mark Jones (twelve), Kevin Jones (eleven), and Heather Jones (nine) were at Mount Carmel on February 28, but they were sent out on March 3, 4, and 5. Their mother, David Jones's ex-wife, Kathy Jones, had left Mount Carmel, perhaps around 1989. David Jones died in the fire.

Rachel Howell Koresh, a daughter of Perry and Mary Belle Jones, was David Koresh's wife. She and David were married in 1984 when she was fourteen.[18] They had three children. Cyrus Howell Koresh (eight) was David's oldest son. Star Howell Koresh (six) was the first daughter. Bobbie Lane Koresh (two), a girl, was their youngest child. Michele Jones (eighteen) was the youngest daughter of Perry and Mary Belle.[19] She had three children with David: Serenity Sea Jones (four), and twin girls, Chica Jones and Little One Jones (two). Rachel and Michele and their children died in the fire.

If someone asked David how many wives he had, he would say one. The other women had children by him, but they were not in the same category as his wife. Theologically, his answer of one wife may even supersede Rachel. He taught that in the next life we will have our perfect mates, so the coupling here is temporary. We believe the Kingdom will be on earth, and people gathered in or raised from the dead will possess this earth as their paradise. The ones who will go to heaven will have a God-appointed union with a perfect mate who will come from within themselves, like Eve came from within Adam. As David taught it, in the Kingdom, especially for those who go to heaven, the true partner will be from oneself and therefore identically matched. The perfect mate has to be developed in this lifetime. Your whole life is geared to becoming more like God, more in His image, your mind aiming to be like God. By the time you get your reward it will be a perfect match from within.

Jeff Little (thirty-two) came over from Hawaii but was originally from Michigan. He was a computer whiz who worked for big companies like Sony. He married Nicole Gent to give her citizenship. There was no relationship technically. For the same reason, Greg Summers married Aisha Gyarfas, Peter Hipsman married Novellette Sinclair, and Jimmy Riddle married Ruth Ottman.

Douglas Wayne Martin (forty-two) was married to Sheila Martin (forty-six), who was a Branch Davidian from Boston. Wayne was from New York City and had been raised a Seventh-day Adventist. They met when Sheila was working in New York City. Wayne obtained his law degree from Harvard Law School. Wayne, Sheila, and their kids joined us when we were at the camp in Palestine, and then they moved with us to Mount Carmel. He left a good job as a law librarian in Durham, North Carolina, to join us.[20]

Wayne wasn't licensed to practice law in Texas when he first came and had to prepare for the bar exam. In the interim, for about a year, he worked for me as a roofer. He was overweight when he started. Sheila said he lost about a hundred pounds doing the roofing work. On the first day, poor Wayne could hardly stand up on the roof. He sat for much of the time in the shade under a tree. It was 120 degrees Fahrenheit up on that roof. Wayne persevered and kept coming to work. Later he had a law office downtown. He did court-appointed cases, but he finally closed that office and worked from an office in the building at Mount Carmel. Wayne made the 911 call on February 28 during the ATF raid in an effort to get the shooting stopped.

Wayne and Sheila's children were Wayne Joseph Martin (twenty), Anita Marie Martin (eighteen), Sheila Reneé Martin (fifteen), Lisa Marie Martin (thirteen), Jamie Martin (ten), Daniel Martin (six), and Kimberly Martin (four). Jamie was severely disabled due to spinal meningitis contracted when he was a baby. Jamie survived the ATF raid and was sent out on the evening of March 1. Daniel and Kimberly were sent out on the morning of March 2, and Sheila came out on March 21. Wayne Martin, all three of the oldest girls, and the oldest boy died in the fire. Jamie died in 1998 and is buried next to his father and siblings in the McLennan County Restland Cemetery in Waco. The only two that Sheila has left are Daniel and Kimberly, and they all live in Waco.

Juliette Santoyo (thirty), daughter of Ofelia Santoyo (sixty-two), was Mexican American. Ofelia came out on March 21, but Juliette and her five children, Audrey Martinez (thirteen), Abigail Martinez (eleven), Joseph Martinez (eight), Isaiah Barrios (four), and Crystal Barrios (three), stayed inside the building and died in the fire. Isaiah was nicknamed "Taco."

The man I considered my best friend was James Riddle (thirty-two). He went by "Jimmy." At one point his whole family was at Mount Carmel studying under David. Jimmy had four sisters, including Rita Riddle. His mother would have been at Mount Carmel at the time of the ATF raid, except she and Janet Kendrick were minding the property at Palestine. On February 28, there was only Jimmy Riddle and his sister Rita Riddle (thirty-five) and her daughter, Misty Ferguson (seventeen), at Mount Carmel. Rita came out on March 21. Jimmy died on April 19. We believe that Jimmy was one of the ones who tried to escape the fire from the back of the building, that he was shot and killed outside and then his body pushed back inside by a tank.[21] Misty was severely burned but escaped the fire.

The Schneiders were Steve (forty-three) and Judy (forty-one). Judy was a top-notch office worker. In Honolulu Steve was teaching comparative religions at the University of Hawaii. At the time Bonnie Haldeman and

I were in Hawaii in 1987 to revitalize a bakery, Steve was traveling with David, and Judy was still in Hawaii. They came to Texas when we were staying at Palestine, and they returned to Mount Carmel with us. Judy had a child with David named Mayanah (two), pronounced "Myna." They called her a little myna bird. Judy was shot on February 28 by a bullet that split her finger and skipped up her arm. She was pretty outspoken.[22] They tried to negotiate her out for treatment. She said she would come out for them to sew it up if they promised she could go right back to Mount Carmel. They would not agree to that. They said: The doctors are concerned you will get infection and lose your finger. She said: I guess we'll have to chop it off. It sounds crude, but we knew that a lot of the things said by negotiators on the phone were not sincere and only manipulation. We knew when they were saying what they thought we wanted to hear.

Scott Sonobe (thirty-five) was Japanese American. His wife, Floracita (thirty-four), was Filipina American. We called her Cita. They had two little girls, Angelica Sonobe (six) and Crystal Sonobe (three), and they were the first children to be sent out, at 8:55 p.m. on February 28. On that night Cita was the one who walked or drove children down the driveway to be turned over to the agents waiting on the road. Scott was wounded on February 28 but recovered. Scott and Cita died in the fire.

Jaydean Wendel (thirty-four) was shot and killed on February 28. Her husband, Mark Wendel (forty), survived the shoot-out with ATF agents but died in the fire. They were from Hawaii. Jaydean was the only one of the people from Hawaii who was actually born there. Mark was well educated. When we were in California he got a job where he was in charge of landscaping for a whole school district in Orange County. Their children, Jaunessa (eight), Tamara (five), Landon (four), and Patron (five months), were sent out on March 1.

THE BUILDING

I can describe the building from memory, but I can't give measurements. [See figures 3 and 4 in the appendix.][23]

The front door, on the west side of the building, was where the ATF agents came out of the cattle trailers at the start of the raid on February 28, 1993. There was only one door to the building on the front, and it was close to the southwest corner. The front door opened into a foyer that continued into a hallway, which led into the chapel. The hallway going into the chapel was in line with the front door. The opening to the chapel had no door.

The machine shop [#6 in figure 3] was located in rooms behind the chapel on the first floor, on the swimming pool side of the chapel. From the stage in the chapel there was a little doorway that went into the back.

You could go through there, and there was another door leading into the machine shop.

The hallway going from the foyer into the chapel was intersected by a long hallway that ran straight down the middle of the longest front part of the building. On the first floor, this long hall went from one end to the other, roughly running north and south. On either side of the hall, on the west (front side) and east (back side), were rooms.

Coming in the front door you entered the foyer. The foyer was behind the windows on each side of the front door. Armchairs and bookcases with encyclopedias and other books were to the right. To the left was the upright piano. There might have been some more chairs on the left. Then further on the left you came to a stairway that went up to the second floor.

The front stairway took a turn going up. It was set back from the front wall on the first floor. By the time it turned further up, it ran up the front wall and went past a window on the second floor.

After coming in the front door, instead of going into the chapel, if you turned right (south) into the long hall there were two doors on your left, on the east side of the hallway. The first doorway was for the computer room [#16 in figure 3 in appendix]. The second doorway was for Wayne Martin's office [#17 in figure 3] at the end of the hall. Directly opposite his office, on the front southwest corner of the building, was the sewing room [#18 in figure 3]. It had originally been a bedroom for one of the older ladies, but she wasn't all that keen on it, and eventually she and several other ladies went to live in David Jones's trailer at Beaver Lake [see figure 1 in appendix]. This room was turned into a sewing room, which was the workplace for the Mag Bag business. "Mag Bag" was the brand name that they put on the hunting vests that the women sewed.

If you went back down the hall going toward the opposite (north) end of the front part of the building, the first room you came to on your right was called the phone room [#15 in figure 3]. It also had armchairs. The public phone was there, as opposed to, for instance, Wayne Martin's office, which also had a telephone. The second door you came to on your right was Steve Schneider's room [#13 in figure 3].

Then there was a blank wall on the right. Beyond that was a big rectangular-shaped opening, with no door, which went into the serving area of the kitchen. By the time you got there, you were in the center of the building where the four-story tower was located. The center tower consisted of three stories built on top of a concrete vault on the first floor, making it four stories. You couldn't access the upper levels of that central tower from the first floor—you had to be on the second floor to do that.

The vault had been part of a previous building—the Administration Building—that the Davidians had built back in the 1950s. The Administration Building was still there when I first came to Mount Carmel in 1966 to be with the Branch Davidians under Ben Roden. We used the Administration Building for different things over the years.[24] In 1983 the Administration Building burned down due to an electrical fire in the ceiling. The only thing that survived was the vault, and nothing inside it burned. All the church records and files and other things that were in the vault were not touched by the 1983 fire.

David built the large building around this vault. The door of the vault faced west, toward the front of the building. I'm not sure when, but he took the big metal door off the vault and incorporated the vault into the kitchen. I think the reason he took the door off was because he brought in a big metal walk-in cooler, which they put inside the vault to the right [#4 in figure 3 in appendix]. Then shelves were put in the vault to store food and things. David built a small partition just inside the door of the vault probably in October or November of '92. The cooler was still in there, but he brought a lot of the food out and stored it on other shelves, either in the cafeteria or in a little adjunct built onto the kitchen [#5 in figure 3]. Unbeknownst to most of us, David brought the guns down from one of his rooms upstairs over the chapel [#21b in figure 4 in appendix] and stored them in the vault inside the partitioned area. They were put in there either on the floor or on racks.

The kitchen in front of the vault was where we had big commercial stoves, ranges, and pizza-making ovens, a huge popcorn maker, and a bread mixer. Then there was a stainless steel serving area where you could slide a tray along the rails, and all of the food was spread out along there for serving. In front of that was an open area where people lined up to get their food. The line would come out into the main hallway through the rectangular-shaped opening.

The north end of the hall was initially built as a gymnasium. So many people turned up for Passover in 1992 we wondered where everyone was going to sleep. So we worked day and night to subdivide the gymnasium into upper and lower levels. We divided the length of it into rooms on the front and back (west and east sides) of the long hall. The first floor was considered the men's dormitory, and upstairs was the women's dormitory.

In this new section on the first floor, instead of having regular bedrooms David built bunk beds. Each room had two bunk beds. These rooms, unlike the ones closer to the front door, did not have doors on them. They had carpet on the floor, but there were no built-in closets. You made do with something to hang your clothes on, but by that time, most people had pared down whatever excess furniture or baggage they had. By 1993 it had all been put out in the gymnasium, which had been built behind the chapel after the first gymnasium was turned into bedrooms. Things were stored out there until they could be disposed of or utilized.

There was a door across the hall going into the men's dorm section on the northern end of the first floor, which blocked people from wandering in. From there on, the rooms were open. If you wanted privacy, you hung a blanket or something. Most rooms had three or four guys in them. I was in the second room on the left past the door, or the third window from the far north end [#10 in figure 3 in appendix].[25] If you were looking at the front of the building prior to the FBI tanks doing their damage, there was a tree growing right outside my window. [Part of the tree is visible in photo 13.]

The end of the hall ran into a large room that took up the whole north end of the men's dorm floor [#8 in figure 3]. Shortly before the ATF raid, one part of it had been turned into a studio for Cliff Sellors. He had his art supplies stored to the left, the west side. To the right, on the east side, were tools. On the far north wall was a trapdoor that led into the buried school bus, which functioned as a tunnel going into the storm shelter we were building.

Across the hallway from the four rooms in the men's dorm area on the front of the building were four other rooms on the east side of the hall, three of which were used for bedrooms. The first room you came to as you went through the door that designated the men's dorm area was a room that was used for weights and exercise equipment [#11 in figure 3]. There were three more rooms on that side of the hall. Two of them butted up against the wall that was part of the cafeteria, so they didn't have windows. The very last dorm room had a window [#9 in figure 3] because the cafeteria didn't go the whole length of the building. David had a big platform out there holding three 1,500-gallon plastic water tanks [#3 in figure 3], which were shot up by the ATF agents on the helicopters during the raid. Just the year before the raid we had our well fixed, and I believe one pipe went into the cafeteria so they could wash dishes. So we had running water in the cafeteria, but not in the rest of the building.

One of the men who was in the last dorm room on the east side of the hall [#9] was Winston Blake. He was shot sitting in his room on his bunk bed. You couldn't see out of his room and you couldn't see in because the water tanks blocked the window. A little light came into the room because the tanks weren't jammed right up to the building. The ATF agents shot up our water tanks, and Winston happened to get shot sitting on the other side in his room.

At different times there had been women staying on the first floor, but as more and more people came, eventually it got to where all the women were upstairs except for Kathy Schroeder and her three boys and daughter. She was in the room on the front, or west, side of the hall, before you went through the door into the men's dormitory area [#12 in figure 3].

Unlike the hall on the first floor that was straight, the hall on the second floor jogged around. The rooms on the second floor for mothers and their children were bigger than the rooms the men had. [See figure 4 in appendix.]

When you came out of the stairs onto the second floor, you had to turn left to walk to the main hallway. If you then turned right (south), the hall went past two rooms and turned right again, making an L-shape. Sheila Martin's room was at the end, on the southwest front corner of the building [#23 in figure 4 in appendix].

Mothers with children had the rooms on the second floor on the front (west side) of the building. Some of the other older ladies were in rooms on the back (east side) of the second floor, which looked out over the cafeteria in one section. Women without children were primarily in the two three-story towers on the ends of the building. Ladders were used to go up in the towers.

David moved several times. He moved initially, I think, from the two rooms over the back end of the chapel [#21a and #21b in figure 4] into the central tower. At one time we had a lot of the younger women who didn't have children staying in the central tower. Then there came a point when some of them moved out and David, I think, took the very top floor. At another time—maybe it was only during the siege—he moved into one of the front rooms on the second floor. By that time, of course, people were being negotiated out and living situations were totally different from what they had been before.

I'm not exactly sure where David's room was at the time of the ATF raid, whether he was still in the tower or not. After the raid took place and David was wounded, he spent most of the time in the short little hallway on the second floor that led back to the central tower [#19 in figure 4]. He was lying on the floor for days, probably weeks, thinking he was dying, so he didn't use a bedroom.

During the siege we heard that a helicopter had crashed, not because we had shot it, but it had gone down. I tried to look out a window without exposing myself and getting shot, but I couldn't see anything. I finally went up to the top floor of the central tower. There was a bed there, but it didn't look like a room that was currently being used as a bedroom. I'd say it was a room that David had occupied sometime prior to that. David Jones was up there keeping watch. That was the only time I went up there. That room had a big bed in it and maybe a closet or two. The room was fairly bare since the bed took up the whole section.

EVENTS LEADING UP TO THE ATF RAID

The year or two before the ATF raid on February 28, 1993, David told us: The way things are shaping up, we may not get to Israel. The devil doesn't want us to go, so he is going to block it. It looks like persecution is coming.[26] David's focus shifted from our going to Israel to preparing for the trouble he saw coming.[27] Increasingly we began to notice things that indicated that we were being watched and something was being planned.

To my knowledge there was no systematic training at Mount Carmel about how to use weapons. The rifles that David got in the big order were disassembled and in crates. I don't know whether or not they were put together. I don't know how many he had except for what the government said,[28] and I don't know if that is factual. I didn't see the purchase order or how many were delivered.

I never saw a shooting range or training program where people went out until they got good in the handling of weapons. There was a big heap of dirt in the back of the building, perhaps from digging the swimming pool. Sometimes David would put tin cans up on the dirt pile and shoot at them. There were times when David would put a rifle together and he would go out back and test it. If there were people out there with him he might say: Do you want to try this? He did that with me one time. I fired, and he said: You're wasting bullets. And he took it back.

There were times when David handed out certain things. They got a good deal on a bunch of holsters for sidearms once, and he gave all the guys one. I think I had a holster for less than twenty-four hours before he asked for all of them back. I didn't get a gun to put in it. I don't know what they did with the holsters. Maybe they were taken to a gun show the next week. There were occasions like that when people were given things, but there was no real training, no forced marches, no boot camp. Mount Carmel was not a military camp.

Apparently at some point in 1992 David made a deal with Henry McMahon, a local licensed gun dealer. Henry convinced David that gun legislation was going to ban assault rifles. The way the law was written, if you already had the weapons when the deadline came, you could still sell them, but you could not import or manufacture any beyond that point. He told David that this would be a good investment. He could buy them and wait for the date,[29] and after that the price might quadruple. David decided to go ahead with buying them as an investment. When they arrived they were all disassembled from what I understand. I wasn't in on anything to do with the guns. Out of the approximately 130 people at Mount Carmel, I doubt if there were more than three or four who had been in the machine shop.

The weapons were bought with the idea that they would bring in money. That was consistent with other things that David did to make money or to find work for different ones in the group. He floated a bakery in Hawaii. We had a restaurant near the Baylor campus. Not all of these things lasted a long time, but they were different ventures that were opened and worked for a while. We had a crew that installed and maintained sprinkler systems in a California school district. There was a group called the Yard Birds that did yard work. Even when I ran the roofing crew, it was David who got it started. He started a lot of things, and once they got going he would bow out and start other projects.

David's room upstairs at the back of the chapel was off limits unless we were invited. I went up there a couple of times to give him a back adjustment. The men were not supposed to go up and wander around the second floor because the women lived up there. At first, the guns that had been purchased were stored upstairs next to David's room.[30]

One of the neighbors reported hearing automatic gunfire to the sheriff's department. David explained that he had gotten a device called a hellfire switch, which was attached to the gun and simulated the sound of an automatic weapon. He said he was trying it out. David was told at the sheriff's department that those things were legal. I do not recall hearing it firing.

In late 1992 Mark Spoon lived in the one-family house across the road and worked for the Double EE Ranch. We had a good rapport with him and his family. They would sometimes come over to Mount Carmel for David's Bible studies or to watch movies. Their kids played with our kids on the go-carts.

He came over one night and said: I've got a project I have to do; I was wondering if some of the guys could help. He said that the owner of the Double EE Ranch wanted him to do a lot of repair and remodeling work on the house next to his, which was vacant. [See figures 1 and 2 in appendix.] David said sure. A whole bunch of our guys went over there. We thought it was going to be a one-day job. After they worked for a day they realized that this was going to be a big project. So David said: You can't all go. There are projects here that we are working on. I think David limited it to four guys and finally cut it down to two.

In the process of helping they asked Mr. Spoon: What's all this renovation for? Is Mr. Perry[31] going to rent out this house? Spoon said: No, he says he is not going to rent it. I don't know why he wants this work done. Maybe when we get it done he will move my family into the empty house and then renovate mine. One night Spoon came over and said: Mr. Perry says there is a woman who works as a maid at the ranch, and she and her fourteen-year-old son will be moving in.

David had rototilled a section all the way around the inside of the Mount Carmel fence line to make a track. The women would walk and the guys would jog on it. Jaime Castillo went out and jogged one night. When he came back into the building I happened to be in the foyer. He said: There's something strange going on. I asked: What are you talking about? He said: Mr. Spoon said that a lady and her son were going to move into the house, but there are a bunch of guys over there. As I was coming around the front fence, I saw men, maybe in their thirties or forties, unloading things and taking them into the house. They have no furniture, they have no suitcases. But they have long boxes that look like rifle cases.

David said to Neil Vaega: Take a six-pack of beer and welcome them to the neighborhood. Tell them we are the neighbors across the road. After a while Neil came back and said: Something weird is going on. When asked: What is it? He said: I went over there and there were no lights on. It was all pitch black inside, but there were cars in the carport. I knocked on the door. Eventually the door opened just a crack and a man said: What do you want? I said: We're your neighbors. I just want to welcome you to the neighborhood. Neil told me: I thought something was wrong. He said the guy growled back something like: You can't come in. I've got my girlfriend here! Neil said to him: I brought a six-pack and some chips. The man said, maybe some other time, and kind of slammed the door. Then he opened the door back up, reached out, grabbed the six-pack, and shut the door again. Neil went over to Mr. Spoon's house and asked: What's going on with your next-door neighbor? Spoon didn't seem to know and was a bit concerned because the neighbor was acting strange.

After Neil came back and told us, David said: I think we are being watched. He never once, to my knowledge, said they were ATF or FBI. The only concern he seemed to project was that maybe they were with the INS[32] because we had so many people from different countries. He said: When you go for walks don't just go off on your own because you may be picked up. We do not know who they are or what they are doing.

Two of the men came over with the excuse of wanting to buy our horse walker. You hook a horse to it, and it has a motor and it goes around in circles. We had a horse walker in the field across from the chapel, which had been there since the Rodens' time. That was their excuse to get on our property and see what we were up to. While one of them was talking to David, the other one was running around looking in the pit where we were building the storm shelter. He was gawking, and it looked suspicious.

Somehow we learned that they were claiming they were students at Texas State Technical College (TSTC) [for location, see figure 1 in appendix]. Perhaps they told David, or perhaps Mr. Spoon told that to David. Wayne Martin got the numbers from the license plates on their cars. He called the school and asked: Do you have any students with these license plate numbers? They said no.[33]

We knew that something was going on. A couple of the men came over, and David took them through the building. One of them said that he went to a flea market or a gun show and he bought a rifle. David said: I'd like to see it. David said that the man pulled out this gun and gave it to him. David looked at it, stripped it all the way down, and put it back together again. He said the guy's eyes popped out of his head. David looked at him and said: You didn't buy this at a flea market. This is a sniper rifle. You do not just find these in flea markets and gun shows. He said the men were kind of dumbfounded that he was familiar with the rifle.[34]

That was the way David was. Whenever David put his mind to do something, he would learn everything about it. If he got into carpentry, he tried to learn everything there was about construction. If he got into fixing cars, he would fix cars, talk cars, and all the rest of it. It was the same with music. Once he started to buy weapons, he really familiarized himself with them.

Paul Fatta came back from Austin one time with an Italian gun in a glass case. He was pleased with himself. He thought this gun was one of a kind and that David would like it for his personal collection. David looked at it and said: It is Italian, but it is a piece of junk. I know you tried, Paul, but you didn't pull that good a deal. It is not an antique, it is not a collector's item, and it is not working. Occasionally David went to the gun shows. As with a lot of things that David started, he would let other people carry them out. He didn't want to travel halfway down to the bottom of Texas and spend two or three days at a gun show if he felt he needed to give Bible studies or do something else important.

I don't remember if it was the same or another day, but these men from across the street came over to Mount Carmel with their rifles. David took the men out back and they were all shooting together for a while.[35] After a while one of the men, who called himself Robert Gonzalez, but who was really Robert Rodriguez, said that he was interested in learning what David was teaching in his Bible studies. Robert started coming over and having Bible studies with David. We had the impression that Robert understood what David was talking about and that it was making sense to him.

On Saturday, February 27, the day before the ATF raid, Robert spent most of the day with us in Bible studies. As it was drawing to a close in the evening, Robert said he was going out of town for several days. He said: Man, I sure hate missing these studies. I wish I could attend them all. David said: You are welcome to attend them all if you want to. In fact, you could move in with us. That way you would be here at any given time during the day or night. Robert said: When I come back I might take you up on that.

On that Saturday, the *Waco Tribune-Herald* published the first story in the "Sinful Messiah" series by Mark England and Darlene McCormick.[36] The stories were supposed to be published in the *Tribune-Herald* over seven days. On that Sabbath we discussed some of the things said about David and us in the article. We thought, uh-oh, this is pretty trashy.[37] We wondered if people from town would come out and try to make trouble.

EXPERIENCES DURING THE RAID BY THE BUREAU OF ALCOHOL, TOBACCO, AND FIREARMS ON FEBRUARY 28, 1993, AND IMMEDIATELY AFTERWARD

Even though he had said he was going out of town, Robert used the second article in the "Sinful Messiah" series as an excuse to come back to Mount Carmel early the next morning, Sunday, February 28. The ATF wanted him to get a last look before they launched the raid. He brought a copy of the Sunday newspaper with him.

In the meantime—I don't now whether this was before or after Robert arrived with a copy of the *Tribune-Herald*—Don Bunds and David Jones left Mount Carmel to go get copies of the newspaper. On Double EE Ranch Road, Don Bunds turned left, going toward Farm Road 2491, and David Jones turned right, going toward Old Mexia Road [see figure 1 in appendix].

David Jones is the mailman you hear about in the accounts of what happened on that day. He had a mail route and he had a car with the lights on the top, or it might just have had a sign marked "US Mail." He went down the road and saw a vehicle stopped. David Jones asked: Do you need some help? The man said he was looking for Mount Carmel. David Jones said: You are not too far away. What do you need? The man wore a shirt with KWTX-TV on it. He was a cameraman for the television station. He said that we have a tip that something big is going on down there. There is going to be a raid.[38] David Jones drove to his trailer at Beaver Lake [see figure 1] and phoned his father, Perry Jones, at Mount Carmel.

Perry did not want to interrupt David, because he and Robert were sitting in the foyer talking. It was a common understanding that if David was giving a Bible study you did not go in and interrupt. Eventually Perry was agitated enough to interrupt. He went over and told David there was long-distance call from England. He made it important so David would say, just a minute, I'll be back. When David walked toward the phone room, Perry said, actually my son says that something is going to happen because the press are out here.

Robert Rodriguez has testified later that David Koresh came back and said something about the ATF and the National Guard: They got me once, and they will not get me again.[39] This makes no sense because neither the ATF nor any of the other federal agencies had ever arrested David.[40]

David later said that Robert got real anxious. He said: I better go. I'm supposed to go eat breakfast and I have to go somewhere. As he went out the door, David said good luck to you, or something to that effect. He did not try to take him hostage or anything. He just let him go. People who were there said that Robert went out the door, jumped in his truck, and was honking his horn all the way up the driveway.[41]

Robert drove across the road, and from what we learned later, he went running into the house yelling: Where's Chuck? They said: He is at the staging area.[42] I do not know if Robert tried to call. He was not in the house long. The next thing, he came out, jumped in his car, and went speeding down the road. Apparently he drove all the way to the staging area to try to get them to call off the raid.

In the meantime, unbeknownst to us, behind the Mount Carmel property, there were about seventeen ATF agents who were hiding there in a big barn. Three National Guard helicopters had gone out and were circling between Mount Carmel and Farm Road 2491 [see figure 1 in appendix], waiting for the agents in the cattle trailers to arrive. It was about 9:45 a.m. when the trucks pulling the cattle trailers drove in the front driveway.

When Robert left Mount Carmel I was in my room at the front of the building on the first floor. My room's window was the third one from the north end [#10 in figure 3 in appendix]. There was a tree growing outside my window. I heard a lot of people in the cafeteria, which was across the hall. I could hear voices that sounded kind of agitated. I thought: What's going on? So I walked down the hall a little bit and around the corner into the cafeteria. There were maybe a dozen people there. They are all saying: We just got word that something is going on. Maybe it will be a raid. About that time David walked through the serving area entrance into the cafeteria. He said: We just got a report that some law enforcement agency is coming out. I want you all to go back to your rooms and stay calm. I'll go down to the front door and talk to them.

I went back to my room. I could hear David's steps going down the hall toward the front door. Two or three men, including Perry Jones, went down to the door with him. Then all of a sudden I heard David say: Hey, wait a minute! There are women and children in here! Then all hell broke loose—just a barrage of shots from outside coming in.[43] It sounded like a bloodbath. I thought: Oh my God.

I went running down the hall. By the time I got just past the open doorway going into the serving area, I saw Perry Jones crawling on his hands and knees screaming that he had been shot. I stopped and asked Perry: Are you okay? Are you going to be all right? He said: I'm shot! He was screaming at the top of his voice. I said: Calm down, Perry. Stay right there. Don't move. I'll be right back. I asked: Is anybody else shot? He said: They shot David. I told Perry to wait. I went running.

I expected to see bodies all over the floor. When I went down there the foyer was empty. Not a soul was in there. People were standing in the hallway at the far end of the building near Wayne Martin's office [#17 in figure 3]. They did not want to be in any of the front rooms because there were bullets coming into the rooms on that corner of the building. They screamed at me: Get down! Get down! They are shooting through the walls!

I was kind of saying to myself: Yeah, I can see that. I was not crouching and crawling, I was just going down the hall upright. When I got to the foyer it was empty; I thought: That's weird. I thought Perry said David was shot.

I went back to Perry and said: I thought you said David was shot. Perry said he was, but he went upstairs—up the front stairs. I said: C'mon, we need to get you to a bed. By this time Livingston Malcolm came from the men's dorm area. I said: Livingston, give me a hand with Perry. We need to get him to a bed. He said: Let's put him in his room. Perry's room was close to where we were. I said: There's no point putting him in there, he's already shot. If the bullets are coming in all the front walls and windows, he's just likely to get shot again. We needed to get him to a room on the backside of the hall, further into the building.

I picked Perry up on his left side and Livingston got him by his other arm. When Livingston started to lift him Perry let out a shriek of pain. Later someone told me that Perry's arm was broken, or that a bullet had gone into his arm. I don't know if they knew what they were talking about. Perry kind of stumbled and we half dragged him, half walked him into Kevin Whitecliff's room, which was across the hall from my room, away from the front where all the shooting was taking place.

We laid Perry down on Kevin Whitecliff's bed. There were three guys in the hall asking: What's going on? What's going on? I said: Somebody is shooting. Perry is hurt. We put him in the bed. I said: You guys try to quiet Perry down. If he needs water, do what you can to comfort him. I'll be back.

Perry said his wound was in the stomach. There was blood everywhere, on his shirt and everything. I kick myself to this day: Why didn't I take his shirt off and look at it? But there were three other guys with him, so I figured they would take care of him.

About the time I came out of the room someone said: Winston is dead. Or Winston is shot, something like that. I asked: Where is he? They said: He is in his room [#9 in figure 3 in appendix].

As I walked toward Winston Blake's room I heard water running. I thought: What's that? We did not have running water in the building other than into the cafeteria. I thought: What is all that water running? I turned into the room and there was Winston lying on the floor, right up against his bed. The windows were all shot out. On a downward angle, the carpet was wringing wet and there was blood everywhere. I knelt down and tried to find a pulse on his neck, but I could not find one. I figured he was dead. I came back out.

I went back to see Perry at some point, and he was begging for something for the pain. No one had much of anything. Perry was still holding his stomach with his hand and screaming like crazy. He was screaming for something for the pain so I thought: Where can I get him something? I remembered that a sample pack containing two aspirin or two Tylenol had come in the mail. I went and got them and said: Perry, this is all that I can find right now, but here take these. I went out again.

I think that as I was passing the doorway to the cafeteria I could see people looking out the back door toward the swimming pool. I cannot remember now whether I went over there or whether I was just passing by. As I looked through the doorway I saw a helicopter kind of banking and turning. Later the ATF agents said the three National Guard helicopters did not get any closer than a football field to the building. This helicopter was right over the swimming pool.

I went on down the hall. By the time I got to the far end, Wayne Martin was in the middle of making a 911 call from his office. He spent a lot of time talking with sheriff's deputy, Lieutenant Larry Lynch. Sometimes Lynch would want some information or a decision and Wayne would say: I need to ask David. I do not have the authority to agree to this. He needed someone to run upstairs to ask David. Greg Summers and I alternated running upstairs to convey these messages to David.[44]

I think I might have been the first one to go upstairs as a result of the 911 call. The first time I went up the front stairs, when I got to the women's level on the second floor I could not even get down the hallway. The women had all the kids out in the hall and they were lying on top of them trying to protect them. I had to run back down the front stairs, go along the men's hallway, and up the stairs in the cafeteria. [See figure 3 in appendix.] A little bit up the main hallway on the second floor, there was another hall that went back into the central tower [#19 in figure 4 in appendix]. David was lying on the floor of that hallway. A bullet had gone through his left side and another bullet had gone through his wrist.

David had been shot in the wrist at the front door. I have heard several different versions of how he got shot in the side. I don't know which one of them is correct. I don't know how he got from the point where he was supposed to have been shot in the side all the way to where he was lying on the floor where I saw him.

One story says that after the shooting started, David ran up the front stairs and crossed the catwalk across the top of the ceiling of the chapel [#22 in figure 4], which came out into the two rooms [#21a and #21b in figure 4] on the second floor you see ATF agents entering in the video footage. These two rooms used to be David's rooms. The ATF agents who used ladders to go up to the second floor were breaking into rooms that were basically empty. David had already moved into a room somewhere on the second floor and he had moved the weapons to the concrete vault next to the kitchen on the first floor. This story goes that when David got to his old room he saw an agent lying on the floor wounded. He bent over and was trying to comfort him. He was saying we will get you some help. The story goes that the agent rolled over and shot him at point blank range. I did not hear this version of how David was shot until after I got out of jail after being acquitted in the criminal trial in 1994. It is supposed to have come from David's attorney, Dick DeGuerin. I have never checked with his lawyer to see if that is accurate.

When I saw David he was in a bad way. He thought his hip was broken and he thought he was dying. The idea of David being shot way at the back of the building in his old room and crawling all the way to the little hallway in the center of the building does not make much sense.

All during the siege and waiting for trial in jail, I thought that David got shot as he went past a window on the second floor at the top of the front stairs [see figure 4 in appendix]. If you look at close-up photographs of the building on the day of the raid, there was a flag hanging in the window at the top of the stairs. It was a Branch Davidian flag. It wasn't a kosher Branch Davidian flag. Ben Roden had wanted a flag with what he called the ensign—the rod and the branch—a family tree–type of emblem. Some Branch Davidians up north, perhaps in Massachusetts or New York, went to a lot of trouble to make that flag. They came to Mount Carmel and presented it to Ben. It had a beautiful satiny gold background. I think it had fringe all around it. Even though he thanked them for it, he said the colors were wrong and he never flew it. David had found this flag and on the day of the ATF raid it was hanging in the window. How long it had been there I don't remember. I had the impression that David got hit by gunfire as he went past that window as he ran up the stairs.

All I know is that I saw the wound in his side. It went from front to back.[45] While David was lying on the floor he thought he was done for. Some of the women were gathered around him and they were getting pillows. At some point David made a phone call. I do not know whether it was while shooting was still going on or right after it stopped. He called his mother and left a message on her answering machine saying that he thought he was dying.[46]

There was one point where I went to see how Perry was doing. He was still screaming. I tried to calm him down. He said: I can't stand the pain. Ask David if I can be put out of my misery. Please, please, I can't stand it. I said: Okay, hang in there. I will go. I went up to see David again. I said: Perry is in a bad way. He's screaming and it's kind of unnerving for everyone who can hear him, it's so shrill. He is so delirious that he wants something to be done to put him out of his misery. David said: You tell him to hang in there. We are going to get help. Just tell him to grit his teeth and we are working on it. I went down and told Perry what David had said. Maybe that is when I got him the Tylenol, I do not remember. I said: David said hang in there, just wait. Not long afterwards someone told me that Perry was dead.

The government said that somebody shot Perry. Either that or somebody gave him a gun and he shot himself. The Tarrant County, Texas, medical examiner's autopsy report said that other than this head wound or mouth wound, Perry had no wounds whatsoever.[47] That does not make any sense. There was blood all over the place. Perry was screaming he had been shot, and you are telling me that he did not have any other wounds whatsoever, that this was just an assassination? Why would a guy be screaming if he had not been hit?[48]

The only place where I saw any of our people shooting, and I think I only saw two people, was in the area of the kitchen as I was passing by. I did not see anyone shooting from the chapel, the front of the building, or upstairs.

When I was down at Wayne Martin's office and we were involved in the 911 call, Wayne told me that at one point he heard noise outside his window. He said that when he raised the window and looked out, there was an agent immediately outside looking back at him. He said he just closed the window and moved out of his office in case the agent should start shooting at him. Wayne and two or three other guys were standing in the hallway by the time I got there. There were bullets coming into the sewing room on the front southwest corner [#18 in figure 3 in appendix]. Most of the gunfire was directed at the second floor, which was where the women and children were.

Wayne called 911 as soon as the shooting started. McLennan County Deputy Sheriff Larry Lynch[49] was put on the line. We did not know who Larry Lynch was at the time. I could hear his voice on the speakerphone. During a lot of that call Wayne was agitated. He was yelling across the room to his desk trying to respond to Lynch.[50]

It took quite a long time for Larry Lynch to get ahold of the ATF commanders. Then we started to negotiate to get a cease-fire. They were telling us they could not reach most of their people. After the initial major barrage of gunfire, the shots started to get more sporadic. It took quite a while, I think maybe it was a couple of hours into the shooting, when we thought we had a cease-fire. We were yelling out the windows at the agents: Cease fire! We've got a cease-fire! We're trying to get a cease-fire! We were running all around the building saying, "Cease fire! Cease fire!" We had to get the word out to our people and their people.

The ATF agents did not trust us. They figured the cease-fire was just a ruse to trick them into standing up so we could kill them all. At one point we thought we had the cease-fire in place. All of a sudden a shot rang out from inside. Wayne said: Go find out who is shooting.

I ran up the front stairs yelling: Cease fire! Cease fire! Cease fire! I got to the top of the stairs on the second floor, and two teenage girls were standing in the hall. I said: Cease fire! They said: We are not shooting. I said: Somebody inside fired a shot. They said: It's Scott. I said: Tell him to quit it.

We have a cease-fire. They said something like: We have tried, but he can't hear us. I asked: Where is he?

There was a cutout doorway in the wall of the second floor hallway. You could go through it to walk across the boards making the catwalk across the top of the chapel ceiling [#22 in figure 4]. You could go across this walkway and come to a doorway in the wall on the other side, which went into what had been David's rooms [#21a and #21b in figure 4].

I looked down that walkway to the other end and saw Scott Sonobe sitting on the floor with his back against the wall of David's old bedroom [#21a in figure 4 in appendix]. I yelled at him, but he could not hear me. It seemed like he was deaf. I crossed over to reach him, not knowing if he was going to shoot me, what state of panic he was in. On my way I yelled: Scott! Do not shoot! I got over there and saw that he had been shot. He was propped up against the wall, almost passing out.

I had to get right in Scott's face. I said: Do not shoot. There is a cease-fire. I asked him: What are you shooting at? He said: They came in the window and I ran out the door. I didn't think they saw me, but they shot me.[51]

Later we found out that Jeff Little, who had been downstairs at the back of the chapel, had started to come up the stairs leading from the back of the stage to the second-floor room [#21a in figure 4], just about where Scott was. There was a lightbulb hanging at the foot of the stairs. When Jeff passed that light he threw his shadow upstairs, and when Scott saw the shadow he started shooting. Jeff said: Yeah, I started to go up there and shots started coming down toward me. I just went back downstairs and rolled under the stage.

I asked: Scott, do you think you are going to make it? He said he thought so. I think he was shot in the leg or the thigh.[52] He felt a bit cold, so I got him a blanket. I said: Now don't be shooting. It is all agreed on. There is no more shooting and they are not coming in to get you. Just lie there and we will try to get you some help later. I went back to Wayne and told him about Scott and that the shooting was a mistake. Wayne told Larry Lynch.

By the time we actually got to the point where both sides agreed there was a cease-fire, it was negotiated that the ATF agents could retrieve their men who were down and hurt in different locations.[53] When the ATF agents finally left, we could see them carrying people. I think one guy you see in the footage is one of the agents who died. Another one was hobbling and being assisted to get off the property. The KWTX-TV guys followed them off the property; some bodies and some wounded were put in their van.[54]

All through the shoot-out, even though it was obvious we were under attack, I did not see who those people were. I did not see them drive up. I did not see them jump out of the cattle trailers. As I was running back and forth checking on people and trying to help Wayne with the cease-fire arrangement, I was moving around the building a certain amount. I remember asking people: Who is out there? Where are they? I tried to look out a front window without exposing myself, but I could not see anyone. They were crouched down behind the vehicles behind the fence. I think I saw boots sticking out from behind a car.

When we got the cease-fire in effect I looked out. I think I was in the foyer. All the agents started rising up from behind the vehicles. Some of them were right up next to the building. They moved away and climbed over the fence. To me it was a big crowd. I thought to myself: Oh my God. Where are all these people coming from?[55]

I was shocked at the number of people I saw moving out. They had their hands in the air and they were moving out as we watched them. They were going across the open field in front of the building, heading toward the front gate. I was shocked at the mass of manpower. All of a sudden another big crowd of them came from the back of the building.[56]

It was very impressive to see them all moving across the field together. Even with all the shooting I had not seen any of these people, and I did not realize how many of them there were. It kind of blew my mind. I think the general consensus that seemed to permeate the people in the foyer area was: Whew! They left, but we don't know what is going to happen now.

Like the government itself said later, the ATF agents were supposed to be serving a warrant to search the building and a warrant to take David into custody. The warrants should not have been, technically, even signed. The warrants should not have been served in a "no-knock" "dynamic entry." There are a lot of things you can argue about the rights and the wrongs of the warrants. To serve warrants was allegedly the reason for the ATF agents to come out to Mount Carmel.[57]

The minute a law enforcement agent gets shot at or hit, from their perspective all of a sudden it is a different ball game. It is no longer just a regular "serving a warrant" situation. We knew that. I have known that for years. The minute someone defends himself against an officer or runs from an officer, especially if an officer goes down, whether it is just a punch in the nose or a shot, then it is almost a free-for-all. So our feeling after the ATF agents left the immediate proximity of the building was that we were in for it; they were going to come back in force, probably that night. That was the general feeling: They will be back tonight. So the word was passed around by mouth that we needed to be vigilant. We did not want to be taken by surprise. We needed to be on watch. We did not want them sneaking up on us in the dark.[58]

From the start, beginning with the 911 call and ongoing throughout the siege, negotiations were taking place. There were negotiations that if agents would read a short statement from David on the radio,[59] some small children would be released. Children began going out in twos from that point on.

The first children who went out were Scott and Cita Sonobe's two little girls. If I remember correctly, Cita walked them down the driveway and up to the front gate, where they were handed over to someone in a car. I think that was the only time children were walked out. From then on they said they didn't want to expose social workers, or whoever was meeting the children, to gunfire. There was no gunfire going on. Ever since the cease-fire there was no threat to their safety at all, but they were acting as if that was the case. From then on, each set of children negotiated out was put in one of our vehicles, which turned out to be Misty Ferguson's car, and Cita drove them up to the gate, turned left on Double EE Ranch Road, drove the short distance to the intersection with Farm Road 2491 at the water towers [see figure 1 in appendix], and then handed them over.

That went on for a period of time. Angelica Sonobe and Crystal Sonobe, and Renae Fagan and Neharah Fagan, went out on February 28 between 9:00 and 10:00 p.m. The next day, March 1, Jaunessa Wendel, Landon Wendel, Patron Wendel, Tamara Wendel, Scott Mabb, Christyn Mabb, Jacob Mabb, and Bryan Schroeder went out at various times. That evening Jamie Martin and Joshua Sylvia went out at 11:05 p.m. On March 3, 4, and 5, the final three children were sent out: Mark Jones, Kevin Jones, and Heather Jones.[60]

BRANCH DAVIDIAN DEATHS AT
MOUNT CARMEL ON FEBRUARY 28, 1993

Perry Jones died on the day of the ATF raid. Peter Gent was shot up on top of the water tower [#1 in figure 3 in appendix] by our swimming pool.

Peter Hipsman was shot out over the top of the gymnasium at the back of our building, on the overhead walkway that ran over the gym, that the agents called the dog run [#20 in figure 4 in appendix]. If you went in a continuous line on the catwalk [#22 in figure 4] that went over the chapel, past David's two rooms [#21a and #21b in figure 4], you got onto another ceiling walkway that went over the gymnasium. I don't know why the agents called it a dog run. There were no dogs in it. It was a little hallway that ran across the top of the gym. It had a window at the end through which one could look out behind the building beyond the swimming pool.

It was my understanding that Peter Hipsman got shot in the area of the dog run. All through the siege I didn't know where he was when he got shot. All I knew was that he was upstairs somewhere. Apparently, on the day of the raid, some of the ATF agents got into the gymnasium and could hear people. They couldn't see anything. They just sprayed bullets all along there when they heard footsteps. Peter was shot up pretty bad in the stomach from what I understand.

Winston Blake was killed in his room [#9 in figure 3 in appendix] when they strafed the water tanks outside at the back. The bullets went through into his room and killed him.

Jaydean Wendel was shot on the second floor in a room on the front.

So at Mount Carmel we had Perry Jones, Winston Blake, Peter Hipsman, Peter Gent, and Jaydean Wendel dead. Mike Schroeder was killed by ATF agents later in the day as he was walking back to Mount Carmel.

Death of Mike Schroeder

We heard about Mike Schroeder's death in the news either that evening or the next day. The first news reports said that three men tried to escape Mount Carmel and one was killed, which of course was wrong. The details of what happened did not come out for a lot of us until the criminal trial in 1994.

Bob Kendrick was staying at the car shop [see figure 1 in appendix] overnight, and Mike Schroeder was there. They were the main ones working on the cars. Sometimes others would go and help them, but on the day of the ATF raid, those two had been there all night. Norman Allison had also been there for a night or two.

When the raid went down, I don't know if they heard it on the news, but some exchange took place. A phone call was made by them or us in which they were told what had happened. From what I understand, Mike was anxious to get out to Mount Carmel. His wife, Kathy, and his son and her other children were there.

They tried to come up Farm Road 2491, but they ran into the roadblocks, so they doubled back, and from what I understand, all three of them ended up on the other side of Mount Carmel near Highway 84 and Old Mexia Road [see figure 1]. They went over to the trailer park where some of the ladies, including my mother, were living in David Jones's trailer. They stopped there and tried to figure out how to get to Mount Carmel. There were police everywhere. They decided to walk through the fields [see figure 1]. Unbeknownst to them, there were seventeen ATF agents in a barn on the Double EE Ranch property at the back of ours. They had been there watching since 7:30 in the morning.

Mike Schroeder, Bob Kendrick, and Norman Allison started to approach Mount Carmel by walking along a creek, which eventually flows under a dirt road. They worked their way across the field, came to the creek, and started to walk along the creek bed, which brought them to some positions slightly below the Double EE Ranch barn, according to the agents who testified in our trial—observers or snipers or whatever they were.[61] At least two of them, I'd say, were snipers, because they were dressed in camouflage with grass and leaves stuck all over them. The rest might have been in their regular uniforms.

These officers had received a radio contact to abandon the position and go back to the staging area. So they left the barn and were going across the field to get to the road when someone yelled out: There's a man down in the creek! From what I understand, they all hit face down in the grass. Someone up front started shooting, so they all began shooting. Mike Schroeder was the guy they saw. Mike, being young and more eager to get back to Mount Carmel, was way out in front of the other two. All three were in the creek bed, but they were not together. Norman Allison was quite a way behind, and Bob Kendrick, who was old and had a heart condition, was somewhere back in the rear.

The ATF agents claimed that Mike Schroeder shot at them. No one testified that he had a particular weapon on him, although they claimed he shot at them. I did hear someone allege that he had a flare pistol. It doesn't make a whole lot of sense that if you spot a bunch of agents firing at you, you shoot back with a flare pistol. There's a hole in that story. For a long time we heard that Mike Schroeder's body had five or six shots in the back—two of them in the back of the head.[62] It hardly seems like a shooting situation with him facing them.

After Mike Schroeder was shot, the ATF agents heard a noise in the creek bed, so they were screaming: Come out with your hands up! Out stepped Norman Allison. He approached them across an open field. They told him to get down on his hands and knees, face down, and submit, which he did. They arrested him and took him away.

Bob Kendrick, way in the back, figured things were not going well, so he walked through the brush and went back to the trailer where the older ladies were. Later he heard statements that law enforcement agents were looking for him, so he gave himself up.

As more news began to come out about Mike Schroeder, there were allegations about his body. During the trial it was reported that some of the evidence regarding Mike was lost. They couldn't find the stocking cap he was wearing when he was shot.[63] There were weird allegations that his body was hung on a fence. We know that it was several days before they went and picked up his body, and the excuse was they couldn't retrieve him because someone in our building might shoot at them.[64] From the top of our building you could barely see the roof of the barn where these agents had been holed up all day, let alone the creek, which is further down the hill. That story doesn't hold any water with me.

THE FIFTY-ONE-DAY SIEGE

People stood watch that first night and during the following days and nights in the siege. At least one person in an area of the building would stay awake, not necessarily looking out the window, while other people in the area tried to nap, which was hard to do with the racket made by the tanks and the loudspeakers. At least one person would be awake at all times in any given area.

I stayed in the chapel. Probably at any given time there were three or four people in the chapel. People remained scattered throughout the building for the rest of the fifty-one days. That does not mean they did not leave to go eat or to go back to their rooms. But they maintained these areas so that a warning could go out if agents came crashing through a wall or a window.

After the first day, Marjorie Thomas and Shari, my daughter, came down to the chapel and stayed with me. Kevin Whitecliff was in the chapel for most of the time until he went out during the negotiations. I think one of the main reasons he was in there was because he could not spend time in his room. We had put Perry Jones in his bed, and I don't think he liked the idea that the bed had been soaked in blood and somebody had died there. Kevin had a problem with varicose veins and couldn't stand up for too long. He was sitting in a La-Z-Boy-type armchair most of the time he was in the chapel. Shari and Marjorie stayed in the chapel probably up until April 17, when word came down from David that he did not want women staying overnight on the first floor.

Wayne Martin, Floyd Houtman, and maybe one or two others stayed near Wayne's office. Pablo Cohen and Lisa Farris were in the foyer. I'm sure there were women staying in the cafeteria. Livingston Malcolm and Raymond Friesen were in Steve Schneider's room.

Many of the children were negotiated out early in the siege. It started that first night. David's immediate children were upstairs with their mothers, and Melissa Morrison was there with her mother, Rosemary. Ofelia Santoyo's five grandchildren were also upstairs with their mother, Juliette Santoyo. Those were the children under age ten who stayed there. There were also teenagers who were with family members.

FBI agents took over from the ATF on March 1. If you walked around the perimeter of the building and looked in different directions, you could count agents all over the place. There were seventeen on one ridge in the back beyond the swimming pool. If you looked through binoculars, you could see three different sniper positions near the dairy barn on Mount Carmel property. [See figure 2 in appendix.] We knew we were surrounded.

FBI negotiators, whom I consider to be professional liars, have the job to be Mr. Nice Guy to talk you out of any situation. If you are a bank robber and you have taken hostages, the negotiator will promise pizza, a getaway plane, stacks of money, whatever it takes to defuse the situation. If a guy is standing on a ledge getting ready to jump off, the negotiator is going to try to talk him down. That is what they were doing with us: You can do this, David, if you come out now.

But the FBI agents who were actually handling the situation on the ground probably had an attitude: We need to beat the heck out of them; we need to get even for our brothers who got hurt, or for the trouble you have caused us. That came across in their actions.[65]

We were dealing with a couple of different mentalities. The negotiators said to us in effect: While we have no control or jurisdiction over these other agents, we have good intent. But they knew that whatever they were saying to us would probably not be fulfilled.[66]

The FBI negotiators tried to get as many of our people as possible on the phone. By that time I had a slight attitude—not a real bad one—but when anyone asked me if I wanted to talk to a negotiator, I said I was not interested. I had a feeling that I was performing services that were necessary. I was burying the waste and garbage. So somewhere in the back of my mind, without it being an order or discussing it with anyone, I had this thought that I would probably be one of the last ones out. It was not that I was a hardhead or a diehard. I just thought: They are negotiating the little kids out, then negotiating the old ladies out; when they have gone through all of the people who need to come out—there were people still in there who were older than me and there were still children—I thought I would be one of the last ones out. So initially I was not keen on talking with negotiators. I could see their doubletalk and broken promises, and I wasn't interested.

Relatives from outside were allowed to send in audiotapes. I think David Thibodeau got a tape from his mother. I'm not sure whether Sherri Jewell or someone else got a tape. I think they sent in tapes for two or three people. After those tapes came in, someone came and said to me: The FBI would like to talk to you. I said I was not interested. They said: They've got a message from your daughter. That kind of caught my attention. My daughter Karen had been out in California. So I asked: Really? Why don't they just send the tape in like they've sent all the others? The person said: It's not a tape.

I got on the phone. I am sure there is a recording of it somewhere, and I might not have it straight. This is just memory I'm going by, and the impressions that were made on me at the time. I got on the phone and the guy was asking me: Are you okay? Are you wounded? He was going on and on and on. I said: Yeah, everything's okay. I think he asked me: When are you going to come out? I said: Why do I need to come out? This is where I live. I'm home. Eventually we're all going to come out.

I can't quote him word for word, but the impression that I picked up from what he was saying was, we've got to search the building, and if you come on out and we do our job, the sooner you can all get back home. He was going through all this and I was listening, really not too impressed. Finally I said: You know, the only reason I got on this phone is because I was told you have a message from my daughter. He said: Oh yeah, yeah. I asked: Why didn't you send it in? He said: It's not a tape, I can tell you what it is. I said: Okay. He said: She just wanted to know how you are doing. I thought to myself: You led the person you talked to before me to believe that you had an important message for me, and she just asked if I'm okay? It kind of ticked me off.

The FBI brought the tanks in on March 1. I remember that the whole building began to shake and vibrate and there was a loud rumble in the distance. My first thoughts were: It feels like an earthquake. I had been in three different earthquakes in California. Then I thought: That's weird, because we don't have earthquakes much in Texas.

Some of us looked out from the south side of the chapel. The chapel had windows with opaque stipple glass, which we had probably taken from the bathrooms of some of the little houses at Mount Carmel that we had demolished. You couldn't see through those windows. Anytime you wanted to look out the windows in the chapel, you had to raise them or go outside. Someone raised one of the windows and we looked out.

There was a big convoy of long trailers with tanks on them going down Farm Road 2491 [see figure 1 in appendix]. They were half a mile from Mount Carmel and yet the ground and the building were vibrating and shaking. The news reported that tanks were being brought in. We had a set of *World Book Encyclopedias* in the foyer, and Lisa Farris began to look up tanks. She read out loud the capabilities of some of the tanks. Someone remarked: If they start shooting at us with these things this building is going to look like Swiss cheese.

David was very concerned about the tanks coming onto Mount Carmel property. When the tanks arrived, the negotiators promised that they would not come on the property. They said the tanks were there only to hold the perimeter. In other words, they were saying: We will surround you with tanks, but we are not going to approach you with them; the tanks are not going to come on the property.

The tanks were on the property most of the time, laying barbed wire around us, trucking men back and forth between the front of the property and the back, tearing up things, tipping over our fuel supplies, pushing our building supplies into piles, pushing people's cars up on to a big heap of wood they made. They used the tanks on the property throughout the siege and on the last day, April 19.

One of the things that I was slightly concerned about was that when this was all over and we went to jail, there would be a trial. I was kind of looking toward the future and hoping that was going to work out all right. One of the things in my mind was: I am going to be able to say that I wasn't shooting from my room, because my room does not have any bullet holes in it. My window was one of the few on the front that was intact. I thought: That should give me a pretty good alibi. I was not shooting at them for sure. I figured that this window would be good evidence on my behalf. But toward the end of the siege, they decided they were going to use the tanks to take out the front fence and move all the cars from the front. They had an agenda in mind, so they were getting the ground all around us cleared. They started bulldozing trees, vehicles, fences, and what have you. Lo and behold, they decided to take out the tree that grew outside my window. The tank knocked the tree down. As the tree was falling over, a branch smashed my window. There went my alibi as far as not shooting from my room.[67]

David negotiated that if he made an audiotape conveying his theology and if they played it at prime time, we would all come out. The tape was taken out by Catherine Matteson on March 2, who went out with Margaret Lawson and Daniel and Kimberly Martin, at 8:10 a.m.[68]

When we heard that there was a plan for us to come out, everyone was pretty excited. As scary and dangerous as the situation was, we hoped it could be resolved soon. We went and packed bags and brought them to where we were staying, which for me was the chapel. Kevin Whitecliff had a big old bag.

I was leery about the safety of our coming out as a group. I sat in the chapel and talked to Shari. I told her that I had a really bad feeling about all of us coming out at once. If they opened fire on us, we would be massacred. I said to Shari: I think we will kind of hold back and see what happens to the first ones. We'll wait to see if there is any shooting. If shooting starts, those at the back will have a bit of advantage in getting back inside the building and putting some walls between us.

Despite that trepidation, I was still kind of naïve about what was going to happen to us. I went down to the cafeteria and fixed a brown-paper-bag lunch for both of us. I thought we would go outside and sit on the lawn for a few hours while they searched the building. Looking back on it now, I don't know why I was so stupid; we actually got a lunch to take with us.

That particular negotiated exit fell through. First of all, David said they had not kept their end of the bargain—they hadn't played the tape in prime time. David also said that God had said to wait.[69] We were waiting on God. Some word would come through David as to what God instructed. It became a holding pattern. In the meantime, people were still being negotiated out on a fairly regular basis.

The FBI told the media that David had reneged on the deal.[70] In order to put more pressure on us, they cut off the telephone lines. The only phone line left was direct to the negotiators. They cut off the electricity from time to time and permanently on March 12.[71] They had already shot up our water supply, so we had no water.

We collected rainwater to drink. There was a little alcove right beside the chapel that was kind of out of sight [see figure 3 in appendix], or at least the part right up close to the building was out of sight of the snipers positioned in the dairy at the back of the property. This alcove was also out of sight of the two houses across Double EE Ranch Road. The snipers along the fence lines couldn't see it either, so it was a little protected area. People went out and put buckets around that narrow concrete courtyard to be filled by rainwater running off the roof. That was the only water we had for drinking. It rained quite a bit during the siege, but not every day, so the water was rationed. Most of the time you were lucky if you got eight ounces in a day. We had a little water for drinking, but we didn't have water for washing.

Probably on March 2, when everyone thought we would be going out soon, someone went around writing welcome signs for the FBI with red paint on the inside walls. They were derogatory to the FBI but not nasty. Some of it was painted on the back wall of the chapel. When David heard about it he was furious. He said: This building is our evidence to support what we have been saying about the ATF agents doing most of the shooting. This is not the attitude we want to portray to them. I have said all along that the agents are souls to be saved as much as anyone.[72] Young Wayne Martin, Sheila Martin's oldest son, was given the job of painting over the messages with white paint. Poor kid. He was rolling white paint over red, and the red kept bleeding through. I don't know how many coats he put on until finally the red letters could hardly be seen.

If David had planned that we were going to go out in a blaze of glory, or shoot our way out with a big historical end, he wouldn't have been emphasizing that the building would testify to our innocence after we went to jail. If he had planned we would all be dead or the building would be burned up, he wouldn't have cared what the building looked like.

The word came down that we had to do something with the bodies, and I was asked to go out and dig graves for them. I was surprised that the bodies were not stiff. I had the idea of rigor mortis causing bodies to stiffen up and stay that way, but they don't. They get limber again.

Even though there had been rain, the ground in the storm shelter we had been constructing at the north end of the building [see figure 3 in appendix] was dry. I went out through the buried school bus and the concrete tunnel into the storm shelter. I began to dig in the unfinished part of the storm shelter that had no roof. Someone came out after I had part of a hole dug and said: Don't be doing that out in the open. They could come up and grab you. They said I was too exposed and far away from the rest of the people inside. So I quit that hole and came back into the part of the storm shelter that had a roof, and began to dig another hole in the corner.

It was hard going. I had originally planned to dig four graves. We only had four bodies at that time. Peter Gent's body was still up on the water tower [#1 in figure 3]. I dug one hole all the way down and didn't really have time to make sure it had straight sides. I noticed that the hole was starting to get narrower at the bottom.

People inside were getting concerned that it was taking so long and I was too exposed. So we decided to put all four bodies in the one hole until we could do something about them later. When I was about finished with the hole I said: Go get help to bring the bodies down.

Winston's body was the largest. He was tall and he was also pretty hefty. Jaydean was the smallest, and then Perry. Peter Hipsman was fairly lanky, maybe six feet, but not as heavy as Winston. So I determined to put Jaydean on the bottom and Perry next—the two smallest ones on the bottom because of the narrowing of the hole. Peter Hipsman was the third one, and Winston was put on top. By then I was worn out and I got some help to fill the hole in. We ended up with a mound, and we put a wheelbarrow upside down on top—I forget why now. It turned out that later on this section of the storm shelter filled up with water. We couldn't tell if it was rainwater or if the tanks had somehow damaged a spring or pipeline.

Later it was negotiated that we could get Peter Gent's body down from the water tower and hand it over to the FBI agents. I was told that we could retrieve the body and they would send a tank or something to the front door, and we would hand it out and they would take him away.

Jimmy Riddle, Mark Wendel, and I crawled out on our stomachs over to the foot of the water tower, which was located next to the swimming pool. There was a cinder-block utility building [#2 in figure 3 in appendix] that we had built up against the water tower. A hole had been cut in the side of the water tower. Peter Gent had been working on the inside scraping and removing rust, because we had only just had our well fixed. The tower was being cleaned up inside, and to do the work, scaffolding had been built inside.

Mark Wendel went to the water tower and got in through the square hole that had been cut. He climbed up to the top and tied a rope around Peter Gent's body and lowered him down to the cinder-block building where Jimmy Riddle and I were waiting. We put him in a zip-up sleeping bag preparatory to carrying him back to the building and eventually handing him over to the FBI.

When the body came down on the rope, I thought that Peter had been shot through the head in the vicinity of the eye because his face was just a mass of blood. With so much pressure and stress I didn't take the time to look closely. I assumed he had been shot in the head.[73]

While we were putting him in the sleeping bag, a guy yelled from the back door of the cafeteria: Leave him there! Come back inside quick! Leave him there! We crawled back trying to keep our heads down in case we were targets. We got back inside and were told that the FBI had called it off. Their statement now was that they were not interested in salvaging the dead; they were more interested in negotiating out the living. Just leave him there.[74]

These negotiations were going on hour after hour, sometimes continuously. At some point it was negotiated that they didn't want us to hand

Peter Gent's body over to them, but they granted us permission to bury him. It was agreed that three of our guys could go out front and dig a grave across the driveway. Kevin Whitecliff, Brad Branch, and a young teenage guy from Australia, Oliver Gyarfas, were picked to go out and dig this grave. I remember that they went around asking all the women if they had any plastic flowers to mark the grave. Tanks were being driven up and down and they didn't want the grave to be run over. They collected a bunch of plastic flowers. It didn't seem like they were gone long so it must have been a fairly shallow grave. We had to go back out and get Peter's body and bring him in. They took him out front, put him in the hole, filled it in, and put the flowers all around to indicate the grave was there.[75]

Prior to burying Peter Gent we had permission to move the bodies of five Malamute dogs from a fenced-in area by the front door. They had been killed by ATF agents on February 28. The dogs were inside a hog-wire fence that ran between the front fence and the front door [see figure 3 in appendix]. The agents' excuse for shooting the younger ones, the four pups, who were almost a year old—almost full-grown—was that they were baring their teeth at them and barking. Then they shot the mother, who was chained to the flagpole [#14 in figure 3]. She was no threat to anyone. She was barking at them for killing her kids, and so they shot her, too. They were all inside that fenced area. She had a new litter, which was eleven or twelve pups— just little bitty ones—in a kennel. They were not shot.

The dead dogs were lying where they fell, and the flies were beginning to come and the smell was getting bad. In the negotiation it was agreed that one person could come out, carry the dead dogs across the driveway, and put them on the grass on the other side. It was agreed that Greg Summers and Cliff Sellors would go out. Greg had been the one who fed the dogs. They carried all the dead dogs across the driveway.

It was unknown to me that there was an agreement not to do anything outside except for these two. I had been coming out of the building from the time of the raid onward, going out a chapel window or maybe out the front door, retrieving things that ATF agents had dropped. I picked up flashlights, helmets, and guns. Probably the first things that I took in were the ladders that ATF agents had used to get onto the chapel roof to go into David's old rooms [#21a and #21b in figure 4 in appendix]. I said: If they're coming back tonight they had better bring some new ladders, because we are not going to help them get up on our roof. I crawled out the window and took the ladders into the chapel.

When Greg and Cliff were taking the dead dogs across the driveway, I happened to go out a window and was picking up things outside the chapel, where I saw near the corner of the building that one of the agents had dropped a shield. It had a panel you could see through and a little light on the top. It was big and I guess it was supposed to deflect bullets. I went out and grabbed that. When I returned I was chewed out by Steve Schneider, who said that I had jeopardized Greg and Cliff's lives. While they were outside a negotiator was on the phone screaming that there were *three* guys out there.[76] I didn't even know what was going on around by the front door. From then on I stopped going out to retrieve things. They were getting pretty touchy. The FBI agents were very stringent about what we could or couldn't do.

I never heard negotiations directly. When Steve was on the phone in the foyer talking to negotiators, you could hear his side and he would reiterate what they said, either while it was going on or afterwards.[77] It wasn't like it was on a speakerphone where everyone could hear it. I never got to hear directly any negotiation they did with David, who was upstairs.

We got Peter Gent buried on March 8. It seemed like the tanks ran over his grave and ran over our dogs from then on. I've since been told that if the tanks had run over him in a shallow grave he would have been crushed to smithereens, but his body wasn't.[78] Maybe the tanks straddled it, but it looked like they were running over the grave. I know they ran over the dogs. To me that was done in spite. They didn't need to run over the dogs. There was plenty of open ground and a driveway they could travel on.

On March 12, Kathy Schroeder and Oliver Gyarfas went out. On March 19, Brad Branch and Kevin Whitecliff were negotiated out.[79] By this time we knew that everyone who went out was going to jail. That was very obvious. Adults who went out were usually allowed to call back to Mount Carmel from jail.

David said: I don't want you taking bags of clothes out because you are not going to be able to keep them. The minute Kevin Whitecliff heard that he was the next one going out he gave all his clothes away. That's what some people were doing, saying: You need them more than I do, because I am going where I won't be able to have them. I think I had some of Kevin's clothes on when I finally came out on April 19.

After Kathy Schroeder and Oliver Gyarfas went out on March 12, the FBI cut the electricity off permanently.[80] Once they did that, our frozen food and fresh food had to be eaten in a hurry or be wasted. After that we went into rationing mode. Water was already rationed but the food had not been. We had MREs for the rest of the time.

As more and more people were negotiated out, David contacted Sheriff Harwell. He said: You are having to house so many of my people you shouldn't have the burden to feed them. I have food here that I'm willing to send down to you. When he told him it was MREs, the sheriff said he had a whole basement full of those things and he didn't need them.

While we had electricity everyone had a radio and some had small TVs that we used to get the news. Without electricity, people were listening to their radios using batteries. Not too long into it, David sent word down that since we didn't know how long we would need the batteries, people would be designated to listen to the news, take notes, and come tell the rest of us.

To put more and more pressure on us, the tanks bulldozed all of our building supplies into a big heap across the little driveway that went behind the building. They bulldozed several little outlying buildings we had on the south end onto the heap as well. They began to push people's cars up there, including the car we were using to bring the kids out. We were inside watching this going on and wondering: Why are they heaping everything up? Are they going to set it on fire or what? It looked ominous.

The tanks knocked down all of our fuel tanks on the south side of the building, and we thought: Oh, this is great. They are soaking the whole area in gasoline and diesel, and they have all that wood and the cars piled up. If they set this on fire and the wind blows the wrong way we are gone—the whole building will go.

We had big silver tanks containing gasoline up on pedestals [see figure 2 in appendix]. We also had a whole row—maybe a dozen—of fifty-five-gallon drums of different fuels, either diesel or gasoline, along the driveway as well. It came out in court later on that when the agent who was bulldozing all this stuff knocked over the fuel tanks, one of them ruptured and fell back onto the tank and drenched the men inside. They took off in a panic thinking that if we shot at them, a bullet could spark and they would be torched. They took off to clean themselves up and dry the tank out. We didn't know that. All we knew was that the tank left the scene. From that point on I don't think we noticed any particular work on the heap they had created.[81]

The FBI brought in spotlights and loudspeakers.[82] They put one set of speakers in front of the building across the driveway, and they set up another set of speakers out toward the back of the swimming pool. They played all kinds of noises on the speakers. They also used the speakers for messages they wanted to convey to us. They wanted to undermine our allegiance to David. They figured they would tell us how it really was as opposed to lies from David. They used the speakers to make announcements. There were times they would get on the loudspeaker and say they did not want anybody in the tower; they would consider that a threatening gesture. They did not want anybody looking out the windows at them when they drove by in tanks.[83]

Each adult who went out was arrested, but when they got to jail they could call back and let us know they were okay. Kathy Schroeder was taped when she called back in. I don't know if she was reading from a script, but she made some kind of statement she was okay and I can guarantee they will treat you okay if you come out. They played that over and over to us and said: Whatever David is telling you, this is what your sister is saying. Why don't you listen to her?[84]

The first time they played both sets of speakers, it was so loud you couldn't make out what was being said. They eventually woke up to the fact that one set of speakers was interfering with the other, so they cut the back one off. They didn't take it away, but it was not used for the rest of the siege.

Before the ATF raid, David had recently bought two big, heavy generators. They were pretty much still in the crates. One had been taken into the machine shop, and the other one was still out in the backyard. During the siege some of the guys manipulated the one from the machine shop into the chapel. Some of them who knew what they were doing got the generator out of the crate, and they tinkered with it until they managed to get it running. We thought: We are going to have electricity and get the refrigerator running again, but that was not what happened.

By that time David had managed to get up on his feet and hobble around a little bit.[85] I guess David was getting sick of all the noise they were piping in at us—rabbits being killed, warped-up music, Nancy Sinatra singing "These Boots Are Made for Walking," Tibetan monks chanting, Christmas carols, telephones ringing, reveille—all the noises they were putting on us to cause sleep deprivation.[86] He said: I guess two can play at this game. If we are going to be kept awake by their racket, we'll see what happens when they get it turned on them. They dragged his sound equipment into the foyer. They moved the upright piano to block the view. Then they opened the door. David and the guys with their instruments played back at them, as loud as anybody could stand, directed out the front door at the house across the road.

That was the only time I know of that the generator was used. Whether we ran out of gas to power it, or just what, I'm not sure. It wasn't used to put electric lights on or to turn the refrigerator on again, which would not have helped much because all the food in the refrigerator was pretty much gone. It had been either eaten or thrown away.

There are some interesting anecdotes about what went on during the siege. At one point we formed something like a bucket brigade outside, only it was not for buckets. We climbed out the windows of the chapel and kind of ran the gauntlet over to the outside door going into the gymnasium, hoping they would not shoot us. We formed a line into the gymnasium, where a lot of supplies were stored. There was no inside door to get into the gym from the chapel; you had to go outside and enter the gym from an outside door. We formed this line and we got as much stuff as we could—supplies for the women, first-aid supplies, sleeping bags, Coleman lanterns and fuel, bags of food, dog food, and chicken feed. We passed the things along the line. We salvaged all of this stuff, which eventually, like so many of the decisions that were made, turned into more of a detriment than a help. Bringing in all that fuel turned out to work against us.

I think David Jones was feeding the dogs. Earlier in the siege, for some reason he decided to dump a whole fifty-pound bag of dog food out the chapel window and said: Here, let them help themselves. We asked: What are they going to eat when all this is gone? He had not thought of that. He was also sneaking out the back every day, going across the lawn, trying to keep his head down and out of view of the snipers, to feed the chickens. Well, he ran out of chicken feed.

In the meantime, upstairs on the second floor most of the women's rooms in the front of the building had the windows shot up and bullet holes in the front wall. The women were complaining that with all the wind and rain coming in it was pretty cold and damp. They wanted us to see if we could fix it. Someone came up with the idea, let's get all the boxes of potatoes out of the kitchen. We lined the whole front wall on the second floor with boxes of potatoes to block the rain and wind from coming in.[87] The damp made them sprout, so when David Jones ran out of chicken feed, he started going upstairs every day and picking all the eyes off the potatoes to feed to the chickens. [See chicken coop in figure 3 in appendix.] Eventually, the potatoes began to break down because of the dampness. I think they were also attracting rats. The women complained about the smell: Can we please get rid of the potatoes? So we took the potatoes and dumped them outside. It was decided that we had to put something in their place along the front wall.

We did not want to keep exposing ourselves outside to go into the gymnasium. We took one four-by-eight piece of Sheetrock or plywood off the wall at the far end of the machine shop. After we took that off, we could walk into the gym. We went out there and brought in bales of hay to put up against the front windows on the second floor. Just like bringing the fuel in, bringing in the bales of hay turned out to be a detriment when the fire started. We made some mistakes, but we were doing the best we could with what we had under the circumstances.

In our trial, the government put on this big story about us having sniper nests, because after the fire here were all these wires that had been on the hay bales around the window areas. They figured we had stacked up the hay to make what they called shooting positions. The bales of hay were there for a different reason than what they were trying to make out.

At some point during the siege, they brought in three tanks in formation, one behind the other, with another tank blocking our view of the gap between them. They were laying razor wire around the building. They were encircling us with razor wire that was supposed to stop us from escaping or going out in all directions. We had no plan to do that anyway.

Some of their mentality was really strange when you think back on some of the maneuvers. Here we had not been a threat since the first day when we retaliated to their shooting at us. No matter what damage they were doing, no matter the uncomfortable position they were putting us in, other than talking on the phone saying we do not like it, or will you please be considerate, no one had threatened them. Yet they were continuing to apply pressure.[88]

I got to where I was only getting about an hour or two of sleep every twenty-four hours. People began to put something in their ears—either regular earplugs or cotton or something else—to cut the noise down. They would try to get some sleep that way. I found myself sitting up most of the night acting as a watcher. The trouble was that during the day I stayed up, too. So whatever sleep I was getting was just pure fatigue, when I passed out because I couldn't stand up anymore. So much was going on and changing that I found myself awake again in an hour, standing up and walking around.

I don't recall that David gave a Bible study to the whole congregation during the siege. He may have given individual studies at times, such as talking to the negotiators or the Friday night study he gave me a couple of days before the fire. Especially in the early part of the siege, David was in no condition to give Bible studies. He got to a point where he could get up and hobble around, but he wasn't able to preach standing up or even sitting down. Since we were surrounded by agents on all sides, we were in watch mode. There was plenty of praying. There was a lot of studying our Bibles privately, a lot of reading.

I don't remember if it was early or late in the siege, but a message was sent down by David asking us to read Nahum 2, and something in Micah, chapter 2 or 4. The message was: David wants you to read these two chapters and to be in prayer that God will only permit the lesser of the two evils.[89] I read them and to me they both looked bad and I couldn't tell that one looked better than the other. So I didn't know what particular set of circumstances I was supposed to pray for.

Nahum deals with the Assyrian coming in and dashing things. Nahum 2:1–4 says:

> He that dasheth in pieces is come up before thy face: keep the munition, watch the way, make thy loins strong, fortify thy power mightily.
> For the Lord hath turned away the excellency of Jacob, as the excellency of Israel: for the emptiers have emptied them out, and marred their vine branches.
> The shield of his mighty men is made red, the valiant men are in scarlet: the chariots shall be with flaming torches in the day of his preparation, and the fir trees shall be terribly shaken.
> The chariots shall rage in the streets, they shall jostle one against another in the broad ways: they shall seem like torches, they shall run like the lightnings.

This scripture is saying the Lord is turning away the excellency of Jacob. In other words, Jacob is in trouble. If you get into the book of Jeremiah, Jacob, being a group, is asked: Why are you crying? You deserve everything that is coming to you. Jeremiah 30:6 says: *Wherefore do I see every man with his hands on his loins as a woman in travail, and all faces are turned into paleness.* It says in Jeremiah 30:7 it is the time of Jacob's trouble. But he will be saved out of it. In other words, it is not a punishment that will cost him his life, or not his salvation anyway. God will bring him through this situation in one form or another, and ultimately save him. Nahum 2 is a pretty bleak chapter in terms of how far is God going to let this go?

We were in a situation where outside forces had come in and attacked us. We were a group of people who had been primarily studying prophecies relating to military forces coming into Israel, Jerusalem in particular, before the Lord intervenes and sets up His Kingdom. But here we were physically in a situation in Texas—not in Israel, but in the United States—and where did that fit in the story?

David didn't give any interpretation that day. We were told to read and pray to God for the lesser of these two situations, that God would be merciful and we would get the better of the deal. After reading it I couldn't see that either one was better than the other. Maybe I was distracted. That is the only thing that I can recall that we were told as a group to study. It was left up to everybody to get their act together and discipline themselves as to how much time they spent studying or praying.

I don't recall hearing during or even just before the siege that we were going to be going through the Fifth Seal.[90] I remember that right after the ATF raid someone asked David about the people who had been killed on the first day. David said: Nobody else has to die. God said this is enough. In other words, God has accepted these people and that's it.

So we were very hopeful every time it was arranged that people would go out that the prospect was life. But more did die. You can't ask David about it, because he is one of them. More people died than those who were left. It is only a minority who lived on beyond the fire.

During the siege David asked Cliff Sellors—who was one of my better or closer friends—to redraw all of Victor Houteff's charts. We had hung dark material over the windows to block the spotlights at night, or to stop the sun from coming in, or maybe the wind, probably for different reasons. Cliff took all that down in one of the rooms so he could get as much sunlight as possible. He set up his easel and he was reworking all the charts. There were dozens of them, and Cliff was redrawing each of them in color.

Victor Houteff had printed small eight-and-a-half-inch by eleven-inch booklets for the members. The Davidian "hunters," or ministers who traveled around giving Bible studies, carried with them charts on cloth with artwork that probably dated to the 1930s. The charts were about three feet by about two or two and a half feet long, and they were attached to a rail at the top so they could be flipped.

The charts Cliff was making were quite possibly the same size. He could have colored Victor Houteff's charts if the intent was to dress them up a bit. But Cliff was actually redrawing all of them and putting them in color. He was doing a good job from what I can remember, but none of that has survived.

Why would David instruct Cliff to do this as a project if the plan was that we were all going to die? Cliff spent hours and hours working on them. You might reason that it was just a project to keep Cliff's mind off the fact that he was going to die, but we did not know that. In fact, when David negotiated on April 14 that we would come out after he wrote his little book on the Seven Seals, we rejoiced, thinking it was finally over, God had finally given the green light. We knew we were going to jail. It was not like we were walking into the Promised Land. We knew where we were headed, but we were relieved to know this privation was about to be finished, and whatever was going to be next was right there waiting for us.

On March 21, seven people came out—Rita Riddle, Gladys Ottman, Sheila Martin, James Lawter, Ofelia Santoyo, Victorine Hollingsworth, and Annetta Richards. It turned out that Livingstone Fagan was the last one to go out before the last day on April 19. When Livingstone went out on March 23, he wasn't allowed to call back in. In fact, there was a dead blackout on the news about his coming out. So people began to balk when Steve Schneider went around yelling: Who is going out today? Who wants to leave? Everyone figured that the FBI was not keeping what had been arranged by the negotiators, the agents in the tanks have got attitudes,[91] they're doing things to us that are totally unnecessary and lying about it in the press briefings. A lot of the people began saying: God says wait, let's just wait. But we were all hoping that this would be resolved.

The Final Week

On March 2, the third day of the fifty-one days, David said that God said to wait. He was waiting to see what God directed him to do. As I have mentioned, in the meantime there were negotiations taking place. Some of the people were coming out—the children and some of the adults had been coming out between February 28 and March 23.[92]

On April 14 David told the FBI that God told him that the waiting period was over if he could write out his understanding of the Seven Seals,[93] which would amount to the meaning of the whole book of Revelation basically. If they would let him write it, God said we could all come out. The negotiators asked him how long it would take. From the way it was related to us, David said on April 16: I've been working on the First Seal for a couple of days. It is complete, but it needs to be typed up. At that rate, if it takes a couple of days for each Seal, it will take a couple of weeks or so. From what

I understand, the negotiators said: Fine, we are willing to wait two more weeks if we can settle this thing peacefully without any more bloodshed.[94] They agreed to it, and they sent some supplies in so he could accomplish getting it typed up. I am not sure what all that entailed, batteries for a computer or whatever. Whether it involved more than that I'm not sure. They sent supplies in on April 18.[95]

The week before April 19, the FBI agents on the ground had stepped up the kind of things they were doing, and several people had been flash-banged. In other words, they had thrown these flash-bang devices at people anytime they stepped outside the building. I think they lobbed them at David Jones, because he stepped out onto a rooftop from one of the windows. Someone else mentioned they had come out and the agents had started throwing these flash-bangs at them. They did the same thing even when it was negotiated that Steve Schneider could go out and pick up supplies. It was not like Steve just stepped out for a breath of fresh air. They brought these supplies in a tank, and Steve went out the front door and went over to the tank, picked them up, and came back. By the time he got back to the door they had thrown two of these things. He said it scared the daylights out of him, right at the front door.[96]

Everything they told us was: All we want to do is get everybody out. No more bloodshed. Everything that is done is in the interest of the children. They used these phrases throughout the siege like they were the good guys and we just weren't cooperating. The truth of the matter is that a lot of what they were doing affected the children as much as the adults, like the noise, cutting off electricity, food and water rationing. Ultimately, on the last day you get all the things they were doing, the gassing and running the tanks in the building. A lot of what they said about their concern for us and for the children and settling things in a proper manner doesn't follow through when you look back and analyze it.[97] By flash-banging whoever stepped outside the doors or windows, they were certainly setting up an attitude pattern where we did not trust them. I certainly didn't trust them.

When the word went around that David had made the negotiation to write the Seals and we would all go out together, there was real rejoicing that finally this was over, it has all been resolved. There were just a few days left and we would be out of there. We knew it wasn't like we were going to walk out and everything would be hunky-dory. We knew we were going to jail. But at least this severe lifestyle we were forced to live—rationing and no water and not being able to take a bath and go to the bathroom properly—would be over. If we did go to jail, we would deal with that when it came.

I was not aware of it at the time, but during the night of April 18 David and some of the women worked on typing up the First Seal. The only way that most of us who survived found out that anyone was working on it was the fact that Ruth Riddle was one of the nine people who escaped the fire on the nineteenth, and she brought it out saved on a disk. When Ruth was arrested, the agents probably took it off her.

I think it is somewhat of a miracle that this document ended up being given to James Tabor and Phil Arnold.[98] I think Phil Arnold put the document out on eight-and-a-half-inch by eleven-inch paper. It is printed in the back of the book *Why Waco?* by Tabor and Eugene Gallagher.[99] I have seen some people who have put it out in little skinny booklets. We later had it printed on eight-and-a-half-inch by eleven-inch paper folded to make a small booklet. The fact that we even got our hands on a copy is kind of a miracle. They could have destroyed it and held up the statement that David was not writing anything, he was just stalling for time, since that is what they have alleged.

I guess David felt that things were not necessarily getting a whole lot better. He had this negotiation with the FBI whereby he would write out his understanding of the Seven Seals and we would all come out, and they were telling us that they were willing to wait until the manuscript was finished. In the meantime, I do not know that David trusted the agents on the ground. They had certainly gone against everything else that had been negotiated.

About two days before the fire, David was talking to me pretty much one on one. He said nothing was going the way he had visualized it. The government was trying to say he did all this to make his own prophecies come true. If that is what he foresaw and felt he had to orchestrate, I don't think he would be saying this is not the way I envisioned it, or I don't know where this is going to end up. God had not shown him this immediate situation or the way things were going in the siege. Sometimes prophets don't get to see all that far into the future. Sometimes they are given a certain series of scriptures or prophecies or scenarios, and they may assume or presume that they have an idea of how it's going to be, but most times it doesn't go the way they personally view it. I don't recall David ever spelling out ahead of time the way it went in 1993 and then saying: This is right on the money, see, it proves I am right. In fact, the plan was that we were coming out if certain things were done.

Just how imminent David thought another attack was I do not know, but word came down that he wanted the women back upstairs at night.[100] He figured that way they would have some warning or some kind of chance if agents came crashing in. The women could be down on the first floor in the daytime.

FBI ASSAULT ON APRIL 19, 1993

On the last day, April 19, they started gassing about the crack of dawn. I had been sick all day on the eighteenth and I had gone back to my room to rest, but I couldn't sleep during the night. Early in the morning on April 19, I got up and went down into the chapel. Because of the big spotlights FBI agents were shining on us during the night, I was able to work on a transcription of one of David's audiotaped sermons. We had no electricity, and probably by that time I did not even have a flashlight. I sat over on the south side of the chapel, and the light coming in the window was enough for me to write. That was what I was working on when around six o'clock someone came on the loudspeakers. He said that the siege was over; we needed to come out; this is over, we're not waiting any longer. He informed us that they would start to insert gas into the building. Of course, the loudness of the noise woke a lot of people up, and the ones who didn't wake up as a result of it were woken up by the others, so pretty much everyone was wide awake by a few minutes after six. Steve Schneider went running around shouting: Get your gas masks![101]

A lot of the supplies stored in the gymnasium had been brought into the chapel. Most of the supplies were dispersed and divided among different people who needed sleeping bags and medical supplies and what have you. A big black sack full of gas masks was in the chapel, so people put them on.

I was unfamiliar with how they worked. I put the mask on and it had a little thing that said, take this tag off, but I didn't read all the instructions. What it said was save the tag and put it back on when you quit using it. If you do not put it back on, the filters will last only about thirty minutes, then they're full. I had put the cover or tag thing down somewhere and I couldn't find it. Pretty soon I could hardly breathe through the mask because the filter was full of gas, so I took it off. My face started burning from the gas, so I put the gas mask back on and thought: I would rather suck air through a clogged filter than to have my face all burned.[102]

I noticed that some of the other guys who were either in the chapel or passing through had gotten the gas on their skin. If it got on your skin it really burned. Grown men were almost in tears from the gas getting on their bare skin. One guy was begging for someone to find water so he could wash it off, and I said: I don't think I would put any water on that, it might just spread it and cause it to be worse. The reason I said that was not because I was familiar with the gas, but because they have blister bugs in Texas. I had been sprayed once by one of those bugs, and when I put my arm under the tap the whole thing ballooned up like one big blister.[103]

The minute the gassing started I grabbed every coat or jacket I could find so I had several layers on. I put a helmet on that I had brought in from outside—it was probably one of the ATF helmets. So I was fairly well covered, except I did not have any gloves, which would be part of my undoing. When the building caught on fire, it was my hands that got burned the worst. I was burned down the side of my neck and one ankle, but my hands were more exposed than anything else.

From what I have come to understand since April 19, 1993, the plan that Attorney General Janet Reno had signed off on was that there would be spraying of gas from these CEVs—combat engineering vehicles—as they call the tanks, which would poke holes in the building and put their booms through windows or walls and spray the gas from bottle-type containers that were strapped on. That was to go on for forty-eight hours. At the end of that time, if we had not come out, then the tanks would start firing in what they call ferret rounds. The ferret rounds were supposed to have been used only at the end of two days, but they started firing the ferret rounds right after the tanks started inserting the gas.[104] So we were getting two or three days of this CS gas pumped in within a matter of hours.[105]

Ferret rounds kind of sound like mortars, but they look like small rockets. They'd come flying through the glass of the windows, and they would just whiz past your head until they hit something solid. Then they would break and start hissing. One of them stuck in the wall of the chapel behind the pews, and you could hear it hissing inside the wall. There was another one that scooted under the pews into a corner and it, too, was hissing.

I heard a story from one of the survivors that one of the ferret rounds was fired into the cafeteria, and Jimmy Riddle was there wearing some kind of goggles or mask. It hit him in the face with enough force to knock him down.

It turned out that they used up all the gas, which was supposed to be sprayed over forty-eight hours, before the morning was even over. They used it up in a matter of a few hours.[106] According to the manufacturer's warning on these things, we found out later, you shouldn't even use the gas indoors. The United States signed a treaty saying that they would not use CS gas on enemies in warfare.[107] About the only thing it should be used for, if you are going to use it, would be for quelling a street riot or something like that, to drive the crowds back, and that way there would be plenty of ventilation.[108]

I believe that we were kind of an exercise for the federal agents. A lot of different kinds of equipment and devices were used on us, perhaps for the first time. The situation at Mount Carmel gave the agents the opportunity to experience using them and see the results. It was not only a revenge thing for the deaths of four ATF agents on February 28; it was not only what some might think was a law enforcement mission. I think there was more to it than that. They were testing equipment to see how things worked. But they were also testing to see what they could get away with in relation to the public and the media. If in the future they decided to use these things, they would have learned from our situation what they needed to modify, or what they could just go right ahead and do.

On the morning of April 19, it was not just a case of tanks poking little holes in the building. If you look at news footage from that day, there was a whole lot of demolishing going on—tearing sections of the building away, dragging walls down, and punching holes in the building. [See photos.] That was not just to insert gas. They began to penetrate the building more and more with the tanks. If you look at footage, it got to the point that a tank was disappearing all the way into the gymnasium, or each time a tank came through the front door area it penetrated deeper and deeper. I think about the last time a tank came into the direction of the chapel, the nozzle or the boom, or whatever you call it, was right in the chapel, which meant the tank was twenty or thirty feet from the front door. That's major penetration. All that was tearing up the building since tanks weigh several tons. They were destroying the floor, destroying anything else they were running over. They were certainly knocking down walls.

At some point during that morning the women who had young children were told to go downstairs and into what had been the vault in the Administration Building that had burned down in 1983. The vault was made of concrete, and in 1983 it had protected everything inside it. The agents called it "the bunker," but David had been using it for a variety of things, including a pantry. The vault was a poured cement structure with rebar[109] located at the base of the building's central tower. Perhaps David thought that since the tanks were smashing up the building all around us, the children and their mothers would be safer in there.

We found out later that during the morning of April 19 the tanks drove through the front bedrooms on the first floor to get to the entrance to the vault and sprayed CS gas into the vault pretty much at point-blank range. It must have been pretty miserable in there because there was no ventilation. The gas might have been deflected a little by the Sheetrock partition inside the vault [see figure 3 in appendix], but it could go around it and fill up that area. The fire and the smoke would have sucked up all the oxygen in there. The vault turned out to be a death trap for those who were in there.[110]

Unfortunately, a decision was made to put the children and their mothers in the vault, and certainly that might have protected them at least somewhat from the tanks crashing in. At least the concrete would have been stronger than the paper-thin walls. But the vault turned out to be a cul-de-sac with no ventilation. With the door off there was not a whole lot of protection from the gas or the smoke. I think most of them were probably dead from asphyxiation before the fire reached them. A lot of people in there died from smoke inhalation.[111]

As the tanks pushed on the front of the building throughout that morning there was one point where I decided I wanted to retrieve my drinking water. When we were given water during the siege it was rationed to us, but sometimes I saved mine in a glass jar with a screw lid on it. I knew I had a little bit of water left in my room up at the other end of the building on the first floor. I went up there and noticed as I passed that a lot of the rooms in the men's section on the first floor had been penetrated through the front wall by the tanks.

There were two bunk beds in my room on either side of the window. When I got to my room I saw that a tank had pushed the front wall in where I had the bottom bunk. If you were looking at the wall from the outside, my bed would have been on the left side of the window. The tank had made a hole that I could see daylight through, and it had collapsed the bunk beds. I had a bookcase at the head of my bed and that was pushed over and smashed. There were books and things strewn all over the bed. I retrieved the water and went back to the chapel.

Later you could hardly get up the hallway at all, because the tanks had pushed the walls back into the hall and there was Sheetrock and two-by-fours pretty much blocking our ability to get to the far end. There was quite a lot of chaos.

Renos Avraam and Mark Wendel had been staying upstairs, either in David's old room or over the gymnasium, keeping watch out the back window. The two of them passed through the chapel. As they came through they said: It is getting so rickety up there we can't stay any longer. So they abandoned wherever they had been staying, sleeping and keeping watch all through the siege. Renos ended up upstairs, because that is where he came out during the fire.[112]

If you look at the footage of what was going on at the back of the building, eventually half to two-thirds of the gymnasium collapsed in a big heap, which included the hallway and the dog run that ran over the top of the gymnasium. I don't know of anyone who was buried by rubble in that particular part of the building.

While the gas was coming in I only got up and moved if I had to. I was still kind of sick from the day before. As much as possible I was lying on the floor between the pews trying to stay out of the line of the gas being sprayed in and the ferret rounds. I wasn't feeling good at all.

After the fire started around noon we moved away from the area we thought it was located. There was no evidence of it, but someone yelled out that the building was on fire, and it is quite possible that somebody asked: Where? I don't recall hearing that, but I know that instinctively those of us who were still in the chapel moved away from the front of the building, which was what we had been doing all morning. When a tank came in from the front door and sprayed gas, we moved as far away from it as we could by backing up and getting up on the stage. Then when a tank came in from the back and sprayed, we would move back to the front of the chapel. So we were going back and forth pretty much all morning.

When we heard that the building was on fire we got up on the stage and looked behind a partition David had built across the stage where he had installed a big-screen TV. There was a narrow passageway right behind it. When we went through the doorway that had been cut in the partition and looked, we could see there was a hole in the south side of the chapel wall. There was a big heap of Sheetrock and two-by-fours inside the hole. You couldn't walk straight up to the hole because of all the rubble. [#7 in figure 3 in appendix.]

I remember walking up near the hole, and David Thibodeau[113] was with me, and we were kind of looking out. We were the first two to get there. We could see tanks and men with guns standing outside the tanks. The men were not pointing their guns at us. They were just standing there up against a tree or against the tank, but the guns were in their hands. The men were all dressed in camo so we could not tell if they were FBI or army or what, because they all looked the same.

There was this hesitancy. There was no smell of smoke, there was no heat, certainly no visible flames. Thoughts were going through my head like: If we come running out or jump out, will someone shoot us? We didn't know. With all the flash-bang grenades that had been thrown at us during the siege and other things that had gone on leading up to this day, we weren't sure how they would respond. David Thibodeau and I stopped and talked about it, assessing the situation.

In the meantime, other people are crowding in behind us. It ended up with I guess about nine or ten men in the narrow passageway created by the partition. I remember that Wayne Martin was one of the last to come in there. He was wearing a gas mask. He came in and stood with his back up against the wall, and then he took his gas mask off and slid down into a sitting position, like he was really tired. I do not know what was going through his mind. He just slid down to the floor, sitting up. People were saying: What do we do, Wayne? What do you reckon we ought to do? All I can remember Wayne saying was, I think you'd better pray, or something like that.

There was still no evidence of where the fire was or how engulfed the building was. I turned around and looked out the hole, and all of this smoke came down the outside wall of the chapel, from the front of the building toward the back, and when it got to the hole it was sucked into where we were. Everything turned black almost instantly. It not only turned black, but there was this tremendous heat over the top of our heads, up above the ceiling somewhere. It was just a heavy, heavy pressure and heat, but there was no evidence of flames. The pressure was so much that you did not consciously think it would be a good idea to get down on the floor where the air was cleaner. It forced you down, like you got hit with a two-hundred-pound sack of flour. So I found myself face down on the floor, rolling around with my hands under my armpits trying to protect them, because I had no gloves on. I remember thinking: God, if you are going to do a miracle, you'd better do it quick, because it is getting hot in here.

I was rolling around, really suffering from the heat, and it began to register: The guys further back in the building were screaming. I knew who they were and I thought: We have got to get out of here somehow. So in spite of the pressure and the heat, I got up and lurched toward the hole in the wall. It was not all that obvious where it was located, so I lurched in the general direction of where I figured it was. I slithered out over the rubble and somehow ended up landing on my feet outside, with my back against the opening in the wall of the chapel.

I looked at myself. My jacket was melting all over me and smoking. The skin was rolling off my hands. It was not blistering, it was just rolling off. I turned around and looked at the hole, and it was a big mass of flames. The thought that went through my head was: No one is coming out of there now. I felt like I was the only one who had managed to get out.

I thought: I can't just stand here, because if I stand as close as I am right here I will burn up anyway. It was pretty obvious the building was starting to be fully engulfed. I could see, as the wind blew and the smoke gave a little bit, that the flames were way back in there. So I figured I'd better get away from the building.[114]

I staggered away from the building and ran into the razor wire that they had put around us. I had watched them lay it all around the building using three tanks. On the day of the fire, with everything that was going on and the fact that I had been sick for twenty-four hours or so, I guess I was not thinking too well. So I came out and ran into this wire. I thought: What do I do now?

I looked to my left toward the back of the property. The wire went around the back of the building and I couldn't see anyone down there. Then I looked up to my right toward the front gate, and I saw four guys walking up the driveway with their hands in the air. I thought: They look like our guys. I looked again: Wow, that looks like Jaime and Thibodeau and Derek. I may not have recognized Renos at the time. He had jumped off the front roof. He had come out of a window on the second floor and jumped down onto the ground and met the three of them, who had come out from where I was. He met them at the corner of the building, and they proceeded to walk up the driveway to the front of the property. I thought: Wow, I'm not the only one who got out. Before I saw them I was totally ignorant of the fact that three people had gone out of the hole ahead of me. I did not hear them. I didn't hear anyone say, "Let's go," or "Follow me." When I saw them I decided that I would just follow them: Wherever they go, that's okay.

I came out the little driveway on the side of the building and got onto the main driveway that ran along the front of the building. As I turned the corner to get out onto the driveway, one of the agents outside a tank started screaming at me to come over to him. My left ankle was all blistered, the skin was rolling off my hands, and my face was burned down the right side of my neck where the mask had been. I guess I took the mask off after I got out. It was kind of melting onto my face. I stumbled over to him. The ground around the building was just like it had been plowed.

There is an interesting anecdote going back to the time before the ATF raid. I had been planting and tending a garden out beyond the swimming pool at the back. I used to go out there every day and bury peelings and things from the kitchen, and I had a lot of different things growing out there—garlic, asparagus, onions, and other things. David met me out there one time on my way out and said: You know you are wasting your time, don't you? I didn't have a clue what he was talking about, and I asked: What do you mean? He said: You planting this garden. I asked: Why? He said: It's all going to be plowed under. That was all he said, and he walked away. I went to Jimmy Riddle, who did a lot of mowing with the tractor and shredder. I asked: Jimmy, do you have orders to plow the back field where I have my garden? He said: No, David hasn't said anything to me about plowing. I thought: That's strange.

When I came out of the building on the nineteenth of April I kind of understood, or at least I interpreted, that somehow either David had a premonition or God had said something to him that I was never going to get to reap my garden. I was never going to see it again. David said the garden would end up getting plowed under, and it turned out that is what the tanks did. If you look at aerial pictures of the building prior to the raid, the grass is green and there are trees and little buildings on the south side. In the aerial views of the building after the fire, and even before that during the siege, the land gets barer and barer and more churned up.

So I hobbled over to this guy through all this churned-up ground and he was screaming at me: Where are the kids? Where are the kids? And I said: I don't know. I have no idea where they are. He was cussing me out, telling me if I made a false move he was going to blow my so-and-so head off. But he said: You're gonna remember this day for the rest of your life. I thought: At least that is a true statement. Whatever transpires, I am going to remember this day probably a whole lot better than many other days.

Because I could not tell him where the kids were, he told me to follow the guys going up the driveway. There would be people up at the gate to tell me where to go and what to do. I staggered up there and he was still yelling: Don't make a false move or you'll be shot!

By the time I got up to the gate they already had the four guys lying facedown on the gravel in the turnaround of the driveway. Their hands were cuffed at their backs with plastic strips. When I got there they told me to lie down and start a new row, so I lay down with my head to their feet. They handcuffed me. Someone was taking pictures, asking my name and so forth. I remember looking toward the building. I do not know how long I had been lying there. The next thing that registered was a big fireball going up from somewhere in the middle of the building. It was a big, huge fireball, and I thought: Oh my God.

All through that day my emotions had been going up and down like a yo-yo. When I first got out, I thought I was the only one. Then when I saw the guys walking up to the front and I thought, I'm not the only one so maybe a lot of people are going to get out and maybe they are coming out all over the place; I felt a little higher, more confident, more hopeful. Then I saw the fireball go off, and I thought: No one is getting out of there now. That seemed to be the last straw for me. I saw the central tower fall over and the place burn up.[115]

In the meantime, while I was lying there they brought Ruth Riddle up. They put her face down beside me to my left. There was some guy screaming at her: Tell us your name! Tell us your name! She was not responding. I didn't know it at the time, but she was about out of it. She had jumped out of a second-floor window and broken her ankle when she hit the ground. Because the tanks had knocked the front out of the building, when she hit the ground she fell back into one of the rooms, which was on fire, and her knees were burned. Of the three women who survived, Ruth was the least burned, but she was burned and had sustained a broken ankle. This guy was screaming at Ruth and she was not saying a word, so he got mad. He grabbed her by the hair and was jerking her head back and forth: Tell us your name! Tell us your name!

I was facing Ruth, watching this. I heard a voice off to my right basically say: You'd better not be doing that, they're taking pictures. So he let her hair go, and he turned to me and said: She is not being cooperative, tell us her name. I said: I don't know why she's not telling you her name, but if she chooses not to that's her right. You see it in the movies, you know: You have the right to remain silent. That was kind of going through my mind. It was no problem to me to tell them my name. I said: If she doesn't want to tell you, I'm not going to either.

Shortly after that I heard a voice, whether it was the same guy or not I don't know, but someone behind me said: This guy needs some attention. So they picked me up and put me into a Bradley. I was laid on the floor. It's like lying on a sheet of corrugated iron. The tank started going down the road and I was bouncing all over the place because there were no shocks or rubber tires. It was a real rough ride. I guess I passed out.

I thought the tank took me all the way to the medical tent. Years later, Mike McNulty,[116] who did a lot of research and got all kinds of information, said: I have pictures of you arriving at the medical tent in an ambulance.

I said: No, they put me in a tank to take me there. He said: Well, I have pictures of you in an ambulance. I said: I don't remember any ambulance. Perhaps the tank took me down to the water towers on Farm Road 2491 [see figure 1 in appendix] and then switched me over. I must have passed out because I don't remember a transfer.

I remember they brought me into the medical tent and put me on a table. I don't know where the medical tent was. It was in a field somewhere. I can remember someone being in the bed just over from me. I don't know who it was. I remember seeing Derek Lovelock sitting about where the pole of the tent was. He was sitting on a chair; his arm was all burned. I do remember a little of being in the tent, but I don't remember how I got there. There is a gap there somewhere.

When I became conscious in the tent they were telling me to lie flat. I guess my throat was burned from sucking on the hot smoke, or raw flames for all I know. I couldn't swallow. It was like my throat was closed up. I could breathe, but I couldn't swallow. I kept trying to raise my head up, and they kept trying to keep me flat. I was kind of gagging. It was a bit of a battle between me trying to sit up and them trying to force me flat, and in the meantime they were pumping me full of morphine. I think I had about three doses of that stuff with needles. I finally convinced them I needed to have my head elevated. They gave me a pillow, but I didn't get much benefit from it.

I'm not sure if it was at the tent or when I was lying in the gravel, but at some point I remember people stripping me. They didn't undress me, they just took scissors and cut everything off. I was stark naked. You don't worry about being embarrassed in those conditions, I guess.

There were doctors. It was hard to tell who was who, because sometimes someone would introduce himself, but there were also ATF and FBI people there. The tent seemed to be pretty crowded.

Shortly thereafter they decided I needed to go to the burn ward in Parkland Hospital, which is in Dallas. I remember them putting me on a stretcher and four guys carrying me out. From the door of the tent it went uphill, and at the top of the hill was a helicopter. I remember being carried up that hill and the sun was dazzling bright. They put me in the helicopter and everybody was jumping in there—ATF agents and doctors and guards or whoever.

I was lying on the floor, and they were all sitting on either side of me facing me. It began to lift and I remember asking: How long is this trip going to take? I vaguely remember someone saying about forty minutes, and that's all I remember of the helicopter ride. The press wrote it up that I walked into the hospital totally cognizant, but I don't remember any of that.

HOSPITAL

The next thing I knew I was in the hospital room. Whenever I came to—I'm not sure of the order of things—but the TV was on and there was a news reporter doing a report with the building burning down behind him, and he was saying that he had just gotten a report that twenty or thirty people had come out. I wondered where they were, because I knew of only six of us who made it out.

There was a nurse who was very friendly who spent time talking and walking with me. Someone told me that I was not the only one there from Waco. I was wondering about Shari, my daughter, knowing there was no way she could have made it out of there, but some people did, so maybe she did. It went back and forth in my mind for the next day.

They told me they had two young ladies from Mount Carmel in the burn unit. I asked: Please let me see them. I was all bandaged up and sedated and hooked up to a catheter. They said no, you are in no condition to get around. I said: Please, it might be my daughter. They said: You can't get up, but there are two of them. If we describe them do you think you can tell us who they are?

They said that one of them was a tall black woman, about thirty years old, and she was burned pretty badly, maybe 65 percent of her body. I had spent the whole siege with my daughter and Marjorie Thomas. Marjorie was the tallest one I could think of, and she was on my mind because I had spent so much time with her. I said: Maybe she's Marjorie Thomas from England. It turned out she was Marjorie.

Then they said: We have a white girl, possibly about sixteen, blonde hair. Of course I thought, Shari, Shari. She was the only one I wanted to think of, I guess. I asked: Please let me see her. She might be my daughter. They said: No, no. They didn't want me to get up. I was thinking maybe they had a necklace or piece of clothing or something I would recognize. Eventually they came back with a big mop of hair: Is this your daughter's?

I was almost in tears. I said: No, unless the fire has changed the color of her hair somewhat. For the life of me I couldn't think of who it might be. When they said, maybe about sixteen, I thought: That's close enough. My daughter is eighteen. That's close enough! They later found out she was Misty Ferguson, Rita Riddle's daughter. They still wouldn't let me see either one of them.

The whole time I was in the hospital I had ankle chains on even though I had a burn on my ankle. They hadn't noted the burn on my ankle on my chart, so I had steel leg cuffs and every time I moved it rubbed on the burn on my left ankle.

They came and said they had to operate to do something with my hands. I didn't have a thing. I said: I can't afford to pay you.

When I had the skin grafts they took the skin off my left leg from the hip to the knee in strips and ran it through a machine that put little holes in it so it would stretch. They put lots of some kind of cream on my hands, which were totally raw meat, to get them ready. When they actually do the graft, they put these strips of skin on and then just staple them. You can even see the little dots on my hands where the holes were when they ran the skin through the machine. They are permanent scars. So they just stapled the skin on and wrapped my hands. They had to change the dressing every day.

When I was in bed at night the leg that had the skin removed would just draw up. In the morning I couldn't move it to get up. I had to sit up and swivel around to force the leg down. After a bit they wanted me to exercise so the leg would not atrophy. I remember hobbling down the hall with the nurse one time and all I had on was the gown with the open back. I don't know why they don't put zippers on those things. Anyway, she looked behind me one day and said: Oh, you're all exposed. I said: Aw, don't worry about it. I lost my morality a long time ago. She said: I think you mean your modesty, don't you? I said: Yeah, that too.

First of all I wasn't conscious that I was exposed, but then I couldn't care less in the condition I was in. I had ATF agents sitting outside my door and ankle chains on the whole time I was in the hospital. The nurses came in every day to change the bandages.

I could hardly do anything for myself. They took me to the shower rooms and I had to sit in a metal tub and they would hose me down. I tried to take a shower one day and almost passed out. I couldn't stand the humidity from the steam. They put me in there on my own and they gave me a button to push. I was about sliding down the wall when I hit the button and they came and got me. They never tried that again.

They took me to a room with three or four or five other burn patients. They put a rubber sheet around you, or they may not, depending on what condition you are in.

When I first got there I thought I was in a bad way. I was feeling sorry for myself, but after a couple of days I realized almost everybody in there was burned much worse than I was, so I began to think I needed to thank God I was as well off as I was.

Two little black boys were so badly burned that they couldn't lie down and they couldn't put any clothes on. There were two little red wagons at the nurse's counter, and the little boys just sat in those screaming and crying most of the time. They were just little bitty kids. I felt so terrible.

One day they took me for a shower and one of the little boys was there, and he was just hollering. You know, when they hire nurses and people like that for certain jobs, they need to screen them for attitudes. It's not just a case of having an RN or LVN degree.[117] This nurse bathing the little boy was so annoyed and grumpy. She was telling the little kid: Shut up. You don't need to be making that noise. Of course, he just screamed more and more. Eventually some other nurse came in and picked him up and held him close in spite of his burns and loved him. He calmed right down. She said: What you are doing is not the way to handle a little child. He doesn't understand why you are upset. I said: That nurse does not need to be in this ward, especially dealing with babies or little kids.

They took me out one day to take me to court. I was sick and in bad shape. They put me in a wheelchair, and ATF agents took me off to court. I was supposed to be arraigned, I guess. I had a court-appointed lawyer. I had never seen him before. He told me it was a simple procedure, you just plead not guilty. I said: I'm not in any condition to plead anything. I'm not in any condition to pay attention. They kept me waiting in a cell in the back of the courthouse. I was sick. I couldn't eat. There was a desktop on the front of the wheelchair, and I just laid my head on it, all bent over.

When they took me into court and started the proceedings, either the lawyer said something or the judge saw how bad I was, because he said to take me back to the hospital and we would do this another day. The ATF agents were mad as could be. All the way from the hospital to the courthouse they were planning what they were going to do once they unloaded me. The minute I was arraigned I was off their hands. The federal marshals would take over and do whatever running around with me had to be done. But now they were still stuck with me because the judge didn't make a decision. They were mad. I had messed up their plans.

I got put back in the bed. The hospital administrators seemed to be pretty nice. One—I don't know who she was—kept saying: Don't worry about the guards outside. We are not going to let them do anything to you. You are under our jurisdiction. We are about seeing that you get well. They kept telling me this, leading up to and after the grafting operation. They did not want me to panic or have my blood pressure up. They said: Don't worry, they have been told to back off. After three weeks of being there, I was still in bad shape. I had bandages on both hands the size of footballs.

I will tell two little stories about my time in the hospital.

In the first one, a nurse came in to dress my hands, and I asked: Do you think you can do something about this ankle chain that is rubbing against the burn on my left ankle? It feels like it's getting infected. She looked down there and said: Oh, that's terrible. I asked: How come they haven't been dressing my ankle? She said: It's not on your chart. It wasn't the same degree of burn. So they started wrapping it.

In the second story, I noticed that each day when they came in to wrap my ankle, they had to wrap around and under the chain. The ATF agents would not take the chain off. After dressing the ankle, they threw the rest of the roll of bandage in the garbage. Once it's opened it's not sterile anymore, so they throw it away. One day they were just about to throw it away and I asked: Do you think you could use some of that on my other ankle? Oh, are you burned on the other ankle, too? I said: No, I'm not burned on the right foot, but these ankle chains are rubbing it. From then on they started wrapping both legs, even though one wasn't burned.

One day when I was walking up the hall with my nurse, I saw a nurse, a man, and somebody in a wheelchair who looked like a mummy, bandaged from head to foot with dark glasses and a brimmed hat on. We stepped aside to let them pass. My nurse didn't tell me a thing. We had talked about Marjorie and Misty during our little walks, but I had never been allowed to visit them. I only knew whatever the nurse told me. The wheelchair got about level with me and they stopped. I think it was the man who spoke to me first. He said: Clive, we just wanted to say goodbye. It was Misty's father. He had come to pick her up and he was taking her out of there.

After they left I turned to the nurse and said: There's not much of Misty you can see, but I know there is something wrong that you haven't told me. Then she admitted to me that they had amputated all of Misty's fingers. You could just tell from the way she had her hand on the wheelchair that it wasn't as long as it should have been. We heard later, I think her mother told us the story, that her father had taken her to a Shriners hospital in Ohio. From what we were told, the doctors at the Shriners hospital said they could have saved those fingers, which of course upset the family.

REFLECTIONS ON SHARI AND OTHER PEOPLE WHO DIED

At one point during the siege when Shari and I were in the chapel together, Shari was scared. She was concerned and said: Dad, if things don't go the way we are hoping, like we will come out and go to jail, if they come in here and start killing people and I get wounded, or if the tanks come in here and I'm injured and I'm not dead, don't let me lie there suffering. Will you put me out of my misery? I said: Don't talk like that, Shari. Everything's going to work out. Maybe it would have worked out if she had stayed with me.

From what I heard from Renos Avraam, on April 19 he was talking to her in the hallway on the second floor. He got up and left her when David walked by and went into the front room. Renos followed David into the room. They were in there talking when all of a sudden smoke started coming in under the door. He said David and Steve Schneider walked out into the hall to see where the smoke was coming from.

After the building burned down, Shari was not found on the first-floor level. If she had continued sitting out in the hallway on the second floor where Renos left her and was killed by the fire, when that floor burned through she would have ended on the ground level. Instead, she was found on top of the vault along with nine or so other people, most with bullet holes in them. They said she had a towel wrapped around her arm. I don't know if she had started burning and tried to protect herself with a wet towel, and I don't know whether she asked someone to put her out of her misery because she was in pain.

The room on top of the vault was a cul-de-sac [see figure 4 in appendix]. If the hall was blocked because of damage the tanks made or because the fire was there, they could not run out in the hall and try to find a way in the dark to go down some stairs to get out. Why they didn't try to go out a window I don't know.

On the other hand, I have to consider what we were being told on loudspeakers prior to the last day. We were told by the FBI: We don't want anyone in the tower. We'll consider that a threatening gesture. There was to be no one in the tower or they would deal with it. They did not want people looking out of windows. They would consider that a threatening gesture. The message was to stay back from the windows.

If you have nine people running away from the fire or the smoke, and they find their way into the second-floor level of the tower with snipers all around the back side of the building who can see people in there, there's no telling whether or not they were shooting at them. I don't know whether some of those people were killed by agents, or by each other because they felt trapped and couldn't get out and they'd rather die a quick death. I don't know the answer to that.

If Shari had somebody shoot her, that could be a choice she made. She had voiced it to me. She wasn't scared of dying, but she was scared of lingering pain, and I wasn't there where she was.

I didn't even know where she was, so I didn't rescue her. I feel bad about that. But then I didn't rescue even the other people who were close to me at the time. By the time you're caught up in the whole thing and you're burning, and you're hearing people behind you screaming, you react—almost like an automatic reaction—for self-preservation. It's not a case of "Everybody follow me, we're getting out of here." Three people went out that hole ahead of me. I didn't even know they had left. I didn't see them and I didn't hear them. Nobody said: Everybody join hands and the guy who can find the hole will lead you out.

David Thibodeau said to me that he feels bad because Raymond Friesen asked him: What shall we do now? He put him off a little bit, told him don't worry, all we can do is pray, everything's going to be all right.[118] There was a hesitation on Raymond's part. He didn't make it out. He's dead. David Thibodeau feels bad because Raymond had asked him: What should I do?

None of the people who died in the little narrow corridor area in the chapel had bullet holes in them. If they had, those of us who came out from that area would have been accused of shooting them and running off and leaving them. They died of smoke inhalation or burned to death.

We reflect, why didn't we all come out quicker than we did, or long before it even was totally engulfed? I don't know the answer to that. There are a lot of things you might wish or hope were different.

It's all right for people to ask, "Why didn't you come out earlier?" or, "Why didn't you come out right in the beginning?" There were a lot of different factors involved. We were trusting in God, we were praying for miracles, we were looking to a leader for guidance. We were waiting on the government to fulfill what they were promising. As far as agreements, the FBI agents were not coming through any better than we were. They became demanding toward the end. It wasn't a case of "Who wants to leave?" They started saying things like: We're going to pull up a whole bunch of buses and we want twenty-two people today. Who did they think they were? Where did they get off calling the shots? What if the people didn't want to leave? Why didn't they want to leave? Maybe they didn't trust the agents.

They asked Juliette Santoyo, who had five kids in there: Why don't you send your kids out? She answered: I would, but they don't want to go. They want to be with me. They said: Fine, why don't you all come out? Why don't you bring your children out and you can all be together? She said: You know that's a lie, because I'll be going to jail and they'll be going to foster homes or somewhere. They said: Oh, no, no, no. She said: Don't say no, no. That was the exact fact of what was happening.

6

Jail, Two Trials, and Changes at Mount Carmel

JAIL

While I was in the hospital the staff promised me that ATF agents would not be allowed to take me out until the hospital people deemed I was ready to go. They didn't tell me when they deemed it. One day hospital staff came in and said they were going to transfer me, and I thought they meant to some other clinic or some other part of the hospital, when federal marshals walked in with a dark blue jumpsuit for me to put on. They transferred me from Dallas all the way back to Waco, where I was put in the McLennan County jail.

They started by putting me in what they call a medical cell. It's like solitary confinement. There is no view of the outside. It is cement on all sides, and there is a slit in the door with just a little panel of glass. The lights are on all the time. You have cameras on you, and it's freezing cold. No matter what time of year, they have the thermostat turned down to unbearable. You have one blanket and you have a plastic kind of mattress thing and that's about it—concrete floor and concrete walls.

Outside of freezing to death, I did pretty well in there. I was more focused. I prayed a lot more. I finally got a Bible—a big-print Bible. It was like I had two big footballs on my hands trying to hold a Bible up. I had no glasses. I couldn't remember why. I kept thinking they must have melted in the fire. I must have lost them.

I asked the nurse if I could get some glasses. She answered: If we give you glasses, we have six hundred people here who need glasses. I said: If they all need glasses, what's wrong with that?

I managed to tell my mother one day when she was visiting that I needed glasses. She went to my lawyer, and my lawyer went to the federal marshals, and the federal marshals leaned on the sheriff's department a little bit, and they finally agreed to let me go out with a sheriff's deputy to an optometrist and get some glasses. They arranged with my mother to be there to pay for it, but we were not permitted to have conversation.

In the McLennan County jail there are two buildings—a newer wing and an older wing. The nurse's quarter is in the old wing. All the prisoners in the old building are allowed to see a visitor on the fifth floor, where you sit with a glass between you and the visitor and talk on the phone.

When you get moved to general population, or High Five, which is the newer section, they don't have phones. When people come to visit they bring them all the way up to the area you are in, which is all metal walls, and they have little holes with a grill about level with your navel, and then they have a little slit window. You look through the window to see who is on the other side, and then you have to duck your head down and yell through this slit. There is no speaker in it. Then you jump up to look to see if they heard you. Then you put your ear down there to hear. It was miserable. I hated visiting in that section.

For the first month or so, they arranged to take me out twice a week to a sports clinic, where they put my hands in a whirlpool for half an hour. Then I was taken back. Derek Lovelock came also.

That was the first time I had seen Derek since I had been in the medical tent. His arm was burned from wrist to elbow, and it looked just like pizza. They had not taken him to a hospital. I guess they dressed it in the tent and he went straight to jail.

The medical treatment they give you in the jail is almost nonexistent. They have a doctor who comes around once a week and maybe tells the nurse you can have a pill, but that's about it. At the sports clinic, Derek would hold his arm in the water, and I would hold my hands in it, and then they would rewrap them. They told Derek his bandage needed to be changed and new cream put on every day. The nurses at the jail wouldn't do it. They might change a bandage but no creams. By the next time Derek went to the sports clinic the bandage was stuck to it, so it was raw every time. Without any salve, his arm looked pretty bad most of the time I saw him.

When we were going to the sports clinic I would beg the deputy driving us to go up Third Street, because it runs along the river where there are trees. The route he normally took was devoid of anything green, a real run-down street, and I just wanted to see something green, something alive.

It turned out that the cell I was in had held Kathy Schroeder for a while. While she was in there she had a TV and VCR so they could ask her to identify people. When I came, they took the VCR out but left the TV. As much as I have hated golf all my life, I got to where I was willing to watch golf because at least I could see trees and grass.

When you went to the booking desk at the jail, there was a blackboard with all the rules on it. You were supposed to get two showers a week, which I wasn't getting. You were supposed to have access to the law library, which didn't exist, apparently, and you were supposed to have access to the regular reading library. It was eight or nine months before they admitted there was a library, and all it amounted to was a rolling cart with books. You were also supposed to have recreation twice a week. Recreation was on the roof. For some reason they wouldn't take me out of my cell for recreation at any time during the day. They would not take me to the roof when anyone else was there. If they took me at all, it was at 8:00 or 9:00 at night. They never explained. That was their orders.

When I was taken up there, the guy would kind of push me out onto the roof and he would get back inside. I would stand there hoping that a bird would land so I could see something living, or hoping that a plane would fly over. Otherwise, I just stood in the darkness. I didn't play basketball, and I could hardly walk because my leg kept drawing up. I really didn't care much for rec other than to get out. I could get more exercise in my cell.

So going to the sports clinic was a bit of an outing. They would pull into the parking lot of the clinic, I would get out, and instead of shuffling straight in the door I would stand there looking at a tree. They would say: C'mon hurry up! I'd say: Just give me another minute. They'd say: What's the problem? I said: I just want to look at the tree a little longer. I really did. I missed green stuff.

CRIMINAL TRIAL IN 1994

There didn't seem to be any rhyme or reason as to who was put on trial[1] and who wasn't, because they had all the adults who came out in custody for various periods. David Thibodeau, Derek Lovelock, and Oliver Gyarfas were not indicted.

Bob Kendrick and Norman Allison were charged in what they called the "second shooting." They were two of the three who had tried to get back to Mount Carmel later on February 28 when Mike Schroeder was killed.

Paul Fatta was a defendant. He was not at Mount Carmel throughout the whole thing because he had gone to a gun show in Austin on the morning of February 28.

The men who were defendants who had been at Mount Carmel were Renos Avraam, Brad Branch, Jaime Castillo, Graeme Craddock, Livingstone Fagan, Kevin Whitecliff, and myself.

The only woman they put on trial with the men was Ruth Riddle. Ruth was tried for allegedly picking up a weapon. What came out in the trial was that she was in an upstairs room and someone called up: Is there a gun up there? Ruth said yes. She picked it up and handed it to someone. No one tried to find out who the person receiving the gun was, and Ruth was not put on the stand. They had indicted Kathy Schroeder, but because she agreed to testify for the prosecution she was not in the trial.

Each of the eleven defendants had different circumstances, but all of us were being tried on the first two or three counts. The first count was conspiracy to murder federal agents. We were told that would be a twenty-year sentence if we were found guilty. The second count was aiding and abetting the murder of federal agents, which was supposed to be another twenty-year sentence. The third count was having a weapon during the commission of a violent crime, specifically conspiracy to murder federal agents. We were told that carried a five- to ten-year sentence. Then there were lesser charges for other circumstances.[2]

Each of the eleven defendants pretty much had a different lawyer. One group of lawyers consisted of buddies from Houston. There was Mike DeGuerin, Rocket Rosen, and there was my lawyer, Dan Cogdell. There were some lawyers from Austin and one or two from Waco. It was a hodge-podge of attorneys, and to some extent they did not have a coordinated game plan.

My lawyer told me point blank that he was not there to defend David Koresh or to defend any of the other people on trial. He was there to defend only me. That was the way most of them handled it, and it played to our disadvantage at times because one or two of them would jump up and say, these others might have been shooting, but my client wasn't; or, these others might have lit the fire, but my client was fresh out of matches—things like that. Nothing was brought out that any of us were involved in the fire.

Partway through the trial, or going into the trial, my lawyer told me: They are going to blame you for the fire. I asked: Based on what? He said: They don't have any evidence. They're looking for scapegoats to blame for different sections of what happened. They are going to say you were the one who lit the fire. I asked: Why? He said: The only thing they've got to go on is that your hands were burned. I asked: Why don't they blame Misty Ferguson? What makes them think the lighter of the fire would have necessarily been burned at all? Anyway, about halfway through the trial, my lawyer said: They're dropping it. They are not going after you on the fire. I asked: Oh, why? It was as much why are they dropping it, as why did they pick me in the first place? He said: They have no evidence. They've got nothing to go on.

The government put on about six weeks of testimony and evidence.[3] Judge Walter S. Smith, Jr., of the United States District Court for the Western District of Texas, Waco Division, presided. The trial was held in San Antonio instead of Waco.

A lot of the testimony was redundant and I thought a waste of time. They brought an awful lot of mom-and-pop-type gun dealers to the stand, which didn't prove one thing or another, and some of them had no connection to us. The prosecuting attorneys showed the jury lots of guns and presented the testimony of various agents.

The first ATF agent who ran to the front door on February 28, I think his name was Ballesteros,[4] said the minute he got to the front door shots came from inside and he got splinters in his hand from the wooden door. As the story unfolded, we found out that the minute the shooting started, he hit the deck and rolled off the porch onto the ground just to the right of the door. So for a long time during the trial they were saying the front door was a wooden door. Then it was determined it wasn't a wooden door, and if he got splinters they were probably from the plywood porch that he rolled on.

They maintained first that the door was wood, and that they couldn't produce the door because it had burned up. They went around and around about the door, and finally it was claimed that the door was aluminum. Okay, they said, it melted. They should have stuck to that story and said both doors melted, but lo and behold, partway through the trial, they decided to bring the other half of the front door in, the side with very few bullet holes in it. They were still sticking to their story that they couldn't produce the right-hand door because it was aluminum and it had melted. When they brought the door in, one of the defense attorneys walked over with a big magnet and stuck it on the door. He said: This is not an aluminum door, this is a steel door.[5] They had egg on their faces. Plus, they had all the other metal doors that were in the building. There were doors that went into the gymnasium from the outside of the building, and there was one outside door, I think, going into the machine shop [see figure 3 in appendix]. Actually, all the exterior doors were metal. There were other doors inside that were made of wood. So that story didn't hold up.

There were also stories as to why they didn't catch David when he was off the property. All of these stories fell apart or were made to look stupid.

At one point, one of our lawyers stood up and asked the government lawyer: Will you quit calling them a cult and Mount Carmel a compound? It's derogatory. The response to that was: We'll quit calling it a compound, or we'll quit calling them a cult, if you quit calling us the government. This was kind of childish, you know.

They got up one time and demanded that our lawyers quit using the word "grenade" for the flash-bang things the agents were lobbing at us.[6] They said: They're not grenades, they're diversionary devices. They claimed: They're not harmful. They won't hurt you. They would get into an argument about whether or not they were thrown. They said: We didn't throw them through the windows, we carefully placed them.

They kept trying to maintain that these things were harmless and that all they did was give off a lot of light and noise to disorient people. When we finally did get to put a witness on, it was a woman from Arizona who had nothing to do with us. She was visiting a friend when agents raided the wrong house. She was sitting in the living room and they threw these things in. One blew her arm off and tore up her neck. You could hardly hear her speak. Her voice was all messed up and her arm was damaged. The arm had been sewn back on, but she didn't have much use of it. It made a pretty big impression.[7] Don't say these things are harmless.

All through the trial the prosecution kept pounding away at just how many guns we had, and all these terrible people and all of this stuff that we were supposed to have done.

Two ATF agents said that they saw Livingstone Fagan shoot at them. They were off to the north end of the building. After one was shot he rolled into a ditch. Under cross-examination about that particular shooting, there were different versions of what was supposed to have happened. The other ATF agent said he ran around the north end of the building and he was met by three guys—all with goggles on, and when he first saw them he thought they were ATF agents—and then they fired at him. He said that two of them were white, one was black, and the black guy was real tall. Livingstone is about my size. He is a thin, relatively small guy. A couple of us were willing to swear that Livingstone was not out in the yard or at that end of the building. We told our lawyers to tell the judge we wanted to get on the stand and testify on Livingstone's behalf. The judge wouldn't let us do it. He said we were co-defendants and couldn't testify on behalf of a co-defendant. We asked for a separate trial for Livingstone based on extenuating circumstances so then we could testify. The judge denied that because he said our testimony would be self-serving. All testimony is self-serving whether it's from the government or from the defense. Anyone who gets up and testifies tries to help someone or prove something. Saying testimony is denied because it would be self-serving is kind of ridiculous.

Livingstone did not match the description of the man who allegedly did the shooting, but he was the only black Branch Davidian they had their hands on. All the others died in the fire, so he was the scapegoat who paid. The agents could identify Livingstone even with his face covered with some kind of mask or goggles, and yet they couldn't identify the two white guys. I mean, you could just imagine fifty to a hundred years ago that Livingstone would have been lynched whether or not he did anything. He just happened to be the convenient scapegoat. That's the way it came across to me.[8]

The prosecution put an FBI agent on the witness stand who was in the house across Double EE Ranch Road on April 19 [see figure 2 in appendix].

He testified that he was able to see through the front door at the end of the Mount Carmel driveway.[9] He said: I saw a man making this motion with his hands. It was a swinging, back-and-forth motion. He said: It looked like he was pouring something. I saw flames leap up, three or four feet. One of our attorneys asked: Did any of the other agents who were in the house with you at the time see this? He answered: No. The attorney asked: Did you contact any of the other sniper positions to verify they had seen the same thing? He answered: No. The attorney said: Describe the front. A tank had already knocked the front door in, and the upright piano in the foyer had fallen over. So he was describing an upright piano lying on its back. Under cross-examination, they took him through a series of photos. He was asked: Is this how it looked at the time you saw a man making a pouring motion? It was determined through a process of elimination that the time he was talking about had to be ten o'clock in the morning. After that time the tank went all the way through the foyer into the chapel. So everything he described as being visible—the doors, the piano, and the guy who was behind them somehow—would have all been crushed by the time the fire started. He was basically saying a person poured fuel and lit a fire at ten o'clock in the morning and nobody saw any smoke until after noon. Plus, the front door area wasn't where the first smoke came from anyway. It came from the second floor in Sheila Martin's old room on the southwest corner [#23 in figure 4 in appendix].

Under cross-examination, our lawyers did a lot of damage to the government's case, exposing lies or stupid statements, but when it came to putting on a defense they were a little bit self-confident because they just didn't make a major effort. None of us defendants were put on the stand, because our lawyers said that the government had to prove the accusations they were making beyond a shadow of a doubt. Our lawyers thought the prosecution had not done a very good job, so they didn't have to put up much of a defense. We had a day and a half for the defense summation.[10]

After the jury deliberated for two and a half days, they reached their verdicts. When the jury returned to the courtroom, Sarah Bain, the forewoman, went through the defendants' names one at a time. On the first charge—conspiracy to murder federal agents—everyone was found not guilty. On the second charge—aiding and abetting the murder of federal agents—everyone was found not guilty.

On the second charge, unbeknownst to us, our lawyers had gone to the judge and argued: There is nothing written into these indictments that gives our people the right to plead self-defense. We think that should be there. In response to the arguments of the government attorneys, Judge Smith included voluntary manslaughter along with self-defense in the second count. I asked my attorney: What is voluntary manslaughter?[11] We knew nothing about the voluntary manslaughter count.

Bob Kendrick, Norman Allison, and I were found not guilty on all of the charges. Five were found guilty of carrying a weapon during the commission of a violent crime (count three), and seven were found guilty of aiding and abetting voluntary manslaughter (part of count two). Paul Fatta was sent to prison because he had bought some of the guns and his name was on some receipts.[12] Graeme Craddock was convicted of holding an explosive grenade on April 19 (counts seven and eight).

When the jury started thinking about the third count—using and carrying a firearm while committing a crime of violence, specifically to murder federal agents[13]—it sounded like there was a bit of division among them. I'm just giving you my version of it, because obviously I wasn't inside hearing the discussion. Some wanted to acquit and some were saying we've got to go by the preponderance of the evidence. According to what was presented in the trial, one of the defendants admitted having a gun, and several ATF witnesses said they saw so-and-so with a gun, so things like that caused the jurors to say it looks like some of them are guilty.

After the forewoman had read all of the verdicts and the judge dismissed the jury, the minute they left the courtroom both sets of lawyers jumped up to the bench and asked: How can they be guilty of having a weapon during the commission of a crime if they're not guilty of the crime? From what we were told, the judge said the jury had made a mistake. He said that he had explained to the jury that they had to convict on count one in order to convict on count three, having a weapon during the commission of an offense.[14] The judge said the jurors didn't understand what they were doing, and it would be a big deal to go find them because they were all dispersed. He told the attorneys that he would waive the conviction on the third count rather than bring the jurors back and tell them they had made a mistake, which would have meant they would have to vote not guilty on it. He said he would just waive count three to save himself and the jury the trouble of doing it over.

A couple of people had no other charges. Ruth Riddle was one, and she was technically free. But she was rearrested two days later as she was clearing immigration to return to Canada, because the judge had reinstated count three.[15] They put her back in jail. When Judge Smith sentenced everyone on June 17, 1994, he gave Ruth five years because a Texas Ranger said she picked up a gun on February 28. The Ranger interviewed her at the hospital when she was all doped up. She was about to go in and have her broken ankle set. She didn't know what was going on. She was about to pass out, so what she said or didn't say, we don't know. It was not tape-recorded, and it was his word against her memory, which wasn't too good. The point was, she was not a shooter. She was not someone standing there and waiting in ambush for the ATF agents. Ruth went to jail for five years on the charge that she picked up a weapon during the shoot-out.

During the sentencing, the judge said that since the jury had found defendants guilty of carrying a weapon in the commission of a crime that it was the jury's intent to find them guilty of the first count—conspiracy to murder federal agents.[16] The judge reinstated the first count and pronounced long sentences. What he did was walk in and say: I believe you're guilty of everything. Of course, there was no jury there to say that's not what we said. He just overrode them. On that basis he gave Renos Avraam, Brad Branch, Jaime Castillo, Livingstone Fagan, and Kevin Whitecliff forty years in prison.

He gave Graeme Craddock twenty years, Paul Fatta fifteen years, and Ruth Riddle five years.

He even sentenced Kathy Schroeder, who hadn't gone through the trial, to three years. She had made a deal through her lawyer. Kathy admitted that after the shooting, and maybe even after the ATF had left, she went around and asked everyone did they have a gun or did they need ammunition. She took it upon herself, I guess, to arm some people with weapons, after the thing was over. There was one woman, I think, from England, I can't remember which one, but one woman had apparently gone to David and asked: Should I have a gun? Considering what's happened, should I have a gun? He answered: Do you think you need one? She said: I don't know. He said: If you feel you need one, go ask Kathy to get you one. So she did. On the strength of that, Kathy went around and started giving everyone a gun who didn't have one. When David heard about it, he was very upset. I was in the chapel at the time, and I remember especially some of the women coming in there with weapons. The next thing the word came down from David. He was upstairs, shot, lying on the floor thinking he was dying. Someone came down and said: David's real upset that everybody's ransacking the supply of guns and ammunition, handing them all out. He wants all the guns put back. If you didn't have a gun before when the shooting was going on, he wants you to put it back. They didn't put them back. They just dropped them. So for the next hour or so people had to pick them up and put them back in the storeroom.

That was all I admitted to. They asked: Did you ever pick up a gun? I said: Yeah, when it was all over. People were dropping guns, because David told them they shouldn't have them. We picked up some guns that were dropped in the chapel and we took them to the vault, and that was the first time I even knew the guns were in that part of the building.

When the trial was over and the jury found me not guilty on all counts, I went through a variety of emotions. I felt greatly relieved on the one hand, and on the other hand I felt guilty. It was like coming out of the fire and realizing you have lived and others haven't. You feel bad about it. I felt: Why am I being singled out? Why did I make it and others didn't? Why did I come out of the trial not guilty?

The defense attorneys had a party, not a big bash, but they were drinking champagne and toasting each other. I felt kind of bad. They really had nothing to boast about as far as winning, because they hadn't won. All of the defendants were not released. They weren't all found not guilty. It just didn't seem fair or right. It was a hollow victory and a premature celebration in my view.

The government lawyers kind of walked around with their tails between their legs for a little bit, but they ultimately got the victory. With the turnaround in the sentencing, they got what they wanted. They had their scapegoats locked up in prison for major lengths of time.

In the trial, the defense attorneys did a relatively good job of chopping up some of the testimony put on by the prosecution. But after the sentencing, at the time of the first appeal, they didn't go after the verdicts at all. They were only appealing the sentences. The appellate court sent it back to Judge Smith for resentencing, which implied the sentences needed to change. Of course, he gave most of the guys the same forty years again. By the time it went to the Supreme Court for the second time, they cut the forty-year sentences down to fifteen years. Graeme Craddock's sentence was reduced to fifteen years, and Paul Fatta continued to be stuck with a fifteen-year sentence.

By the time most of the guys in prison had their sentences reduced in 2000, both of the women—Kathy Schroeder, who had been given three years, and Ruth Riddle, who had five years—had already served their sentences and were free. Ruth Riddle was sent back to Canada, with the stipulation that she couldn't come back to the United States for twenty years or something like that. After most of the guys were released in 2006 after serving thirteen and a half years in prison, the Americans were put on parole and the others were deported to their countries. Graeme Craddock was sent back to Australia. Livingstone Fagan served the entire fifteen years, because he was deemed uncooperative by the authorities.[17] After serving his sentence he was sent back to England.

RELEASE AND RETURN TO WACO

After being acquitted, the attorneys put us in a hotel in San Antonio for one or two nights, and then I think I went over to a lady's place where Mother had been staying. I might have spent one night there, and then we went back to Waco. I needed to renew my driver's license, because everything I had for identification was gone.

In Waco we stayed at the Brittany Hotel for maybe two nights,[18] and then we heard about Dr. Millay, who was a naturopathic-type doctor who had been giving treatment to some of the Branches long before the raid. I guess you would call him a patriot. He offered us a place to stay at his house.

My daughter Karen, who had come from California, my mother, and I lived there for a while. I didn't work most of the time we were staying at Millay's place. We were living on Mother's pension from Australia. We stayed there for maybe the rest of the year. Then he started talking about wanting to move and he put his house up for sale, so we got an apartment. Karen wanted to apply for a job at a health food store. I took her over there for an interview, and the owner ended up saying he'd hire both of us. I worked there for eight years until the store closed down.

It took me until 1999 to decide I'd better go live at Mount Carmel. We had already planted crape myrtle trees there in front of where the building had been for the 1995 memorial, one each for the Branch Davidians who died in 1993.[19] When Jamie Martin died in 1998, a tree was planted for him.

Amo Roden, George Roden's former common-law wife, and Tom Drake were living near the front gate at Mount Carmel amid an accumulation of junky cars and shacks. They were claiming to be Branch Davidians and told visitors their version of what happened in 1993.[20] They both left for a period of time, which is when I got a trailer and Mother and I moved onto the property in February of 1999. I figured someone needed to be there to tell our side of the story.[21]

Toward the end of 1999 two men from Austin, Alex Jones and Mike Hanson, came to Mount Carmel offering to build something for the survivors. Rather than have them build a house, I suggested they build a chapel where the survivors could worship. They immediately set about raising money and volunteers to accomplish this. By April 19, 2000, we were able to dedicate this chapel as part of our memorial service. We had previously built a small structure at the front of the property, which we used as a visitor's center. It displayed photographs, articles salvaged from the fire, and the model of the building made by Matthew Wittmer, along with books for sale on the debacle that had taken place.

CIVIL TRIAL IN 2000

After the criminal trial I began to hear that some of the survivors and relatives of those who died were hiring lawyers to file a wrongful death lawsuit against the government. My attorney said he didn't handle that sort of case. His partner advised me to look up Michael Caddell in Houston.

When I spoke to Mr. Caddell by phone, I said: I hear you are taking some clients for a civil case against the government in regard to Mount Carmel. He said he was. I said: You've been recommended by my lawyer. Do you have some things that you can send me, so I can decide whether I want to sign up with you? He sent me a big resume brochure. He was not only a top-notch lawyer in Houston, but as a sideline he had a company that built federal prisons. That seemed to me to be a conflict of interest, plus he didn't seem very keen on having me as his client, so I never signed with him.

In the meantime, Gordon Novell out of New Orleans looked us up. He said he could get some lawyers in Louisiana to represent us. Eventually, however, Gordon Novell talked us into signing with Ramsey Clark out of New York, with the attorneys in New Orleans providing the funds. Ramsey Clark was the former attorney general under President Lyndon Johnson. Gordon Novell was the investigator.

Meanwhile Kirk Lyons[22] jumped the gun on everybody and filed the first lawsuit against the government, on behalf of Misty Ferguson, in Waco. When the other lawyers—Mike Caddell, Ramsey, and some others—started to have pretrial hearings, they filed in Houston. The government used the fact that Kirk Lyons's case was filed in Waco to say the trial ought to be held in Waco. The judge in Houston, who seemed in favor of justice, pretty well laid down the law to the government that she was sick of their excuses as to why they couldn't hand over evidence and discovery when they were asked to, and hand it over on time. I guess they got to her because she switched the case to Waco. It went back into the hands of Judge Walter S. Smith, Jr., the judge in the criminal trial. Kirk Lyons and other lawyers started handing their clients over to Mike Caddell, especially if they only had one or two. Ramsey Clark refused to relinquish his clients. He had most of the surviving church members or families of deceased members.[23]

Caddell really didn't want to represent survivors. He wanted to go on behalf of the families of the deceased children. The children were his big focus, but then he had a lot of clients handed to him who were the families of adults who had died. He had most of the children and a quite a few families that were not connected to us in any way theologically. They were not former or current members.

One slow process after another resulted in just about all of Ramsey's clients being kicked out of the case, but not officially, only verbally. Ramsey's suit was listed as Deborah Brown et al. against the government. Deborah Brown is my ex-wife. She was suing on behalf of Shari. Everybody else was listed under her. For months and months and months we didn't know if the judge was going to allow us into the trial. Then, I think a week before it went to trial, he let us back in, because by exempting us he left himself open to an appeal saying that we were prevented from coming to trial. He didn't want that. All that time, not making it a written directive that we were excluded from the trial prevented us from access to discovery and these various terms they have for getting evidence and access to the documents and so forth. But we had been doing our own investigating and trying to get as much material together as we could.

The judge exempted all of the government agents from the case, from Janet Reno on down, on the grounds that they could not be sued because they were just doing their jobs. The only one who was kept on a little longer was Lon Horiuchi, who was the FBI sniper who killed Vicki Weaver at Ruby Ridge in 1992 and was at Mount Carmel in the house across Double EE Ranch Road on April 19.[24] Smith kept him on for a little while, and then he was released also. By the time the case went to trial at the end of June 2000, we were suing "the government"—whoever they were—but no people by name: no agents, no heads of departments, no official government personalities.

Smith restricted the trial to talking about the ATF raid on February 28, but we couldn't talk about the training of ATF agents and the practice session at Fort Hood or any of the people who were involved in planning the raid. We couldn't talk about day two through day fifty, pretty much. We could talk about day fifty-one, April 19, but even then there were areas we weren't allowed to get into. We were very limited as to what could be brought up.

I have to admit that Caddell had his ducks in a row at the trial. He was very good, but he would take his questioning of some people up to a certain point, and then he wouldn't take it to the end to prove the point. That was frustrating.

Ramsey was sick during the trial and did not present his material in a fast or hard-driving manner. He ended up leaving partway through the trial to go back to New York because of his health. Some other lawyers stepped in.

The judge had limited the jury to five people. I think he had six and he dismissed one. He let us know that they were just an advisory jury. If he liked what they came up with, he would go along with it, but if he didn't like their verdict, he would counteract it. They had no real authority. Day after day he denied or refused to allow certain things to be presented.[25] Expert witness after expert witness was denied.

The members of the jury made a verdict that pleased Judge Smith, and he dismissed them. The government was exonerated. We had all committed suicide, and we didn't deserve anything. The press wanted to know: Were we disappointed? Yes, we were disappointed, but we were not surprised. Look at who the judge was. It was obvious we weren't going to get a fair hearing.

For us, it wasn't about money. The purpose of going to trial for many of us was to bring out the truth. The government had lied about what happened for so long,[26] we thought that with the investigation and all that had been brought out over the years leading up to the civil trial, now would be our chance to present this evidence. Even that was denied.

In his motion to appeal the decision in the civil trial,[27] Caddell made an issue of the judge's remarks about Livingstone Fagan's mother as an example of his bias against us. During a conference of the attorneys at the bench, Judge Smith called Livingstone Fagan a "lying, murdering son-of-a-bitch."[28] The way Caddell put it was, your remark about Livingstone Fagan's mother was uncalled for. The judge responded, I apologize for referring to his mother—should he have one.[29] That was almost as bad as what he said originally.

FLIR Tapes

Caddell used the FBI's FLIR footage to argue there had been shooting at the back of the building on April 19 that prevented people from escaping the fire.[30] The government did a purported reenactment of the FLIR at Fort Hood to which Caddell was invited.[31]

Later Mike McNulty did some FLIR reenactment testing for his movie, *The F.L.I.R. Project,*[32] and brought out some different aspects of what could or could not have happened, or possibly did or didn't happen. McNulty showed there were flaws with the reenactment at Fort Hood. The government tried to prove that the flashes behind the building during the tank assault on April 19 were from sunlight reflecting on sheets of tin or broken glass on the ground. They still stick to that story. What they do not take into account is that on April 19, film was being shot from a moving plane. The plane was going around in circles over Mount Carmel, so the sun would not have been shining at the same angle all the time. FLIR footage shot from a moving plane wouldn't get these constant flashes that several experts have described as automatic gunfire.

Not only that, McNulty in his investigation shows from other government footage—regular film taken from planes and other places—actual people can be seen outside the tanks, crouched down in the rubble of the gymnasium that was being destroyed.[33] That, coupled with the evidence from the FLIR tapes, pretty well indicates there were people firing, from close-up positions at the back, preventing people from coming out.

McNulty shows in his latest documentary, *The F.L.I.R. Project,* that the whole FBI operation at Mount Carmel, aside from just trying to make the ATF agents look good and cover up their wrongdoing, became a vast technological experiment. They were trying out all kinds of equipment for a wartime situation. It gave them ample opportunity to test technology, such as robotic vehicles, listening devices, and the use of FLIR to pick up body heat.

McNulty shows aerial pictures of people positioned in the area of the storm shelter, who were invisible as long as they didn't move. They had suits on that could not be picked up by FLIR photography because they cut down body heat. It's only as people move forward, change their positions, and walk across the roof of the storm shelter that all of a sudden these little ghosty images are visible. All of a sudden you see them: Hey, that was a guy! Other than that, they blend in with the terrain in such a way that you can't see them with the FLIR imagery. You might see there's a person there with a naked eye if you're actually looking there.

There were federal agents on the ground during the final day, outside the tanks in sniper-shooting positions. Not just over on that one side near the gymnasium they were destroying, but also on the other side, situated on the storm shelter roof.

The question has always been: Why did no one get out of the cafeteria? If anyone had a good chance of getting out, the cafeteria was a likely place, considering the fact that it had two doors—one facing the swimming pool, and one facing north on the end of the building [see figure 3]. Tanks had not destroyed that part of the building.[34] There were people jumping out of windows and off the roof in the front. There were people coming out of the hole in the chapel wall [#7 in figure 3 in appendix].[35] Yet everyone in the cafeteria died by being burned or shot.

I don't think federal agents at Mount Carmel had the intention to save lives or get people to come out. I believe there is a devil. I believe that some people allow themselves to be influenced by the powers of darkness to do terrible things. There are others who are caught unconsciously, you might say, in the aims of the devil to destroy God's people.

When it comes to law enforcement, there are many good law enforcement officers who think they're serving their country or protecting their neighborhood or whatever, but they're trained in such a way that if they feel threatened or they get word that there's an officer in danger, or an officer down, all of a sudden it's: You deserve whatever we do to you. It's a gang mentality to get even.[36] That was our fear at Mount Carmel in 1993.

CHANGES AT MOUNT CARMEL

After I got out of jail, on April 22, 1994, we put together a Board of Trustees for the General Association of Branch Davidian Seventh-day Adventists made up of those who were interested among the surviving members of David's group to take care of the Mount Carmel property.[37] Then in 1999 we sent out a letter and signature form for people to indicate they accepted the board as being in charge of the property.[38] We got back seventy-five or eighty responses from survivors and former Branch Davidians in agreement. When we had the signatures together we decided to go to court and ask the judge to recognize the board of trustees. We did that because otherwise we could not deal with the city for water and sewerage and other things, because they wanted to know who was legally responsible for the bills.

We thought it would be easily done. Those who were not in favor of David had walked away. But when we went to court, we ran into opposition. Amo Roden filed against us, and a guy from California named Douglas Mitchell filed against us. Neither of them represented a group of people or former Branch Davidians. It went back and forth with different filings and hearings, and finally Amo demanded a jury trial.

When we went to court on May 5, 2000, Doug was ruled out, and then the jury came back and said they could not decide who represented the General Association of the Branch Davidian Seventh-day Adventists. Our board of trustees, consisting of Ofelia Santoyo, Edna Doyle, Catherine Matteson, Bonnie Haldeman, Sheila Martin, Karen Doyle Graham, David Thibodeau, and myself, with Mary Jones and Kathy Jones as alternates, was not found to be trustees of the association. Likewise Amo Paul Bishop Roden was not found to be a trustee.[39] We talked to several of the jurors afterward, and they said it was confusing. Then someone put it out on the Internet that we had won the case. People were calling me to congratulate us. I went to the courthouse to check the status of our case and they said no one had won.

The jury recognized that the General Association of Branch Davidian Seventh-day Adventists as a church owned Mount Carmel. The contest was about who were the Branch Davidians and who would be recognized as the administrators. I paid the taxes, worked on the landscape, and had lived on the property all along. Amo and Doug tried to show that we were not true Branch Davidians because we had accepted David.

From 1999 to 2006 I lived at Mount Carmel in order to have someone there who could give our version of what happened in 1993. Theological and practical disagreements with Charles Pace, who leads a group now living on the back portion of the property, contributed to my moving away from Mount Carmel to an apartment in Waco at the beginning of 2006.

The subject of property taxes came up in 2005. I told Charlie I had received the tax bill. He said they were not going to help with the taxes that year. I told Charlie I was not going to pay the taxes and have no say in what was going on at Mount Carmel. Charlie was doing things to the property, making decisions about the property, and inviting people whom I had made an effort to keep off the property because they were trouble.

I prayed about it. I considered quite a few options. I ended up renting an apartment downtown and moving away from Mount Carmel in 2006.[40]

Certainly I had a lot of second thoughts, not necessarily regrets but, you know, I have forty years devoted to or involved in that piece of property. I've been there since 1966 off and on. My mother is buried there. My daughter died there as a result of the siege and the fire. I've got more history in Mount Carmel than anyone else except Mary Belle Jones. She was there before me, but everybody else that is still alive pretty much has less history there than I do.

The Mount Carmel property belongs to God. In 1984 David chose to walk away rather than fight it out with George Roden. God ended up taking care of it. Once we realized that Lois Roden had died and George was no longer living there and running all of the members off, then we came back, and we were there up until 1993.

I got a lot of reaction from people scattered around the country when I suggested that I might leave. A lot of people said that they wished I would stay. I explained to them that it's all right saying you ought to hang in there, and it means this, and it means that, and it's important, but with no help it's a major deal, spiritually, physically, financially, and every other way, for one person to try to hold the fort. I had hoped that by holding onto the property and being an anchor, when the guys got out of prison they might be able to come there. There would be a place for them. But that did not work out.

Also, I'm getting old. I turned seventy in 2011. I figure we'll see what God allows to happen. If God's not happy with what goes on there, then He can deal with it and maybe things can be different in the future. Since the property at Mount Carmel belongs to God, and since it has been used for so many years by God through his messengers, I believe in the future there's a further use or role for Mount Carmel to play. I don't believe that's in my power to bring about, however.[41]

If there is to be a future for what David started, using the people he had as his students, then God's going to have to do something pretty soon, because they are dying out. They are getting old, and one by one they are passing off the scene. Pretty soon there won't be any first-generation students left, especially the ones who are still trying to hang on to the teachings and live the life.

If God wants to do something in the future, He's going to have to start all over from scratch—which He's done before. I don't limit God. But on the other hand, if God is going to do something with the people that He trained, or who stepped out in faith and endeavored to do what was requested of them, then God needs to do something fairly soon.

7

Survivors of the Siege—Where We Are Today

I didn't become a Davidian out of a search for heaven or just because I was a disgruntled Seventh-day Adventist. I didn't join the Branch because I was mad at the Davidians. You join because you hear truth. The Spirit impresses you that this is for you; this is what you need to pay attention to and what you need to comply with and get involved with. God respects that.

I've messed up plenty of times in my life. I gave up on God for a time. I went out in the world and did my thing, and I am probably doing plenty of things right now that I know better than to do even if it is, you might say, not of God. This is what I told David when he first started teaching. He said: You need this message. I replied: I've tried to follow every message I believe is of God. I don't need a message, I need a miracle. He said: No, you need this message. And after listening to it and accepting it and seeing how it developed, I agreed with him. It was very enlightening.

I'm a different person for having joined with David, more so than for having joined Victor Houteff or Ben Roden's message. I'm a better person in more ways than one. I used to be introverted; I hadn't traveled before. I'm not shy to talk to anybody anymore. I have traveled.

When I first became a Davidian I was sixteen, and I thought I was being persecuted at my job and persecuted by the Seventh-day Adventist Church because they kicked me out, which ruined my education. I felt pretty sorry for myself. Then one day I guess the Spirit addressed me: If you're going to stay in the position you are now where you dread going to work, and you dread having to be with people you don't like, then you're going to be miserable the rest of your life. You'd better change your attitude. You'd better learn to like others.

People have asked me: What's the best job you've ever had? I answered: This one. I made up my mind way back when I was a teenager to love whatever I do. I enjoyed every job, whether it was show business, digging ditches, printing money for the Reserve Bank of Australia, working in a bakery, working in a plant nursery, painting houses, doing roofing, or printing at Mount Carmel. I've done dirty jobs and clean jobs. I've never been rich, but I'd like to try that, too. I enjoy what I do. I'm not happy with everything that goes on, I'm not happy with everybody, but I don't let that get me down.

For those who have followed our story, whether in this book or some other book, whether in newspapers, television, or whatever source, you will be aware of just how many of our people died in 1993 as a result of the raid by the ATF and the following siege and assault by the FBI. Six died on February 28 because of the raid. Seventy-six died in the fire on April 19. What most people may not be so informed about is what has become of those who survived that catastrophe.

From February 28 to March 23 in the siege, thirty-five people exited the building as a result of negotiations. On April 19 another nine managed to escape the building during the fire. Here is an update on those forty-four survivors.

Angelica (six) and Crystal (three) Sonobe were the first two children to be brought out by their mother, Cita, on February 28. They were sent to the Methodist Children's Home in Waco and later given into the custody of Scott Sonobe's parents in Hawaii. They were subsequently adopted by a family in Hawaii and then moved with them to Virginia. They have graduated from college, and Angelica works as a case manager assisting homeless young mothers, and Crystal works as a graphic artist. Crystal has so far exhibited her artwork in one art show. They recently reunited with their mother's side of the family.

Renae (six) and Neharah (four) Fagan, the children of Livingstone and Yvette Fagan, were also sent out on the evening of February 28 and went to the Methodist Children's Home. After their mother and grandmother died in the fire, and with their father in prison, they were sent back to England. Livingstone was not able to see them in person for fifteen years until after he was released from prison in 2007. I understand they are doing well.

On March 1, which was a Monday, Jamie Martin (ten) was sent out along with Joshua Sylvia (seven). Jamie was Sheila and Wayne Martin's invalid son who suffered from bacterial meningitis as an infant, which left him blind and severely handicapped. Jamie passed away February 11, 1998.

Joshua Sylvia was eventually sent to live with Lorraine Sylvia's sister, his aunt, and it took three trips to the courts here in Waco before his father, Stan Sylvia, was able to get custody of his son. Stan and Joshua live in Massachusetts.

Also on March 1 the four children of Jaydean and Mark Wendel departed the building. Jaunessa (eight), Tamara (five), Landon (four), and Patron (five months) likewise ended up at the Methodist Children's Home for a time. They were later given to Jaydean's sister to care for. They were living in Washington state the last time I heard. I have not seen Jaunessa since she came to Waco for a deposition for the civil trial in 2000.

Kathryn and Mike Schroeder's four children also came out on March 1. The three oldest, Scott (eleven), Jacob (nine), and Christyn (seven) Mabb, were from Kathy's former marriage. They were given into the custody of their father in Florida. Jacob is now married with one child and lives in Florida. Scott also lives in Florida with no children. Chrissy has two children and is currently expecting a third. Bryan (age three in 1993), the only child of Kathy and Mike, recently graduated from Air Force training in San Antonio, Texas, and is now stationed in Biloxi, Mississippi.

On March 2 Catherine Matteson (seventy-seven) was sent out by David Koresh with a taped sermon that he wanted to be played on national radio. She came out with Margaret Lawson (seventy-five), and Daniel (six) and Kimberly (four) Martin, children of Wayne and Sheila Martin. Catherine and Margaret were arrested and charged with murder, but the charges were dropped. After the fire, Catherine settled in Waco and passed away in October 2009 at the age of ninety-three. Margaret moved back to Washington state to be near her family, where I visited with her twice, once in 2000 and again the next year. I have not had any news as to her status since that time. As for Daniel and Kimberly, they continue to live in the Waco area where they both attend college.

A young girl from England, Natalie Nobrega (eleven), was sent out by her mother, Theresa Nobrega, on March 2. She was returned to England, where she lived with her father. When Natalie came back to give a deposition in relation to the civil trial in 2000, I asked how she was doing in school, and she answered: I'm not in school. I'm a school teacher! She has recently had a baby, so I'm told by her dad.

Joann Vaega (seven), the daughter of Neil and Margarida Vaega from Hawaii, was sent out on March 2. After losing both parents in the fire, she was returned to Hawaii under the care of her half-sister. She currently lives in California and has a son.

Over the next three days, March 3 through March 5, the children of David and Kathy Jones exited the building, one of them bringing the dozen or so small puppies that survived the shooting of their mother and siblings on February 28 by ATF agents. All three of them, Mark (twelve), Kevin (eleven), and Heather (nine), who was the last to leave, currently live in Texas. Both Kevin and Heather have children. Mark is still single.

Between the Sonobe girls on February 28 and Heather Jones on March 5, eighteen children were sent out in the first week.

On March 12, Kathy Schroeder (thirty-four) and Oliver Gyarfas (nineteen) departed Mount Carmel. Kathy would ultimately be given a three-year sentence even though she did not go through the criminal trial in 1994. She served her time in Florida and upon her release managed to get her youngest son back. She continues to live in Florida and has had another child. Oliver Gyarfas was released from jail fairly early without being charged and was deported back to Australia. He is married with a family and survived a terrible car accident a number of years back.

Brad Branch (thirty-five) and Kevin Whitecliff (thirty-one), who helped bury Peter Gent across the driveway from the main building, exited Mount Carmel on March 19. They were part of the eleven who went to trial in San Antonio. They were originally given forty-year sentences, which were appealed and eventually reduced to fifteen years. They were both released in 2006 and currently live in the San Antonio, Texas, area.

March 21 was probably the biggest exodus of the siege. Seven adults came out that day. They were Sheila Martin (forty-six), Annetta Richards (sixty-four), Rita Riddle (thirty-five), Gladys Ottman (sixty-seven), James Lawter (seventy), Ofelia Santoyo (sixty-two), and Victorine Hollingsworth (fifty-nine). None of these people were indicted and therefore did not have to endure the criminal trial. Sheila Martin currently lives in the Waco area. Annetta Richards returned to Canada, where she lives today. Rita Riddle stayed in the Waco area until after the criminal trial and then returned to North Carolina. Gladys Ottman lives in Ontario, where she returned after being released. Ofelia Santoyo still lives near Waco, having returned to live at Mount Carmel with the Charles Pace group a number of years ago. Most of these women spent quite some time in custody at the Salvation Army halfway house before being set free. Victorine Hollingsworth of Guyana, but who came over from England, returned to the UK. She has passed away in the intervening years. James Lawter returned to North Carolina, where he has since passed away.

The last one to be negotiated out during the siege was Livingstone Fagan (thirty-four) on March 23. He was charged and tried in San Antonio and was given a forty-year sentence that was reduced to fifteen years upon appeal. He suffered many hardships and persecutions in several different federal prisons before being released in 2007. He served the longest of all of the prisoners. He was deported back to England, where he lives today.

The fire on April 19, 1993, took the lives of all but nine who were in the building on that day. Three women and six men were the only ones to make it out.

Misty Ferguson (seventeen) is the daughter of Rita Riddle. She jumped from a two-story window. She sustained terrible burns and was sent to Parkland Memorial Hospital in Dallas. All of her fingers were amputated before her father came and took her out. She had to undergo many skin grafts, both at Parkland and later on at a Shriners Hospital in Ohio. She went back to North Carolina to live and recuperate. I got to visit with her a couple of times but have not had any recent contact.

Ruth Riddle (twenty-nine), the daughter of Gladys Ottman, also jumped from a second-story window to escape the fire and broke her ankle in the process. She was the only female fire survivor that was charged and went through the trial in San Antonio. She was given a five-year sentence and spent most of her time serving in Connecticut. Upon her release, she was deported back to Canada, where she has since married and had a child.

Marjorie Thomas (thirty) also escaped from the second floor, sustaining burns over about 65 percent of her body. She eventually went back to England. I have not seen Marjorie since she came back for a deposition for the 2000 civil trial in Waco.

The six men who escaped the fire are Derek Lovelock (thirty-seven), Jaime Castillo (twenty-four), David Thibodeau (twenty-four), Renos Avraam (twenty-nine), Graeme Craddock (thirty-one), and myself.

Derek was burned on his arm in the fire, but unlike the women and myself, was not sent to the burn ward of any hospital. Instead he was treated on-site and sent to the county jail. He was held there in solitary for a number of months, until such time when his father died back in England. Derek was finally released and deported back to England, where he lives to this day.

Jaime Castillo spent nearly a year in the county jail awaiting trial. After the trial where he was sentenced to forty years, he was shipped around to several federal facilities until his release in 2006. Upon his release, he chose to return to California to be near his family. He died in 2008 from hepatitis C.

David Thibodeau was not charged and eventually returned to Maine, where he currently lives.

Renos Avraam jumped from the second-floor level to escape the fire. He was part of the trial in San Antonio and was sentenced to forty years, which was later reduced to fifteen. Upon his release, he returned to England. I have no direct contact with him at the present time.

Graeme Craddock, who was a schoolteacher from Australia, took shelter from the fire in the cinderblock utility building next to the water tower and was therefore probably the last one of the nine to be arrested. He was part of the San Antonio trial and was sentenced to fifteen years. Upon his release he returned to Australia, where he lives today.

Quite a number of our members were not at the Mount Carmel property on the day of the ATF raid on February 28, 1993.

Paul Fatta (thirty-seven) and his son Kalani (fourteen) were not at Mount Carmel because they had gone to a gun show in Austin, Texas. Paul was still charged, tried, and sentenced to forty years, which was reduced to fifteen.

Upon his release in 2006, he returned to southern California, where he lives today.

Don Bunds (sixty-three) left the property on the morning of the raid to go buy a newspaper. He was arrested and held downtown throughout the siege. Later on he returned to California, where he passed away in 2010 from kidney failure.

Bob Kendrick (sixty-three), Norman Allison, and Mike Schroeder (twenty-nine) were working at our auto repair shop on February 28. That evening they made an effort to return to Mount Carmel. On the property at the back of Mount Carmel, Mike was gunned down by ATF agents, Norman Allison was arrested, and Bob Kendrick escaped. He later turned himself in, and he and Norman spent the next twelve months in jail awaiting trial. At the end of the San Antonio trial, Bob, Norman, and myself were all found not guilty and released. Norman returned to England. Bob currently lives in North Carolina with his wife, Janet.

A number of the older ladies were not on the property at the time of the raid, having moved to a trailer park at Beaver Lake some months before. They were Concepción Acuña, Tillie Friesen, and Trudy Meyer. My mother, Edna Doyle (seventy-seven), was sent to help Mary Belle Jones take care of them. All of these ladies, except for Mary Jones, have since passed away.

Myrtle Riddle, mother of Rita and Jimmy Riddle, and Janet Kendrick were at the camp near Palestine, East Texas, at the time of the ATF raid. They both live in North Carolina at the present time.

My daughter Karen Doyle, Janet McBean, sister of John-Mark McBean, and Stan Sylvia, husband of Lorraine Sylvia and father of Joshua and Rachel Sylvia, were also not at Mount Carmel, having been asked to stay in California to watch the house in Pomona. Janet McBean still lives in California, my daughter lives and works in Pennsylvania, and Stan lives in Massachusetts.

Bonnie and Roy Haldeman, David's mother and stepfather, had moved from Mount Carmel to Waco in 1991 and returned to East Texas the early part of 1992. Roger Haldeman, David's half-brother, was not at Mount Carmel at the time his parents left but moved back after that and then left again two weeks before the raid. Roy Haldeman died in 2001, and Bonnie was murdered in 2009. They are buried next to David in a cemetery near Tyler, Texas.

A number of other believers from England and Australia had returned to their countries of origin prior to the raid.

None of the survivors received any help from the government as a result of what they had suffered. The orphans received no help for schooling. Our elderly people were left to fend for themselves, many of them dying in nursing homes around the country, cut off from believers of like faith and forced to eat foods that they had not been exposed to before.[1] Alone and abandoned!

As each year passes it remains to be seen just how long it will be before there are no more original students of David Koresh. There is a whole new generation of believers. Who knows just how long it will be before God steps in to set things straight and require justice for the wrongs that have been done to all those who would follow and serve Him?

Appendix

Reconstructing Mount Carmel Center

Proportion and Memory

Matthew D. Wittmer

Clive Doyle has often reminded me that there was never a master blueprint of David Koresh's large building at Mount Carmel Center outside Waco, Texas. Clive says that many areas inside the building were repurposed as the community grew and as construction developed between 1990 and 1993. If any design layouts were drafted for or during its construction, none have surfaced since the April 19, 1993, fire.

Clive Doyle's autobiography presents an opportunity to provide freshly reconstructed diagrams of the Mount Carmel Center property and building as they appeared in 1993. Most of the previously published interior floor plans have been conceptual and state that they are "not to scale," thus when cross-referenced, inconsistencies in exterior proportions are revealed. By creating new diagrams that mirror the property and the building's proportions by utilizing aerial photographs as guides, and by integrating Clive Doyle's recollections of the interior layout to rectify previous floor plan oversights, concise diagrams of the property and the building are presented here to complement Clive's narrative. Details that have heretofore not been published are also incorporated into figures 1 through 4, such as where many of the automobiles were parked, where elevated fuel tanks were located, where chickens were kept, where and how bunk beds were positioned in dorm rooms, and how picnic tables were positioned inside the cafeteria.

Most of the Branch Davidians who built and knew the most about David Koresh's Mount Carmel Center lived in the large building and were killed during the assault by agents with the Bureau of Alcohol, Tobacco, and Firearms on February 28, 1993, and during the assault by agents with the Federal Bureau of Investigation on April 19, 1993, that culminated in the fire. Personal photographs and belongings that could have revealed details about the building's design were also destroyed in the fire.[1] The four sources of information that remain today—survivors, accessible photography, remaining concrete structures, and previous diagram efforts—each provide selective information about the building and the Mount Carmel property in 1993. Pulling elements from each of these sources has enabled the reconstruction of accurately proportioned diagrams for this book.

FIGURE 1: MAP OF AREA SURROUNDING MOUNT CARMEL CENTER IN 1993

Figure 1 is based on an aerial Google map, and dots were chosen to represent points of interest to prevent any misconception of a structure's scale. Personal odometer readings clock the drive from Loop 340 to the Mount Carmel property driveway at approximately six miles. Clive explained where David Jones's trailer was located at Beaver Lake in 1993, and its location is included in figure 1 to show the route that Michael Schroeder walked back to Mount Carmel on February 28 when he was shot and killed by ATF agents.

FIGURE 2: MOUNT CARMEL CENTER PROPERTY, FEBRUARY–APRIL 1993

The location of all the buildings on and around the Mount Carmel property in 1993 is not forthcoming or clear in publications about the events in 1993, so readers are provided with this information in figure 2. This figure's overall structure is based on an aerial photograph of the property taken directly over the residence during the siege. The photo was taken at a significantly high overhead vantage point; therefore, smaller details for figure 2 were ascertained from helicopter video footage shot on February 28 and March 3, 1993, and from aerial photographs taken before and during the siege.[2] The scale and placement of the automobiles in front of the large building were taken from an aerial photograph published in the *Report of the Department of the Treasury*,[3] and the size of those vehicles was then replicated for the vehicles parked farther north of the building along the old property driveway, since these vehicles can be seen in the helicopter footage.

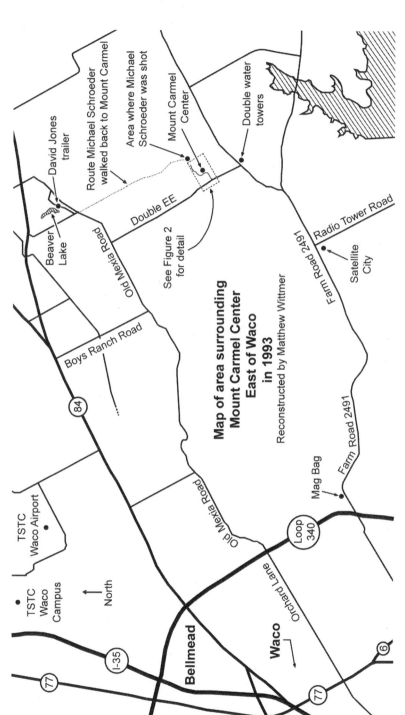

Figure 1. Map of Area Surrounding Mount Carmel Center, East of Waco, in 1993.

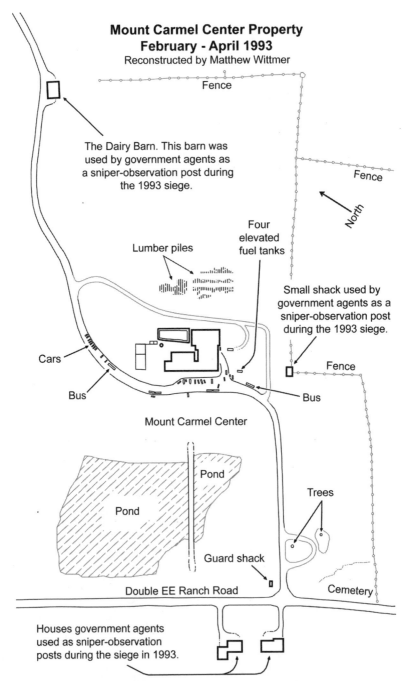

Mount Carmel Center Property
February - April 1993
Reconstructed by Matthew Wittmer

Fence

The Dairy Barn. This barn was used by government agents as a sniper-observation post during the 1993 siege.

Fence

North

Four elevated fuel tanks

Lumber piles

Small shack used by government agents as a sniper-observation post during the 1993 siege.

Cars

Fence

Bus

Bus

Mount Carmel Center

Pond

Trees

Pond

Guard shack

Double EE Ranch Road

Cemetery

Houses government agents used as sniper-observation posts during the siege in 1993.

Figure 2.   Mount Carmel Center Property, February–April 1993.

FIGURES 3 AND 4: GROUND-LEVEL
LAYOUT AND SECOND-LEVEL LAYOUT

To create figure 3 and figure 4, ten previously drafted interior floor layouts of the large building at Mount Carmel were analyzed.[4] This analysis reveals significant differences in the overall building proportions and interior layouts. I discussed these discrepancies with Clive to clarify what he remembered as being accurate. I then drafted both floor layouts according to Clive's memory and elements from the previous layouts that best correlated with his recollections.

For figure 3, the ground-level layout, an exterior wall outline for the entire building was drafted by drawing directly on top of a relatively clear and detailed overhead aerial photograph of the building's rooftop,[5] taking into account the space where the roof extended over each exterior wall. This ensures that the interior layouts exist within an accurate exterior contour shape of the building. Interior wall layouts were then reconstructed inside the outer shape according to the number of rooms and arrangement that Clive confirmed to the best of his memory. Some previous layouts were generally aligned with Clive's recollection of the layout in the building. The building layouts created for the civil trial and the ATF map found by Ken Fawcett had the greatest similarity to how Clive remembers the interior of the building. However, some parts of the first floor, such as the rooms behind the partition at the back of the stage in the chapel, remain difficult to confirm because they have been diagramed differently in various sources and there is relatively no photographic evidence of the inside of the building to reference. Clive was unable to recall enough of the precise layout of the rooms in the area behind the chapel's stage to create a diagram from his description. Diagrams in the books by Dick Reavis and David Thibodeau do not display a wall behind the chapel stage, while diagrams from the civil trial—both defense and plaintiffs's exhibits, the floor plans discarded by ATF agents and found by Ken Fawcett, diagrams in Quintere and Mowrer's "Fire Development Analysis," and Vector Data System's diagrams in the Danforth Report—each show that such a wall existed. They all also show room areas east of this wall. Clive often refers to this wall behind the chapel stage as a "partition wall that David built," and he remembers that an entryway existed in the north end of that wall. That "partition wall" and the entry on the north end can be seen in the raw footage that the crew of the Australian television show *A Current Affair* filmed when videotaping one of David's sermons inside the chapel.[6] Figure 3, therefore, includes this partition wall, as the civil trial and ATF floor plans do, but unlike those diagrams, figure 3 shows the entryway where Clive says it existed and where it can be seen in the video footage. In discussing the layout of the chapel with Clive, he stressed to me that it is important to understand that the chapel's alignment mirrored that of a former chapel that had existed close to the property's front gate. The pulpit in David's chapel was on the east end, while the former chapel's pulpit was on the west end.

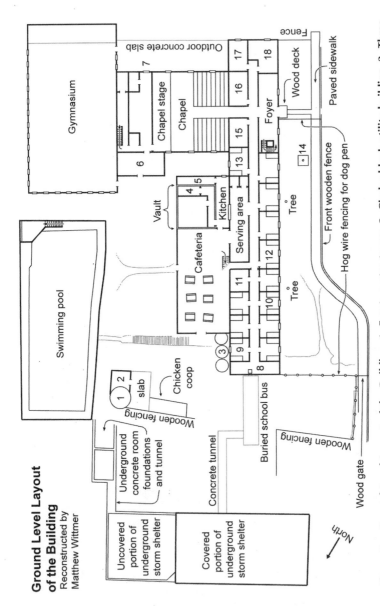

Ground Level Layout of the Building

Reconstructed by Matthew Wittmer

Figure 3. Ground-Level Layout of the Building. 1. Empty water tower. 2. Cinder-block utility building. 3. Three 1,500-gallon water tanks. 4. Walk-in cooler. 5. Small adjunct built onto the kitchen. 6. Machine shop. 7. Area where Clive Doyle escaped the burning chapel on April 19, 1993. 8. Cliff Sellors's art supply area and trapdoor leading to the buried school bus. 9. Winston Blake's room. 10. Clive Doyle's room. 11. Weight room. 12. Kathy Schroeder's room. 13. Steve Schneider's room. 14. Flagpole. 15. Telephone room. 16. Computer room. 17. Wayne Martin's office. 18. Sewing room.

**Second Level Layout
of the Building**
Reconstructed by
Matthew Wittmer

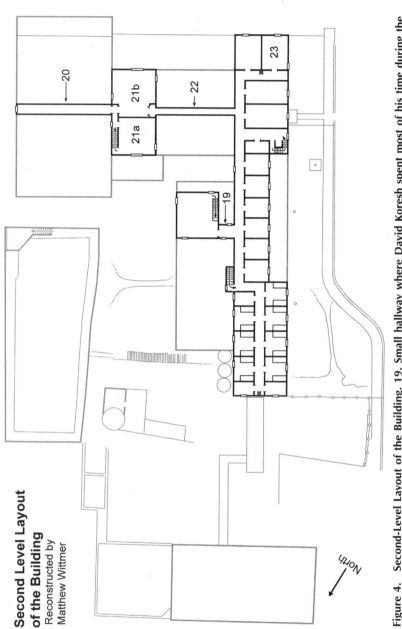

North

Figure 4.   Second-Level Layout of the Building. 19. Small hallway where David Koresh spent most of his time during the siege. 20. Walkway above the gym referred to by agents as the "dog run." 21a. David Koresh's former bedroom. 21b. David Koresh's former gun room. 22. Catwalk above the chapel ceiling. 23. Sheila Martin's room.

The number and size of the rooms on the first floor also vary in previous diagrams, as does the scale of the north end room where Cliff Sellors stored his art supplies. I have re-created the number of rooms Clive remembers and have tried to accommodate the scale of the rooms he remembers as well. Equally varying in previous diagrams is how the stairwell ascended upward from the cafeteria to the second floor on the east side of the north end of the residential rooms. Figure 3 diagrams it as a single set of stairs ascending north, though it quite possibly could have taken one to four turns as it ascended to the second floor.

Figure 4, the layout of the second level—the floor where David Koresh lived with the mothers and their children—has been diagrammed with greater difficulty than the first level. Clive stresses that he did not go up to the second floor very often since it was the women's floor, and the previously drawn floor plans have varied greatly. The second-floor plans in the Treasury Report, Dick Reavis's book, and survivor David Thibodeau's book position the centrally located residential rooms on the east side of the central hallway, putting the hallway running along the six central windows that faced out the front of the building. However, Clive remembers these rooms as being situated along the west side of that central hallway, which therefore ran along the east exterior wall of the second-floor women's quarters. He remembers those six front rooms as each having one of the six windows overlooking the front of the building to the west.

The diagrams in the Treasury Report, the "Fire Development Analysis," and Carol Moore's book depict the south end of the second floor as having a hall that split the north/south hallway with equidistant rooms on the east and west sides. The ATF map Ken Fawcett discovered, the diagrams created for the civil trial, the Dick Reavis diagram, and the diagram in David Thibodeau's book depict the main hall running southward alongside the east exterior wall of the building, which then turned ninety degrees toward the west exterior wall, ending at Sheila Martin's room (#23 in figure 4) on the southwest corner of the building. This is how it is diagramed in figure 4. This schematic necessitates that two large rooms existed with their short side adjacent to the west exterior wall with a single front window for each.[7] Clive has confirmed that figure 4's layout is the way he remembers the south end of the upstairs floor.

BARRIERS OF PHOTOGRAPHIC
IMAGERY AND LIMITS OF INFORMATION

Much of the photography taken of Mount Carmel Center during the siege was captured from significant distances using zoom lenses, which complicates ascertaining precise proportions for replicating shapes and placement of structures on the property. The Vector Data Systems report included in the Danforth Report acknowledges that their process of reconstructing "mensuration" of the building was limited to referencing nineteen photographs of the building, and that their team had no access to photographic negatives nor to knowledge of the types of cameras that had been used. Furthermore, Vector Data Systems mentions that radial distortion caused by zoom lenses and the "obliquity of aerial imagery" each further complicates the accuracy in reconstructing accurate proportions and measurements.[8]

James G. Quintere and Frederick Mowrer's "Fire Development Analysis" credits Andrew Stokes of the FBI for providing them with the dimensions of the Mount Carmel Center building, but how Stokes obtained measurements is not indicated.[9] "Report of Fire Scene Investigation" by Paul T. Gray, John T. Ricketts, William S. Case, and Thomas W. Hitchings states that the Mount Carmel building had a "ground floor area of approximately 12,500 square feet" and describes dimensions that mirror the measurements on numerous building sketches in Quintere and Mowrer's "Fire Development Analysis," but again no mention is made of how these measurements were acquired.[10]

USE OF COMPARATIVE ANALYSIS TO RECONSTRUCT THE LARGE BUILDING AT MOUNT CARMEL CENTER

The Vector Data Systems "Mensuration Report" states that comparative analysis methods were used to estimate the building's measurements, whereby the known size of building materials and military equipment seen in photographs were used to estimate measurements of the building. Comparative analysis is a central feature to basic observational drawing skills,[11] and it is why the aerial image in the Treasury Report is comparatively valuable for its clarity in ascertaining the general proportions of the outer contours of the building. Comparative analysis was utilized to create all four figures in this book. It builds on the comparative analysis I used earlier in 1999 to construct a memorial model of the exterior of the building, which I made for Clive Doyle's Visitor's Center at Mount Carmel.[12] The process of comparative analysis, then, has been a central tool for reconstructing the main structure at Mount Carmel because no such measurements, or the building, exist.

Recreating the layout of Mount Carmel Center requires careful study of the accessible evidence of the buildings: photographs, survivor memories, previous diagram efforts, and the remaining concrete foundations of previous structures. Despite the limitations of each of these sources and despite their scant availability, each source presents attributes that, when cross referenced, enable an approximation of how the large building at Mount Carmel Center was most likely designed and positioned back in 1993.

Notes

CHAPTER 1

1. For instance, Jaime Castillo, a survivor of the fire who subsequently served thirteen and a half years in federal prison, died in 2008 at age forty.

Bonnie Haldeman (1944–2009), David Koresh's mother, was murdered by her mentally ill sister on January 23, 2009. Her oral history is recorded in Bonnie Haldeman, *Memories of the Branch Davidians: The Autobiography of David Koresh's Mother*, ed. Catherine Wessinger (Waco: Baylor University Press, 2007).

Catherine Matteson, who was sent out of the residence during the siege in 1993 with an audiotape of a sermon by David Koresh, died in Waco at age ninety-three on October 6, 2009. Transcripts of Catherine Matteson's interviews with Catherine Wessinger have been placed in the Texas Collection, Baylor University.

Prior to these deaths, a number of other elderly Branch Davidians had passed away, including Clive Doyle's mother, Edna Doyle, on July 1, 2001, at age eighty-six.

2. See also Sheila Martin, *When They Were Mine: Memoirs of a Branch Davidian Wife and Mother*, ed. Catherine Wessinger (Waco: Baylor University Press, 2009).

3. Ben Roden (1902–1978) in 1965 created the Branch Davidian community on property called Mount Carmel Center located eight miles outside Waco, Texas, as an offshoot of an earlier community in Waco known as the Davidians, founded by Victor Houteff (1885–1955); in turn, the Davidians had split off from the Seventh-day Adventist Church in the 1930s. Mount Carmel Center was the location of the events involving David Koresh's Branch Davidians in 1993. Clive Doyle came to Mount Carmel Center from Australia in 1966 at age twenty-five, when Ben Roden was the Branch Davidian prophet.

4. Ben Roden taught that the Branch Davidians would relocate to Israel to await the end-time events. They never moved to Israel, as Clive recounts in this book.

5. Quotation marks are not placed around Clive Doyle's recollection of conversations and statements in this book since these are his paraphrases of recalled statements.

CHAPTER 2

1. "Light" is a reference to additional understanding of scripture revealed through a prophet.

2. Victor Houteff (1885–1955) broke from the Seventh-day Adventist Church in the United States to found a group known as the Davidian Seventh-day Adventists. In 1935 he settled the Davidians in a community in Waco, Texas, on property that he named Mount Carmel Center. His wife, Florence Houteff, took leadership of the Davidians from the death of her husband in 1955 until 1962, when she dissolved the organization. In 1957 Florence Houteff sold most of the property in town next to Lake Waco and purchased 941.69 acres near Elk, Texas, eight miles east of Waco, where the community relocated. This property, also named Mount Carmel Center, was known as New Mount Carmel; the property in town next to Lake Waco was called Old Mount Carmel.

3. "Offshoot" is the term used by Adventists to refer to groups that break away from the Seventh-day Adventist Church to present their own teachings.

4. Acts 9:36–42 describes Dorcas (Aramaic, Tabitha) as a disciple in Joppa who performed works of charity and who was raised from the dead by Peter.

5. After the death of her husband, Victor Houteff, Florence Houteff predicted, based on her husband's teachings, that in forty-two months (Rev. 11:2) God would violently chastise the Seventh-day Adventists who did not accept the Davidian message, and then Davidians would be relocated miraculously to God's kingdom in the Holy Land. The belief in a violent punishment of Adventists was based on Ezekiel 9. Australians understood that this event would take place in 1958, forty-two months after Victor Houteff's death on February 5, 1955. Florence Houteff came to emphasize that it would occur on April 22, 1959; as that date came closer, American Davidians gathered on the New Mount Carmel property in expectation of the miraculous events. Therefore, Australian Davidians experienced disappointment in relation to the prophecy earlier than the American Davidians.

On Florence Houteff's leadership of the Davidian Seventh-day Adventists, see William L. Pitts Jr., "Women Leaders in the Davidian and Branch Davidian Traditions," *Nova Religio* 12, no. 4 (May 2009): 54–58.

6. Ellen G. White (1827–1915, née Harmon) was seventeen years old when the believers in the movement sparked by William Miller anticipating the second coming of Christ experienced the Great Disappointment on October 22, 1844. After the Great Disappointment White began having visions, and she became a traveling speaker with her husband, James White, as Adventists reinterpreted their understanding of what had happened on October 22, 1844, and the imminent end-time events. The Seventh-day Adventist Church, which was formally organized in 1863, regards Ellen White as a prophet.

7. Adventists, Davidians, and Branch Davidians use "the world" to refer to sinful society outside the church.

8. The anticipation of the American Davidians was still building for the predicted events to happen on April 22, 1959.

9. Jesus's parable of the prodigal son is found in Luke 15:11–32.

10. After the disappointment on April 22, 1959, Florence Houteff and the church board dissolved the General Association of Davidian Seventh-day Adventists and sold the bulk of the 941.69 acres of the New Mount Carmel property, leaving 77.86 acres that became the Mount Carmel of the Branch Davidians. Jamaicans attracted to Victor Houteff's message have reconstituted the Davidians in Waco. The number of acres for the Mount Carmel property is taken from Clive Doyle's letter to Catherine Wessinger, December 10, 2004, and accompanying legal documents contained in the Mount Carmel Property Documents folder in the Texas Collection, Baylor University.

11. This was after the General Association of Davidian Seventh-day Adventists had been dissolved by Florence Houteff and the board of trustees.

12. Ben Roden organized the General Association of Branch Davidian Seventh-day Adventists in 1955 and took occupation of the remaining 77.86 acres of the Mount Carmel property near Elk, Texas, outside Waco. He bought the property for the church in 1973 and sold it to the trustees of the general association to administer. See documents, which are discussed in Mount Carmel Property Documents folder. For a historical property map depicting the buildings that have been on this 77.86 acres of the New Mount Carmel Center property, see the website of Matthew Wittmer at http://stormbound.org/waco.html.

13. Rev. 11:1–13.

14. Branch Davidians often refer to their prophets, as well as one another, by the appellation "brother" or "sister", thus, "Brother Roden" refers to Ben Roden, "Sister Roden" refers to his wife, Lois Roden. Ellen White is often called "Sister White." This terminology was not used by David Koresh's Branch Davidians to refer to one another or to David Koresh, although they used this old terminology to refer to respected elders from the days of Ellen White, Victor Houteff, and Ben and Lois Roden.

15. Rev. 7:4–8; 14:1–5.

16. According to Clive, Tom Street Sr. was Victor Houteff's attorney.

17. Ellen G. White's writings teach a "health message" based on the dietary laws in Leviticus 11 and other prescriptions she revealed for a healthful diet and life.

18. Deut. 28:13.

19. Ben Roden had instituted the observation of Jewish feasts in addition to Passover, observed by the Davidians.

CHAPTER 3

1. First the Davidians and then the Branch Davidians under Ben and Lois Roden lived in houses at Mount Carmel Center. A church was located close to the front gate, and an Administration Building, which burned down in 1983, was located farther back in the property where David Koresh would build his large building. The Davidians had constructed barracks to house the people who gathered in anticipation of the prophecy about April 22, 1959, which during the Rodens' tenure were

used mainly for storage. David Koresh's Branch Davidians tore down these buildings as they constructed the single large building in the early 1990s. There is no city water available at Mount Carmel and the area can become very dry, so fires have been a common occurrence through the years.

2. See a pictorial history of Victor Houteff's Mount Carmel Center at "History of Mount Carmel: Photo Album," Shepherd's Rod Information Center, accessed September 4, 2011, http://www.shepherds-rod.org/photo/.

3. In Exodus 3:14 in the King James Version of the Bible, God identifies himself to Moses as "I AM THAT I AM," and this is followed by God telling Moses to tell the children of Israel, "I AM hath sent me unto you."

4. Mental illness manifested later on. Mental health records for George Roden are found in the Joe Roberts Collection, Texas Collection, Baylor University.

5. At that time in Texas, girls could be married at age fourteen with parental permission.

6. August 17 happens to be David Koresh's birthday. Vernon Wayne Howell was born on August 17, 1959.

7. Tillie and Raymond Friesen were Branch Davidians. In 1993 Raymond was living in David Koresh's large building at Mount Carmel, and he died in the fire on April 19. Tillie Friesen was living in a trailer at a nearby trailer park at Beaver Lake (see figure 1 in appendix) with a couple of other older women. She subsequently died and was buried in the Mount Carmel property cemetery near the front gate.

8. Catherine Matteson was living in Phoenix when first she heard Ben Roden give Bible studies there. She became convinced he was a prophet, and she became a Branch Davidian. She grew up a nominal Catholic. Her spiritual search as an adult led her to becoming a Baptist, then a Seventh-day Adventist, then a Davidian, and finally a Branch Davidian. Matteson transcript no. 1, Catherine Matteson interview with Catherine Wessinger on October 1, 2004, in Waco, Texas, in the Texas Collection, Baylor University.

9. Mount Carmel is about eight miles from Bellmead, a city in the Waco metropolitan area in McLennan County, Texas (see figure 1 in appendix).

10. The Davidian family in Boston that introduced Sheila Martin to their beliefs also used the surname Ben David. Sheila Martin, *When They Were Mine: Memoirs of a Branch Davidian Wife and Mother*, ed. Catherine Wessinger (Waco: Baylor University Press, 2009), 7.

11. See Matthew Wittmer's website at http://stormbound.org/waco.html for a historical property map depicting the history of the buildings at New Mount Carmel Center.

12. The governing document of the General Association of the Davidian Seventh-day Adventists founded by Victor Houteff was *The Leviticus of the Davidian Seventh-day Adventists* (n.p.: 1943). Ben Roden articulated his claim that his group was the continuation of that association and that he was changing its name, on biblical grounds, to the General Association of the Branch Davidian Seventh-day Adventists in *The Leviticus of the Davidian Seventh-day Adventists, The Branch Supplement* (New Mount Carmel Center, Waco, TX: Universal Publishing Association, 1972). In both *The Leviticus* of Victor Houteff and *The Leviticus, Branch Supplement* of Ben Roden, the president of the general association was a prophet. Ben Roden's *Leviticus* sets up an executive council to advise the president, who was also the chairman of the

executive council. *The Leviticus, Branch Supplement*, 13–14, indicates that Ben Roden expected to transfer the office of president to "Jesus the Branch," "the antitypical David, the king of Israel," when he returned. Documents 1 and 6 in the Mount Carmel Property Documents folder, Matthew D. Wittmer Collection, Texas Collection, Baylor University.

Like Seventh-day Adventists, Davidians and Branch Davidians see figures and events in the Bible as "types" that will appear later as "antitypes" in the fulfillment of prophecy.

13. Receiver's deed dated February 22, 1973, records the sale of 77.86 acres of land in McLennan County, Texas, by Tom Street, Receiver, to Benjamin Roden, Lois Roden, and George B. Roden, Trustees for the General Association of Branch Davidian Seventh-day Adventists. Document 3 in the Mount Carmel Property Documents folder.

Before this sale, a confusing Document 4 in the Mount Carmel Property Documents folder, notarized on January 19, 1973, by Perry D. Jones, a Branch Davidian who would later become David Koresh's father-in-law, sells "941.69" acres of the Mount Carmel land (of which all but the 77.86 acres had been sold earlier under Florence Houteff) to "Trustees Ben L. Roden, Lois I. Roden, George B. Roden, of The Branch Davidian Seventh-day Adventists, an Association constituting a Church." Despite the error in the number of acres and the fact that this document was notarized before the Rodens legally acquired the property, it is clear from this document and the receiver's deed that Ben Roden intended for Mount Carmel to be owned by the Church, the General Association of the Branch Davidian Seventh-day Adventists. By selling the property to himself, his wife, and his son, George Roden, as trustees of the church, the stage was set for George to claim ownership of the property, and even later for Amo Paul Bishop Roden (b. 1943), who alleges she was George Roden's common-law wife, to claim ownership as opposed to the survivors of the David Koresh group of Branch Davidians. See further discussion in subsequent notes.

14. Conflict between spouses, especially over child custody, when one of them leaves a religious community is very common.

15. For his early life, see Bonnie Haldeman, *Memories of the Branch Davidians: The Autobiography of David Koresh's Mother*, ed. Catherine Wessinger (Waco: Baylor University Press, 2007), 1–30. Branch Davidian survivors call him "David," even when referring to the period before he changed his name.

16. Court Order, *The Branch Davidian Seventh Day Adventists Association v. George Roden*, 19th Judicial District Court of McLennan County, Texas, No. 79-1124-1, signed June 19, 1979, Document 5a in Mount Carmel Property Documents folder, states that Lois I. Roden is the president of the association and that George B. Roden is permanently enjoined from holding himself out as the association's president and also from selling the property or anything of value belonging to the plaintiff association.

17. According to Catherine Matteson, David handed her the letter and said, "Have Lois sign this." Catherine showed the letter to Lois Roden, and she did not want to sign it. Catherine reported that she told her, "Lois, you know you have to sign it, so why don't you just sign it?" Lois signed the letter and it was sent to all the Branches. Catherine Matteson's interpretation of Lois Roden's hesitation was

that "she had already lost her Spirit of Prophecy," and that she was starting to favor George again. Matteson Transcript no. 2, interview of Catherine Matteson by Catherine Wessinger, October 11, 2004, in Waco, Texas, in the Texas Collection, Baylor University.

18. *Shekinah* is a feminine word in Hebrew that refers to God's divine presence. For Branch Davidians this is a reference to the feminine Holy Spirit. Clive printed Lois Roden's tracts and her journal, *SHEkinah*, which ran from 1980 to 1983, in which news articles and short essays by cutting-edge Christian feminist theologians, Bible scholars, and historians were reprinted. The Branch Davidians considered *SHEkinah* a "sounding board" for feminist ideas, which appeared to attract Lois and in which she found support for her leadership of the Branch Davidians. Although the Branch Davidians accepted Lois's teaching that the Holy Spirit is feminine and strong women were members of the group, feminist ideas in general were not accepted by the Branch Davidians. On Lois Roden's tenure as Branch Davidian prophet and her ultimate loss of the Spirit of Prophecy in the eyes of the core group, including Clive, see William L. Pitts, "Women Leaders in the Davidian and Branch Davidian Traditions," *Nova Religio* 12, no. 4 (May): 59–66. Clive discusses *SHEkinah* in Doyle Transcript no. 9, Clive Doyle interview with Catherine Wessinger, October 8, 2004, at Mount Carmel. Ten thousand to twelve thousand copies were printed of each issue and mailed to Davidians, Branch Davidians, Adventists, and colleges and universities around the world.

19. This was a double issue, *SHEkinah* 4, nos. 3–4 (July–December 1983).

20. The photograph is on the "Notes from the Editor" page. Her large glasses cast dark shadows over her eyes.

21. Beginning with Ellen G. White in the Seventh-day Adventist tradition, and continuing in Victor Houteff's Davidians and Ben and Lois Roden's Branch Davidians, a prophet is regarded as someone who receives inspiration or "light" to interpret the Bible's prophecies.

22. The Branch Davidian survivors refer to this as Lois losing the "Spirit of Prophecy," implying that David had received the Spirit of Prophecy and supplanted Lois as prophet. Matteson Transcript no. 2; Doyle Transcript no. 17, interview of Clive Doyle by Catherine Wessinger, October 12, 2004, at Mount Carmel.

23. Vernon Howell and Lois Roden were lovers for a time. Clive reports that Lois had, at age seventy, become pregnant but lost the fetus. Doyle Transcript no. 9.

24. Vernon Howell married Rachel Jones, the fourteen-year-old daughter of Perry and Mary Belle Jones, on January 18, 1984.

25. Lois Roden had instituted the Emblems being taken every day at 9:00 a.m. and 3:00 p.m. There were no priests involved. As Sheila Martin puts it, "We were the priests in our own homes." Martin, *When They Were Mine*, 22–23, quotation on 23.

26. Passover is an eight-day holiday in the Jewish calendar, which was observed by the Branch Davidians along with other Jewish feasts.

27. Sheila Martin became a Davidian Seventh-day Adventist when she was a teenager in Boston. Later she became a Branch Davidian under the messages of Ben Roden and then Lois Roden. Her husband, Wayne Martin, was a Harvard-educated attorney who also had a master's degree in library science from Columbia University. He was assistant professor and law librarian at North Carolina Central University in Durham, North Carolina. Wayne had been raised in the Seventh-day

Adventist Church but over time drifted away. Their youngest son, James Desmond Charles Martin, was born on May 31, 1982, and about five months later contracted meningitis, which left him severely disabled, causing a spiritual crisis for his parents. During the difficult period of Jamie's illness, when it was unclear whether he would live or die, Sheila called Mount Carmel frequently to talk to Lois Roden and also to Vernon Howell (David Koresh). She describes David as being very empathetic. In January 1984 Wayne listened to an audiotape of David teaching and became interested. Sheila attended David's teachings at Passover in the spring of 1984 and brought Jamie with her. She reports that Jamie cried throughout the meetings, but David told her to stay in the room. He held Jamie frequently to comfort him. After Sheila's visit to Texas in 1984, David and Novellette Sinclair, a Branch Davidian from Canada, visited the Martins in Durham, where David presented his message directly to Wayne Martin. When the Martins visited for the 1985 Passover, the Branch Davidians who had accepted that the Spirit of Prophecy had moved from Lois Roden to David were living temporarily at a campground at Mexia, Texas. Subsequently, Wayne Martin quit his job, bought a school bus, and drove his family back to join the group, which had settled at a camp they constructed at Palestine, Texas, where they lived in the bus until the Branch Davidians moved back to Mount Carmel in 1988. Martin, *When They Were Mine*, 7–34.

28. Vernon Howell (David Koresh) married Rachel Jones, the daughter of Perry and Mary Belle Jones, in 1984 when she was fourteen years old, with the permission of her parents.

29. Bonnie Haldeman recalled that on a visit she saw Floyd Houtman, his wife and children, Novellette Sinclair, the Doyles, David Bunds, and his sister Robyn Bunds living in the house, and David and Rachel living in the bus behind the house. Haldeman, *Memories of the Branch Davidians*, 28.

30. While he was in Israel he received the "Cyrus message," that he was God's son who had received the Christ Spirit and would play the key role in the end-time events to establish the Davidic kingdom in the Holy Land. He taught that he was identified with the Lamb in the book of Revelation and the Seventh Angel in Rev. 10:7. "Koresh" is Hebrew for Cyrus. On his experience in Israel, see James Tabor, "David Koresh and the Branch Davidians," Apocalypticism Explained, accessed September 2, 2011, http://www.pbs.org/wgbh/pages/frontline/shows/apocalypse/explanation/cults.html.

Cyrus was the great Persian king who, through his military victories, created the Achaemenid Empire. He defeated the Babylonian Empire in 539 B.C.E., bringing to an end the "Babylonian captivity" of Jews who had been brought to Babylon when the first Jerusalem Temple was destroyed by the Babylonians in 586 B.C.E. Cyrus gave permission for the Jews who wished to do so to return to their homeland and rebuild their temple, which was accomplished by 520 B.C.E. The Hebrew Bible (the Christian Old Testament) therefore depicts Cyrus as a savior of God's people. Cyrus is termed a "messiah," God's "anointed," in Isaiah 45:1. In the Christian Bible, the Hebrew word *messiah* became *christos* in Greek, so this passage was read by David Koresh and the Branch Davidians as a reference to Cyrus as Christ. In Isaiah 45, Cyrus is described as the individual selected by God to defeat Babylon. "Babylon" is an important theme in the Old Testament book of Daniel and the New Testament book of Revelation, which are very important in Branch Davidian theology. David taught that he was the Christ prefigured by the historical Cyrus who would defeat "Babylon," the corrupt world, in the apocalyptic events described in Revelation and other books of the Bible.

The meanings of the term "messiah" developed in the course of the history of Judaism and later in early Christianity. According to James D. Tabor and Eugene V. Gallagher, *Why Waco? Cults and the Battle for Religious Freedom in America* (Berkeley and Los Angeles: University of California Press, 1995), 59: "The term 'messiah' is used for a variety of figures in the Hebrew Bible and basically means 'one who is chosen or appointed for a special mission.'" They point out that in Psalm 105:15 Abraham, Isaac, and Jacob are called messiahs. The term "messiah" referred to the consecration of a king or priest by ritually pouring oil over his head. This term came to be applied to the kings of the people of Israel. See 1 Samuel 10:1 where Saul, the first king of Israel, is consecrated by the pouring of oil by the prophet Samuel.

31. Clive is referring to Floyd Houtman's family. His wife and children subsequently left the Branch Davidians. Floyd Houtman was with the Branch Davidians at Mount Carmel during the events in 1993 and died in the fire on April 19.

32. Under Lois Roden the group was known as the Living Waters Branch.

33. Martin, *When They Were Mine*, 33.

34. See Sheila's recollections of the Palestine experience in Martin, *When They Were Mine*, 33–41; Bonnie Haldeman's recollections in Haldeman, *Memories of the Branch Davidians*, 33–38, 47–48, 50–54, 58; Catherine Matteson's recollections in Matteson Transcript no. 2 and Matteson Transcript no. 3, interview of Catherine Matteson by Catherine Wessinger, November 26, 2004, in Waco, Texas. The Palestine period is one that they looked back on fondly.

35. There have been two Davidian groups in South Carolina for some time, one of which is headed by Don Adair. He has published hardback reproductions of much of the Davidian literature, such as *The Shepherd's Rod* tract compendium and *The Symbolic Code* series. He has a "Search Key Words" page at the Mt. Carmel Center website, accessed September 4, 2011, http://www.davidian.org/keywords.htm.

36. Mark Swett told co-editor Matthew Wittmer that he obtained cassette audiotapes that were taken from the Palestine property during the siege in 1993. One of them had a nine-minute recording of Rachel Howell giving birth with Vernon Howell's assistance. The birth and the voice of Vernon (David Koresh) are audible. According to Swett, who digitized the tape, the child is Cyrus. A copy saved on CD is in the Mark Swett Collection in the Texas Collection, Baylor University.

37. David was also promoting his music in California, which he used to attract young people to his message. See David Thibodeau and Leon Whiteson, *A Place Called Waco: A Survivor's Story* (New York: Public Affairs, 1999), 14–24.

38. Haldeman, *Memories of the Branch Davidians*, 44.

39. Clive and Bonnie Haldeman were given the job of revitalizing a bakery that had been donated to the group by Neil and Margarida Vaega. They also got to know the young people living in Hawaii who had started following David. Haldeman, *Memories of the Branch Davidians*, 48–50.

40. A longer version of this story is told, in Clive's words, in Haldeman, *Memories of the Branch Davidians*, 55–59. The men who went with David to photograph the remains of Anna Hughes included Floyd Houtman, Stan Sylvia, David Jones, and

Paul Fatta. David, Paul Fatta, and David Jones got out on bail. The other men had to wait in jail until the case came to trial. The charge was attempted murder. David and his men said they were shooting in self-defense.

41. Order of Contempt, *The Branch Davidian Seventh Day Adventist Association v. George Roden*, 19th Judicial District Court of McLennan County, Texas, No. 79-1124-1, signed September 20, 1988, Document 9 in Mount Carmel Property Documents folder. When George was released from jail he moved to Odessa, Texas. There he killed Dale Adair, Don Adair's brother, in 1989, and he spent the rest of his life confined to the Big Spring State Hospital, where he died from a heart attack at age sixty in 1998. Dick Reavis, *The Ashes of Waco: An Investigation* (New York: Simon & Schuster, 1995), 82; Catherine Wessinger, *How the Millennium Comes Violently: From Jonestown to Heaven's Gate* (New York: Seven Bridges Press, 2000), 117n130.

42. Probably with legal assistance from Wayne Martin and financial assistance from wealthy followers, perhaps Paul Fatta, David took other steps to assert legal control over Mount Carmel. Ben and Lois Roden and George Roden had never paid property taxes on Mount Carmel, and in August 1987 the Axtell Independent School District sued George Roden as the surviving trustee of the original General Association of the Branch Davidian Seventh-day Adventists for the owed taxes. On December 15, 1988, Raymond Friesen, Perry Dale Jones, Clive Doyle, Woodrow W. Kendrick, Bill Worrow, and Donald E. Bunds signed a notarized statement as members of the executive council of the General Association of the Branch Davidian Seventh-day Adventists that Vernon Wayne Howell was the association's president and trustee. On January 11, 1988, David paid the $23,569.15 in owed taxes and received a release of judgment on behalf of the association. Letter from Clive Doyle, December 10, 2004, and Documents 9, 10, 11 in the Mount Carmel Property Documents folder.

43. See the historical property map on Matthew Wittmer's website at http://stormbound.org/waco.html.

44. This house was also filled with pornography in connection with a mail-order business. David took the meth lab paraphernalia to the sheriff's department, and he would not let anyone move into that house. Haldeman, *Memories of the Branch Davidians*, 61–62.

Although David Koresh had turned these materials in to the sheriff's department, during its preparations for the raid on Mount Carmel carried out on February 28, 1993, the Bureau of Alcohol, Tobacco, and Firearms (ATF) alleged that the Branch Davidians were operating a methamphetamine lab, so the ATF could obtain training from Army Special Forces and the use of National Guard helicopters in the raid. According to the Posse Comitatus Act of 1878 it is illegal for the military to be used in actions against civilians except for specific exceptions, one of which, according to later law, is an illegal drug nexus. The congressional report issued in 1996 concluded that the behavior of the ATF agents while conducting the raid, including the use of pyrotechnic flash-bang grenades, contradicted safety protocols for law enforcement agents when entering a site where an active meth lab with highly flammable and poisonous chemicals is located. The report concluded that the ATF agents planning the raid were aware that David Koresh's Branch Davidians were not operating a meth lab at Mount Carmel. House of Representatives Report 104-749, *Investigation into the*

Activities of Federal Law Enforcement Agencies toward the Branch Davidians (Washington, DC: US Government Printing Office, 1996), 43–50.

45. Haldeman, *Memories of the Branch Davidians*, 60–61, talks about how filthy the houses were and the work they did to clean them up and make them fit to live in.

46. Amo Paul Bishop Roden engages in *pro se* litigation, meaning that she composes and files legal documents in accordance with the ideology of the antigovernment "Common Law" or "Freeman" movement. This is probably what she means when she says she was George Roden's "common law" wife. This body of alternative knowledge has meanings specific to the movement that are not recognized by American courts. On the Common Law movement in the United States, see the chapter on the Montana Freemen in Wessinger, *How the Millennium Comes Violently*, 158–217; Documents 19 and 20 in the Mount Carmel Property Documents folder are examples of Amo Roden's legal documents influenced by Common Law thought.

George Roden was still legally married to Carmen Roden when he and Amo married in 1987 by signing a contract. Amo describes how she agreed to the marriage after George presented her with his essay on the Mosaic law of polygamy. Amo Roden, "George Roden," The Writings of Amo Roden, accessed September 3, 2011, http://wacocult.tripod.com/amo/george.html. In the following years, Amo Roden would periodically assert ownership of Mount Carmel based on her claim to be a Branch Davidian under George as well as his common law wife. See the discussions in chapter 4.

Amo had a daughter by George Roden, whose name is given in the Pauper's Oath that is part of Document 17 in the Mount Carmel Property Documents folder.

47. See Haldeman, *Memories of the Branch Davidians*, 66.

48. See the historical property map depicting these former buildings at Mount Carmel on Matthew Wittmer's website at http://stormbound.org/waco.html.

49. Ben Roden's organization was called the General Association of the Branch Davidian Seventh-day Adventists. Lois Roden called her church the Living Waters Branch, although the name of the organization was not officially changed. As David attracted young people, he did not assign a particular name to the group. Many considered themselves students studying the Bible and its prophecies with David. The long-time members such as Clive were familiar with the name Branch Davidians.

50. Newbold College.

51. Matt. 13:10–17.

52. Parables of the seed and the sower follow in Matt. 13:18–30.

53. A principle of classified secrets is that information is divulged to individuals based on a need-to-know basis. If they do not need that information for their particular work, they are not informed.

54. Rick Ross was a deprogrammer and continues to be an anticult activist. Tabor and Gallagher, *Why Waco?* 93–96, discusses the "deprogramming" of the young man by Ross.

55. Texas Highway 340. After the ATF raid on February 28, 1993, the press called this building the Mag Bag, but the Branch Davidians never called it that. (See figure 1.)

CHAPTER 4

1. The digitized audiofiles for the "Serpent's Root" lectures, along with other Bible studies given by David Koresh, have been placed in the Texas Collection, Baylor University.

2. Clive can be heard on the recorded audio as he rigorously questions Vernon Howell (David Koresh) about his interpretations of the biblical passages and his understanding of the teachings of Ellen White, Victor Houteff, and also Lois Roden. These recorded studies demonstrate that Howell had absorbed and was building on the teachers who went before him in the Adventist, Davidian, and Branch Davidian line of prophets. In these studies, Howell often read passages from the writings of these individuals.

3. David Koresh, like participants in the nineteenth-century Millerite movement, the Seventh-day Adventist Church that emerged from the Millerite movement, Victor Houteff of the Davidians, and the previous Branch Davidian prophets Ben Roden and Lois Roden, saw certain people and events in the Bible as "types" prefiguring figures and events in the future they termed "antitypes." This typological approach to interpreting the Bible is explained in Kenneth G. C. Newport, *The Branch Davidians of Waco: The History and Beliefs of an Apocalyptic Sect* (Oxford: Oxford University Press, 2006), 34. The Newport volume and James D. Tabor and Eugene V. Gallagher, *Why Waco? Cults and the Battle for Religious Freedom in America* (Berkeley and Los Angeles: University of California Press, 1995), provide treatments of Branch Davidian theology and relevant scriptural passages.

The interviews with Clive Doyle contain more extensive discussions of theology than can be included in this chapter. The corrected transcripts of the thirty-one interviews will be placed in the Texas Collection, Baylor University.

4. David Koresh writes in his unfinished manuscript, "The Seven Seals of the Book of Revelation," in Tabor and Gallagher, *Why Waco?* 197: "The servant of God will find as we continue in our searching of the scriptures that every book of the Bible meets and ends in the book of Revelation."

A short treatment of the Revelation (Apocalypse) of Saint John, its history, and much of the translated text is found in Robert K. Gnuse, "Bible: Revelation," in *Milestone Documents of World Religions: Exploring Traditions of Faith through Primary Sources*, ed. David M. Fahey, vol. 1, *2404 b.c.e.–200 c.e.* (Dallas: Schlager Group, 2011), 425–41.

5. Bible passages quoted in this chapter are from the King James Version of the Bible, the translation used by Branch Davidians.

6. *Shekinah* is a feminine word in Hebrew that referred to the dwelling or presence of God, especially in the sanctuary, first in the tent of meeting and later in the temple in Jerusalem. From 1980 to 1983 Lois Roden published a small journal named *SHEkinah*, which Clive Doyle printed.

7. *Hokhmah*, "wisdom," is a feminine word in Hebrew that is associated with God in the Torah, which Christians know as the Old Testament.

8. In Genesis 28:3 El Shaddai is translated as "God Almighty"; in Genesis 49:25, El Shaddai is also translated as "Almighty," but with reference to God's womb and breasts.

9. Before settling in the land of Canaan, the Israelites' sanctuary for the worship of the God of Israel, containing the Ark of the Covenant, was portable, and it would be placed where the tent of meeting was set up. After settling in the land, the sanctuary and the Ark were set up at Shiloh (Joshua 18:1), where a structure with doors (1 Samuel 3:15) was built. 1 Samuel 4–7 describes the Ark of the Covenant being stolen by the Philistines, who kept it for seven months before returning it to the Israelites. The sanctuary and the Ark were transferred to the temple built by King Solomon in Jerusalem in the tenth century B.C.E. This First Temple was destroyed by the Babylonians in 586 B.C.E., marking the beginning of the Babylonian captivity of Jewish priests and aristocrats.

Seventh-day Adventists and Branch Davidians believe that prior to the destruction of the First Temple, the Ark of the Covenant was hidden in a cave. Citing 2 Maccabees in the Roman Catholic and Eastern Orthodox Bibles, chapter 2, verses 4–7, and Ellen G. White, *The Story of Prophets and Kings as Illustrated in the Captivity and Restoration of Israel* (1917), 453 (located at http://www.whiteestate.org/books/pk/pk.asp and other websites), they believe the prophecy indicated that the Ark of the Covenant would not be returned to Israel until the gathering of God's people in the Last Days.

After the Jews in Babylon were liberated by Cyrus, king of the Persian Empire, when he defeated the Babylonian Empire in 538 B.C.E., the Second Temple was built in Jerusalem by 520 B.C.E. The Ark of the Covenant was not in this Second Temple. This was the temple in existence in Jerusalem during the ministry of Jesus of Nazareth. It was destroyed by the Romans in 70 C.E.

Revelation 11:19 refers to the sanctuary in heaven. The sanctuary figures prominently in Seventh-day Adventist theology.

10. The Greek word *christos* ("christ" in English) was used to translate the Hebrew word *messiah*. It means "anointed" and refers to one who is anointed by God for a special mission. See the discussion of the historical development of the term's meaning in Tabor and Gallagher, *Why Waco?* 55–56; and in James D. Tabor and J. Phillip Arnold, "Commentary on the Koresh Manuscript," in Tabor and Gallagher, *Why Waco?* 205.

11. Bonnie Haldeman, David Koresh's mother, presents her recollections of his childhood and life in *Memories of the Branch Davidians: The Autobiography of David Koresh's Mother*, ed. Catherine Wessinger (Waco: Baylor University Press, 2007).

12. The composite image of the front of the building shown in the photospread shows that a sheet has been hung from a central tower window on which Bible verses have been written. The words on the sheet read: "1st Seal" in red with a line drawn under it, and three passages written in black, Rev. 6:1, 2 (in which the First Seal is opened and the rider on the white horse appears); Ps. 45, Rev. 19 (about the marriage of the Lamb, the marriage supper, and the rider on the white horse and his victory); followed by three psalms written in blue, Ps. 2, Ps. 18, Ps 35; followed by KJV in black letters, for King James Version of the Bible. The verses in Psalm 2:1–2 were often cited by David Koresh: *Why do the heathen rage, and the people imagine a vain thing? The kings of the earth set themselves, and the rulers take counsel together, against the Lord, and against his anointed. . . .*

13. Out of the twenty-three children age fifteen and under who died in the fire on April 19, 1993, fourteen were David Koresh's biological children. This number for

David's children who died includes two near-term infants who were born and died during the CS gas and tank assault and the fire. Sixteen of the twenty-three children who died were age eight and under. "List of Mount Carmel Branch Davidians," in Tabor and Gallagher, *Why Waco?* unnumbered last page (255).

Before he came to Mount Carmel in 1981 he had a daughter with his girlfriend, Linda Campion, whom he wished to marry but was prevented from doing so by her father. In 1990 Robyn Bunds, one of David's nonlegal wives, left the Branch Davidians, taking their son, Shaun. In 1992 Dana Okimoto, another unofficial wife, left the community, taking two sons, Sky and Scooter. Therefore David Koresh has four surviving offspring out of a total of eighteen known children. David Thibodeau and Leon Whiteson, *A Place Called Waco: A Survivor's Story* (New York: Public Affairs, 1999), 40–42; Haldeman, *Memories of the Branch Davidians*, 23–24; David G. Bromley and Catherine Wessinger, "Millennial Visions and Conflict with Society," in *Oxford Handbook of Millennialism*, ed. Catherine Wessinger (New York: Oxford University Press, 2011), 205.

14. See the discussion of the two-horned beast in this chapter.

15. *The Leviticus of the Davidian Seventh-day Adventists* (n.p.: 1943), 3.

16. The Hebrew name Dawid means "beloved."

17. After a coalition of nations was formed to drive the forces of Saddam Hussein of Iraq from Kuwait in the Persian Gulf War, President George H. W. Bush gave a speech before Congress in which he used the term "new world order" to refer to: "A new era—freer from the threat of terror, stronger in the pursuit of justice and more secure in the quest for peace. An era in which the nations of the world, east and west, north and south, can prosper and live in harmony." George H. W. Bush, "Address before a Joint Session of Congress on the Persian Gulf Crisis and the Federal Budget Deficit," September 11, 1990, http://en.wikisource.org/wiki/Toward_a_New_World_Order. Clive specifically mentions President Bush's new world order speech in Doyle transcript no. 28, interview with Catherine Wessinger on August 20, 2006, in Waco.

18. Genesis 11:1–9 tells the story of humans in a city attempting to build a tower to reach the Lord. The Lord destroyed the tower, and since everyone at that time spoke a single language, He scattered the people and made them speak different languages so that humans would not make the attempt again. The city in question reportedly was given the name Babel, after the Hebrew word *balal*, meaning "confusion."

CHAPTER 5

1. See "Lois Roden, Vernon Howell, and George Roden" in chapter 3.

2. Aisha married Greg Summers, an American citizen, so that she could stay in the United States. They did not live together as husband and wife.

3. See Marc Breault and Martin King, *Inside the Cult: A Member's Chilling, Exclusive Account of Madness and Depravity in David Koresh's Compound* (New York: Signet Books, 1993), for an anticult account. For a scholarly account, see James D. Tabor and Eugene V. Gallagher, *Why Waco? Cults and the Battle for Religious Freedom in America* (Berkeley and Los Angeles: University of California Press, 1995), 80–93.

4. Bonnie Haldeman, *Memories of the Branch Davidians: The Autobiography of David Koresh's Mother*, ed. Catherine Wessinger (Waco: Baylor University Press, 2007), 142–43n66.

5. Of the fifth and sixth Branch Davidians who were killed on February 28, Peter Gent's body was retrieved from the water tower later in the siege, and Mike Schroeder was shot and killed by ATF agents outside the Mount Carmel property.

6. Deposition of Livingstone Fagan, February 1, 2000, United States District Court for the Western District of Texas–Waco Division, No. W-96-CA-139, *Isabel G. Andrade et al. v. Phillip J. Chojnacki et al.*, 64, 162.

7. A convenient list of the dates and times that people left the building during the siege is given in Kenneth G. C. Newport, *The Branch Davidians of Waco: The History and Beliefs of an Apocalyptic Sect* (Oxford: Oxford University Press, 2006), 363–64. This information is also found in "Chronological Table of Events," Appendix C in John C. Danforth, Special Counsel, "Final Report to the Deputy Attorney General Concerning the 1993 Confrontation at the Mt. Carmel Complex," November 8, 2000. A full copy of the Danforth Final Report is available in the Wittliff Collections, Texas State University, San Marcos. A pdf version minus the extensive appendices is available at http://www.apologeticsindex.org/pdf/finalreport.pdf, accessed September 6, 2011. This chronological table is by no means complete. In the following notes the FBI's WACMUR Major Event Log, February–July 1993, available in the Lee Hancock Collection, Southwestern Writers Collection, Texas State University, San Marcos, will also be cited. WACMUR, the name for the FBI operation at Mount Carmel, is an acronym for "Waco Murders."

8. Livingstone Fagan's theological writings are found on his website, David Koresh, http://david.koresh-lf-2009.angelfire.com/index.html. His prison composition, "Mt. Carmel: The Unseen Reality," is located on several websites, including the original typescript manuscript in the Dick Reavis Collection in the Southwestern Writers Collection, Texas State University, San Marcos, http://cdm15042 .contentdm.oclc.org/cdm4/item_viewer.php?CISOROOT=/p9010coll4&CISOPTR= 275&CISOBOX=1&REC=2, accessed September 6, 2011. This essay is discussed in Eugene V. Gallagher, "The Persistence of the Millennium: Branch Davidian Expectations of the End after 'Waco,'" *Nova Religio* 3, no. 2 (April 2000): 303–19.

9. A lot of these people converted to David's message as a result of Steve Schneider's trips to England in 1988 and 1990. Newport, *Branch Davidians of Waco*, 198; Steve Schneider, audiotaped Bible studies given in Manchester, England, in 1990, in the Texas Collection, Baylor University.

10. Renos Avraam, teaching under the name Chosen Vessel, claims that he has a prophetic message and is David Koresh's successor. See the discussion in Gallagher, "Persistence of the Millennium." Chosen Vessel predicted that in August 2012 a comet striking the Earth would cause the cataclysmic events described in the book of Revelation. See New Light Publications, http://www.sevenseals.com/index.php, accessed September 6, 2011.

11. Women at Mount Carmel sewed ammunition vests for sale at gun shows. This business was called Mag Bag, and its mailing address was the car repair shop down the road from Mount Carmel, so during the siege reporters started calling the car shop the Mag Bag. The Branch Davidians did not call it that.

12. Haldeman, *Memories of the Branch Davidians*, 36, 47, 52–54, 60, 72.

13. To view the memorial stones for Branch Davidians buried at McLennan County Restland Cemetery, go to Matthew Wittmer's website, http://www.storm-bound.org/waco.html.

14. Matteson Transcript no. 1, interview with Catherine Wessinger in Waco, Texas, on October 1, 2004; Matteson Transcript no. 2, interview with Catherine Wessinger in Waco, Texas, on October 11, 2004; Matteson Transcript no. 4, interview with Catherine Wessinger in Waco, Texas, on November 26, 2004, in the Texas Collection, Baylor University; Catherine Wessinger, *How the Millennium Comes Violently: From Jonestown to Heaven's Gate* (New York: Seven Bridges Press, 2000), 71–72. In her earlier years with the Branch Davidians she called herself Kay Matteson.

15. Haldeman, *Memories of the Branch Davidians.*

16. Kiri Jewell testified in the congressional hearings that her mother took her to a motel room when she was ten, where David Koresh had sexual contact with her. Kiri's allegations contributed to an investigation by a social worker with Texas Child Protective Services, who closed the case for lack of evidence. "Statement of Kiri Jewell," and "Statement of Joyce Sparks," in Joint Hearings, *Activities of Federal Law Enforcement Agencies (Part I), Committee on the Judiciary* Serial No. 72 (Washington, DC: US Government Printing Office, 1996), 147–57, 575–79; Newport, *Branch Davidians of Waco*, 202–3.

17. Interview with Paul Fatta facilitated by Catherine Wessinger at the CESNUR conference at San Diego State University, July 15, 2006, transcript in the possession of Catherine Wessinger.

18. At that time in Texas a fourteen-year-old girl could get married with the permission of her parents. The legal age of marriage with parental consent in Texas was raised to sixteen in 2005 as a result of a bill introduced by Harvey Hilderbran of Schleicher County, where the Yearning for Zion Ranch, a Fundamentalist Church of Jesus Christ of Latter-day Saints community, was located. Individuals who are sixteen or seventeen must have judicial approval or parental consent. Personal communication from Stuart A. Wright, August 24, 2011.

19. Beginning in 1986 Koresh began taking other young women in the community to be his wives and to bear God's children for special roles in the end-time events and the coming Kingdom. Some of these were fourteen years old and younger. Michele Jones became one of Koresh's wives in 1986 when she was twelve, with the permission of her parents.

David Koresh was vulnerable to complaint from the young women who were underage when Koresh initiated his sexual relationship with them and being charged with statutory rape. At that time in Texas, it was a first-degree felony to have sex with a girl under fourteen, and a second-degree felony if a man had sex with a girl under eighteen who was not married to him. Newport, *Branch Davidians of Waco*, 200.

20. See Sheila Martin, *When They Were Mine: Memoirs of a Branch Davidian Wife and Mother*, ed. Catherine Wessinger (Waco: Baylor University Press, 2009).

21. Jimmy Riddle died of a gunshot to the head. His right arm and shoulder blade were sheered off. His autopsy indicated no smoke inhalation or carbon monoxide in his blood. In Rick Van Vleet, Stephen M. Novak, Jason Van Vleet, and Michael McNulty, producers, *Waco: A New Revelation* (MGA Films, 1999), it is reported that when Rita Riddle arranged for a second autopsy on Jimmy's skeletal remains, it was discovered that the portion of the skull with the bullet hole was

missing. See also the discussion of Jimmy Riddle's death in David T. Hardy with Rex Kimball, *This Is Not an Assault: Penetrating the Web of Official Lies Regarding the Waco Incident* (n.p.: Xlibris, 2001), 44–45, 49–50.

22. This is apparent in videotape shot inside the building after the ATF raid, in which Judy Schneider indicts government actions on February 28 and after. Three videotapes shot by the Branch Davidians were compiled into one and named "Inside Mount Carmel," available in the Texas Collection, Baylor University. Selections from this video footage are shown in Dan Gifford, William Gazecki, and Michael McNulty, producers, *Waco: The Rules of Engagement* (Los Angeles: Fifth Estate Productions, 1997).

23. For a visual documentation of Mount Carmel and the changes there since the year 2000, see Matthew D. Wittmer's website, Memorializing Mount Carmel Center East of Waco, Texas, http://www.stormbound.org/waco.html.

24. In Clive's words: The print shop had been at the back end of that building. Catherine Matteson was in charge of audiotaping under Lois Roden, so she had access to a big office near the front door of the Administration Building. There was another section of that building that they sometimes used for school classrooms. Perry Jones had the secretary's office and other things in a hall that ran to the back to the print room. There were toilets and storerooms. Doyle no. 22, transcript of interview of Clive Doyle by Catherine Wessinger on November 27, 2004, at Mount Carmel Center.

25. The long room on the very north end of the men's dorm area, which was dedicated to tool storage and Cliff Sellors's art supplies, as Clive describes next, did not have windows.

26. David was aware that the activities of Marc Breault had led to several investigations. The investigation of Child Protective Services into child abuse had been closed due to lack of evidence. David knew that the ATF was making inquiries about his gun purchases. Two ATF agents, including Davey Aguilera, who wrote the affidavit to secure the warrants for February 28, 1993, had visited Henry McMahon, a firearms dealer, in July 1992 and made inquiries about David's gun purchases. McMahon called David and told him the agents were there asking questions. David said, "Well, if there is a problem tell them to come out here." McMahon asked the agents several times whether they wanted to speak to David, who was on the phone, but they declined. McMahon told the agents they were invited to go out to Mount Carmel to inspect the weapons, and Aguilera said, "We do not need to go out there at this time." "Statement of Henry McMahon," in Joint Hearings, *Activities of Federal Law Enforcement Agencies*, 1:162.

27. Bonnie Haldeman in *Memories of the Branch Davidians*, 73, reports that on a visit to Mount Carmel in 1992 she saw "provisions stacked everywhere." Catherine Matteson reports that most of the women and children were gradually moved to rooms upstairs for protection. Livingstone Fagan and Graeme Craddock report that the thin outer walls were reinforced with poured concrete from the bottom of the windows to the floor to provide protection from gunfire. Craddock reports that supplies were accumulated in anticipation of a siege. Matteson transcript no. 3, interview with Catherine Wessinger on November 26, 2004, in Waco; Deposition of Livingstone Fagan, February 1, 2000; Testimony of Graeme Craddock, United

States District Court, Western District of Texas, Waco Division, Federal Grand Jury Proceedings, April 20, 1993, 5–8, 29–30, 47–48.

David was probably aware that a former member had been counseled by a deprogrammer named Rick Ross. This may have prompted David to move the weapons from one of his rooms over the chapel (#21b in figure 4 in appendix) to the vault. The information gained from this individual may have been the reason ATF agents entered the two rooms over the chapel during the "dynamic entry" on February 28. Doyle transcript no. 12, interview of Clive Doyle by Catherine Wessinger on October 9, 2004, at Mount Carmel. On the role Rick Ross played in the events, see Tabor and Gallagher, *Why Waco?* 93–96, 100.

28. Chris Peacock, Director of Public Affairs, Department of the Treasury, "Memorandum to the Press: Weapons Possessed by the Branch Davidians," July 13, 1995, available at http://www.pbs.org/wgbh/pages/frontline/waco/treasury.html.

29. See "Statement of Henry McMahon," 162; Dick J. Reavis, *The Ashes of Waco: An Investigation* (New York: Simon & Schuster, 1995), 36–38. The gun parts were legal. The infraction that ATF agents suspected, but for which they had no proof, was that David Koresh was having semiautomatic weapons converted to automatic weapons without obtaining the proper licenses and paying the related fees. Carol Moore, *The Davidian Massacre: Disturbing Questions about Waco Which Must Be Answered* (Franklin, TN, and Springfield, VA: Legacy Communications and Gun Owners Foundation, 1995), at http://www.carolmoore.net./waco/TDM-index.html, 48–53, 62–71.

30. Bonnie Haldeman, *Memories of the Branch Davidians*, 73, reports that on a visit David took his stepfather, Roy Haldeman, upstairs "to the gunroom and showed him all the guns." Bonnie was not interested in guns, so she did not go to look. Roy told her "about all of these guns that were collector's items. A lot of them were in cases."

31. Owner of the Double EE Ranch.

32. Immigration and Naturalization Service.

33. David Thibodeau and Leon Whiteson, *A Place Called Waco: A Survivor's Story* (New York: Public Affairs, 1999), 142–44, provides similar, but slightly different, accounts of these interactions with the ATF undercover agents.

Bonnie Haldeman, *Memories of the Branch Davidians*, 74, reports that when she visited Mount Carmel the women told her that they were aware that the men across the street were not students and that they were watching Mount Carmel. They said that the men were older than the usual student age and drove very nice cars, unlike students. They told her, "Helicopters were coming over all the time." "Chronological Table," Danforth Report, 7, 13, 14, 16, 19, states that Texas National Guard flew aerial surveillance missions over Mount Carmel on January 6, February 3, 6,18, and 25, 1993, but does not state the nature of the aircraft. On page 8 it reports that ATF surveillance operations began from a rented house on January 11, 1993.

34. David Thibodeau reports that Robert Rodriguez was the ATF agent who brought the rifle to David Koresh to examine and that it was an AR-15. Thibodeau and Whiteson, *A Place Called Waco*, 145.

35. David Hardy states that this event of ATF agents shooting guns with David Koresh on the Mount Carmel property occurred on February 19, 1993, as reported

in an ATF internal memo. See Hardy with Kimball, *This Is Not an Assault*, 67. Hardy quotes from the ATF memo on pages 174–75, and it is replicated on page 326. The report states that ATF agents Robert Rodriguez and Jeffrey Brzozowski brought two AR-15 rifles to Koresh to examine. The report states that Koresh took them through the building and out back, where he supplied .223 caliber rounds to shoot. Rodriguez permitted Koresh and two other Branch Davidian men to shoot his .38 Super pistol.

Hardy, like Clive Doyle, stresses that there were ample opportunities for ATF agents to arrest David Koresh without launching a dynamic entry on February 28 to serve an arrest warrant and a search warrant. According to Clive Doyle in Doyle transcript no. 13, interview with Catherine Wessinger at Mount Carmel on October 11, 2004 (text is copyedited):

> David did business downtown. He went downtown for haircuts, to buy car parts, things like that. We even had witnesses to that effect—business people, or people who worked at various establishments—who had seen him and had done business with him. Not only that, he went jogging down the gravel road out in front of the property [the Double EE Ranch Road], and sometimes he went down the road in a go-cart.
>
> I do not know the last time he went out, but David and some of the guys in the band would go to town and jam, play with people at different clubs. There are all kinds of situations where David was off the property.
>
> During the criminal trial in 1994, an ATF agent was asked by one of our lawyers: Did you keep a log of everybody that came out of the property? Oh, yes, we logged everything. Then he was asked: Did you ever see a black Camaro going in and out of the gate? Oh yeah. Well, that was David Koresh's car.
>
> The fact of the matter was that the agents were coming over to Mount Carmel from that house across the street on numerous occasions. They were coming over on one excuse or another: to look at things they want to buy, or to show David their guns. They came for Bible studies. It was just a bald-faced lie to say in the trial: We did not know what he looked like. The undercover ATF agents said that in court under oath.

36. See discussion of the "Sinful Messiah" series in Tabor and Gallagher, *Why Waco?* 117–20; and Catherine Wessinger, "The Branch Davidians and Religion Reporting: A Ten-Year Retrospective," in *Expecting the End: Millennialism in Social and Historical Context*, ed. Kenneth G. C. Newport and Crawford Gribben (Waco: Baylor University Press, 2006), 148–274.

37. The first story in the "Sinful Messiah" series alleged that in addition to accumulating weapons, David Koresh engaged in child abuse by spanking small children severely and by having sex with underage girls. Koresh was depicted as being a "cult leader." Wessinger, "Branch Davidians and Religion Reporting," 149.

The Branch Davidians spanked misbehaving children with small wooden paddles. Bonnie Haldeman, *Memories of the Branch Davidians*, 100, says that a child was told what he or she did wrong, paddled lightly, and then "loved." To date, surviving children, now young adults, have not corroborated allegations of severe spankings.

38. "Chronological Table," Danforth Report, 24, indicates that Robert Rodriguez entered the building at Mount Camel at 8:00 a.m., and David Jones encountered KWTX-TV cameraman James Peeler at 8:30 a.m. ATF agents at the undercover house observed David Jones go back to Mount Carmel at 8:40 a.m., after which David

Koresh told Robert Rodriguez that he knew a raid was imminent. Rodriguez left Mount Carmel at 9:05 a.m. to return to the undercover house.

There was also another KWTX-TV vehicle with John McLemore, a reporter, and Dan Mulloney, a cameraman, and three vehicles containing *Waco-Tribune Herald* reporters on the roads outside Mount Carmel that morning. When the ATF raid was carried out at 9:45 a.m., Mulloney and McLemore's vehicle pulled in the Mount Carmel driveway behind the cattle trailers carrying the ATF agents. When shooting broke out, Mulloney and McLemore took cover behind a bus parked to the southwest of the building. The *Waco Tribune-Herald* reporters took cover in a ditch on Double EE Ranch Road. Although ATF agents were shooting video footage and still photos, the videotape taken from the undercover house and the still camera disappeared, and the videotape shot from helicopters developed gaps at key moments. The footage shot by Mulloney is the footage that is seen in news reporting and documentaries about the case. Wessinger, "Branch Davidians and Religion Reporting," 149–50; Hardy with Kimball, *This Is Not an Assault*, 196–98.

39. Rodriguez testified before the congressional hearing in 1995 that David Koresh was shaking visibly when he returned from speaking to Perry Jones, and he said, "Robert, neither the ATF or the National Guard will ever get me. They got me once, and they'll never get me again." "Statement of Robert Rodriguez," in Joint Hearings, *Activities of Federal Law Enforcement Agencies*, 1:749.

40. David Koresh and some of the other men had been arrested in 1987 for getting into a shoot-out with George Roden at Mount Carmel. A trial in 1988 acquitted Koresh's companions of attempted murder, and the jury was hung in relation to Koresh. They were all released. Wessinger, *How the Millennium Comes Violently*, 83.

41. David Thibodeau says that David Koresh told Robert Rodriguez, "They're coming." He said, "You've got to do what you've got to do, Robert." He shook Robert's hand and said, "Good luck." Rodriguez got in his truck and with lights flashing drove down the driveway and across the road to the undercover house. Thibodeau and Whiteson, *A Place Called Waco*, 164. Sheila Martin, who was in her room on the southwest front corner of the second floor, heard a siren coming from Rodriguez's truck and the horn beep four times. Martin, *When They Were Mine*, 51.

42. Robert Rodriguez informed the ATF agents in the undercover house, including Jim Cavanaugh, deputy tactical commander, that the Branch Davidians knew that a raid was imminent. He then called Chuck Sarabyn, assistant special agent in charge, the tactical coordinator who was with the ATF agents at the staging area at the Texas State Technical College (see figure 1 in appendix), to tell him to call off the raid because the Branch Davidians knew they were coming. Sarabyn and Special Agents in Charge Phillip Chojnacki, the incident commander, and Ted Royster decided to proceed with the raid. They ordered the agents to hurry up to prepare to depart. John R. Hall, "Public Narratives and the Apocalyptic Sect: From Jonestown to Mt. Carmel," in *Armageddon in Waco: Critical Perspectives on the Branch Davidian Conflict*, ed. Stuart A. Wright (Chicago: University of Chicago Press, 1995), 227; Joint Hearings, *Activities of Federal Law Enforcement Agencies*, 1:411–12, 427–29. ATF agent Mike Curtis testified in the criminal trial that he heard Sarabyn say, "Let's go! It's show time! Come on, hurry up! They know we're coming!" Summary of

testimony in Jack DeVault, *The Waco Whitewash: The Mt. Carmel Episode Told by an Eyewitness to the Trial* (San Antonio: Rescue Press, 1994), 82. "Show time" was the "initiation code" for the raid to commence. Hardy with Kimball, *This Is Not an Assault*, 144. The name for the raid was Operation Trojan Horse.

43. David Koresh told his account of what happened later on February 28 in an interview on KRLD radio:

> I had the front door open so they could clearly see me. Then what happened was, I told them, I said, "Get back. There's women and children here. I want to talk." About that time, all of a sudden, a nine-millimeter round started firing at the front wall. (David Koresh, KRLD interview audiotape, February 28, 1993, transcription by Catherine Wessinger.)

44. Wayne Martin dialed 911 at 9:48 a.m. shouting, "There are seventy-five men around our building and they're shooting at us in Mount Carmel. Tell them there are children and women in here and to call it off!" Wessinger, *How the Millennium Comes Violently*, 68; Hardy with Kimball, *This Is Not an Assault*, 209.

The first few minutes of Wayne Martin's 911 call are often quoted, but it is less known that the telephone line to Wayne's office was kept open for more than twenty-four hours with Deputy Sheriff Larry Lynch and, after 12:00 p.m., FBI Supervisory Special Agent Byron Sage, negotiating with Wayne Martin while ATF Special Agent Jim Cavanaugh, negotiated with Steve Schneider and the wounded David Koresh. Matthew Wittmer and Catherine Wessinger have listened to all of the 911 tapes recorded during the first twenty-four hours after the initial gunfire the morning of February 28, 1993. After working with Wayne Martin to obtain a cease-fire, the removal of the bodies of the four ATF agents who had been killed and the wounded ATF agents, and the exit of four children that evening, the arrival of Byron Sage signaled the stage in which Sage and Lynch attempted to persuade Wayne to "exercise leadership" and send more children out and resolve the siege. Wayne consistently said that he deferred to the authority of David Koresh, and there were intervals while consultations with David were held. On occasions, it was reported that David was on the telephone speaking with reporters and could not be interrupted. The line to Wayne Martin's office was closed when FBI negotiators took over direct negotiations with David Koresh and Steve Schneider on a secured line that the Branch Davidians could not use to make calls to other parties.

We thank Ken Fawcett for providing us with the digitized audiofiles of the 911 call. Fawcett purchased the audiotapes from the sheriff's department a few months after the April 19, 1993, fire at Mount Carmel.

DeVault, *Waco Whitewash*, 208–35, provides a transcript of the first hour of the 911 call. DeVault points out that during the criminal trial the following statements made by Wayne Martin were excised from the audiotape and transcript presented to the jury: "I have a right to defend myself! They started firing first!" (214); "They started firing at us first!" (235).

That evening David Koresh spoke by telephone to CNN and KRLD radio.

45. David Koresh displayed his wounds on videotape that was sent out to FBI negotiators during the siege. This footage can be seen in Gifford, Gazecki, and McNulty, *Waco: The Rules of Engagement*.

46. Bonnie Haldeman was outside, so she missed his telephone call. The message he left on her answering machine said: "Hello Mama. It's your boy. They shot me and I'm dying, alright? But I'll be back real soon, okay? I'm sorry you did not learn the Seals, but I'll be merciful, okay? I'll see y'all in the skies." Reavis, *Ashes of Waco*, 24.

47. According to the autopsy report the cause of death was "craniocerebral trauma due to gunshot wound to mouth." No other wound was reported. Marc A. Krouse, Autopsy Report for Perry Jones, Case No. MC-80, 930087#, May 5, 1993, available at http://www.public-action.com/SkyWriter/WacoMuseum/death/80/80_aut.html. Contested Branch Davidian autopsies such as that of Perry Jones could not be verified by subsequent examinations because the cooler containing Branch Davidian remains malfunctioned and the bodies became "like soup." Reavis, *Ashes of Waco*, 148–49. Copies of the autopsy reports in pdf format are available in the Texas Collection, Baylor University in the Matthew D. Wittmer Collection.

48. When he and Wayne Martin went outside the building to negotiate face to face with Byron Sage and Sheriff Jack Harwell on March 15, Steve Schneider mentioned how distressing it was when "a sixty-four-year-old man drops to the floor, crying, screaming, bloody. . . ." "Face-to-face" audiotape available in the Mark Swett Collection, Texas Collection, Baylor University.

49. Larry Lynch was elected McLennan County sheriff in 2000. He retired as sheriff in 2012. "Sheriff Larry Lynch to Step Down at End of Current Term," July 6, 2011, The Legendary, http://downdirtyword.blogspot.com/2011/07/sheriff-larry-lynch-to-step-down-after.html.

50. Wayne's wife, Sheila, reports that she heard Wayne shouting from her room upstairs (#23 in figure 4 in appendix). Martin, *When They Were Mine*, 54.

51. In a telephone conversation on December 11, 2011, Clive Doyle explained to Catherine Wessinger that what Scott meant was that he was in the former gun room (#21b in figure 4 in appendix) when the ATF agents came in the window. He ran out the door leading to what federal agents called the "dog run" (#20 in figure 4), but he was shot and wounded by the agents. The ATF agents had vacated the rooms (#21a and #21b) by the time that Clive saw Scott wounded and leaning against the wall of David Koresh's former bedroom (#21a).

52. FBI WACMUR Event Log entry for March 11, 11:34 a.m., states that the bullet was still in Scott Sonobe's thigh.

53. The ATF agents began leaving at 12:12 p.m. "Chronological Table," Danforth Report, 28.

54. Kenneth King, Todd McKeehan (twenty-eight), David Millen, and Conway LeBleu (thirty) were the ATF agents who entered David Koresh's former room on the second floor over the chapel. McKeehan and LeBleu were killed. King and Millen were wounded, and King was severely wounded and nearly died. A second team of agents on the roof entered the other room belonging to Koresh where the guns had previously been stored; this room was on the outside wall of the building. Bill Buford and Glen Jordan were wounded there. Robert Williams (twenty-six) was killed at a location on the ground. Steve Willis (thirty-two) was killed by gunfire at the front of the building. Twenty-seven agents were wounded by bullets and shrapnel. Wessinger, *How the Millennium Comes Violently*, 67–68.

55. A total of seventy-six ATF agents were involved in the raid. Some were in the three National Guard helicopters.

56. At the sentencing in 1994, Kevin Whitecliff said that he did not know the men were ATF until they were leaving and he saw "the letters on their backs." DeVault, *Waco Whitewash*, 182.

57. The affidavit written by ATF agent Davy Aguilera to obtain the warrants from a US magistrate judge alleged that the Branch Davidians were converting semiautomatic weapons to automatic weapons without obtaining the necessary permits, which involved paying fees in taxes. Robert Rodriguez had reported that he had seen no evidence of illegal weapons at Mount Carmel. To obtain the warrants, Aguilera's affidavit alleged that Koresh was a cult leader who abusively spanked small children and sexually abused underage girls, matters that did not come under the jurisdiction of the ATF. Tabor and Gallagher, *Why Waco?* 100–103. The nature of the evidence concerning the guns presented in the affidavit is discussed in Moore, *Davidian Massacre*, 50–63.

58. This nervousness was evident in Wayne Martin's telephone negotiations with Larry Lynch and Byron Sage through the night. Wayne repeatedly demanded that agents be completely off the Mount Carmel property; however, there were still agents in the barn behind the property and across the Double EE Ranch Road in the front. Visible movement among the agents as they changed shifts or drove up and down Double EE Ranch Road caused a lot of concern. Wayne expressed a fear that a helicopter would fly overhead and drop a bomb, causing a fire, probably reflecting awareness of the MOVE incident in Philadelphia in 1985. When helicopters flew over, he was told that they were news reporters and the agents were attempting to clear them out of the airspace over Mount Carmel.

59. Koresh's message was broadcast on KRLD AM radio at 7:38 and 9:11 p.m. "Chronological Table," 32.

60. "Chronological Table," Danforth Report, 32, 35, 38–39; Newport, *Branch Davidians of Waco*, 363.

61. "Forward observer" is a military term that has been appropriated by law enforcement to refer to snipers. The term obscures the fact that these individuals are "observing" through rifle scopes.

62. Michael Schroeder's autopsy has been uploaded to a memorial website, Michael Schroeder 1963–1993, accessed August 18, 2011, http://www.wizardsofaz. com/waco/mikeautop.html. DeVault, *Waco Whitewash*, 125, summarizes the autopsy findings: "His body had suffered six bullet wounds, only one of which was minor. Any of the five others would have knocked Schroeder to the ground, gravely injured. From this we can assume that no later than the second shot, he was knocked down."

63. Examination of the stocking cap for traces of gunpowder would have indicated whether or not the two bullets to Mike's head had been fired at close range. DeVault, *Waco Whitewash*, 125.

64. DeVault, *Waco Whitewash*, 124–25, reports that three days after the ATF raid, federal agents went in a helicopter to photograph Mike Schroeder's corpse wearing the blue stocking cap. When the body was picked up a day or two later, the cap had disappeared.

65. Gary Noesner, who was the head of the FBI negotiating team at Waco until March 23, stated that the actions of the tactical unit, the Hostage Rescue Team

(HRT), undermined the successes the negotiators were having in securing the release of children and the exit of adults, in *CNN Presents: Faith, Fear and Fire*, which aired on April 17, 2011, and in his book, *Stalling for Time: My Life as an FBI Hostage Negotiator* (New York: Random House, 2010). He also articulated his criticism in internal FBI memos, which came to light in 1999. See Lee Hancock, "FBI Missteps Doomed Siege Talks, Memos Say," *Dallas Morning News*, December 30, 1999; Stuart A. Wright, "A Decade after Waco: Reassessing Crisis Negotiations at Mount Carmel in Light of New Government Disclosures," *Nova Religio* 7, no. 2 (November 2003): 101–10; Noesner's memos in the Lee Hancock Collection, Southwestern Writers Collection, Texas State University, San Marcos. Jayne Seminare Docherty has analyzed the FBI negotiations with the Branch Davidians in *Learning Lessons from Waco: When the Parties Bring Their Gods to the Negotiation Table* (Syracuse: Syracuse University Press, 2001).

66. On March 22 at 9:10 a.m., in response to Steve Schneider's anger at the high-decibel noise blasted at them all night, a negotiator told him, "There's two factions here, us [the negotiators] and the tactical. . . ." FBI WACMUR Event Log.

67. Gifford, Gazecki, and McNulty, *Waco: The Rules of Engagement*, shows footage of the tank running over and moving vehicles, overturning and pushing a boat back from the building, knocking down the southern end of the fence, and knocking down the tall tree with green foliage that was outside Clive's window. This footage in the movie is located after the statement of Nicole Gent, holding her son Dayland in her lap, and before the statement of Theresa Nobrega. The composite image of the building in the photospread was taken after the tree and these vehicles were crushed and moved but before the remaining vehicles and the fence were removed by the tanks.

68. Newport, *Branch Davidians of Waco*, 363.

69. The audiotape was played on KRLD radio and on the Christian Broadcasting Network at 2:30 p.m. At 5:59 p.m. the negotiators were told that God had told David to wait. "Chronological Table," Danforth Report, 37.

70. Kathy Schroeder and Victorine Hollingsworth, who came out later during the siege and were interviewed by FBI agents, alleged that some Branch Davidians, believing that Koresh was dying, had developed a plan to carry him out on a stretcher, and then Branch Davidians would commit suicide by gunfire and grenades. Newport, *Branch Davidians of Waco*, 266–69; Reavis, *Ashes of Waco*, 216. This report is disputed by Clive Doyle and other survivors. If some Branch Davidians had developed such a plan, then David's saying that God had said to wait was a positive development.

71. Moore, *Davidian Massacre*, 211. From March 12 on, Steve Schneider expressed anger at the electricity being cut off. He reiterated that cutting the electricity off was a huge setback in the trust-building efforts of the negotiators. He also complained about the cold temperature inside the building. FBI WACMUR Event Log.

72. David was concerned to preserve the building as evidence of the ATF agents shooting at them on February 28. Jack Zimmerman, Steve Schneider's attorney, a retired Marine colonel who had combat service as a commander in Vietnam and who had served as a chief prosecutor, chief defense counsel, and trial judge in the Marine Corps, testified during the 1994 criminal trial that he went inside the building twice during the siege, inspected the building, and interviewed Branch Davidians, who alleged that ATF agents fired first and did most of the shooting, and that agents in the

National Guard helicopters fired down at them. He saw holes made by incoming bullets in the roof of the chapel (while standing on the catwalk) and in the Sheetrock ceiling of the top room in the four-story central tower. He saw bullet holes going both directions in the walls of David's room above the chapel. He saw that the right-hand side of the metal double front door had numerous bullet holes going into the building, with a few bullet holes going outside the door. The left-hand side of the door was stationary, while the right-hand side of the door opened. In testimony in the 1995 congressional hearings, Zimmerman and Dick DeGuerin, David Koresh's attorney, made similar reports on their observations inside the building. DeGuerin characterized himself as a life-long hunter and reported he saw the same physical evidence as Zimmerman. Zimmerman and DeGuerin made the point that the bullet holes coming into the ceiling of the top tower room could have only been made by gunfire from the helicopters or someone standing on the roof. Since no one was standing on the roof of the four-story tower at any time during the raid or siege, they surmised the holes came from gunfire from the helicopters. They begged the congressional committees to obtain from the ATF and FBI videotape made on February 28 and the right-hand side of the front doors but were told that that the committees had been informed that the tape was blank and the right-hand door was missing. Zimmerman considered the ATF plan to assault the residence at Mount Carmel in a "no-knock" entry to be deeply flawed, endangering ATF agents and Branch Davidians, when the search warrant could have been served peacefully and David Koresh could have been arrested on one of the many occasions he left Mount Carmel. DeVault, *Waco White-wash*, 141–42; Testimony of Jack Zimmerman and Dick DeGuerin, in Joint Hearings, *Activities of Federal Law Enforcement Agencies*, 2:18–50.

73. The Branch Davidians and ATF agents disputed the origin of the gunshot that killed Peter Gent. The Branch Davidians alleged that he had been killed by gunfire from the helicopters. ATF agents alleged that Peter Gent was firing on them and he was shot by an agent on the ground. The autopsy report indicates a single bullet wound that traveled from the chest to the heel, suggesting the shot was fired from above. Reavis, *Ashes of Waco*, 132–33; Marc A. Krouse, M.D., Autopsy Report for Peter Gent, Case No. MC-76, 930083#, May 5, 1993, accessed September 9, 2011, http://www.public-action.com/SkyWriter/WacoMuseum/death/76/76_pg01 .gif. The origin of the gunshot that killed Peter Gent is important because it is illegal for the American military, in this case National Guard helicopters, to be involved in assaults against civilians. See discussion of the Posse Comitatus Act in later notes.

74. FBI WACMUR Event Log on March 5, 5:32 p.m., notes that Peter Gent's body had been retrieved. The notation states that the information was received from Steve Schneider at 5:32 p.m., but it is incorrectly entered into the log at 5:32 a.m. (5:32:00). The log uses military time designations.

75. Peter Gent was buried on March 8 at about 11:00 a.m. "Chronological Table," Danforth Report, 41.

76. Negotiation tape no. 42, undated, in the Mark Swett Collection in the Texas Collection at Baylor University records discussion of this incident. ATF commander Jim Cavanaugh told Rachel Koresh, "The guys in the tactical vehicles just told me that three men walked out of the house carrying guns." Rachel said, "No, I don't think that's true." Steve Schneider then checked to find that two men, "Cliff and Greg," had left the building, each was unarmed, and had left only to move the dogs.

After Steve discovered Clive had left the building as well, he told Cavanaugh that a third man "took it upon himself to go out there and collect; he was going to go collect some things that he thought belonged to some of the guys that were here. He totally took it upon himself, we knew nothing about it."

77. After the regular telephone line was cut off, Steve Schneider sometimes negotiated downstairs in the foyer using a phone with a line only to FBI negotiators. Negotiations were conducted upstairs also. Telephone conversation between Clive Doyle and Catherine Wessinger on December 7, 2011.

During the tank and CS gas assault on April 19, 1993, the Branch Davidians indicated that the telephone line to the negotiators had been severed by a tank and signaled that they wished that the line be repaired and negotiations restored. Receipt of this signal was acknowledged by Byron Sage, the negotiator who addressed the Branch Davidians over the loudspeaker. After the fire, FBI agents alleged that Steve Schneider had thrown the telephone out the front door as soon as he received a call from Byron Sage at 5:56 a.m. to tell the Branch Davidians that the tank and CS attack was "not an assault" and they should come out. Catherine Wessinger, "Deaths in the Fire at the Branch Davidians' Mount Carmel: Who Bears Responsibility?" *Nova Religio* 13, no. 2 (November 2009): 39–40; "Chronological Table," Danforth Report, 64.

78. Autopsy photo of Peter Gent, accessed August 4, 2011, http://www.public-action.com/SkyWriter/WacoMuseum/death/76/76_pix.html. In Gifford, Gazecki, and McNulty, *Waco: The Rules of Engagement*, David Thibodeau also tells of how the Branch Davidians were upset by the tanks running over Peter Gent's grave.

79. "Chronological Table," Danforth Report, 41, 43, 45; Moore, *Davidian Massacre*, 211.

80. Electricity was cut off and restored at least a couple of times before it was finally cut off on March 12. "Chronological Table," Danforth Report, 41, 43. FBI WACMUR Event Log, March 12, 1:22 p.m., records Steve Schneider arguing that Kathy Schroeder and Oliver Gyarfas coming out were "tangible results" and that cutting off the electricity undermined the efforts to get people to leave.

81. FBI WACMUR Event Log, March 18, 6:21–6:35 p.m., notes the demolition of the fuel tanks.

82. High-intensity lights were started on the evening of March 14–15. The use of the loudspeakers began on March 17. Wessinger, *How the Millennium Comes Violently*, 73–74; FBI WACMUR Event Log.

In addition to disrupting sleep, the spotlights and loudspeakers were used to prevent Branch Davidians from directing communications outside the building. SA 65 no. 13, undated surveillance audiotape (probably March 13) in the Mark Swett Collection, Texas Collection, Baylor University, records David Koresh and Steve Schneider discussing a Morse code message to be sent using a flashlight. David dictated the following message to Steve: "FBI broke negotiations. Want negotiations from press." The audiotape records Steve giving a soft-spoken man, perhaps Scott Sonobe, instructions on how to flash the Morse code.

This same audiotape records David attempting to raise a response to his calls on what sounds like a CB radio or a ham radio. He says, "This is Seraph. We need a copy. Anybody pick up, please. Over" (5:15 minutes into the tape/digital file). Traffic on the radio can be heard, but no one responds to Seraph. David complains, "Every idiot that don't have nothing to say gets on CB" (6:07 minutes). Clive Doyle reports that before the ATF raid occurred, Wayne Martin and Jeff Little were setting up a radio for communication at Mount Carmel. Telephone conversation with Catherine Wessinger, November 3, 2011.

FBI WACMUR Event Log entry for March 14, 11:05 a.m., gives a transcription of the flashlight Morse code message observed the night before: "SOS SOS SOS SOS FBI Broke Negotiations Want Negotiator From Press." Negotiation conversations and a telephone conversation between Aisha Gyarfas and her brother Oliver Gyarfas, who was in jail, noted in the log after that time indicate that the Branch Davidians considered the termination of their electricity to put a halt to genuine negotiation and the imposition of a strategy of coercion. The log entry for March 14, 4:40 p.m., states that a sign was hung out by Branch Davidians reading: "FBI Broke Negotiations—We Want Press." Later that evening of March 14–15, high-intensity lights were directed at the building and continued to be used until April 19. FBI WACMUR Event Log, March 15, 12:10 a.m.

83. Negotiation tape no. 80, March 7, 1993, in the Mark Swett Collection, records a negotiator telling David and Steve that they see residents inside wearing balaclavas (ski masks) or camouflage face paint looking at agents in the tanks through the building's windows and that the agents perceived this as threatening gestures, which angered Steve and David. Steve clarified that they did not possess balaclavas and that agents had seen "a dark-skinned woman that was looking out a window . . . that had a camouflage jacket on."

84. FBI WACMUR Event Log entry for March 23, 9:45 a.m., records that Steve Schneider complained that the Kathy Schroeder tape was "not liked by those inside."

85. FBI WACMUR Event Log entry, March 18, 11:10 a.m., records Steve Schneider as saying that was the first day that David got out of bed and walked to the phone. The log entry for March 20, 9:16 p.m., notes a telephone consultation between Special Agent in Charge Jeffrey Jamar in Waco and Deputy Assistant Director Danny Coulson in Washington, DC; they agreed that "more productive results" were achieved when the FBI applied pressure to the Branch Davidians, and they agreed that "more pressure is needed." The loud music playing all night began on March 21.

86. FBI WACMUR Event Log entry, March 21, 11:55 p.m., notes that this was the first night that music was played all night on the loudspeakers. Earlier, during that day, seven adults had come out. Steve Schneider reported that no one else would come out that night because of the noise. The entry notes that a generator had been started in the building. A little later David called to say that the noise was slowing down the negotiation process. On March 22, Steve reported that the people were in shock over the loud music all night. At 9:22 a.m., Steve asked, referring to the public and the media, "Will they know what you put us through?" An "Action Taken" note in the log for March 23 states: "Do not say anything on a bullhorn or through the speakers you don't want in the newspaper or on TV." The entries for these dates indicate that the stress and anger levels of Steve and David, the two persons doing the negotiating, went up notably after the loud noise was started. March 23, 7:01 p.m., Steve mentioned lack of sleep. Log entry for March 24, 11:15 a.m., states that HRT (Hostage Rescue Team) agents were playing whatever tapes they had available through the night, but they wanted guidance about what to play and when. The

"Action Taken" notation reads that the negotiation team should give advice about "appropriate tapes" to be played at "appropriate times." On the use of sound in warfare and torture, see Steve Goodman, *Sonic Warfare: Sound, Affect, and the Ecology of Fear* (Cambridge, MA: MIT Press, 2010).

87. This explains David's humorous side comment in an otherwise very serious statement he made to FBI agents via CB radio: "Let's see if we can't work this out. Let's don't get itchy. We won't get itchy. Let's just relax and think about mamas and papas and babies, and thank God for potatoes, and pretty soon, we hopefully can resolve all this. Thank you." SA 65-19, March 15, 1993, surveillance audiotape in Mark Swett Collection.

88. This was a "stress escalation" strategy, which directly counteracted the negotiations that were going on. Stuart A. Wright, "Anatomy of a Government Massacre: Abuses of Hostage-Barricade Protocols during the Waco Standoff," *Terrorism and Political Violence* 11, no. 2 (1999): 39–68.

89. FBI WACMUR Event Log entry for March 2, 12:57 a.m., states that David told a negotiator, "God always gives two ways out."

90. On the evening of February 28, after he had been shot in the ATF raid, David called a KRLD radio talk show and said, "Now the next event—we're in the Fifth Seal now—the next event to take place is that the sun and the stars will be darkened," referring to the events of the Sixth Seal of the book of Revelation. David Koresh, KRLD interview, tape available in the Texas Collection, transcription by Catherine Wessinger.

The Fifth Seal in Revelation 6:9–11 (KJV) reads:

> And when he had opened the fifth seal, I saw under the altar the souls of them that were slain for the word of God, and for the testimony which they held:
> And they cried with a loud voice, saying, How long, O Lord, holy and true, dost thou not judge and avenge our blood on them that dwell on the earth?
> And white robes were given unto every one of them; and it was said unto them, that they should rest for a little season, until their fellow-servants also and their brethren, that should be killed as they were, should be fulfilled.

When Livingstone Fagan came out to explain David Koresh's theology to the FBI, he understood that they were presently in the Fifth Seal, but he stressed that the outcome was not fixed. Whether or not the Branch Davidians would die at Mount Carmel was dependent on decisions made by federal agents and their willingness to listen to David's message. He explained this to FBI agents and also to Drs. James Tabor and J. Phillip Arnold. Deposition of Livingstone Fagan, 64–68; Tabor and Gallagher, *Why Waco?* 13.

Clive said on February 5, 2006 (Doyle transcript no. 26), about the events in 1993:

> No, I don't think it was the Fifth Seal at all. I don't think the Seals have been opened yet in the reality. I think they are constantly being opened in the sense that every prophet who has ever come has given us more explanation of the scriptures, which is what the seals are about, opening the book.
> What I've come to believe is that the Seals are yet to be opened. In order for the Seals, or we'll say, in the picture of the Seals being opened, that John saw two thousand years ago, first of all he's told it is to be hereafter, so what he's seeing is a preview of coming events. I think we've all been seeing previews of coming events. Like I told someone the

other day, Christ said when this gospel of the Kingdom is preached in all over the world for a witness, then shall the end come. I said there is not one church doing that.

In a sense, what took place to us and through us at Mount Carmel was a glimpse of what the world is going to be facing in the future.

91. FBI WACMUR Event Log for March 6, 7:58 p.m., contains a notation that Steve Schneider complained about the agents in the tanks mooning them and "possible destruction" of the cemetery at Mount Carmel.

92. Twenty-one children and fourteen adults came out during the siege.

93. After the eight-day holiday of Passover was over, David sent out a letter to the FBI saying that God told him to write a "little book" with his interpretation of the Seven Seals of the book of Revelation, and then they would all come out. Writing a "little book" would fulfill what the Branch Davidians regarded as a prophecy in Revelation relating to the Seventh Angel, who holds a "little book" (Rev. 10:1–2, 7), identified with Koresh. David's letter is printed in its entirety in DeVault, *Waco Whitewash*, 236.

94. On April 16 David told a negotiator named Dick that he had completed composing his interpretation of the First Seal. David assured Dick that they really would come out when he completed his manuscript on the Seven Seals: "Yes, yes, yes. I never intended to die in here." Transcription in Wessinger, *How the Millennium Comes Violently*, 105. The FBI WACMUR Event Log shows that on April 18, at 7:15 p.m., Steve Schneider told a negotiator that after the manuscript for the First Seal was typed up it could be sent out, as opposed to waiting until the commentary on all Seven Seals was ready.

95. On April 16 and 17 the Branch Davidians asked for word-processing supplies to type up David's manuscript. Wessinger, *How the Millennium Comes Violently*, 77. The FBI WACMUR Event Log entry for April 18, 7:40 p.m., reports that Casio typewriter tapes were sent in.

96. In the criminal trial, Wyatt Toulouse, a member of the FBI's Hostage Rescue Team, the tactical unit, who was stationed behind the building, testified that he witnessed flash-bang grenades being fired at Branch Davidians on four occasions when they came out of the building. DeVault, *Waco Whitewash*, 107.

97. FBI Major Case 80—WACMUR Updated Event Log for April 19, 1993, printed May 24, 1993, in the Lee Hancock Collection, records that at on April 19 at 1:25 a.m., Special Agent Robert Zane made the following notation: "*M.D. specializing in pediatric burns has called offering assistance. [Name redacted by editors], M.D. Galveston Burn Center, specializing in pediatric burns called offering his assistance. He can be reached at [redacted in log]*" (editors' emphasis). The FBI has persisted in arguing that they did not anticipate a fire and injury to the children. This chilling notation in the log for April 19 *prior to the assault* contradicts that. Dr. Hull would have had no independent knowledge of the imminent assault.

98. Dr. James Tabor is professor and chair of the Religious Studies Department at University of North Carolina, Charlotte. Dr. J. Phillip Arnold, Reunion Institute in Houston, had attended FBI press briefings in Waco and attempted to communicate with FBI agents about the Branch Davidians' theology. When not much came from those efforts, on March 15 Arnold discussed the Bible on a KRLD radio program while some Branch Davidians listened. Steve Schneider reported their interest in Arnold's knowledge of the Bible, and he requested that Arnold be permitted to discuss the

Bible's prophecies directly with David Koresh. This was not allowed, but an audiotape of Arnold's radio discussion was sent into the building on March 19. On April 1 Arnold and Tabor discussed the prophecies in the book of Revelation on KRLD radio for the benefit of David Koresh and the Branch Davidians. They offered an interpretation of Revelation that did not require the Branch Davidians to die to fulfill biblical prophecies. When Koresh sent out his letter on April 14 about writing his "little book," he said that after the manuscript was placed in the hands of Tabor and Arnold, the Branch Davidians would come out. Wessinger, *How the Millennium Comes Violently*, 73–76. After the fire, Tabor obtained the disk from Koresh's attorney and transcribed its content. Email from James Tabor to Catherine Wessinger, May 17, 2012.

99. David Koresh, "The Seven Seals of the Book of Revelation," in Tabor and Gallagher, *Why Waco?* 191–203.

100. David Koresh had a big argument with an FBI negotiator named Henry on April 18 about 2:00 p.m., when Koresh called to complain about the tanks destroying property and dragging away cars. Koresh asked, "What do you men really want?" He warned that the FBI agents were "fixing to step across a ribbon" that would "ruin the safety of me and my children." The tape cuts off at the point where Koresh and Henry get into a shouting match. Transcript of audiotape distributed by James Tabor under the title "Last Recorded Words of David Koresh," in Wessinger, *How the Millennium Comes Violently*, 106–12. The relevant negotiation audiotape, no. 240 in the Mark Swett Collection, also cuts off at the crucial heated moment.

101. By this time in the siege, Byron Sage was the primary FBI negotiator. At 5:56 a.m. Sage called into the residence and told Steve Schneider that "this is not an assault" and that the agents would begin to insert "nonlethal tear gas," the Branch Davidians should not fire their weapons, and they should come out. Schneider shouted for everyone to get gas masks. "Chronological Table," Danforth Report, 64. There were only adult-sized gas masks. FBI surveillance device audiotapes record Sage continuing to make these announcements over the loudspeakers as the tanks inserted the gas.

102. David Hardy explains that CS, although called a "tear gas," is a powder, which is:

> a powerful chemical irritant, formally known as o-chlorobenzylidene malonitrile. Upon contact with water—as found in lung and throat tissues, and on the surface of the eye—it breaks down into malononitrile, which in turn breaks down into the lethal chemical group cyanide. The attack of the cyanide causes tissues to release bradykinens, substances that cause pain, tissue swelling (edema) and leakage of fluid from the capillaries. Hardy with Kimball, *This Is Not an Assault*, 264–65.

In other words, according to Stuart A. Wright, "Revisiting the Branch Davidian Mass Suicide Debate," *Nova Religio* 13, no. 2 (November 2009): 8–9, CS gas causes chemical pneumonia, and "absorbed CS is metabolized to cyanide in peripheral tissues." Wright cites an unpublished report by a retired US Army expert who helped develop the "ferret round" delivery system used on April 19 as saying that the use of CS against the Branch Davidians was excessive and probably incapacitated the Branch Davidians "to the point where they were physically unable to exit the gassed areas" (9). Rex Applegate, "Report on FBI Planning and Operations Relating to the CS Gas Assault at Waco, Texas, February 28 to April 19, 1993," unpublished document, Scottsburg, Oregon, 1995.

103. Wright, "Revisiting the Branch Davidian Mass Suicide Debate," 10, points out that when CS comes into contact with water it "it can form hydrogen cyanide fumes."

Wet towels were used to fill the spaces the adult gas masks left around the children's heads. Derek Lovelock, "A Personal View," appendix A in Newport, *Branch Davidians of Waco*, 351–52.

104. Wright, "Revisiting the Branch Davidian Mass Suicide Debate," 10, reports that both the sprayers and the ferret rounds delivered the CS in a suspension of methylene chloride, which "is toxic and may be metabolized by the body to form carbon monoxide. Combustion of methylene chloride can generate toxic gases, including phosgene, an extremely poisonous gas. Burning CS can also produce cyanide." Wright reports: "Forty-four of the Branch Davidian corpses tested positive for cyanide, some with enough to reach concentration levels in the blood to produce a coma or death."

105. Hardy with Kimball, *This Is Not an Assault*, 263–68, describes the plan approved by Attorney General Janet Reno and how the actions of the Hostage Rescue Team on April 19 deviated from that plan. The plan included a clause that if the HRT reported being fired on by the Branch Davidians that the on-site commanders could ratchet up the gassing and demolishing of the building.

House of Representatives Report 104-749, *Activities of Federal Law Enforcement Agencies* (Washington, DC: US Government Printing Office, 1996), 75, concludes:

> [T]he levels of methylene chloride that were present in the [Branch] Davidian residence as a result of the use of the CS riot control agent might have impaired the ability of some of the [Branch] Davidians to be able to leave the residence had they otherwise wished to do so.

106. The assault began at 6:00 a.m. The fire was visible by 12:07 p.m.

107. The United States and 130 other countries signed the Chemical Weapons Convention in January 1993 agreeing not to use CS in warfare. Thibodeau and Whiteson, *A Place Called Waco*, 253. A letter in the Lee Hancock Collection from Gary W. Allen, Director, Torts Branch, Civil Division of the Justice Department, dated September 15, 1999, encloses a memo entitled "Allegation," which states that the Paris Chemical Weapons treaty did not extend to the use of "riot control agents" in law enforcement actions.

108. DeVault, *Waco Whitewash*, 132–33, reprints statements from US Army manuals that CS is a riot control agent, and crowd control agents are not designed to be introduced directly into "barricaded buildings": "Do not use around hospitals or other places where innocent persons may be affected. . . . Do not use where fires may start or asphyxiation may occur."

109. "Rebar," reinforcing bar, refers to steel bars inside the poured cement to strengthen it.

110. Aerial photographs taken from a plane overhead reveal that beginning at 11:31 a.m., a tank drove through the front of the building to the doorway of the vault and gassed that area until 11:55. Subsequently, agents testified that the tank did not insert gas into the vault, but they had been given the order to do so. The Danforth Final Report concluded that CS was dispersed between seventeen and twenty-eight feet away from the open door of the vault and that no deaths occurred

as a result of CS gas. However, shortly after the fire, Bob Ricks, the FBI spokesperson, said at a press conference that the tank had inserted gas directly into the vault. Hardy with Kimball, *This Is Not an Assault*, 275-76, 285; Gifford, Gazecki, and McNulty, *Waco: The Rules of Engagement*; transcript of a lecture given by Bob Ricks to the Tulsa, Oklahoma, Rotary Club on August 25, 1993, in the Lee Hancock Collection; Danforth, "Final Report," 11–14.

In 1999 Colonel Rodney L. Rawlings, who served as the head military liaison for the FBI operation at Mount Carmel, told Lee Hancock of the *Dallas Morning News* that he and FBI agents were listening in real time to audio captured by surveillance devices planted inside the building. He said that this audio helped the agents target areas of the building for gassing. He said that the children and mothers inside the vault could be heard "crying, talking, and praying." Lee Hancock, "Ex-Colonel Says FBI Heard Sect's Fire Plans," *Dallas Morning News*, October 8, 1999; Wessinger, "Deaths in the Fire at the Branch Davidians' Mount Carmel," 44. The analysis by David Hardy puts an order inside the building to light fires after the children and mothers were gassed in the vault and after the tanks closed in on Koresh's location on the second floor. Hardy with Kimball, *This Is Not an Assault*, 283–91.

111. House of Representatives Report 104-749, *Investigation*, 71, concludes:

CS insertion into the enclosed bunker [vault] at a time when women and children were assembled inside could have been a proximate cause of or directly resulted in some or all of the deaths attributed to asphyxiation in the autopsy reports.

After the fire died down, the only structures remaining were the water tower and the vault. KXXV-TV Channel 25 video footage recorded by Ken Fawcett and provided to the editors reveals that a fire continued to blaze within the vault for several hours after the building burned down. Smoke from the vault could be seen for the rest of the afternoon. A tank was pulled up to block the camera's clear view of the activities of the federal agents gathered around the vault. Wessinger, "Deaths in the Fire," 48; the Fawcett digitized video received by the co-editors has been placed in the Texas Collection, Baylor University.

112. Mark Wendel likely also went upstairs. After the fire his body was found close to the bodies of David Koresh and Steve Schneider.

Graeme Craddock testified that he heard Mark Wendel's voice from upstairs call out, "Light the fire!" He heard Pablo Cohen in the chapel shout, "Wait. Wait. Find out." Craddock said that Mark and Pablo continued shouting through the chapel ceiling at each other, and he also heard a command, "Don't light the fire." After the fire started Craddock left the back of the chapel to cross the courtyard and take shelter in the cinderblock utility building next to the water tower (#2 in figure 3 in appendix). Craddock said that before the exchange between Mark Wendel and Pablo Cohen, he saw an unidentified person spreading fuel in the chapel, to which Pablo objected. Wessinger, "Deaths in the Fire," 43–44; Deposition of Graeme Craddock, October 28, 1999, United States District Court for the Western District of Texas, Waco Division, No. W-96-CA-139, *Isabel G. Andrade et al. v. Phillip J. Chojnacki et al.*, 201–5; Deposition of Graeme Craddock, October 29, 1999, 2:254, 259–64, 405.

Government investigators concluded that the fire started in at least three locations within minutes of each other. They also concluded that the CS gas did not contribute to the acceleration of the fire. (They also concluded that the CS gas did not reach toxic levels inside the building, although one of the experts dissented.) See Danforth, "Final Report," 9–15, 118–19, appendices D, E, and F.

For an additional perspective, Wright, "Revisiting the Branch Davidian Mass Suicide Debate," 13, cites a declaration by Richard Sherrow, a former ATF fire and explosion investigator, for the civil case, in which Sherrow concludes, "It is consistent with this evidence that the fire originated from a single point and spread throughout the Mount Carmel structure." According to "Declaration of Richard L. Sherrow," January 17, 1996, at http://www.carolmoore.net/waco/waco-fire.html, "It is also consistent with evidence that the original fire was started by an M728 CEV striking the southwest corner tower of Mount Carmel." Wright points out that FLIR (Forward-Looking Infrared) footage taken from an airplane flying overhead shows that fire appears in the southwest corner second-floor window (#23 in figure 4 in appendix) less than two minutes after the tank struck the building at that location. Wright argues that the evidence is by no means conclusive that one or more Branch Davidians lit the fire.

113. For David Thibodeau's account of his experiences in the fire, see Thibodeau and Whiteson, *A Place Called Waco*, xvi–xviii. After he heard someone shout, "Fire!" he went up the stairs in the back of the chapel to the catwalk. When he reached the hallway on the second floor he observed a huge fireball shoot from the southwest end to the other end of the hall. He then returned to the space behind the partition behind the chapel stage, where he escaped through the hole in the outer wall made by the tank.

114. A total of nine Branch Davidians escaped the fire. Jaime Castillo, Derek Lovelock, and David Thibodeau went out the hole in the wall of the chapel (#7 in figure 3 in appendix) ahead of Clive Doyle. Clive Doyle was the last person out through that hole. Renos Avraam, Misty Ferguson, Ruth Riddle, and Marjorie Thomas jumped from the second floor. Graeme Craddock took shelter in a cinderblock utility building (#2 in figure 3) next to the water tower in the courtyard and came out after the fire died down.

115. Seventy-six Branch Davidians of all ages died in the fire. This number includes twenty-three children age fifteen and younger, including the two infants that died with their pregnant mothers, Aisha Gyarfas and Nicole Gent. David Koresh was the father of these two fetuses and twelve other children who died in the fire.

116. Investigator and filmmaker who co-produced *Waco: Rules of Engagement* (1997) and *Waco: A New Revelation* (2000) and produced *The F.L.I.R. Project* (2001), all dealing with the events at Mount Carmel in 1993 and subsequent events.

117. Registered Nurse (RN) and Licensed Vocational Nurse (LVN; in states outside of Texas and California, they are called Licensed Practical Nurses, LPN).

118. See Thibodeau and Whiteson, *A Place Called Waco*, xvii.

CHAPTER 6

1. James T. Richardson provides a sociological and legal analysis of the criminal trial in 1994 and the civil trial in 2000 in "'Showtime' in Texas: Social Production of the Branch Davidian Trials," *Nova Religio* 5, no. 1 (October 2001): 152–70.

There remains scope for additional scholarly study of the 1994 criminal trial of the Branch Davidians; the trial proceedings are available in the Texas Collection, Baylor University, in the Kirk Lyons Collection. Dick J. Reavis provides an account of the criminal trial in *The Ashes of Waco: An Investigation* (New York: Simon & Schuster, 1995), 278–300. Carol Moore provides a close account of the trial from a Libertarian and gun owners' perspective in *The Davidian Massacre: Disturbing Questions about Waco Which Must Be Answered* (Franklin, TN, and Springfield, VA: Legacy Communications and Gun Owners Foundation, 1995), at http://www.carolmoore .net./waco/TDM-index.html, 437–54. Jack DeVault, a retired US Air Force major and member of the Christian Patriot movement, provides an interesting summary of the testimony and analysis of the criminal trial in *The Waco Whitewash: The Mt. Carmel Episode Told by an Eyewitness to the Trial* (San Antonio: Rescue Press, 1994).

The actions of the FBI against the Randy Weaver family at Ruby Ridge, Idaho, in 1992, and the actions of the ATF and FBI against the Branch Davidians in 1993 gave a big impetus to the Patriot movement's concerns about abuses committed against citizens by American law enforcement agents. Some Patriots identify themselves as Christian Patriots. Others are pagan or nonreligious. Many are former police or military. The number of militias in the movement increased in response to the events at Ruby Ridge and Mount Carmel. There are moderate and extremist elements in the Patriot movement. Timothy McVeigh, a Gulf War veteran who carried out the bombing of the Murrah Federal Building in Oklahoma City, Oklahoma, on April 19, 1995, the second anniversary of the fire at Mount Carmel, participated in these circles. See Stuart A. Wright, *Patriots, Politics, and the Oklahoma City Bombing* (Cambridge: Cambridge University Press, 2007).

2. See Court's Instructions to the Jury, United States District Court for the Western District of Texas, Waco Division, Criminal No. W-93-CR-046, *United States of America v. Brad Eugene Branch et al.*, in DeVault, *Waco Whitewash*, 283–314.

3. The trial began on January 12, 1994. DeVault, *Waco Whitewash*.

4. Roland Ballesteros was shot in the left hand and later had to have part of his thumb amputated. In a deposition, he gave moving testimony of removing the dead ATF agents from the property after the cease-fire had been arranged. He saw himself as participating in the dynamic entry to save the children. He carried candy bars in a pack to soothe the children whom he knew would be terrorized by the no-knock raid. Deposition of Roland Ballesteros, July 11, 1996, United States District Court for the Western Division of Texas, Waco Division, Civil Action No. W-93-CA-138, *John T. Risenhoover v. Cox Texas Publications et al.*, 92–97.

5. The front door was important evidence because the Branch Davidians alleged that it would show that most of the bullet holes in the double doors, especially the right-hand door, were from shots fired outside going into the building. Photographs taken before the fire show that the right-hand door indeed had more bullet holes in it. As Clive describes, the right-hand side of the front door disappeared in or after the fire. The prosecutors brought in the left-hand side of the door as evidence that Branch Davidians standing behind the closed doors shot at the ATF agents.

6. Flash-bang or stun grenades were thrown into the second-floor windows that ATF agents entered on February 28, and FBI agents threw them at Branch Davidians who came out of the building during the siege, sometimes, as with the case of Steve Schneider, when prior permission had been given to come out for a purpose. The

congressional hearings in 1995 heard testimony disputes about the use of flash-bangs at Mount Carmel. Sections of this testimony are included in Dan Gifford, William Gazecki, and Michael McNulty, producers, *Waco: The Rules of Engagement* (Los Angeles: Fifth Estate Productions, 1997).

7. Sandra Sawyer of Denver, Colorado, had been babysitting when the ATF threw in a flash-bang grenade that blew off her arm. DeVault, *Waco Whitewash*, 143.

8. See also Reavis, *Ashes of Waco*, 290–91. The ATF agent who said that Livingstone Fagan shot him was Eric Evers. DeVault, *Waco Whitewash*, 76–81, 90, summarizes the testimony of Evers and an agent named Orchowski against Fagan. Evers's bullet-proof vest protected him from two shots, and he was wounded in the shoulder. Orchowski described the three men as wearing combat goggles and dark clothing such as that worn by ATF agents. Both initially thought that the three men were ATF agents.

In a deposition in conjunction with the civil trial, Fagan stated that at no point on February 28 did he go outside where the two agents accused him of shooting at and wounding one of them. Fagan recounted that on February 28, he heard shooting and saw the helicopters, he saw the wounded Perry Jones and heard his screams, and he was told by Oliver Gyarfas that Winston Blake had been shot and killed in his room. He looked out the back and saw men on the roof of the chapel shooting into one of the second-floor rooms (#21a in figure 4 in appendix). Fagan stated that the first gun he picked up misfired. He obtained another gun and went to the room next to the telephone room (#13 in figure 3 in appendix) overlooking the back courtyard. He said that when the men shot at him he returned fire. He saw one agent fall to the courtyard and subsequently heard him groan when he was carried off by his colleagues during the cease-fire. Deposition of Livingstone Fagan, February 1, 2000, in United States District Court for the Western District of Texas, Waco Division, No. W-96-CA-139, *Isabel G. Andrade et al. v. Phillip J. Chojnacki et al.*, 118–25, 127, 135–43.

The severely wounded ATF agent would have been Kenneth King. Two ATF agents—Todd McKeehan and Conway LeBleu—were killed when they entered the second-floor room from that side of the chapel roof. Livingstone Fagan's shooting at the attackers likely happened after Clive moved to other parts of the building, as he recounts.

9. Special Agent Jack Morrison was looking through the scope of his rifle. DeVault, *Waco Whitewash*, 109–10.

10. Reading the summaries in DeVault, *Waco Whitewash*, one gains the impression that the defense attorneys did ask good questions and make good points in the cross-examinations.

11. Judge Walter Smith defined voluntary manslaughter as being committed when "a human being is unlawfully killed in the sudden heat of passion caused by adequate provocation," thus leaving the self-defense clause vague. The jury apparently understood it as referring to actions taken as self-defense, based on later statements by the jury forewoman, Sarah Bain. Reavis, *Ashes of Waco*, 295; Court's Instructions to the Jury in DeVault, *Waco Whitewash*, 303.

Sarah Bain wrote to Judge Smith on May 11, 1994, to ask for leniency in the sentencing and to explain the jury's thinking about the verdicts. She wrote:

Further, on Count Two (part two): the five individuals found guilty: Brad Eugene Branch, Kevin A. Whitecliff, Jaime Castillo, Livingston [sic] Fagan, and Renos Avraam, were not found guilty of voluntary manslaughter but of aiding and abetting voluntary manslaughter. I implore the Court to recognize that the jury never believed these individuals themselves committed the crime of voluntary manslaughter. Further, we did believe, and the charge to the jury gave credence to the belief that aiding and abetting was a "lesser charge."

For these five individuals, I beg the Court's utmost leniency.

Bain's letter is printed in full in DeVault, *Waco Whitewash*, 175–78, quotation on 177.

12. See Reavis's discussion of the evidence in relation to Paul Fatta's gun show business dealings, *Ashes of Waco*, 291, where he writes: "No evidence was ever brought [in the trial] that Fatta had converted any weapons to automatic fire, or was aware of their conversion." Fatta was found guilty of conspiracy to manufacture automatic weapons and of aiding and abetting the manufacture of automatic weapons. According to Fatta, he should have been sentenced to three years according to the sentencing guidelines. After Judge Smith changed the jury's verdicts, as Clive describes in the following, Fatta was given a sentence of fifteen years based on the preponderance of the evidence and relevant conduct that he was guilty of conspiracy to murder federal agents. Fatta reports that Sarah Bain, the jury forewoman, wrote him in prison, apologizing for his conviction and lengthy sentence. Paul Fatta interview facilitated by Catherine Wessinger, CESNUR conference, San Diego State University, July 15, 2006.

13. Court's Instructions to the Jury, in DeVault, *Waco Whitewash*, 305.

14. Reavis, *Ashes of Waco*, 296.

15. DeVault, *Waco Whitewash*, 166.

16. Reavis, *Ashes of Waco*, 298.

17. Livingstone Fagan, personal communication with Catherine Wessinger, London, 2008. Fagan was kept in solitary confinement for many years of his prison term, and he was severely beaten and subjected to harsh treatment by the guards, particularly at the Leavenworth, Kansas, prison. On one occasion he was hosed down with water and left to shiver for four days in an unheated cell in the winter with air blown on him by an industrial fan. He was also denied meals. At the time of his deposition in 2000, Fagan had been held in solitary confinement for five and a half years out of his six years in prison. Deposition of Livingstone Fagan, February 1, 2000, 157–59.

18. Mark Domangue, the owner of the Brittany Hotel in Waco, provided free accommodations to the survivors while they figured out where they would live. Sheila Martin, *When They Were Mine: Memoirs of a Branch Davidian Wife and Mother*, ed. Catherine Wessinger (Waco: Baylor University Press, 2009), 75; David Thibodeau and Leon Whiteson, *A Place Called Waco: A Survivor's Story* (New York: Public Affairs, 1999), 293–94.

19. See the photographs and historical property map on Matthew Wittmer's website at http://www.stormbound.org/waco.html to see where the crape myrtle trees were located originally and the locations to which they were moved by Charles Pace after Clive moved off the property.

20. Amo Roden was interviewed by James D. Faubion, an anthropologist at Rice University, who published a book about her theology, *The Shadows and Lights of Waco: Millennialism Today* (Princeton: Princeton University Press, 2001).

21. Amo Roden returned periodically to reside on the Mount Carmel property near the front gate. She claimed ownership of the property as a Branch Davidian. Or, if she was not living on the property, she stationed herself by the front gate and handed literature to visitors and asked for donations. Amo painted textual information about the siege on the swimming pool foundation and made several large altars on the property expressing her views. Matthew Wittmer obtained literature from Amo at the Mount Carmel gate in 2000 and photographed her wooden altar that was just inside the front gate at that time. Catherine Wessinger observed her by the front gate on several visits to Mount Carmel in 2004.

22. Attorney Kirk Lyons, affiliated with CAUSE Foundation, in 1996 assisted the FBI in persuading the Montana Freemen to come out of a farm they called Justus Township to be taken into custody after an eighty-one-day standoff. Catherine Wessinger, *How the Millennium Comes Violently: From Jonestown to Heaven's Gate* (New York: Seven Bridges Press, 2000), 191–93. The Southern Poverty Law Center identifies him as a white supremacist neo-Confederate. "Kirk Lyons," Southern Poverty Law Center, accessed August 12, 2011, http://www.splcenter.org/get-informed/intelligence-files/profiles/kirk-lyons.

23. David Hardy explains that there were three sets of attorneys involved with the civil trial. The largest group of clients was represented by Michael Caddell and his wife, Cynthia Chapman. Ramsey Clark represented the next-largest group. James Brannon of Houston represented the third group. Hardy, an attorney in Tucson, Arizona, was asked by Clark to serve with him as co-counsel. David T. Hardy with Rex Kimball, *This Is Not an Assault: Penetrating the Web of Official Lies Regarding the Waco Incident* (n.p.: Xlibris, 2001), 133–34.

24. Lon Horiuchi was the sniper-observer who relayed the code word "Compromise" to indicate that Branch Davidians were firing at the tanks inserting CS gas into the building. Jean E. Rosenfeld, "The Use of the Military at Waco: The Danforth Report in Context," *Nova Religio* 5, no. 1 (October 2001): 185n84. According to the plan approved by Attorney General Janet Reno, gunfire from the Branch Davidians gave the on-site FBI commanders the discretion to accelerate the gassing, which they did. Dick Rogers, the Hostage Rescue Team commander, had also been in charge of the HRT at Ruby Ridge. Special Agent in Charge Jeffrey Jamar had overall command of the operation at Mount Carmel. FBI Major Case 80—WACMUR Updated Event Log for April 19, 1993, indicates that negotiator Byron Sage called inside the building to notify of the insertion of CS gas and to say, "This is not an assault," at 5:56 a.m., and that the code word "Compromise, compromise" was conveyed by a sniper-observer at 6:04 a.m. to report observation of gunshots striking an approaching tank.

25. James T. Richardson explains that a judge has *discretion*, a legal term meaning that the judge can decide the following: what evidence, including questionable evidence, is presented; what evidence is excluded; and what instructions, including ambiguous or confusing ones, will be told to the jurors. Hence through the exercise of discretion the judge can have considerable influence over the outcome of the trial. Richardson, "'Showtime' in Texas," 154. Richardson discusses the exercise of discretion in the civil trial on pp.162–63. Stuart A. Wright, who observed the civil trial, writes of Judge Smith's bias against the Branch Davidians in "Justice Denied: The Waco Civil Trial," *Nova Religio* 5, no. 1 (October 2001): 143–51.

Wright also reports on the civil trial in "Field Notes from Waco: *Isabel Andrade et al v. U.S.,*" *Nova Religio* 4, no. 2 (April 2001): 351–56, and the extensive withholding or destroying of evidence by federal agents that was illuminated in the civil trial. He recounts that Michael Caddell called to the stand David Keys, an officer of the Department of Public Safety who was at Mount Carmel on April 19, 1993. Keys reported that around 3:00 p.m. that afternoon he observed agents load what looked like a door into a U-Haul truck. Television cameras had filmed a tank dragging the front doors away from the building during the demolition of the building. Defense attorneys in the civil trial objected, and Judge Smith stopped Keys's testimony. Wright reports that in a videotaped deposition that was not shown in court, Keys testified that when the U-Haul truck departed it did not turn onto Farm Road 2491 to go into town, which would have taken it past television cameras. A photograph was taken of Keys that shows the U-Haul truck in the background (352–53).

Ken Fawcett also states that the missing right-hand door was carted off in a U-Haul truck; he captured raw satellite feed showing the U-Haul truck arriving and leaving the property following the fire. This VHS recording was digitized by Fawcett and donated to the Texas Collection at Baylor University by Matthew Wittmer.

26. For instance, FBI agents had said in congressional hearings that no pyrotechnic ferret rounds had been used on April 19. A pyrotechnic device operates with a spark and can start a fire. Lee Hancock, "2 Pyrotechnic Devices Fired at Davidians, Ex-Official Says," *Dallas Morning News,* August 24, 1999, reported evidence that pyrotechnic ferret rounds had been fired at Mount Carmel on April 19, which prompted Attorney General Janet Reno to appoint former senator John C. Danforth as special counsel to investigate whether federal agents had contributed to the deaths at Mount Carmel. The Danforth investigation was occurring about the time of the civil trial. John C. Danforth, Special Counsel, "Final Report to the Deputy Attorney General Concerning the 1993 Confrontation at the Mt. Carmel Complex," November 8, 2000, 29–32, concluded that three pyrotechnic devices delivering CS gas had been fired at the storm shelter at 8:08 a.m. on April 19 and therefore did not cause the fire, which started at 12:07 p.m.

27. Caddell and Clark argued for another civil trial on the basis of Judge Smith's bias against the Branch Davidians before the judges of the US Fifth Circuit Court of Appeals in New Orleans on February 10, 2002. The appeal was rejected.

28. Wright, "Justice Denied," 148; Stuart A. Wright, "Waco Redux: Trial and Error," *Religion in the News* 3, no. 3 (Fall 2000), http://www.trincoll.edu/depts/csrpl/rinvol3no3/waco_redux.htm.

29. Doris Fagan died in the fire.

30. FLIR, an acronym for Forward Looking Infrared, is thermal imaging, or infrared film that is sensitive to the temperature of objects being photographed. On April 19 an airplane circled over Mount Carmel as the tanks gassed and destroyed the residence and the fires started. DeVault, *Waco Whitewash,* 129, points out that it has never been explained why FLIR imagery was taken of the assault, and asks whether the FBI was concerned to document the outbreak of a fire. It may have been part of the experimentation of high-tech equipment that Clive believes was being carried out by federal agents at Mount Carmel. For instance, FLIR expert Carlos Ghigliotti, who was communicating with David Hardy before his death before the civil trial,

pointed out that agents on the ground were wearing clothing that concealed their presence from the FLIR until they moved.

In 1997 the film *Waco: The Rules of Engagement* presented the FLIR footage taken over Mount Carmel to the public and included analysis by Dr. Edward Allard that rapid repeated flashes at the back of the building during the tank assault were automatic gunfire directed toward the building. See Hardy with Kimball, *This Is Not an Assault,* for a discussion of the complex issues around the FLIR imagery, the battle of the experts, and the demise of significant experts for the plaintiffs in the civil trial. Hardy also discusses the FLIR evidence at http://www.hardylaw.net/flir.html, accessed August 19, 2011, and the late FLIR expert Carlos Ghigliotti, 2000, at http://www.hardylaw.net/Carlos.html.

Hardy with Kimball, *This Is Not an Assault,* 109–57, discusses how Ghigliotti was retained by the House Government Reform Committee to examine the FLIR footage and make a report. Prior to his unexpected death, Ghigliotti faxed his preliminary report to Hardy, which is found in appendix I, "Preliminary Report of Carlos Ghigliotti to House Government Reform Committee," March 18, 2000, in Hardy with Kimball, *This Is Not an Assault,* 337–42.

Ghigliotti, Edward Allard, and Ferdinand Zegel were the FLIR experts to be called by the plaintiffs' attorneys in the civil trial. Concerning these witnesses, Hardy comments:

> In the meantime, our FLIR expert witnesses suffered an unbelievable casualty rate. In one six-week span, Carlos Ghigliotti died at age 42 of a heart attack, Dr. Allard suffered an incapacitating stroke, and Ferdinand Zegel collapsed and nearly died of blood poisoning, apparently resulting from an infected spider bite (136).

Hardy reports that Ghigliotti was analyzing first-generation Super VHS FLIR footage of a much higher quality than even most FBI agents had seen. After his death, an attorney with the House Government Reform Committee insisted, in the presence of Michael Caddell, that Ghigliotti's sister give him access to Ghigliotti's laboratory so that he could collect property belonging to the committee (109, 140).

The FLIR reenactments at Fort Hood were part of the research by John C. Danforth, Special Counsel, to investigate whether or not there had been wrongdoing on the part of federal agents that caused the deaths of the Branch Davidians. This resulted in the Danforth "Final Report," which includes a discussion of the FLIR footage and analysis by a British firm, Vector Data Systems. Hardy discusses issues concerning the FLIR reenactment on pp. 136–40, 151. In the deposition of Peter Ayres with Vector Data, it came out that Vector Data Systems had no expertise in FLIR analysis, and Ayres agreed that the shape and duration of the flashes were consistent with gunfire. The deposition of Nick Evans, CEO of Vector Data, revealed that Vector Data Systems is owned by Anteon Corporation, which has contracts with the United States government (138–39).

For a critical analysis of the Danforth "Final Report," which does not address the FLIR analysis, see Rosenfeld, "The Use of the Military at Waco," 171–85. Rosenfeld analyzes the Danforth "Final Report" and other government reports on the Branch Davidian case to ascertain whether or not federal agencies illegally contravened the Posse Comitatus Act of 1878, which states: "It shall not be lawful to employ any part of the Army of the United States, as a *posse comitatus,* or otherwise, for the purpose of executing laws, except in such cases and under such circumstances as such employment of such force may be expressly authorized by the Constitution or by Act of Congress" (172). Rosenfeld concludes: "Danforth engaged in a hermeneutical defense of the government. Comparison of these major documents reveals inconsistencies, errors, omissions, terminology, and interpretations that raise questions about violations of the laws separating the armed forces from civilian police operations against United States citizens on U.S. soil" (171).

31. Hardy reports that he did not attend the Fort Hood reenactment because Ghigliotti had pointed out the shortcomings of the protocol to him. Hardy with Kimball, *This Is Not an Assault*, 137.

32. Michael McNulty, producer, *The F.L.I.R. Project* (Fort Collins, CO: COPS Productions, 2001).

33. Hardy discusses Ghigliotti's FLIR footage that showed a gunfight going on in the area of the gymnasium, with two persons on the ground firing into the gymnasium rubble and gunfire coming from individuals in the rubble, who eventually fled back into the building. The gun battle in the area of the collapsed gym began around 11:24 a.m. and continued for about half an hour. Hardy with Kimball, *This Is Not an Assault*, 114–15, 124. According to Ghigliotti's preliminary report, the gun battle involved two individuals coming out of the tank that was demolishing the gym and also providing cover for the shooters and at least one individual in the gym returning fire.

Ghigliotti noted that when a tank entered the front of the building, gunfire was directed at it from the second floor multiple times. The tank inserted its boom into the second floor of the southwest corner tower at 12:05 p.m., and at 12:07 fire was visible from this room's window (#23 in figure 4 in appendix). Meanwhile, shooting continued to be directed toward a subject hiding in the gym at 12:08, and the tank withdrew from the gym at 12:09. Between 12:10 and 12:11 numerous gunshots were fired from the center of the back courtyard into the building toward the cafeteria.

Ghigliotti counted sixty-nine gunshots coming out of the building and fifty-seven gunshots going into the building. He noted three thermal flashes directed toward the building from a weapon with a possible flash-suppressor device. Ghigliotti concluded (all capitals removed): "With only a few exceptions, the Branch Davidians shot at the tanks, only after the tanks penetrated the structure." Appendix I, in Hardy with Kimball, *This Is Not an Assault*, quotation at 341–42.

FLIR analysts' allegations of gunfire directed toward the Branch Davidians are explosive because the alleged purpose of the tank and CS gas assault was to compel the Branch Davidians to exit the building and because of official testimony that no federal agents shot at the Branch Davidians during the assault. Attorney General Janet Reno testified at the 1995 congressional hearings that no federal agents shot at Branch Davidians on April 19, 1993. Statement of Janet Reno, Attorney General, in Joint Hearings, *Activities of Federal Law Enforcement Agencies (Part III)*, Committee on the Judiciary Serial No. 72 (Washington, DC: US Government Printing Office, 1996), 375. Danforth, "Final Report," 17–29, concluded the same. Because of the Posse Comitatus prohibitions, even more explosive would be a revelation that agents firing at the Branch Davidians were military Special Forces or members of the top-secret Delta Force team, who had "observers" on-site. Rosenfeld, "The Use of the Military at Waco," 178–82, discusses the evidence for military assistance

provided during the siege, during planning the final assault and persuading Attorney General Janet Reno to approve it, and on April 19. She points out that "observer" is government shorthand for "sniper-observer" or "forward observer" (178).

34. A tank could not go up close to the cafeteria to insert CS gas or demolish
the building because of the swimming pool and fears that the concrete would give
way under the tank. Jeffrey Jamar, former special agent in charge, in Joint Hearings,
Activities of Federal Law Enforcement Agencies, 2:476.

35. The side of the chapel and the front of the building were in view of the television cameras at the area dubbed Satellite City located three miles away (see figure
1 in appendix).

36. There are numerous examples of this. An egregious case occurred on the
Danziger Bridge in New Orleans on September 4, 2005, six days after Hurricane
Katrina flooded the city. Police officers received a report of gunfire directed toward
other officers on the Danziger Bridge, but arrived to find only unarmed pedestrians
crossing the bridge, and no shooting. The officers opened fire, killing two persons
and critically wounding and maiming four others. A man was stomped by an officer as he lay dying. A wounded man lying on the bridge was shot in the abdomen
at point-blank range. The wounded survived due to prompt attention from Emer-
gency Medical Services personnel who were close by. The aftermath involved false
police reports, planting of a firearm, the false allegation that one of the survivors
was shooting at the officers (the charges were dismissed), manufacture of witnesses,
and perjury on the part of officers. Four officers were found guilty of the shootings
and one officer was found guilty in the cover-up in August 2011. Two other officers
pleaded guilty to participating in the cover-up.

37. Certificate of Resolution dated April 22, 1994, and notarized on April 25,
1994, names Rita Riddle secretary and the following individuals as the other trustees: Clive Doyle, Edna Doyle, Karen Doyle, David Thibodeau, Sheila Martin, Ofelia
Santoya [*sic*], Bob Kendrick, Janet Kendrick, Margaret Lawson, Catherine Matteson,
and Mary Belle Jones. Since according to the Branch Davidian *Leviticus* and bylaws
the office of president "can only be filled by God with someone directly inspired to
do so, and since all other officers are to be appointed by the President," the named
survivors decided not to fill those offices. They were organizing themselves as trustees to act on behalf of the association after the assaults on their community and
resulting deaths of their president and "81 other members." Document 14 in Mount
Carmel Property Documents folder, Texas Collection, Baylor University.

38. The undated letter, Document 14a in the Mount Carmel Property Documents
folder, has the handwritten date of January 31, 1999. It lists the board members
as Clive Doyle, Edna Doyle, David Thibodeau, Karen Graham (nee Doyle), Sheila
Martin, Ofelia Santoyo, Catherine Matteson, and Bonnie Haldeman. Alternates
listed are Mary Jones and Kathy Jones. Signature of the form indicated acceptance
of these individuals as trustees and alternates of the General Association of the
Branch Davidian Seventh-day Adventists "for the purpose of holding and managing
the Mt. Carmel property." It states: "It is my desire that the title to the property in
question be given to the survivors of the 1993 Government siege, and that it be held
in solemn trust by the above named representatives of this Church. I do not wish
title of the property to be held by Amo Drake, Thomas Drake, Douglas Mitchell, or
any other individual claiming to speak on my behalf in this matter." Document 14a

includes a copy of the form signed by Charles Joseph Pace, who currently controls the Mount Carmel property.

39. Order on Plaintiff's Motion for Judgment Notwithstanding the Verdict, *Trustees of the Branch Davidian Seventh Day Adventist Association v. George Buchanan Roden et al.*, District Court of McLennan County, Texas, 74th Judicial District, Case No. 96-1152-3, part of Document 17a in Mount Carmel Property Documents folder.

40. Charles Pace objected to the crape myrtle trees at Mount Carmel, which were planted in front of the new chapel that was built by volunteers in 2000. Each tree had at its foot a memorial stone with the name of a Branch Davidian who died in 1993, with a tree for Jamie Martin, who died in 1998. After Clive moved away from Mount Carmel, Charlie broke and destroyed the stone with David Koresh's name on it and cut down David's tree. On April 19, 2006, the Branch Davidian survivors held the first memorial off of the Mount Carmel property. Charles Pace held a separate memorial at Mount Carmel at which he planned to burn the wood from David's tree. Bonnie Haldeman and Bobby Howell, David Koresh's mother and father, drove to Mount Carmel and loaded up the branches from David's tree into Bobby's truck and left. The Pace group then burned the roots of David's tree. Bonnie told a reporter, "It's just a friggin' tree, but it's a symbol." Cindy V. Culp, "Branch Davidians Caught in Yet Another Power Struggle," *Waco Tribune-Herald*, April 20, 2006.

Charles Pace also moved the memorial stones from underneath each tree and placed them in various arrangements at the front gate. In 2009 every crape myrtle tree had its branches cut back, was dug up, and replanted along the sides of the front driveway. As of 2012 the trees were still surviving.

41. If Charles Pace, or any other occupant of the land, maintains "open, adverse and notorious" possession of the land for ten years, and has paid property taxes during that time, at the end of the ten years that occupant becomes the owner of the property. At the end of ten years Pace will gain adverse possession—adverse in relation to the original owner, the General Association of the Branch Davidian Seventh-day Adventists. Pace or any other claimant to the land could be removed if a corporate attorney reconstituted the General Association as the record title owner with power of attorney to act as the owner of the property. Richard Ruppert, attorney in Houston, Texas, personal communication with Catherine Wessinger, September 11, 2011. On the other hand, Pace may have taken these legal steps himself in relation to the General Association.

CHAPTER 7

1. Branch Davidians observe a general kosher diet. Many have preferred to be vegetarians.

APPENDIX

1. For more information on accessible and inaccessible evidence, see Matthew Wittmer, "Traces of the Mount Carmel Community: Documentation and Access,"

Nova Religio 13, no. 2 (November 2009): 95–113, available at http://stormbound .org/waco.html.

2. Digitized copies of this VHS footage were provided by Ken Fawcett. I have donated digitized moving image copies of these files to the Branch Davidian holdings in the Texas Collection, Baylor University. Photographs were provided by Clive Doyle and Ken Fawcett. Catherine Wessinger provided photographs that were defense exhibits in the Branch Davidians' wrongful death civil trial in 2000.

3. Department of the Treasury, *Report of the Department of the Treasury on the Bureau of Alcohol, Tobacco, and Firearms Investigation of Vernon Wayne Howell Also Known as David Koresh* (Washington, DC: US Government Printing Office, 1993), 99, available at http://www.archive.org/details/reportofdepartme00unit.

4. The diagrams I consulted are found in Department of the Treasury, *Report of the Department of the Treasury*, 47–49; Ron Cole, *Sinister Twilight: A Tragedy Near Waco* (Portland: Augie Enriquez, 1993), 19, 21; Carol Moore, *The Davidian Massacre: Disturbing Questions about Waco Which Must Be Answered* (Franklin, TN, and Springfield, VA: Legacy Communications and Gun Owners Foundation, 1995), 24–25, available at http://www.carolmoore.net./waco/TDM-index.html; "Mount Carmel First and Second Floor Schematic Floor Plans," defense exhibit in the civil trial in 2000; "Plaintiff's Exhibit A: Force 1 Ltd., Mt. Carmel First Floor Plan," January 18, 1995, in the Kirk T. Lyons Collection in the Texas Collection, Baylor University; James G. Quintere and Frederick Mowrer, "Fire Development Analysis, Mount Carmel Branch Davidian Compound Waco, Texas April 19th, 1993," September 8, 1993, 60–64, in the Bill Smith Collection in the Texas Collection, Baylor University; Dick Reavis, *The Ashes of Waco* (New York: Simon & Schuster, 1995), 20–21; first- and second-floor plans that Ken Fawcett discovered ATF agents had discarded in a Waco cafe during the siege, which are reproduced in J. J. Robertson, *Beyond the Flames: The Trials of the Branch Davidians* (San Diego: ProMotion Publishing, 1996), 300–301; David Thibodeau and Leon Whiteson, *A Place Called Waco: A Survivor's Story* (New York: Public Affairs, 1999); Vector Data Systems, "Mensuration Report for the Analysis of Mount Carmel Compound," 1–8, attachment 4 to "Imagery Analysis Report: The Events at Waco, Texas, 19 April 1993, Prepared for the U.S. District Court for the Western District of Texas and the Office of Special Counsel," May 5, 2000, appendix I in John C. Danforth, Special Counsel, "Final Report to the Deputy Attorney General Concerning the 1993 Confrontation at the Mt. Carmel Complex," November 8, 2000, pdf pages 1149–56. The pdf version of the Danforth Report with its appendices has been donated to the Branch Davidian holdings, Wittliff Collection, Texas State University, San Marcos.

5. Department of the Treasury, *Report of the Department of the Treasury*, 99. The images in the print volume are substantially clear compared with the pdf scans of the same report available online.

6. Digitized footage courtesy of Ken Fawcett. This footage is available in the Texas Collection, Baylor University.

7. These windows were the central window above the front door and the window to the right and south of the window above the door.

8. Vector Data Systems, "Mensuration Report," 1–2, in Danforth, "Final Report," pdf pages 1149–50.

9. Quintere and Mowrer, "Fire Development Analysis," 4.

10. Paul T. Gray, John T. Ricketts, William S. Case, and Thomas W. Hitchings, "Report of Fire Scene Investigation," part of Quinterre and Mowrer, "Fire Development Analysis."

11. The author taught beginning and advanced drawing classes in 1998–2000 at the University of Nebraska, Lincoln, while he was a graduate student there.

12. The building model was displayed in the Visitor's Center from 2000 until Clive Doyle moved away from the Mount Carmel property in 2006. The model is now placed in the Wittliff Collections at Texas State University, San Marcos.

Works Cited

Adair, Don. 2011. Search Keywords (website). http://www.davidian.org/keywords .htm. Accessed September 4, 2011.

Allen, Gary W. 1999. Justice Department letter enclosing a memo entitled "Allegation" on the Paris Chemical Weapons treaty. September 15. Lee Hancock Collection, Southwestern Writers Collection, Texas State University, San Marcos.

Ballesteros, Roland. 1996. Deposition, July 11. United States District Court for the Western Division of Texas, Waco Division, Civil Action No. W-93-CA-138, *John T. Risenhoover v. Cox Texas Publications et al.*

Branch Davidians. 1993. "Inside Mount Carmel." Compilation of three videotapes filmed by Branch Davidians during the siege on a single VHS tape. Texas Collection, Baylor University.

Breault, Marc, and Martin King. 1993. *Inside the Cult: A Member's Chilling, Exclusive Account of Madness and Depravity in David Koresh's Compound.* New York: Signet Books.

Bromley, David G., and Catherine Wessinger. 2011. "Millennial Visions and Conflict with Society." In *Oxford Handbook of Millennialism*, ed. Catherine Wessinger, 191–212. New York: Oxford University Press.

Bush, George H. W. 1990. "Address before a Joint Session of Congress on the Persian Gulf Crisis and the Federal Budget Deficit." September 11. http://en.wikisource .org/wiki/Toward_a_New_World_Order.

"Chronological Table of Events." 2000. Appendix C in John C. Danforth, Special Counsel, "Final Report to the Deputy Attorney General Concerning the 1993 Confrontation at the Mt. Carmel Complex." November 8.

Cole, Ron. 1993. *Sinister Twilight: A Tragedy Near Waco.* Portland: Augie Enriquez.

Craddock, Graeme. 1993. Testimony of Graeme Craddock. United States District Court, Western District of Texas, Waco Division, Federal Grand Jury Proceedings. April 20.

243

Craddock, Graeme. 1998. Deposition of Graeme Craddock. United States District Court for the Western District of Texas, Waco Division, No. W-96-CA-139, *Isabel G. Andrade et al. v. Phillip J. Chojnacki et al.* Vols. 1–2. October 28–29.

Culp, Cindy V. 2006. "Branch Davidians Caught in Yet Another Power Struggle." *Waco Tribune-Herald.* April 20.

Danforth, John C., Special Counsel. 2000. "Final Report to the Deputy Attorney General Concerning the 1993 Confrontation at the Mt. Carmel Complex." November 8.

Department of the Treasury. 1993. *Report of the Department of the Treasury on the Bureau of Alcohol, Tobacco, and Firearms Investigation of Vernon Wayne Howell Also Known as David Koresh.* Washington, DC: US Government Printing Office, September. Available at http://www.archive.org/details/reportofdepartme00unit.

DeVault, Jack. 1994. *The Waco Whitewash: The Mt. Carmel Episode Told by an Eyewitness to the Trial.* San Antonio: Rescue Press.

Docherty, Jayne Seminare. 2001. *Learning Lessons from Waco: When the Parties Bring Their Gods to the Negotiation Table.* Syracuse: Syracuse University Press.

"Face-to-face." 1993. Negotiation of Steve Schneider and Wayne Martin with Sheriff Jack Harwell and Byron Sage (FBI). Audiotape available in the Mark Swett Collection, Texas Collection, Baylor University.

Fagan, Livingstone. 2000. Deposition of Livingstone Fagan. United States District Court for the Western District of Texas, Waco Division, No. W-96-CA-139, *Isabel G. Andrade et al. v. Phillip J. Chojnacki et al.* February 1.

———. 2009. David Koresh website. http://david.koresh-lf-2009.angelfire.com/index.html. Accessed November 2, 2011.

Fatta, Paul. 2006. Interview facilitated by Catherine Wessinger at the CESNUR conference at San Diego State University, July 15. Transcript in the possession of Catherine Wessinger.

Faubion, James D. 2001. *The Shadows and Lights of Waco: Millennialism Today.* Princeton: Princeton University Press.

FBI. 1993a. WACMUR Major Event Log, February–July 1993. Available in the Lee Hancock Collection, Southwestern Writers Collection, Texas State University, San Marcos.

———. 1993b. FBI Major Case 80—WACMUR Updated Event Log for April 19, 1993, printed May 24, 1993. Available in the Lee Hancock Collection, Southwestern Writers Collection, Texas State University, San Marcos.

Gallagher, Eugene V. 2000. "The Persistence of the Millennium: Branch Davidian Expectations of the End after 'Waco.'" *Nova Religio* 3, no. 2 (April 2000): 303–19.

Ghigliotti, Carlos. 2000. "Preliminary Report of Carlos Ghigliotti to House Government Reform Committee." March 18. Appendix I in David T. Hardy with Rex Kimball, *This Is Not an Assault: Penetrating the Web of Official Lies Regarding the Waco Incident,* 337–42. N.p.: Xlibris, 2001.

Gifford, Dan, William Gazecki, and Michael McNulty, producers. 1997. *Waco: The Rules of Engagement.* Los Angeles: Fifth Estate Productions.

Goodman, Steve. 2010. *Sonic Warfare: Sound, Affect, and the Ecology of Fear.* Cambridge, MA: MIT Press.

Gray, Paul T., John T. Ricketts, William S. Case, Thomas W. Hitchings. N.d. "Report of Fire Scene Investigation." Available in the Texas Collection, Baylor University.

Haldeman, Bonnie. 2007. *Memories of the Branch Davidians: The Autobiography of David Koresh's Mother*, ed. Catherine Wessinger. Waco: Baylor University Press.

Hall, John R. 1995. "Public Narratives and the Apocalyptic Sect: From Jonestown to Mt. Carmel." In *Armageddon in Waco: Critical Perspectives on the Branch Davidian Conflict*, ed. Stuart A. Wright, 205–35. Chicago: University of Chicago Press.

Hancock, Lee. 1999a. "2 Pyrotechnic Devices Fired at Davidians, Ex-Official Says." *Dallas Morning News*. August 24.

———. 1999b. "FBI Missteps Doomed Siege Talks, Memos Say." *Dallas Morning News*. December 30.

Hardy, David T. 2011a. "FLIR Background." http://www.hardylaw.net/flir.html. Accessed November 3, 2011.

———. 2011b. "Memorial to an Honest Man: Carlos Ghigliotti." http://www.hardylaw.net/Carlos.html. Accessed November 3, 2011.

Hardy, David T., with Rex Kimball. 2001. *This Is Not an Assault: Penetrating the Web of Official Lies Regarding the Waco Incident*. N.p.: Xlibris.

History of Mount Carmel: Photo Album. 2011. http://www.shepherds-rod.org/photo/. Accessed September 4.

House of Representatives. 1996. *Investigation into the Activities of Federal Law Enforcement Agencies toward the Branch Davidians*. Report 104–749. Washington, DC: US Government Printing Office.

Houteff, Victor. 1943. *The Leviticus of the Davidian Seventh-day Adventists*. Author.

Joint Hearings. 1996. *Activities of Federal Law Enforcement Agencies toward the Branch Davidians (Parts 1–3)*. Committee on the Judiciary Serial No. 72. Washington, DC: US Government Printing Office.

Koresh, David. 1993. KRLD interview, February 28. Audiotape available in the Texas Collection, Baylor University.

———. 1995. "The Seven Seals of the Book of Revelation." In *Why Waco? Cults and the Battle for Religious Freedom in America*, by James D. Tabor and Eugene V. Gallagher, 191–203. Berkeley and Los Angeles: University of California Press.

Krouse, Marc A. 1993a. Autopsy Report for Perry Jones. Case No. MC-80, 930087. May 5. Available at http://www.public-action.com/SkyWriter/WacoMuseum/death/80/80_aut.html. Accessed November 3, 2011. Available also in the Matthew D. Wittmer Collection, in the Texas Collection, Baylor University.

———. 1993b. Autopsy Report for Peter Gent. Case No. MC-76, 930083#. May 5. Available at http://www.public-action.com/SkyWriter/WacoMuseum/death/76/76_pg01.gif. Accessed November 3, 2011. Available also in the Texas Collection, Baylor University.

Lovelock, Derek. 2006. "A Personal View." Appendix A in *The Branch Davidians of Waco: The History and Beliefs of an Apocalyptic Sect*, by Kenneth G. C. Newport, 351–52. Oxford: Oxford University Press.

Martin, Sheila. 2009. *When They Were Mine: Memoirs of a Branch Davidian Wife and Mother*, ed. Catherine Wessinger. Waco: Baylor University Press.

McNulty, Michael, producer. 2001. *The F.L.I.R. Project*. Fort Collins, CO: COPS Productions.

Moore, Carol. 1995. *The Davidian Massacre: Disturbing Questions about Waco Which Must Be Answered*. Franklin, TN, and Springfield, VA: Legacy Communications and Gun Owners Foundation. Available at http://www.carolmoore.net./waco/ TDM-index.html. Accessed November 3, 2011.

New Light Publications. 2011. http://www.sevenseals.com/index.php. Accessed September 6.

Newport, Kenneth G. C. 2006. *The Branch Davidians of Waco: The History and Beliefs of an Apocalyptic Sect.* Oxford: Oxford University Press.

Noesner, Gary. 2010. *Stalling for Time: My Life as an FBI Hostage Negotiator.* New York: Random House.

Parks, Jim. 2011. "Sheriff Larry Lynch to Step Down at End of Current Term." The Legendary. July 6. http://downdirtyword.blogspot.com/2011/07/sheriff-larry-lynch-to-step-down-after.html. Accessed November 3, 2011.

Peacock, Chris. 1995. Director of Public Affairs, Department of the Treasury. "Memorandum to the Press: Weapons Possessed by the Branch Davidians." July 13. Available at http://www.pbs.org/wgbh/pages/frontline/waco/treasury.html.

Peerwani, Nizam. 1993. Autopsy Report for Michael Dean Schroeder. Case No. 930053. March 5, 1993. At Michael Schroeder 1963–1993. Available at http://www.wizardsofaz.com/waco/mikeautop.html. Accessed November 3, 2011.

Pitts, Jr., William L. 2009. "Women Leaders in the Davidian and Branch Davidian Traditions." *Nova Religio* 12, no. 4 (May): 50–71.

Quintere, James G., and Frederick Mowrer. 1993. "Fire Development Analysis, Mount Carmel Branch Davidian Compound, Waco, Texas, April 19th, 1993." September 8. Bill Smith Collection in the Texas Collection, Baylor University.

Reavis, Dick. 1995. *The Ashes of Waco: An Investigation.* New York: Simon & Schuster.

Richardson, James T. 2001. "'Showtime' in Texas: Social Production of the Branch Davidian Trials." *Nova Religio* 5, no. 1 (October): 152–70.

Ricks, Bob. 1993. Speech to the Tulsa, Oklahoma, Rotary Club, August 25. Transcript and audiotape in the Lee Hancock Collection, Southwestern Writers Collection, Texas State University, San Marcos.

Robertson, J. J. 1996. *Beyond the Flames: The Trials of the Branch Davidians.* San Diego: ProMotion Publishing.

Roden, Amo. 2011. "George Roden." The Writings of Amo Roden. http://wacocult .tripod.com/amo/george.html. Accessed September 3, 2011.

Roden, Ben. 1972. *The Leviticus of the Davidian Seventh-day Adventists, The Branch Supplement.* New Mount Carmel Center, Waco, TX: Universal Publishing Association.

Rosenfeld, Jean E. 2001. "The Use of the Military at Waco: The Danforth Report in Context." *Nova Religio* 5, no. 1 (October): 171–85.

Segal, Andy, producer. 2011. *CNN Presents: Faith, Fear, and Fire.* Atlanta: CNN Worldwide.

Sherrow, Richard L. 1996. "Declaration of Richard L. Sherrow." January 17. Available at http://www.carolmoore.net/waco/waco-fire.html. Accessed November 3, 2011.

Southern Poverty Law Center. 2011. "Kirk Lyons." http://www.splcenter.org/get-informed/intelligence-files/profiles/kirk-lyons. Accessed November 3, 2011.

Tabor, James. 2011. "David Koresh and the Branch Davidians." http://www.pbs .org/wgbh/pages/frontline/shows/apocalypse/explanation/cults.html. Accessed September 1, 2011.

Tabor, James D., and J. Phillip Arnold. 1995. "Commentary on the Koresh Manuscript." In *Why Waco? Cults and the Battle for Religious Freedom in America,* by James D. Tabor and Eugene V. Gallagher, 205–11. Berkeley and Los Angeles: University of California Press.

Tabor, James D., and Eugene V. Gallagher. 1995. *Why Waco? Cults and the Battle for Religious Freedom in America.* Berkeley and Los Angeles: University of California Press.

Thibodeau, David, and Leon Whiteson. 1999. *A Place Called Waco: A Survivor's Story.* New York: Public Affairs.

Van Vleet, Rick, Stephen M. Novak, Jason Van Vleet, and Michael McNulty, producers. 1999. *Waco: A New Revelation.* MGA Films.

Vector Data Systems. 2000. "Mensuration Report for the Analysis of Mount Carmel Compound," 1–8, pdf. Attachment 4 to "Imagery Analysis Report: The Events at Waco, Texas, 19 April 1993, Prepared for the U.S. District Court for the Western District of Texas and the Office of Special Counsel," May 5, 2000. Appendix I in John C. Danforth, Special Counsel, "Final Report to the Deputy Attorney General Concerning the 1993 Confrontation at the Mt. Carmel Complex," November 8, 2000, pdf pages 1149–56. Available in the Wittliff Collection, Texas State University, San Marcos.

Wessinger, Catherine. 2000. *How the Millennium Comes Violently: From Jonestown to Heaven's Gate.* New York: Seven Bridges Press.

———. 2006. "The Branch Davidians and Religion Reporting: A Ten-Year Retrospective." In *Expecting the End: Millennialism in Social and Historical Context,* ed. Kenneth G. C. Newport and Crawford Gribben, 148–274. Waco: Baylor University Press, 2006.

———. 2009. "Deaths in the Fire at the Branch Davidians' Mount Carmel: Who Bears Responsbility?" *Nova Religio* 13, no. 2 (November): 39–40.

Wittmer, Matthew D. 2009. "Traces of the Mount Carmel Community: Documentation and Access." *Nova Religio* 13, no. 2: 95–113. Available at http://stormbound.org/waco.html.

———. 2011a. Memorializing Mount Carmel Center East of Waco, Texas. http://www.stormbound.org/waco.html. Accessed November 3, 2011.

———. 2011b. Mount Carmel Property, 1950s–2011. http://stormbound.org/waco.html#Historical_Property_Map. Accessed December 22.

Wright, Stuart A., ed. 1995. *Armageddon in Waco: Critical Perspectives on the Branch Davidian Conflict.* Chicago: University of Chicago Press.

———. 1999. "Anatomy of a Government Massacre: Abuses of Hostage-Barricade Protocols during the Waco Standoff." *Terrorism and Political Violence* 11, no. 2: 39–68.

———. 2000. "Waco Redux: Trial and Error." *Religion in the News* 3, no. 3 (Fall). Available at http://www.trincoll.edu/depts/csrpl/rinvol3no3/waco_redux.htm.

———. 2001a. "Field Notes from Waco: *Isabel Andrade et al. v. U.S.*" *Nova Religio* 4, no. 2 (April): 351–56.

———. 2001b. "Justice Denied: The Waco Civil Trial." *Nova Religio* 5, no. 1 (October): 143–51.

———. 2003. "A Decade after Waco: Reassessing Crisis Negotiations at Mount Carmel in Light of New Government Disclosures." *Nova Religio* 7, no. 2 (November): 101–10.

Wright, Stuart A. 2007. *Patriots, Politics, and the Oklahoma City Bombing*. Cambridge: Cambridge University Press.
———. 2009. "Revisiting the Branch Davidian Mass Suicide Debate." *Nova Religio* 13, no. 2 (November): 4–24.

MATERIALS IN ARCHIVES

Martin, Wayne. 1993. Digitized audiofiles of more than twenty-four hours of the 911 call initiated on February 28. Provided by Ken Fawcett, who purchased the audiotapes from the McLennan County Sheriff's Department. Available in the Matthew D. Wittmer Collection, in the Texas Collection, Baylor University.
Matteson no. 1 through no. 4 transcripts. 2004. Catherine Matteson interviews with Catherine Wessinger, in Waco, Texas, in the Texas Collection, Baylor University.
Mount Carmel Property Documents folder in the Matthew D. Wittmer Collection, in the Texas Collection, Baylor University.
Schneider, Steve. 1990. Audiotaped Bible studies given in Manchester, England. Texas Collection, Baylor University.
SHEkinah. 1980–1983. Matthew D. Wittmer Collection in the Texas Collection, Baylor University.
Videotape of live news satellite feed. 1993. Captured, digitized and provided by Ken Fawcett. February 28–April 19. Matthew D. Wittmer Collection, in the Texas Collection, Baylor University.

ARCHIVAL COLLECTIONS

Joe Roberts Collection, Texas Collection, Baylor University.
Lee Hancock Collection. Southwestern Writers Collection. Texas State University, San Marcos. Finding aid at http://www.thewittliffcollections.txstate.edu/research/a-z/hancock.html.
Mark Swett Collection in the Texas Collection, Baylor University.
Matthew D. Wittmer Collection in the Texas Collection, Baylor University.

TRANSCRIPTS

Doyle—Property transcript. 2003. Clive Doyle interview with Catherine Wessinger on August 15 at Mount Carmel Center.
Doyle—Theology transcript. 2003. Clive Doyle interview with Catherine Wessinger on August 15 at Mount Carmel Center.
Doyle no. 1 through no. 25 transcripts. 2004. Clive Doyle interviews with Catherine Wessinger.
Doyle no. 26 through no. 29 transcripts. 2006. Clive Doyle interviews with Catherine Wessinger.

Index

Acuña, Concepción, 6, 63, 104, 106, 186

A Current Affair (Australia), 193

Adminstration Building. *See under* Mount Carmel (New Mount Carmel Center

affidavit for warrants. *See under* ATF

Aguilera, Davy, 214n26, 220n57

Allard, Edward, 236n30

Allison, Norman, 103, 105, 129–30, 165, 170, 186

Alloway, Myrtle, 100

Andrade, Chanel, 106

Andrade, Jennifer, 106

Andrade, Kathy, 106

Anteon Corporation, 236n30

Ark of the Covenant, 77, 210n9

Arnold, J. Phillip, 146, 225n90; March 15 KRLD Radio discussion of theology, 226–27n98; April 1 KRLD Radio discussion with James Tabor, 227n98

ATF: 911 call, 110, 123, 125, 218n44; affidavit for warrants, 1, 214n26, 220n57; aerial surveillance, 215n33; agents in barn on Double EE Ranch, 129; agents killed in the raid, 1, 218n44, 219n54, 232n8;

allegations against agents, 221–22n72; allegations against Branch Davidians, 168, 215n29, 220n57; Army Special Forces training for raid, 175, 207n44; Branch Davidians killed as a result of the raid, 100–101, 103, 106, 108, 111, 114, 128–30, 182, 212n5, 232n8; Branch Davidians knew of investigation, 117–19, 214n26, 214–15n27, 215n33; building was evidence, 135, 221–22n72; cease-fire, 125–28, 218n44, 231n4, 232n8; children affected by raid, 121, 123, 231n4; David Koresh at front door, 121, 218n43; dynamic entry, 127, 215n27, 216n35, 231n4; element of surprise lost, 120–21, 216n38, 217n42; flash-bang grenades, 167–68, 231–32n6; investigation, 2, 117–19, 214n26, 215n33; invited by David Koresh to inspect his weapons, 214n26; items left behind, 137–38; methamphetamine lab allegation, 207n44; National Guard helicopters, 2, 114, 121, 123, 207n44, 221–22n72, 222n73, 232n8; negotiations, 127–28;

no-knock entry, 127, 222n72; number of agents in raid, 219n55; Operation Trojan Horse, 218n42; raid on February 28, 1993, 1–2, 3, 4, 7, 68, 71, 72, 80, 100, 103, 105, 106, 107, 108–11, 114–15, 119, 120–30, 165–68, 170–71, 175, 182, 185–86, 189, 207n44, 215n27, 216n35, 219n51, 219n54, 220n56, 225n90, 231n4, 232n8; raid unnecessary, 167, 214n26, 216n35; second shooting, 165; shooting dogs, 137, 183; shooting of David Koresh, 123–24, 218n45; shooting of Perry Jones, 121–25, 219n48; shooting death of Michael Schroeder, 103, 106, 129–30, 165, 186, 190, 212n5, figure 1 in appendix; Show Time, 217–18n42; undercover house, 117–18, 215n33, 216n38, figure 2 in appendix; undercover agents shooting rifles with David Koresh, 119, 215–16n35; video footage of raid, 217n38, 222n72

autopsies, contested, 125, 219n47, 220n62–63, 222n73

Avraam, Renos, 103, 150, 152, 159, 165, 171, 185, 212n10, 230n114, 232n11

Ayres, Peter, 236n30

Bain, Sarah, 169, 232–33n11, 233n12

Ballesteros, Roland, 167, 231n4

Baranyai, Elizabeth, 99–101

Barrios, Crystal, xiii, 110

Barrios, Isaiah, xiii, 110

Ben David, 48, 202n10

Bennett, Alrick George, 101

Benta, Susan, 101

Blake, Winston, 101, 114, 122, 129, 136, 232n8

Borst, Brad, 63, 106

Borst, Mary Jean, or Jean, 63, 106

Braden, Frank, 20

Branch, Brad, 101, 107, 137, 138, 165, 171, 184, 232n11,

Brannon, James, 234n23

Breault, Marc, 63, 65, 72, 101, 214n26

Brittany Hotel, 172, 233n18

Brown, Deborah, 174. *See also* Slawson, Debbie

Brzozowski, Jeffrey, 216n35

Buford, Bill, 219n54

Bunds, David, 106, 205n29

Bunds, Debbie, 106

Bunds, Donald, 64, 71–72, 106, 120, 186, 207n42

Bunds, Jeannine, 64, 106

Bunds, Robyn, 106, 205n29, 211n13

Bunds, Shaun (Wisdom), 106, 211n13

Bureau of Alcohol, Tobacco, and Firearms (BATF or ATF). *See* ATF

Caddell, Michael, 173–76, 234n23, 235n25, 236n30

Campion, Linda, 211n13

Castillo, Jaime, 105, 117–18, 152, 165, 171, 185, 199n1, 230n114, 232n11

Cavanaugh, Jim, 217n42, 218n44, 222–23n76

Chapman, Cynthia, 234n23

Child Protective Services (Texas), 213n16, 214n26

children: abuse allegations, 213n16, 214n26, 216n37, 220n57; deaths in FBI assault and fire, 230n115; gassing by FBI and deaths on April 19, 1993, 149, 228–29n110, 229n111, 230n115; investigation by Child Protective Services, 213n16; of David Koresh; spanking of, 216n37, 220n57. *See also under* Koresh, David

Chojnacki, Philip, 217n42

Christ, 71, 76–81, 83, 86, 89, 91, 95, 205–6n30; one hundred and twenty disciples of, 91; parables of, 71, 83, 90, 95; resurrection of, 84–85; translation of, 85; twelve apostles of, 85

Christian Broadcasting Network, 221n69

christos, 210n10

Christ Spirit, 76–81, 88, 205n30
civil trial, 2000, 4–5, 173–76, 183, 185,
    193, 196, 230n112, 232n8, 234n23,
    234–35n25, 235–36n30
Clark, Ramsey, 174–75, 234n23
Clinton, Bill, 4
Cogdell, Dan, 166
Cohen, Pablo, 67, 104, 131, 229n112
"compound," as pejorative term, 167
congressional hearings, 4, 213n16,
    217n41, 222n72, 232n6, 237n33
Coulson, Danny, 224n85
Craddock, Graeme, 101, 165, 170,
    171–72, 185, 214n27, 229n112,
    230n114
criminal trial, 1994, 4, 7, 72, 103,
    104, 108, 124, 129, 141, 165–72,
    184–86, 216n35, 217n42, 218n44,
    220n56, 221n72, 226n96; people
    acquitted of all charges, 186, 170;
    sentences, 170–72, 184–85, 232–
    33n11; sentences appealed, 172;
    verdicts, 169–70, 233n12
CS gas, 3, 7, 146–47, 150, 211n13,
    227n101–2, 228n104, 234n24,
    238n34; and fire, 229–30n112;
    banned by international treaty for
    use in warfare, 3, 148, 228n107;
    cyanide, 227n102, 228n103–4,
    235n26; cyanide poisoning of
    Branch Davidians, 228n104; ferret
    rounds, 3, 148, 150, 227n102,
    235n26; methylene chloride,
    228n104–5; not for indoor use,
    148, 228n108; phosgene, 228n104;
    pyrotechnic ferret rounds, 235n26;
    riot control agent, 228n107–8;
    sprayed by CEVs, 148, 150
"cult" stereotype, 5, 10, 19, 167,
    216n37, 220n57
Curtis, Mike, 217n42
Cyrus, 97, 205–6n30, 210n9; as christ,
    205n30
Cyrus message, 205n30

Danforth, John C., 5, 235n26, 236–
    37n30

Danforth Report, 5, 212n7, 228–
    29n110, 235n26, 236–37n30,
    237n33; FLIR reenactments, 236n30
Danziger Bridge shootings in New
    Orleans, 238n36
Davidians, 6, 7, 18–21, 22–23, 25,
    31–32, 40, 41, 44, 47, 48, 62, 86,
    104, 108, 112, 181,199n3, 200n2,
    200n5, 200n7, 201n1, 201n10,
    202n8, 203n12, 204n18, 204n21,
    204n27, 206n35, 209n2, 209n3
Davies, Abedowalo ("Dabo"), 69, 102
DeGuerin, Dick, 124, 222n72
DeGuerin, Mike, 166
Delta Force, 237n33
discretion, exercised by judge, 234n25
Domangue, Mark, 233n18
Dorcas, 20, 200n4
Doyle, Clive: acquitted of all charges,
    4, 7, 170; American citizenship,
    10; a servant of the Lord, 14; ATF
    guards in medical tent, helicopter,
    and hospital, 155, 157–58; ATF raid
    on February 28, 1993, 7, 121–28;
    becoming a Branch Davidian, 6,
    31; belief about David Koresh, his
    death and resurrection, 83, 85; belief
    about David Koresh's children and
    judgment, 87; belief about death
    and resurrection, 83; belief about
    devil, 177; belief about end-time
    war and peace, 94; belief about Fifth
    Seal and events in 1993, 143, 225–
    26n90; belief about prophets, 146;
    belief about the Kingdom, 94; Bible
    study with David Koresh during
    the siege, 142; burying four bodies
    during the siege, 135–36; burn ward,
    Parkland Hospital, Dallas, 155–59,
    163; California, 63–65, 68, 71;
    child custody disputes, 6, 48–52,
    54–57; childhood, 6, 11–21; coming
    to the United States, 6, 36–38;
    conversation with David Koresh
    on April 17, 1993, 146; criminal
    trial, 1994, 165–72; Davidian,
    6, 18–21, 22–23, 25–26, 30–31;

disfellowshipped from Seventh-day
Adventist Church, 20–21; divorce,
6, 48–50; evaluating prophets,
10; executive council of General
Association of Branch Davidian
Seventh-day Adventists, 207n42;
FBI assault on April 19, 1993, 7,
146–55; FBI siege, 130–46; final
reflections, 181–82, 186–87; fireball,
154; fire on April 19, 1993, 4, 7,
150–54; first court appearance, 158;
garden at Mount Carmel, 153; gas
mask, 147; going outside during the
siege, 137–38, 223n76; Hawaii, 66,
111, 206n39; interviews with, 6; jail,
McLennan County, 163–65; jobs
in Australia, 21–22, 25–29, 33–36;
lack of trust in FBI, 145; marriage,
6, 44–48; medical tent, 154–55;
Mexia camp, 60; moves away from
Mount Carmel, 7, 58, 178, 239n40;
moves to Mount Carmel, 6–7, 39–
41, 112–13, 173, 199n3; opinion
of FBI actions at Mount Carmel,
148; opinion of federal agents'
intentions on April 19, 1993, 177;
Palestine camp, 60–63; printing at
Mount Carmel, 41–42, 53, 204n18;
retrieving Peter Gent's body, 136;
return to Waco after being acquitted,
172–73; roofing work, 62, 63,
110, 117; room in large building,
114, 121, 133–34, 150, 221n67;
"Serpent's Root" studies, attending,
75, 209n2; Seventh-day Adventist, 6,
15–21, 25, 30–31; sleep deprivation
during siege, 142; Tasmania, 22–25;
transcripts of interviews with, 6; trip
to Australia with David Koresh in
1986, 65
Doyle, Edna, 6, 11–20, 22–25, 28–30,
50, 51–52, 55, 58, 60, 61, 73, 86,
104, 106 129, 164, 172–73, 178,
186, 199n1, 238n37–38
Doyle, Karen, 6, 47, 49–52, 55–57, 58,
60, 71, 106, 132, 173, 178, 186,
238n37–38

Doyle, Shari, xiii, 6, 7, 48, 50–52,
55–57, 58, 60, 106, 131, 134, 156,
159–60, 174
Drake, Tom, 173, 238n38
Drake, Amo. *See* Roden, Amo Paul
Bishop
dynamic entry. *See under* ATF

Elliott, Beverly, 101
El Shaddai, 77, 209n8
Emblems, 54, 204n25
England, Mark, 119
ensign, 124
Evans, Nick, 236n30
Evers, Eric, 232n8
Ezekiel 9, 32, 200n5

Fagan, Doris, 101–2, 175–76, 235n29
Fagan, Livingstone, xiii, 101–2, 144,
165, 168, 171–72, 175–76, 182,
184, 212n8, 214n27, 225n90,
232n8, 232n11, 233n17
Fagan, Nehara, 101, 128, 182
Fagan, Renae, 101, 128, 182
Fagan, Yvette, 101–2, 182
Farrell, Ernest, 39
Farris, Lisa Marie, 107, 131, 133
Fatta, Kalani, 69, 108, 185
Fatta, Paul, 72, 108, 119, 165, 170–72,
185–86, 207n40, 207n42, 233n12
Fawcett, Ken, xii–xiii, 193, 196, 218n44,
229n111, 235n25, 240n2, 240n4
FBI: allegations that agents shot at
Branch Davidians on April 19,
1993, 110, 176–77, 213–14n21,
235–37n30, 237n33; April 14,
1993, surrender plan offered by
David Koresh, 144–46, 226n93–94;
227n99; April 18, 1993, warning
by David Koresh, FBI "fixing to step
across a ribbon," 227n100; April 19,
1993, assault on Branch Davidians,
3–4, 7, 110, 145, 146–55, 176–77,
182, 189, 210–11n13, 223n77,
227n101–2, 228n103, 228n104–5,
228n106, 228–29n110, 234n24,
235–37n30, 237n33; April 19,

1993, audio captured by surveillance devices, 229n110; April 19, 1993, fire at Mount Carmel, 4, 143, 145, 146, 147, 149, 150–54, 159–61, 189, 229n110, 229–30n112, 230n114; April 19, 1993, pediatric burn specialist on stand-by, 226n97; assault plan approved by Attorney General Janet Reno, 148, 228n105, 234n24; Branch Davidians rejoiced at plan to come out, 145; children, 145, 149, 153, 226n97, 227n100, 229n110, 230n115; concertina wire, 141, 152; David Koresh's incomplete manuscript, 145–46, 227n99; decision to apply pressure, 224n85; electricity cut off, 134, 138, 140, 145, 147, 221n71, 223n80; evidence destroyed or lost, 167, 213–14n21, 231n5, 235n25; FBI false testimony about start of fire, 168–69; fireball, 154; fire in vault, 229n111; fire visible at 12:07 p.m., 228n106; flash-bang grenades, 3, 145, 151, 167–68, 226n96, 231–32n6; FLIR and the fire, 235n30; FLIR photography, 176–77, 230n112, 235–37n30, 237n33; FLIR reenactment, 176, 236n30, 237n31; FLIR reenactment by Michael McNulty, 176; gas masks, 147, 151, 153, 227n101, 228n103; gassing of children and mothers in vault, 149, 228–29n110, 229n111; Hostage Rescue Team (HRT), 220n65, 224n86, 226n96, 228n105, 234n24; loudspeakers, 131, 139–40, 140, 142, 145, 147, 160, 223n77, 223n82, 224n85, 224–25n86, 227n101; lying in congressional hearings about use of pyrotechnic devices, 235n26; March 2, 1993, alleged suicide plan, 221n70; March 2, 1993, deal with David Koresh, 134–35, 144; media, 5, 134; mistrust of agents by Branch Davidians, 145–46; negotiations,

2–3, 111, 131–34, 136–39, 142–46, 161, 182, 218n44–45, 220–21n65, 221n66, 221n71, 222n76, 223n77, 223n80, 223–24n82, 224n83, 224n84–85, 224–25n86, 225n87, 225n88, 226n94, 227n100; number of Branch Davidians who came out during the siege, 144, 182–84, 226n92; number of Branch Davidians who survived the fire, 4, 145, 182, 230n114; number of Branch Davidians who died in the fire, 4, 100–104, 106–11, 182, 230n115; obscene gestures by agents, 3, 226n91; press briefings, 144, 226n98, 229n110; psychological warfare, 3; punished Branch Davidians for coming out, 2–3; pyrotechnic devices, 4, 235n26; requests by Branch Davidians for typing supplies, 144–45, 226n95; siege of Mount Carmel, 2, 7, 111, 130–46, 182; spotlights, 139, 143, 147, 223–24n82; stress escalation, 225n88; tanks, 131, 133–34, 138, 139, 141, 145, 148–54, 159, 160, 169, 176–77, 224n83, 226n91, 227n100–101, 228–29n110, 229n111, 230n112–13, 234n24, 235–36n30, 237n33, 238n34; videotapes sent out by Branch Davidians, 218n45

Federal Bureau of Investigation. *See* FBI
Ferguson, Misty, 110, 128, 156, 159, 166, 174, 184–85, 230n114
ferret rounds. *See* CS gas
Fifth Seal. *See under* Koresh, David, teachings
fire at Mount Carmel, April 19, 1993, 4, 143, 145, 146, 147, 149, 150–54, 159–61, 189, 229n110, 229–30n112, 230n114; deaths, 4, 100–104, 106–11,182, 230n115; FBI agent's false testimony about start of, 168–69, 232n9; continued to blaze in vault, 229n11; number of survivors, 4, 101–3, 105, 145,

182, 230n114; fireball, 154; visible at 12:07 p.m., 228n106
First Seal. *See under* Koresh, David, teachings
flash-bang grenades, 3, 167–68, 231–32n6, 232n7
FLIR photography, 176–77, 235–37n30, 237n33
The F.L.I.R. Project (2001), 176
FLIR reenactment, 236n30, 237n31
FLIR reenactment by Michael McNulty, 176
Friesen, Raymond, 46, 60, 61–62, 104, 131, 160, 202n7, 207n42
Friesen, Tillie, 46, 60, 104, 186, 202n7
Fundamentalist Church of Jesus Christ of Latter-day Saints, 213n18

Gallagher, Eugene V., 146
General Association of Davidian Seventh-day Adventists, 2, 201n10–11, 202n12
General Association of Branch Davidian Seventh-day Adventists, 2, 31, 48, 53, 66, 201n12, 202n12, 203n13, 203n16, 207n41–42, 208n49, 239n41; reorganized in 1994, 177, 178, 238n37–38
Gent, Bruce, 100
Gent, Dayland, 100, 221n67
Gent, Lisa, 100
Gent, Nicole, 100–101, 109, 221n67, 230n115
Gent, Paiges, 100
Gent, Peter, 100–101, 128–29, 135, 136–37, 184, 212n5, 222n74; autopsy of, 222n73, 223n78; grave of, 137–38, 222n75, 223n78
Ghigliotti, Carlos, 235–36n30, 237n31, 237n33
Great Disappointment, October 22, 1844, 200n6
gun trade. *See under* Koresh, David
Gyarfas, Aisha. *See* Summers, Aisha Gyarfas
Gyarfas, Elizabeth, 100

Gyarfas, Oliver, Jr., 100–101, 137, 138, 165, 184, 223n80, 224n82, 232n8
Gyarfas, Oliver, Sr., 100

Haldeman, Bonnie, xii, 6, 65, 103, 105, 178, 186, 199n1, 205n29, 206n39, 210n11, 214n27, 215n30, 215n33, 219n46, 238n38, 239n40
Haldeman, Roger, 105, 186
Haldeman, Roy, 105, 186, 215n30
Hanson, Mike, 173
Hardial, Sandra, 102
Hardy, David, 234n23, 235–36n30, 237n31, 237n33
Harwell, Jack, 138, 219n48
Henry, Diana, 102
Henry, Paulina, 102
Henry, Phillip, 69, 102
Henry, Stephen, 102
Henry, Vanessa, 102
Henry, Zilla, 102
Hipsman, Novellette Sinclair. *See* Sinclair, Novellette
Hipsman, Peter, 107, 109, 128–29, 136
Hollingsworth, Victorine, 102, 144, 184, 221n70
Holy Spirit, 52, 75, 76–78, 80, 85, 88, 90, 91, 94, 99, 181, 204n18; angel at the altar (Rev. 8:3–5), 91
Horiuchi, Lon, 175, 234n24
Houteff, Florence, 22, 32, 40, 41, 220n2, 200n5, 201n10–11, 203n13; disappointment in Australia, 25–26, 32; disappointment in the United States, April 22, 1959, 32, 201n8, 201n10; forty-two months prophecy, 22, 25, 32
Houteff, Victor, 6, 18, 20, 22, 31, 40, 62, 89, 94, 103, 104, 108, 143–44, 181, 199n3, 200n2, 200n5, 201n10, 201n14, 201n16, 202n12, 204n21, 209n2–3
House Government Reform Committee, 236n30
Houtman, Floyd, 59, 60–61, 71, 107–8, 131, 205n29, 206n31, 206n40

Howell, Bobbie Lane. *See* Koresh, Bobbie Lane
Howell, Bobby, 239n40
Howell, Cyrus. *See* Koresh, Cyrus Howell
Howell, Rachel. *See* Koresh, Rachel Howell
Howell, Star. *See* Koresh, Star Howell
Howell, Vernon: becomes a Branch Davidian, 2, 6, 52, 99; birthday, 202n6; changes name to David Koresh, 52; daughter with Linda Campion, 211n13; president and trustee of the General Association of Branch Davidian Seventh-day Adventists, 207n42; "The Serpent's Root" studies, 75, 209n1–2. *See also* Koresh, David
Hughes, Anna, 65, 206n40
Hussein, Saddam, 211n17

Jamar, Jeffrey, 224n85, 234n24, 238n34
Jesus. *See* Yahshua; Christ Spirit
Jewell, Kiri, 108, 213n16
Jewell, Sherri, 108, 132, 213n16
Jones, Alex, 173
Jones, Chica, and Little One (twins), 109
Jones, David Michael, 108–9, 115, 120, 141, 145, 183, 190, 206–7n40, 216n38; trailer, 99, 104, 106, 108, 112, 120, 129–30, 186, 190, figure 1 in appendix
Jones, Heather, 109, 128, 183
Jones, Kathy, 109, 178, 183, 238n38
Jones, Kevin, 109, 128, 183
Jones, Mark, 109, 128, 183
Jones, Mary Belle, or Mary, 58, 60, 104, 106, 108–9, 178, 186, 204n24, 205n28, 238n37–38
Jones, Michele, 60, 109, 213n19
Jones, Perry Dale, 54, 58, 60, 64, 104, 108–9, 120, 121–25, 128–29, 131, 136, 203n13, 205n28, 207n42, 214n24, 217n39, 219n48, 232n8; contested autopsy, 124–25, 219n47

Jones, Rachel. *See* Koresh, Rachel Howell
Jones, Serenity Sea, 109
Jordan, Glen, 219n54
Joyce, David, 44, 48

Kendrick, Janet, 58, 59, 60, 105, 186, 238n37
Kendrick, Woodrow (Bob), 58, 59, 60, 73, 103, 105, 129–30, 165, 170, 186, 207n42, 238n37
Keys, David, 235n25
King, Kenneth, 219n54, 232n8
Koresh, Bobbie Lane, 109
Koresh, Cyrus Howell, 58, 60, 64, 109, 206n36
Koresh, David: and Lois Roden, 53–54, 59–60, 203–4n17, 204n23; April 14, 1993, surrender plan, 144–46, 226n93–94, 227n99; April 17, 1993, conversation with Clive Doyle, 146; April 18, 1993, warning to FBI, "fixing to step across a ribbon," 227n100; April 19, 1993, 159; ATF raid, February 28, 1993, 1–2, 120–27, 171, 216–17n38, 218n43–44; at Mexia camp, 60; at Mount Carmel, 201n1, 52, 66–72, 99–111, 113, 115–19; at Palestine camp, 60–63, 65, 206n36; Bible studies, 9–10, 73; black Camaro, 216n35; CB calls during siege, 223n82, 225n87; child abuse allegations, 213n16, 214n26, 216n37, 220n57; children as twenty-four elders, 87; children of, 87, 210–11n13, 213n19, 227n100, 230n115; children surviving, 211n13; conflict with George Roden, 53–54, 58–60, 99, 178; cooperation with law enforcement agents, 55–57; crape myrtle tree, 239n40; death in fire on April 19, 1993, 229n112; demonized, 4–5; entrepreneurial activities, 116–17; FBI siege, 131, 133–35, 138–40, 142–46; grave,

186; guns, 72–73, 108, 116, 117, 119, 214n26, 215n34; gun parts, 215n29; gun trade, 72–73, 108, 116, 119, 214n26, 215n29, 233n12; hellfire switch, 117; helps Clive Doyle get his daughters back, 54–57; in Australia, 65, 67, 99–100; in California, 63–65, 107, 206n37; in England, 67, 68–69; in Israel, 52, 58, 67, 205n30; in jail, 207n40; invites ATF agents to inspect his weapon 214n26; last telephone call to his mother, 124, 219n46; left Mount Carmel frequently, 216n35; "Let George Do It" booklet, 67; March 2, 1993, agreement with FBI, 134, 221n69; March 2, 1993, audiotaped sermon, 134, 183, 221n69; March 18, 1993, first day up after being shot, 224n85; moves away from Mount Carmel, 58; music, 100, 104, 105, 107, 119, 140, 216n35; name change, 2; plays loud music at FBI agents, 140; Seraph, 223n82; "The Serpent's Root" studies, 75, 209n1–2; Seventh Angel, 82, 205n30, 226n93; shootout with George Roden, 65–66, 206–7n41, 217n40; SOS message during siege, 223–24n82; Spirit of Prophecy, 204n22; statements to Robert Rodriguez, 120, 217n39, 217n41; statutory rape vulnerability, 213n19; trial for shootout with George Roden, 66, 207n40, 217n40; unfinished manuscript, 145–46, 227n99; visions, 73; wives, 100–101, 106–9, 111, 219n19; wounded in ATF raid, 115, 218n45; "You need this message," 181. *See also* Howell, Vernon; Koresh, David, teachings

Koresh, David, teachings: agents are souls to be saved, 135; antitypical approach to interpreting scripture, 209n3; approach to scripture, 75–

76, 209n3; April 14, 1993, surrender offer, 144–46, 226n93–94, 227n98; April 17, 1993, conversation with Clive Doyle, 146; Armageddon, 97; assault predicted/expected, 115–16, 142–43, 146, 227n100; the Assyrian (United Nations led by the United States), 92–96, 142; Babylon, 93–94, 97; Babylon the Great (new world order, one-world government), 77, 94, 96–98; baptism of fire, 85; book sealed with seven seals, 76, 80, 82–83; carcass, 81; children of light, 69; the Father, 76–77, 79–84; Daniel, book of, 98; David, King, of Latter Days, 89; the devil, 78, 86, 91–92, 96–98, 115; dirty birds, 96; Elihu, 78; false prophet, 97; Feast of Tabernacles, 90, 95; Fifth Seal, 143, 225n90; First Seal, 144, 145, 210n12, 226n94; four beasts (in book of Revelation), 83, 86, 87; four beasts (in Daniel 7:3–8), 92; "God always gives two ways out," 142–43, 225n89; God is light, 69; "God's in the saving business," 91; Gog and Magog, 97; harvests of souls, 71, 83–91, 97; feasts and the harvests, 90; first fruits and wave loaves, 89–90; summer fruits (second fruits), 89, 90–91, 95; heaven on earth, 95; highway to Jerusalem, 94; incomplete manuscript, 145–46; Isaiah, book of, 75–76, 77, 90, 93–94; Jacob's trouble, 142–43; Jerusalem, city of David, 93, 95; Job, the book of, 78; Joel 2, 93; Joel 2:28–29, 91, 97; the Kingdom, 86, 88–90 93–98, 109, 143; king of the north, 93; KRLD Radio interview, 225n90; the Lamb, 76, 80–83, 85–86, 88–96, 205n30; lamb-like beast, 92; leopard-like beast (first beast in book of Revelation), 91–92, 96; Light, 79; "little book" on Seven Seals, 82,

144–46, 226n93–94, 227n98–99; the Lord standing on Mount of Olives, 93, 95–96; male and female natures of one God, 76–80, 83, 88; martyrs, 84–85, 87, 88, 93; Matthew 24, 90; Melchizedek, 78; the millennium, 97–98; the Mother, 77–79, 81; Mount Zion, 82, 86, 88–91, 94, 95; Nahum 2, 142–43; new world order, 96; one body, 69, 70; one hundred and forty-four thousand, 82, 88, 89–91, 94–95, 201n15; one hundred and twenty disciples, 89, 91; the One on the throne (the rock), 76, 78, 79–83, 90; Passover and wave sheaf, 83, 88–90; Pentecost, 85, 89–91; perfect mate, 88, 96, 109; prophecy about the ground being plowed under, 153; Psalms, 210n12; resurrection, 84–85, 89, 93; Revelation, book of, 76–77, 79–98, 144, 209n4, 210n9, 225n90, 226n93, 227n99; rider on the black horse, 82; rider on the pale horse, 82; rider on the red horse, 82; rider on the white horse, 82, 210n12; the sanctuary, 77, 83, 89, 201n9; Seven Seals, 76, 80, 82, 86–87, 105, 144, 146, 209n4, 219n46; "The Seven Seals of the Book of Revelation" (unfinished manuscript), 146, 209n4, 227n99; Seventh Angel, 82, 205n30, 226n93; Sixth Seal, 85, 93, 225n90; the Son, 76–81, 88; Spirit of God, 69, 73; translation (raising into heaven), 85, 86; twenty-four elders, 83, 86–88; two-horned beast (second beast in book of Revelation, the United States), 88, 96–97; two hundred million martyrs of the ages, 85–86, 87, 93; United States, 94; wave sheaf, 83–90, 93–94, 109; the Wife, 81, 88, 91; Wisdom (*hokhmah*), 77, 209n7; woman clothed with the sun, 77–78; Zechariah 14, 90, 93, 95, 97. *See also* Holy Spirit; the

Lamb; Passover; resurrection; wave sheaf
Koresh, meaning of, 205n30
Koresh, Rachel Howell, 58, 59, 60, 63, 64, 109, 204n24, 205n28–29, 206n36, 222n76
Koresh, Star Howell, 109
KRLD Radio, 218n44, 220n59, 221n69, 225n90, 226–27n98
KWTX-TV, 120, 126, 216–17n38
KXXV-TV, 229n111

the Lamb, 76, 80–83, 85–86, 88–96, 205n30; army of, 93; marriage of, 81, 88–89, 210n12; marriage supper of, 88, 94, 95, 210n12; on Mount Zion, 88–91, 94, 95; resurrection of, 85
Lawson, Margaret, 105, 134, 183, 238n37
Lawter, James, 104, 144, 184
LeBleu, Conway, 219n54, 232n8
Lee Hancock Collection, xii
Little, Jeff, 71, 109, 126, 223n82
Living Waters Branch, 206n32, 208n49
Lovelock, Derek, 102, 152, 155, 164–65, 185, 230n114
Lynch, Larry, 123, 125–26, 218n44, 219n49, 220n58
Lyons, Kirk, 174, 234n22

Mag Bag, 73, 106, 112, 208n55, 212n11, figure 1 in appendix
Malamute dogs, 137
Mark Swett Collection, xii
marriage age for girls in Texas, 202n5, 213n18
Martin, Anita Marie, 110
Martin, Daniel, 6, 105, 110, 134, 183
Martin, Diane, 102
Martin, Jamie, 6, 54, 110, 128, 182, 205n27, 239n40
Martin, Kimberly, 6, 105, 110, 134, 183
Martin, Lisa Marie, 110
Martin, Sheila, xiv, 6, 54, 60, 62, 102, 109–10, 115, 135, 144, 178,

182–84, 196, 202n10, 204n25, 204–5n27, 217n41, 219n50, 238n37, 238n88

Martin, Sheila Reneé, 110

Martin, Wayne, xii, 6, 60, 62, 102, 109–10, 118, 123, 125–26, 131, 151, 182–83, 204–5n27, 207n42, 218n44, 219n48, 219n50, 220n58, 223n82

Martin, Wayne Joseph, 110, 135

Martinez, Abigail, xi, 110

Martinez, Audrey, xi, 110

Martinez, Joseph, xi, 110

Martinez, Juliette. *See* Santoyo, Juliette

Matteson, Catherine, xii, 6, 47, 58, 60, 86, 105, 134, 178, 183, 199n1, 202n8, 203–4n17, 213n14, 214n24, 214n27, 238n37–38

McBean, Janet, 102, 106, 186

McBean, John-Mark, 102, 186

McCormick, Darlene, 119

McKeehan, Todd, 219n54, 232n8

McLemore, John, 217n38

McLennan County Restland Cemetery, 104, 105, 110, 213n13

McMahon, Henry, 116, 214n26

McNulty, Michael, 154–55, 176

McVeigh, Timothy, 231n1

methamphetamine lab. *See under* ATF; Mount Carmel (New Mount Carmel Center)

Meyer, Trudy, 63, 104, 106, 186

Millay, Dr., 172–73

Millen, David, 219n54

Miller, William, 200n6

Millerite movement, 209n3

Mitchell, Douglas, 177, 238n38

Mexia campground, 60, 205n27

Monbelly, Bernadette, 102

Morrison, Jack, 232n9

Morrison, Melissa, 102, 131

Morrison, Rosemary, 102, 131

Mount Carmel (New Mount Carmel Center): Administration Building, 40, 44, 53, 54, 112–13, 149, 201n1, 214n24; burned, 54, 113, 149; ATF raid on February 28, 1993, 1–2, 3, 4, 7, 68, 71, 72, 80, 100, 103, 105, 106, 107, 108–11, 114–15, 119, 120–30, 165–68, 170–71, 175, 182, 185–86, 189, 207n44, 215n27, 216n35, 219n51, 219n54, 220n56, 225n90, 231n4, 232n8; barracks, 66; belongs to God, 178–79; Branch Davidians return to, 62, 63, 66–67, 105, 179, 205n27; building was evidence, 135, 167, 221–22n72, 231n5; buried bus tunnel, 68, 114, 135, figure 3 in appendix; bus, parked, 217n38, figure 2 in appendix; cafeteria, 67–68, 113, 114, 115, 121, 123, 131, 134, 136, 148, 177, 189, 196, 238n34, figure 3 in appendix; catwalk, 123, 126, 128, 222n72, 230n113, figure 4 in appendix; CB radio, 223–24n82, 225n87; chicken coop, 141, figure 3 in appendix; Clive Doyle's garden, 153; Clive Doyle moves away from, 7, 58, 178, 239n40; Clive Doyle moves to, 6–7, 39–41, 112–13, 173, 199n3; Clive Doyle's room, 114, 121, 133–34, 150, 221n67, figure 3 in appendix; cemetery, 65, 104, 202n7, 226n91; chapel (original), 54, 66, 67, 75, 201n1; chapel (constructed by David Koresh), 68, 70, 72, 73, 111–12, 113, 115, 117, 118, 123, 125, 126, 128, 131, 133, 134, 135, 137, 140–41, 147–52, 159–60, 169, 171, 177, 193, 215n27, 219n54, 222n72, 229n112, 230n113, 232n8, 238n85, figure 3 in appendix; chapel (constructed by volunteers), 173, 239n40; cinder-block utility building, 136, 185; 229n112, 230n114, figure 3 in appendix; Cliff Sellors' art supply room, 114, 196, 214n25, figure 3 in appendix; Coleman lanterns and fuel, 140; computer room, 112, figure 3 in appendix; courtyard (alcove between kitchen and chapel), 134–35,

229n112, 230n114, 232n8, figure 3 in appendix; crape myrtle trees, 173, 233n19, 239n40; dairy, 67, 131, 135, figure 2 in appendix; Davidian disappointment on April 22, 1959, 32, 200n5, 201n8; David Koresh's rooms, 72, 73, 113, 115, 117, 123–24, 126, 128, 137, 150, 219n51, 219n54, 222n72, 232n8, figure 4 in appendix; dog run, 128, 150, 219n51, figure 4 in appendix; driveway, 152–53, 169, 184, figure 2 in appendix; FBI assault on April 19, 1993, 3–4, 7, 110, 145, 146–55, 176–77, 182, 189, 210–11n13, 223n77, 227n101–2, 228n103–6, 228–29n110, 234n24, 235–37n30, 237n33; FBI siege of, 130–46; fire on April 19, 1993, 4, 143, 145, 146, 147, 149, 150–54, 159–61, 189, 229n110, 229–30n112, 230n114; flagpole, 137, figure 3 in appendix; foyer, 111–12, 117, 120, 121–22, 127, 131, 133, 138, 140, 169, 223n77, figure 3 in appendix; front doors (double), 111–12, 123, 137, 140, 145, 149, 167, 169, 222n72, 223n77, 231n5, 235n25, figure 3 in appendix; fuel tanks, 133, 139, 223n81, figure 2 in appendix; gassing of children and their mothers in vault on April 19, 1993, 149, 228–29n110, 229n111; generators, 140, 224n86; guard shack, 67, figure 2 in appendix; guns, 72, 116, 117, 215n29; guns storage, 72, 113, 117, 171, 215n27, 215n30, 219n51, 219n54; gymnasium, 68, 72, 113, 128, 140–41, 147, 149–50, 167, 176–77, 237n33, figure 3 in appendix, figure 4 in appendix; hay bales, 141; houses, 66, 67, 105, 201–2n1; Kathy Schroeder's room, figure 3 in appendix; kitchen, 112, 113, 123, 125, figure 3 in appendix; large building, 69–70,

99–111, 189–98, figures 2, 3, 4 in appendix; lifestyle at, 69–70, 99–111; location, 202n9, figure 1 in appendix; machine shop, 72, 111–12, 116, 140–41, 167, figure 3 in appendix; Mag Bag business, 73, 106, 112, 208n55, 212n11, figure 1 in appendix; methamphetamine lab during George Roden's tenure, 67, 207n44; model of building, 173, 197; number of Branch Davidians who came out during siege, 2, 144, 226n92; number of residents, 72, 99; ownership of, 2, 207n42; pantry (in vault), 149, figure 3 in appendix; phone room, 112, 120, 232n8, figure 3 in appendix; post-1993 property disputes, 177–79, 239n41; potatoes, 141, 225n87; property taxes, 207n42; provisions, 214n27; purchased, and partially sold, by Florence Houteff, 32–33, 40, 200n2, 201n10; purchased by Ben Roden, 33, 48, 201n12, 203n13; Reconstructing Mount Carmel Center, 189–98; Roden years, 39–43, 48, 199n3; sewing room, 112, 125, figure 3 in appendix; Sheila Martin's room, 115, 169, 196, 219n50, figure 4 in appendix; shootout with George Roden, 65–66, 206–7n41, 217n40; Steve Schneider's room, 112, 131, 232n8, figure 3 in appendix; storm shelter, 68, 114, 118, 135–36, 176–77, 235n26, figure 3 in appendix; swimming pool, 68, 70, 72, 123, 128, 131, 136, 139, 153, 177, 234n21, figure 3 in appendix; tool storage area, 114, 214n25; a training ground, 68; track, 117; trap door, 114, figure 3 in appendix; tower, central, 112, 115, 123, 139, 149, 154, 160, 222n72, figure 4 in appendix; towers, end, 115; vault, 3–4, 112–13, 123, 149, 160, 171, 215n27, 228–29n110,

229n111, figure 3 in appendix; Visitor's Center, 173, 197, 241n12; walls reinforced with concrete, 214n27; water, 114, 122, 134–35, 138; water tanks (plastic), 114, 122, 129, figure 3 in appendix; water tower, 128, 135, 136, 185, 229n111–12, 230n114, figure 3 in appendix; Wayne Martin's office, 110, 112, 121, 123, 125, figure 3 in appendix; weight room, 114, figure 3 in appendix; well, 136; Winston Blake's room, 114, 122, 129, figure 3 in appendix. *See also* fire at Mount Carmel, April 19, 1993; Passover

Mount Carmel (Old Mount Carmel Center), 40, 200n2

Mount Carmel Center. *See* Mount Carmel (New Mount Carmel Center)

Mount of Olives, 93, 95–96

Mount Zion, 82, 86, 88–91, 94, 95

MOVE, 220n58

Mulloney, Dan, 217n38

Murray, Sonia, 102

Newbold College, 68, 101, 102, 208n50

new light, 15, 62, 200n1, 204n21

new world order, 96, 211n17

Nobrega, Natalie, 103, 183

Nobrega, Theresa, 103, 183, 221n67

Noesner, Gary, 220–21n65

Novell, Gordon, 174

observer (military term), 238n33

offshoot, 18, 20, 200n3

Okimoto, Dana, 211n13

Okimoto, Jared (Scooter), 211n13

Okimoto, Sky, 211n13

Oklahoma City bombing (1995), 231n1

one hundred and forty-four thousand, 32, 82, 88, 89–91, 94–95, 201n15

one hundred and twenty disciples, 89, 91

Ottman, Gladys, 103–4, 144, 184, 185

Ottman, Ruth. *See* Riddle, Ruth Ottman

Pace, Charles, 106, 178, 184, 239n38, 239n40–41

Palestine camp, 60–63, 65, 99, 103, 105, 108, 110, 111, 186, 205n27

Passover, 3, 54, 60, 67, 71–72, 83, 88–89, 90, 99, 103, 113, 201n19, 204n26, 205n27, 226n93; and wave sheaf, 83, 88–90; in 1984, 54, 99, 205n27; in 1985, 60, 205n27; in 1992, 71–72, 103, 113; in 1993, 226n93

Patriot movement, 231n1

pauper's cemetery. *See* McLennan County Restland Cemetery

Peeler, James, 216n38

Persian Gulf War, 211n17

Posse Comitatus Act, 207n44, 222n73, 236–37n30, 237n33

pyrotechnic devices. *See under* FBI

Reno, Janet, 3, 4, 5, 148, 174, 228n105, 234n24, 235n26, 237–38n33

resurrection, 84–85, 89, 93; final, 98; first (Rev. 20:4–6), 84, 85; of Christ and wave sheaf (Matt. 27:52–53), 84, 93; of David Koresh, 83; of the blessed, 90, 98; of the Lamb and wave sheaf, 85; in Daniel 12:2, 84; in Ezekiel 37:1–14, 84; second (Rev. 20:12–13), 84

Revelation, book of, 3, 76–77, 79–98, 144, 209n4, 210n9, 225n90, 226n93, 227n99

Richards, Annetta, 144, 184

Ricks, Bob, 229n110

Riddle, Jimmy, 60, 64–65, 71, 105, 109, 110, 136, 148, 153, 186, 213–14n21

Riddle, Myrtle, 186

Riddle, Rita, 110, 144, 156, 184, 186, 213n21, 238n37

Riddle, Ruth Ottman, 103–4, 109, 145–46, 154, 166, 170–72, 185, 230n114

Roden, Amo Paul Bishop, 67, 173, 177–78, 203n13, 208n46, 234n21, 238n38

Roden, Ben, 2, 6, 10, 31–33, 34–36, 39–43, 44, 46–47, 48, 49–50, 52, 62, 67, 68, 77, 104, 105, 107, 108, 113, 124, 181, 199n3–4, 201n1, 201n12, 201n14, 201n19, 202n8, 202–3n12, 203n13, 204n21, 204n27, 207n42, 208n49, 209n3; feasts, 201n19

Roden, Benny, 43, 53

Roden, Carmen, 39, 41, 208n46

Roden, George, 7, 39, 40, 42–44, 52–54, 58–60, 62, 65–66, 99, 107–8, 173, 178, 202n4, 203n13, 204n17, 207n41–42, 208n46, 217n40; restraining order against, 52–53, 66, 203n16, 207n41

Roden, Jane, 44, 53

Roden, John, 44

Roden, Lois, 2, 6–7, 32, 39–41, 43, 44, 45–47, 52–54, 58–60, 62, 66, 68, 72, 75, 77, 103–4, 105, 107, 178, 201n1, 201n14, 203n13, 203n16, 203–4n17, 204n18, 204n21–22, 204n25, 204n27, 206n32, 207n42, 208n49, 209n2–3, 209n6, 214n24; death of, 60, 178

Roden, Rebecca, 40

Rodriguez, Robert, 119–21, 215n34, 216n35, 216–17n38, 217n39, 217n41–42, 220n57; invited to move to Mount Carmel, 119

Rogers, Dick, 234n24

Rogers, Helen, 108

Rosen, Rocket, 166

Rosie, 64–65

Ross, Rick, 72, 208n54, 215n27

Royster, Ted, 217n42

Ruby Ridge, Idaho incident (1992), 231n1, 234n24

Sage, Byron, 218n44, 219n48, 220n58, 223n77, 227n101, 234n24

Santoyo, Juliette, xi, 110, 131, 161

Santoyo, Ofelia, xi, 6, 63, 106, 110, 131, 144, 178, 184, 238n37–38

Sarabyn, Chuck, 217n42

Satellite City, 238n35, figure 1 in appendix

Schneider, Judy, 107, 110–11, 214n22

Schneider, Mayanah, 111

Schneider, Steve, 2–3, 106, 110–11, 138, 144–45, 147, 159, 218n44, 219n48, 221n71–72, 222n74, 222–23n76, 223n77, 223n80, 223n82, 224n83–86, 226n98, 227n101, 229n112, 231n6

Schroeder, Bryan, 106, 128, 183

Schroeder, Kathy, 106, 114, 129, 138, 139, 164, 166, 171–72, 183–84, 221n70, 223n80, 224n84

Schroeder, Michael, xi, 73, 103, 105–6, 129–30, 165, 183, 186, 190, 212n5, 220n62–64, figure 1 in appendix

Sellors, Cliff, 71, 196, 102–3, 137–38, 143–44, 214n25, 222n76; redrawing Victor Houteff's charts, 143–44

Seven Seals, 3, 76, 80, 82, 86–87, 105, 144, 146, 209n4, 219n46

Seventh Angel, 82, 205n30, 226n93

Seventh-day Adventist Church, 1, 6, 15–21, 22–23, 25, 29–30, 31–32, 34, 42, 44, 46, 62, 65, 77, 80, 86, 97, 101, 102, 104, 109, 181, 199n3, 200n2–3, 200n6–7, 202n8, 203n12, 204n18, 204n21, 204–5n27, 209n2–3, 210n9; 1964 expectation, 15–16

Seventh-day Adventist Reform Movement, 63, 104, 106

Shaw, Edward, 34, 37, 39, 43, 44

Shaw, Ian, 34

Shaw, Lesley, 25–26, 34, 35, 36, 37, 39, 43–44, 46, 48

SHEkinah, 53, 204n18–19, 204n20, 209n6

The Shepherd's Rod, 18, 206n35
Sherrow, Richard, 230n112
Sinclair, Novellette, 103, 108, 109,
    205n27, 205n29
"Sinful Messiah" series, 119–20,
    216n37
Slawson, Athan, 46–47, 49, 50–51
Slawson, Barbara, 45, 47, 49, 50–51
Slawson, Debbie, 45–46, 48–52, 54–
    57. *See also* Brown, Deborah
Smith, Daniel, 19–21, 22
Smith, Guy, 100
Smith, Jean, 35, 99–100
Smith, Walter S., Jr., 166, 169–72,
    174–75, 232n11, 233n12, 234–
    35n25
Somerton, Rod, 34, 37, 39, 43–44
Sonobe, Angelica, xiii, 111, 128, 182
Sonobe, Crystal, xiii, 111, 128, 182
Sonobe, Floracita ("Cita"), xiii, 111,
    128, 182
Sonobe, Scott, xiii, 111, 125, 128, 182,
    219n51–52, 223n82
Spirit. *See* Holy Spirit
Spirit of Prophecy, 105, 204n17–18,
    204n22, 205n27
Spoon, Mark, 117–18
Steed, Fred, 31
Street, Tom, Jr., 33, 201n16, 203n13
Summers, Aisha Gyarfas, 100–101,
    109, 211n2, 224n82,
    230n115
Summers, Greg, 107, 109, 123, 137–
    38, 211n2, 222n76
Summers, Startle, 100
Swett, Mark, 206n36
Sylvia, Hollywood, 107
Sylvia, Joshua, 107, 128, 182, 186
Sylvia, Lorraine ("Larry"), 60, 107, 182,
    186
Sylvia, Rachel, 107, 186
Sylvia, Stan, 60–61, 106, 107–8, 182,
    186, 206n40

Tabor, James, 146, 225n90, 226–
    27n98; April 1, 1993, KRLD Radio

discussion with J. Phillip Arnold,
    227n98
Texas State Technical College, 118,
    217n42, figure 1 in appendix
Thibodeau, David, 6, 105, 132,
    151, 152, 160, 165, 178, 185,
    193, 196, 215n34, 217n41,
    223n78, 230n113–14,
    238n37–38
Thomas, Marjorie, 102, 131, 156, 159,
    185, 230n114
Toulouse, Wyatt, 226n96
trailer at Beaver Lake, 99, 104, 106,
    108, 112, 120, 129–30, 186, 190,
    figure 1 in appendix
two witnesses, 31, 201n13

Vaega, Joann, 106, 183
Vaega, Margarida, 106, 183, 206n39
Vaega, Neil, 101, 106, 118, 183,
    206n39
vault at Mount Carmel. *See under*
    Mount Carmel (New Mount Carmel
    Center)
Vector Data Systems, 193, 197,
    236n30

WACMUR, 212n7
Waco: The Rules of Engagement (1997),
    236n30
Waco Tribune-Herald, 119–20,
    217n38
wave sheaf, 83–90, 93–94, 109; the
    Church, 88; go with Christ to
    heaven, 95, 109; living wave sheaf,
    85–87, 90; twenty-four elders part
    of, 87–88; will get perfect mates,
    109
Weaver, Randy, 231n1
Wendel, Jaydean, 111, 129, 136,
    183
Wendel, Juanessa, 111, 128, 183
Wendel, Landon, 111, 128, 183
Wendel, Mark, 111, 136, 150, 183,
    229n112
Wendel, Tamara, 111, 128, 183

Wendel, Patron, 111, 128, 183
Wheatley, John, 26
White, Ellen G., 23, 200n6, 201n14, 201n17, 204n21, 209n2, 210n9
White, James, 200n6
Whitecliff, Kevin, 100, 122, 131, 134, 137, 138, 165, 171, 184, 220n56, 232n11
wilderness, 68
Williams, Robert, 219n54
Willis, Steve, 219n54

the world, 24, 26, 34, 43, 44, 92, 97, 181, 200n7
Worrow, Bill, 72, 207n42

Yahshua, 76, 78, 79, 81, 82, 90. *See also* Christ
Yard Birds, 117
Yearning for Zion Ranch, 213n18

Zane, Robert, 226n97
Zegel, Ferdinand, 235n30
Zimmerman, Jack, 221–22n72

About the Authors

Clive Doyle lives in Waco, Texas. His mailing address is P.O. Box 144, Axtell, Texas 76624. His email address is mtcarmelbook2@gmail.com.

Catherine Wessinger lives in New Orleans, Louisiana. Her email address is wessing@loyno.edu.

Matthew D. Wittmer lives in Los Angeles, California. He may be contacted through his website, http://stormbound.org.